AFRICA

Unity,
Sovereignty,
and Sorrow

AFRICA

Unity,
Sovereignty,
and Sorrow

Pierre Englebert

LYNNE
RIENNER
PUBLISHERS

BOULDER
LONDON

Published in the United States of America in 2009 by
Lynne Rienner Publishers, Inc.
1800 30th Street, Boulder, Colorado 80301
www.rienner.com

and in the United Kingdom by
Lynne Rienner Publishers, Inc.
3 Henrietta Street, Covent Garden, London WC2E 8LU

Library of Congress Cataloging-in-Publication Data
Englebert, Pierre, 1962–
  Africa : unity, sovereignty, and sorrow / Pierre Englebert.
    p. cm.
  Includes bibliographical references and index.
  ISBN 978-1-58826-646-0 (hardcover) — ISBN 978-1-58826-623-1 (pbk.)
  1. Africa, Sub-Saharan—Politics and government—21st century. I. Title.
  JQ1875.E57 2009
  320.967—dc22

                                                                      2009002520

British Cataloguing in Publication Data
A Cataloguing in Publication record for this book
is available from the British Library.

Printed and bound in the United States of America

  The paper used in this publication meets the requirements
     of the American National Standard for Permanence of
     Paper for Printed Library Materials Z39.48-1992.

  5 4 3 2 1

Tables and Figures

Tables

Figures

Acknowledgments

I wish to express my sincere gratitude to those who helped me in the conception, research, writing, and editing of this book. They are many.

As my full-time research assistant in 2005 and 2006, Katharine Boyle drafted several case studies, particularly those on Southern Sudan and Nigeria, and compiled and analyzed the data used in Chapter 2. Her work was of the highest quality, and she contributed several significant ideas on Nigeria. Other research assistants who worked on parts of this project over the past few years were Monica Boduszynski, Maggie Fick, Rebecca Hummel, Sinead Hunt, Lisa Mueller, Joanna Schenke, Jeanne Segil, and Stacy Tarango, all of whom were Pomona College students who have since gone on to great things. Evelyn Khalili, the administrative assistant in Pomona's Politics Department and a good friend, provided frequent support. Kerstin Steiner, at the Claremont Graduate University, greatly helped with the latter stages of research, revisions, and editing.

In my travels to develop the book, I was able to rely on the kindness, expertise, and hospitality of many people. I have many debts in particular in the Democratic Republic of Congo. In Goma, I received help from Jean-Charles Dupin and Vital Katembo. It was also in Goma that I was lucky to meet Denis Tull, an esteemed colleague who has since become a dear friend. In Kinshasa, I relied on the generous hospitality of Francesca Bomboko, Kevin Hartigan, and Dominique Morel. Francesca and her BERCI center also proved to be an immense resource for my research. In Kisangani, Alphonse Maindo, Bienvenu Panda, Ediba Yengeme, and Nestor Yombo-Djema went above and beyond the call of duty on my behalf and have become good friends. In Lubumbashi, I enjoyed the assistance and friendship of Reubens Mulenga and the generosity of Dieudonné Been Masudi Kingombe, as well as the hospitality of Elengesa Ndunguna and the staff at the University of Lubumbashi. In addition, my work in Congo has benefited from the knowledge and generosity of Paule Bouvier,

Mauro deLorenzo, Kate Farnsworth, Olivier Kamitatu, Dismas Kitenge, Theodore Trefon, Ernest Wamba dia Wamba, Herbert Weiss, and Stephanie Wolters. Paule Bouvier was my first professor of African politics when I was an undergraduate at the University of Brussels, and it was a joy to be able to do fieldwork with her in Kinshasa and Kisangani in 2005.

In Senegal, Pape Badiane and Abdou Karim Sylla provided great company and assistance. The staff at the West African Research Center was kind and helpful. Momar Comba Diop offered analytical insights and numerous contacts. Vincent Foucher was kind enough to share his knowledge of Casamance and many of his contacts. In preparing for the trip to Senegal, I received useful suggestions and contacts from Linda Beck, Samba Ka, and Leigh Swagart.

For the research on Zambia, Daniel Posner and Richard Sklar were very generous with their connections and research suggestions. Geoffrey Ndaradzi was a good traveling companion. In Mongu, Frederic Mubitelela Mupatu was kindly "delegated" to me by the Barotseland authorities and turned an initially stalled visit into a highly productive one. Natheniel Mubukwanu was also generous with his time and his contacts. In Lusaka, Abhi Sharma and his family were both helpful and hospitable, and Michelle Foust provided insights and useful contacts.

In Congo-Brazzaville, I enjoyed and benefited from the company of my friend James Ron. The brave staff of Catholic Relief Service provided us with generous assistance and unusual access, and we also took advantage of the analyses and numerous connections of John Clark and James Swan. Later, Rémy Bazenguissa-Ganga kindly shared his knowledge of the country's politics.

In Uganda, I am grateful above all to Phoebe Kajubi, who went from being a research assistant to a colleague and is now a good family friend. Her family, including Zephaniah Kajubi and Peruth Nakibirango Ssendaula, Norah Nakirigya, and Betty and Bernard Muramuzi, gave me a home away from home. My thanks also to Aili Mari Tripp, Ruth Nalumaga, Mikael Karlstrom, Peter Maiga, and the personnel at the Kabaka Foundation.

My research on Cameroon was kindly facilitated by Francis Nyamnjoh and abetted by the senior thesis research of Maggie Fick at Pomona College. Nico Fru Awason was also helpful.

I interviewed many dozens of people in developing this book. They had nothing to gain from it, yet they were generous with their time, knowledge, advice, and opinions. They provided the raw material for my analyses, and I owe them a great professional debt.

I am also much indebted to the friends and colleagues who graciously read and commented on all or parts of my manuscript. Nadia Horning and Denis Tull read the entire manuscript and provided critical but supportive comments that helped me to write a much better book. They are true friends and I owe them big. Crawford Young read four chapters, and I cannot thank him enough for the care he took in commenting on them at great length out of pure kindness. The detailed suggestions and corrections of these three readers not only considerably improved my analyses, but also helped me to avoid several blunders. Two anonymous reviewers for Lynne Rienner Publishers also offered useful suggestions. Thanks to their careful reading, I was able to significantly improve the original manuscript. Colleagues and friends at the Working Group on African Political Economy (WGAPE) showed their usual incisive minds in commenting on Chapter 4 and led me to clarify important parts of the argument. Mette Kjaer also gave useful feedback on that chapter, as did Laurie Brand on the introduction. I benefited from Nita Rudra's methodological insights for the regressions in Chapter 2. My thanks also go to David Menefee-Libey, who endured oral versions of most of the book during our runs, frequently raised challenging questions, and offered useful suggestions. My sincere gratitude also goes to Richard Joseph, Célestin Monga, Francis Nyamnjoh, and Michael Ross, who generously agreed to read the final manuscript and shared their impressions.

I had the chance to present parts of the argument at several venues over the past few years, where I received feedback that helped me to improve the book. For giving me these opportunities, I thank the following people and their institutions: Laurie Brand, Christopher Darlington, Ulf Engel, Carol Graham, Nadia Horning and her students, Patrick James, Richard Joseph, Stathis Kalivas and his students, Peter Lewis, Alphonse Maindo, Andreas Mehler, Ted Miguel, Muna Ndulo, René Otayek, Daniel Posner, Lise Rakner, Frances Stewart, Denis Tull, Nic van de Walle and his students, and Rachel Warner. I am also grateful for the several opportunities I had to present my argument to my colleagues and students at the Claremont Colleges.

Research for this book was funded by a generous and patiently administered grant from the Smith-Richardson Foundation. The beautiful Denison Library at Scripps College provided a frequent writing hideaway, as did Claremont's many inviting coffee bars and my beloved backyard. I am delighted to be publishing once again with Lynne Rienner. I am grateful for her confidence in my work and advocacy of it. We students of the continent are lucky to have her, and I am honored to be in her catalog. Working with her superb staff—particularly Shena Redmond, Sonia Smith, and Claire Vlcek—was a privilege.

En route to Africa or on my way back, I often arranged for a stopover in Brussels, where I grew up and where the food is good. There, I relished the hospitality of my mother, Hélène Van Campenhoudt, as well as that of my dear friends Thierry Bonus, Bénédicte Goffinet, and Eric Philippart. Most of all, I thank my wife, Beth, for more than I can write. It is a great life, and I am lucky to share it with her. And, for the joy and wonder of their existence, I dedicate this book to our children, Luke, Tom, Bridget, and Jack.

—*Pierre Englebert*

1

The Resilience
of the African State

By and large, the states of sub-Saharan Africa are failures. Of course, not all of them are failed states where disorder and violence are rampant. And, of course, there is variation among them, with some showing greater concern for their citizens' welfare than others. Most of them, however, have not brought about or facilitated much economic or human development for their populations since independence. Often, they have caused their people much havoc, misery, uncertainty, and fear. With some exceptions, African states have been, mildly or acutely, the enemies of Africans. Parasitic or predatory, they suck resources out of their societies. At the same time, weak and dysfunctional, many of them are unable or unwilling to sustainably provide the rule of law, safety, and basic property rights that have, since Hobbes, justified the very existence of states in the modern world.

This condition of failure-cum-predation is now well established, and there is little to add to the voluminous and informative literature on this subject.[1] Yet, there is a paradoxical feature of Africa's weak states that has received much less attention: they will not go away. For all their catastrophic failures, weak African states are still around. With the partial exception of Somalia, state collapse has yet to lead to state disintegration on the continent. There have been almost no changes to African boundaries since 1960. Dictators and democratic governments have come and gone, as have countries' names and their international alliances. Some states have received more and more aid, others have sunk to levels of unthinkable destitution. But all of them are implausibly still there, by and large as they were at the dusk of colonial times.

This is not to say there have not been significant changes in Africa since the 1960s. For one, the relative political openness—if not always democratic nature—of some regimes stands in sharp contrast to the dictatorships and military juntas of the postindependence decades. If nothing else, freedom of expression has expanded nearly everywhere despite continual challenges. There have also been instances of protest and grassroots mobilization against incompetent and repressive regimes, and a rich associative life has developed since the late 1980s, which testifies to creative strategies of adaptation and resistance. On a more somber note, the violence that has prevailed in many countries since the 1990s has also swept clean some preexisting social and political configurations. Finally, many governments have committed to aid-sponsored programs to improve governance, reduce corruption, and promote human welfare. A 2008 World Bank report, for example, highlighted the continent's recent economic growth and suggested some causal links to improved governance.[2]

Yet, the scale of political and economic change in Africa is easily overstated. More often than not, elections have not brought about alternations in power. More often than not, they have not been free and fair. More often than not, democratically elected elites have failed to implement meaningful change and have returned to the clientelistic and authoritarian politics of yore.[3] Not surprisingly, therefore, surveys of African public opinion show a rise in disenchantment with democracy, and electoral participation has seen declines everywhere.[4] Similarly, the vibrancy of associative life has not usually translated into substantive reforms of the state. Instead, nonstate actors of different hues have often ended up contributing one way or another to the reproduction of weak African states. Moreover, in striking contrast with the historical consolidation of states in Western Europe, the violent conflicts that have ravaged so many regions of Africa since the early 1990s have rarely triggered significant political progress.[5] In fact, it is usually hard to identify the stakes of these conflicts beyond factional struggles and control of natural resources.[6] In most cases, they have been settled, through international oversight, in power-sharing agreements that have brought rebels and the corrupt leaders they were fighting together in broad dysfunctional and predatory coalitions.[7] It would also be hard to argue that the one significant social change that has come at the hands of these conflicts—the transformation of some alienated youth into a new class of warlords and militiamen—has represented a form of political progress or contributes to improved governance. Finally, most packages of economic and civil service reforms, most anticorruption programs, and most poverty-reduction strategies have met at best with partial implementation, and have left Africans by and large as deprived, if not more so, as they were at the dawn of their independence.[8] A closer look at the data behind the 2008 World Bank report indicates that inflated oil prices account for recent growth more than any other factor, and that there has been no significant average improvement in the quality of governance across the continent over the past ten years.[9]

Thus, while postcolonial Africa has not lacked upheaval, I argue that it is in fact characterized by structural inertia. Apparent transformations and prevailing volatility have contributed little progress, little systemic change, and little substantive improvement across the board. Territorial delimitations have remained frozen, and modes of governance based on personal rule, ethnic al-

being instrumentalized. On the contrary, it is the last remnant of public order in weak and failed states—sovereignty—that Africans instrumentalize.

The essential building blocks of my argument are thus that (1) legal command is the domestic expression of international legal sovereignty; (2) the exercise of legal command is widely distributed within countries wherever appendages of the state are present; (3) because of the exogenous nature of African sovereignty, African legal command resists the erosion of state capacity that plagues weak and failed states; (4) as a result, its exchange value in terms of extraction and domination endures in times of failure and promotes continued societal attachment to dysfunctional state institutions. Taken altogether, these elements conspire to create a structure of acquiescence to the state. Because of the benefits of legal command relative to the few nonstate opportunities for advancement and accumulation, African political elites, regional leaders, and other communal contenders face compelling incentives to surrender subnational particularistic claims and compete instead for access to the sovereign state, irrespective of the latter's history of violence toward them. The voicing of cultural grievances may be used in mobilizing local support for their strategies, but the resolution of these grievances is rarely on these elites' agenda.

*   *   *

One could reasonably ask why it matters that African states are unlikely to face deep societal challenges like separatism and other forms of collective political "exit."[21] Isn't this after all good news? Isn't it one fewer problem to worry about for the continent? Should we somehow wish for African countries to fall apart? It is not the point of this book to advocate for such outcome or to problematize attachment to postcolonial states per se. Yet, the lack of relationship in Africa between state failure and state dissolution is informative by its apparent deviation from worldwide patterns, as illustrated in Chapter 2. If we can understand why there is no institutional sanction to state failure, repression, and underdevelopment in Africa, we will have reached a better understanding of the nature of African statehood and of its developmental failure. This is an analytical issue. We may not wish for separatist conflicts, but we can still ask why Africa's subnational communities do not challenge their states more often. Separatism is not per se good or evil—yet it is the manifestation of a communal wish to exit from the state, which is, in the end, a mode of accountability. Given, among other things, the prevailing failures of African states, the contending cultural allegiances of their populations, the prevalence of conflict, and the relative absence of credible options for "voice," it is surprising that Africans refrain from exit to such a degree. It is this book's contention that an understanding of the attachment of African societies to African states can shed light on the prevailing structures that constrain and condition political and economic action on the continent and help us come to a better understanding of the nature of politics in Africa and the roots of the continent's broad failure to sustainably bring about welfare to its populations.

This last statement brings us back to this chapter's opening sentence, where I labeled the majority of African states as failures. Some will see this as harsh judgment and might suggest that this book's argument is more about the basket cases of African states—countries such as the Democratic Republic of Congo (DRC), Liberia, Sierra Leone, Chad, the Central African Republic, Sudan, Somalia, or Burundi—than about the majority of the continent. They will call our attention to the more successful performers—like Botswana, Mauritius, or South Africa—and those whose treatment of their population has been more benign—like Benin, Ghana, Mali, Mozambique, Uganda, or Tanzania. They will also single out the large majority of somewhat functioning states, which may not be developmental successes, but are not either catastrophic failures. Quite a few African countries appear indeed as hybrids, with some dysfunctional aspects but also part of their institutional apparatus operating by Weberian norms.

These people might well be right. I do not deny that there are significant variations in political and economic performance across the region.[22] In fact, in a previous project, I tried to account for the causes of such variations.[23] Botswana and Mauritius are indeed truly exceptional, and South Africa is sufficiently unique to warrant separate discussion. This book's argument is not about these countries. It is, indeed, first and foremost, about Africa's weakest states. Yet, its argument might also be relevant to most other African states, even those that have not reached the depths of utter failure. Consider indeed that, apart from Botswana, Mauritius, and South Africa, no African country has so far managed to successfully develop. Some fifty years after gaining their independence, most of them still rely on the export of a few primary commodities as the engine of their economy. Even a country like Senegal, often perceived as exemplary, remains overwhelmingly dependent on exports of fish and peanuts. Elsewhere it is cotton, coffee, pineapples, tea, or cocoa. In others, it is oil, gold, copper, or diamonds. The point is that the majority of African states may not be failed, but they have failed at establishing any sustainable foundation for economic growth beyond their colonial legacy of raw-material extraction.[24] In fact, the majority of African states can hardly afford their own existence. One often hears the argument that they should not be partitioned because smaller states would not be viable. But existing African states already are not usually viable. About half of them receive at least 10 percent of their gross domestic product (GDP) in foreign aid, and eleven receive more than 20 percent.[25] Aid is usually their main source of government revenue. Even the budgets of relatively successful countries like Ghana and Uganda are more than 50 percent dependent on foreign aid.[26]

Although my argument, which centrally features predation, will no doubt be better suited to the worst failures than to the continent as a whole, it also hopes to shed light on the well-documented and widespread corruption and abuses by state authorities in places like Angola, Nigeria, Cameroon, Congo-Brazzaville, or Equatorial Guinea. These may not be considered failed states but they certainly are largely privatized enterprises of predation and extraction that have done very little for their populations. The ease with which alleged African success stories can collapse should also caution us against making too much of existing variations in performance. Côte d'Ivoire was a model in development circles until the early 1990s. And Zimbabwe once augured well of the possibilities for African development.

My premise is that African states may not all be failed, but many of them have failed in significant parts at their essential mission of providing security, basic welfare, and development. One can thus think of African states in general as weak. Although there are gradations in the actual extent of their weakness at any one time—with some completely collapsed and others functioning better—these are differences in performance that may result from a host of factors but are not necessarily differences in the nature of the states themselves. It is my contention that most African states are vulnerable to failure and reproduction along the logic I describe in this book. Variations among them in this respect may be more a matter of degree (and time) than of intrinsic quality. This being said, the weaker the state, the more paradoxical its reproduction and the more relevant this book's argument. At the very least, therefore, I hope to help make sense of the resilience of Africa's most failed states.

*   *   *

The book begins, in Part 1, with the question of unity, describing the empirical trends it seeks to explain. Chapter 2 documents the unusual territorial resilience of Africa's weak states and shows that, according to patterns in other regions, Africa should have two to five times its actual level of secessionist conflict. Chapter 3 then illustrates how, despite a certain vibrancy of associative life across the continent, dysfunctional state institutions tend to endure and maintain a surprising degree of authority. Often, local elites, civil society groups, and even rebels contribute to their reproduction.

Part 2 sets out to account for this paradoxical resilience by developing a theory of state reproduction based on legal command. Chapter 4 contains the core theoretical argument. It discusses the external origins of African sovereignty, articulates the manner in which it translates into domestic legal command, and shows the mechanisms by which legal command is exchanged for resources and political domination. Chapter 5 offers four illustrations of the resulting compliance of African peripheral elites with the postcolonial state project. They are Barotseland in Zambia; Anglophone Cameroon; the Kivu provinces of the DRC; and the Delta and Biafra regions of Nigeria. Chapter 6 confronts the argument to the reality of existing African separatist movements. If legal command is such a resource to Africans, why are there secession attempts at all on the continent?

Through the examination of several case studies—Casamance, Eritrea, Ethiopia, Somaliland, Southern Sudan, and the Tuaregs—it identifies variations in time and space in the nature of African sovereignty and in opportunities for its domestic distribution, which fine-tune the argument.

The sovereign reproduction of Africa's weak states comes at a price, for it also alters their nature. Part 3 addresses the consequences of the legal command–based reproduction of African states. In Chapter 7, I show that the sovereign structuration of African social life gives rise to a particularly harmful form of nationalist discourse characterized by its tendency to alienate, divide, and exclude more than it unites. In Chapter 8, I highlight the negative effects of the sovereignty regime on democracy, governance, and the economy. In conclusion, Chapter 9 asks what is to be done. It makes some arguably eccentric suggestions, which I call policy fantasies. All of them are based on the claim that, if sovereignty is at the root of African state dysfunctionality, its effects must somehow be deflated. Their goal is to suggest policy mechanisms that would make the self-serving incentives of African elites compatible with the promotion of the welfare of their citizens. One way to do this is to revoke the unconditional international recognition of Africa's postcolonies and promote the conditions for the rise of domestic sovereignty or empirical statehood in Africa. Another, which I borrow from Jeffrey Herbst, is to link international recognition to the provision of services to citizens, whether by existing states or by other public or nonstate actors.[27] A final approach is to shed sovereignty of its dichotomous nature and dilute it among multiple actors in order to promote institutional competition—and, hence, quality—among them.

Notes

1. See, among many others, Rotberg, *State Failure*; Rotberg, *When States Fail*; Ellis, "How to Rebuild"; Addison, *From Conflict to Recovery*; Zartman, *Collapsed States*; Herbst and Mills, "Africa's Big Dysfunctional States"; and Chabal and Daloz, *Africa Works*.
2. World Bank, *Africa Development Indicators 2007*.
3. Van de Walle, "Presidentialism and Clientelism."
4. Afrobarometer, "Citizens and the State"; Soudan, "Pourquoi les Africains."
5. For a classical statement on the role of violence in European state formation, see Tilly, *Coercion*. For the lack of political "productivity" of African conflicts, see Reno, "Shadow States."
6. Gleditsch et al., "Armed Conflict."
7. Tull and Mehler, "The Hidden Costs."
8. Van de Walle, *African Economies*.
9. See Chapter 8.
10. Hyden, "Problems and Prospects."
11. See, for some of the best examples, Médard, "The Underdeveloped State"; Sandbrook, "Patrons, Clients, and Factions"; Jackson and Rosberg, "Personal Rule"; Joseph, *Democracy;* and van de Walle, "Neopatrimonialism and Democracy."

12. The concept of "fusion of elites" was introduced by Sklar, *Nigerian Political Parties,* to explain social class formation in Nigeria and, more generally, tropical Africa. The similar concept of "reciprocal assimilation of elites" was coined by Bayart, *L'Etat au Cameroun* (elaborated upon later in *The State in Africa*) to describe how African states became embedded in society and how they reproduce.

13. Young, "Nationalism and Ethnicity"; Boone, "Open-Economy State Building."

14. See Reno, *Warlord Politics*; Chabal and Daloz, *Africa Works*; Bayart, Ellis and Hibou, *Criminalization of the State*; and Roitman, *Fiscal Disobedience.*

15. On autochthony, see *African Studies Review,* "Special Issue: Autochthony." On predictions of such challenges, see Forrest, "State Inversion," 45–56.

16. Jackson and Rosberg, "Why Africa's Weak States Persist."

17. Reno, "How Sovereignty Matters."

18. On the historically unusual production of inequality by the postcolonial African state, see Bayart, *The State in Africa,* particularly Chapter 2.

19. Krasner, *Sovereignty,* 10–20.

20. Chabal and Daloz, *Africa Works*; Mbembe, *On the Postcolony.*

21. Hirschman, *Exit, Voice and Loyalty.*

22. It is also true that many African states saw a period of relative consolidation in the 1960s and early 1970s, which recorded social and institutional progress (see Cooper, *Africa Since 1940,* 100–130).

23. Englebert, *State Legitimacy.*

24. The policies of developed countries and the structure of international trade account in part for this failure.

25. World Bank, *African Development Indicators* (data for 2003).

26. Ayodele et al., "African Perspectives on Aid."

27. Herbst, *States and Power*; Herbst, "Let Them Fail."

Part 1
Unity

Some two thousand years ago, the historian Pliny the Elder wrote the well-known quip *ex Africa semper aliquid novi*—there is always something new out of Africa. When it comes to contemporary deep politics, however, the next two chapters argue that Pliny was somewhat off the mark and that "out of Africa, never anything new" would be more appropriate and only slightly exaggerated. What is indeed remarkably puzzling about African politics, beyond its surface of apparent instability, is the resilience of its political geography and institutional structures. The map of Europe has seen many more changes since 1960 than the map of Africa, where the emancipation of Eritrea from Ethiopia constitutes the only instance of new state formation—and an ambiguous one at that given Eritrea's distinct colonial status from Ethiopia. Apart from this, name changes are the only things giving cartographers headaches when it comes to the continent. Beyond geography, it is equally surprising that the institutional apparatus of failed African states typically endures, irrespective of how dysfunctional, repressive, exploitative, or parasitic the state has been. State failure does not equate institutional vacuum. Not only do state actors continue to carry authority and perform public roles through public institutions, but many Africans in turn appear to continue to acquiesce to these institutions' existence and to their agents' prerogatives, despite the burden they tend to represent in their lives. More often than not, authorities that might credibly challenge the state, such as chiefs or rebels, end up contributing to its reproduction. Even in countries afflicted by massive civil conflicts, the most common pattern is for rebels to maintain the institutions of the state in the regions they control and in their daily routines. In other words, despite an irrefutable vibrancy of nonstate associations and a few salient exceptions, there appears to be little original social contracting in contemporary Africa. Stifling creative endogenous institutional evolution, there is a strong resilience of inherited institutional arrangements.

The next two chapters describe this paradoxical unity of the weak African state, its territorial integrity and institutional hegemony. They offer a reading of African politics that cuts through the noise of surface upheavals and highlights instead the stability of the African postcolony.

2
The Puzzle of
Territorial Integrity

Over and over again since 1960, the demise of African states has been heralded. Over and over again the continent's numerous rebellions have been explained in ethnic and separatist terms, and the explosion or dissolution of postcolonial states has been anticipated by some and warned against by others. It seems indeed that Africa's quasi states hang on to life by a mere thread, weak, failed, and otherwise collapsed as they are. And yet, they are all still there. Although many have demonstrated their incapacity to provide for themselves, and not a few have literally crashed and burned, they endure. Not only have they resisted the erosion of time and politics, but they have in fact been the object of few challenges. Indeed, political violence may be widespread in Africa, but its goals are rarely ever to revolutionize, dismantle, or do away with the state.[1] In fact, between 1960 and 2006, only ten of sub-Saharan Africa's forty-eight states experienced any secessionist conflict by the most generous definition of the term, and most of these conflicts were short-lived, rather minor in scope, and unsuccessful. In contrast, over the same period, thirty-two African states provided the stage for at least one nonsecessionist domestic conflict, many of which were drawn out and rather significant. Most other regions of the world display a greater propensity for separatism. If one adds up all the country-years of domestic conflict since 1960 by region, the proportion of them with separatist content amounts to 44 percent in the Middle East and North Africa, 47 percent in Asia, and 84 percent in Europe, as against 29 percent in sub-Saharan Africa.[2]

The relative scarcity of African separatism is particularly puzzling since African states are youthful and very heterogeneous; they dispose of large and decentralized reserves of natural resources, which could sustain separatist groups; and they have a poor record of providing for their citizens. African states are also more culturally alien to their populations than most states in other regions of the world. Moreover, politics on the continent often amounts to zero-sum games, as states are captured by one ethnic group or coalition, which frequently exerts its domination over others, largely excluding them from state benefits, if not persecuting them.[3] That these dominated groups do not resort to exit strategies with greater frequency is perplexing, especially given the continent's propensity for other types of violent conflict.

The Surprising Scarcity of Separatism in Africa

One can count Africa's wars of secession on one's fingers.[4] The breakup of Eritrea from Ethiopia in 1993, after some thirty years of warfare, was the only successful one, and it amounted as much to a case of decolonization as to one of separatism.[5] Other attempts have included Katanga and South Kasai in the DRC, Biafra in Nigeria, Casamance in Senegal, Southern Sudan, and several regions of Ethiopia. Although Somaliland has de facto seceded from collapsed Somalia since 1991, it has yet to be recognized by any other state. Table 2.1 provides a complete listing.

Africa's frequency of separatist conflict lies well below that of most other regions, despite the fact that African states reached independence more recently than their counterparts elsewhere and could have been expected to face challenges to their territorial reach or legitimacy. Only Latin America ends up with a smaller proportion of territorial civil conflicts than Africa. But most Latin American countries have more homogeneous populations and have ex-

Table 2.1 Africa's Secessionist Conflicts, 1960–2006

Country	Region	Years of Violence	Intensity
Angola	Cabinda	1991, 1994, 1996–1998, 2002, 2004	Minor
Comoros	Anjouan	1997	Minor
DRC	Katanga	1960–1962	Minor
	South Kasai	1960–1962	Minor
Ethiopia	Eritrea	1962–1991	War
	Ogaden	1975–1983, 1996, 1998–2002, 2004–2006	War
	Afar	1989–1991, 1996	Minor
	Oromia	1989–1991, 1999–2006	Minor
Mali	Tuaregs	1990, 1994	Minor
Niger	Tuaregs	1992, 1994, 1997	Minor
Nigeria	Biafra	1967–1970	War
	Niger Delta	2004	Minor
Senegal	Casamance	1990–2003	Intermediate
Somalia	Somaliland	1989–1991	N.A.
Sudan	Southern Sudan	1963–1972, 1983–2005	War

Note: Based on Gleditsch et al., "Armed Conflict 1946–2001" (including categorization as minor, intermediate, or war). The timing of violence corresponds to at least twenty-five reported deaths per year. The Somali National Movement (SNM) insurgency in Somaliland is not listed as a separatist conflict by the Peace Research Institute of Oslo (PRIO) data set and not disaggregated from other simultaneous conflicts.

erted domination over them based on class more often than race, ethnicity, or regionalism.[6] Their indigenous population groups are less regionally concentrated than most African ethnic groups and, until recently, less politically salient and organized.[7]

As indicated in Table 2.2, the probability of a secessionist conflict in any given year is similar among Africa, Europe, and the Middle East (6–8 percent, against 16 percent for Asia). But, as mentioned earlier, Africa has had more instances of civil conflict altogether (forty-nine in all) than any other region between 1960 and 2006.[8] As a result, the proportion of secessionist conflicts among all instances of domestic warfare is significantly smaller in Africa than it is in Asia, Europe, or North Africa and the Middle East.

This is a puzzling deficit. Looking at the 1990s alone, a period of intense restructuring in the world system following the end of the Cold War, subnational regions in other parts of the world seemed more inclined to disengage from the state. In India, where colonial heritage, religious diversity, and ethnic heterogeneity are reminiscent of Africa, separatism is nothing short of endemic, with the Kashmiris, the Assamese, the Sikhs, the Tripuras, and the Nagas involved in violent secessionist conflicts. In Myanmar, where the government is highly repressive, the privileged mode of political contestation of minorities such as the Karens, the Shans, the Kachins, the Arakanese, and the Mons is secession. And there are numerous more cases of highly violent and sustained separatist conflicts in Asia, including those waged by the Sri Lankan Tamils, the Moros of the Philippines, Aceh (and previously East Timor) in Indonesia, the Chittagong Hill Tribes of Bangladesh, and the Bougainvilleans of Papua New Guinea.

In the former Soviet Union, which provided in 1991 one of the few examples of state collapse outside of Africa, most peripheral republics quickly affirmed their sovereignty.[9] To different degrees, they unilaterally declared their independence, adopted constitutions, asserted their legal supremacy over the central state, refused to send conscripts to Moscow's armies, and proclaimed

Table 2.2 The Likelihood of Secession, 1960–2000

Region	Overall Probability of Secessionist Conflict (%)	Proportion of Secessions Among All Conflicts (%)
Asia	16	47
Europe	6	84
Latin America and Caribbean	0	0
North Africa and Middle East	8	44
Sub-Saharan Africa	6	29

Note: Based on data from Gleditsch et al., "Armed Conflict 1946–2001." The probability of secessionist conflict is calculated in proportion to all available country-years ($n = 7,886$). The proportion of secessionist conflicts among all conflicts is calculated in proportion to all country-years of conflicts ($n = 1,040$).

their rights to natural resources and their own currency.[10] Within these re-publics, further groups have since struggled for their own independence, such as the Avars and Chechens of Russia, the Abkhazians and South Ossetians of Georgia, and the Armenians of Azerbaijan. In fact, this centrifugal trend is nothing new to the region. Armenians and Azerbaijanis had already engaged in secessionist conflict before the fall of the Soviet Union. Going even further back in time, many peripheral communities had seized the opportunity of the collapse of Tsarist Russia in 1917 to claim their independence in what Viva Bartkus calls a "deluge of secession crises."[11] Because the conditions at the time were so reminiscent of those prevailing in large parts of Africa today and the local responses so diametrically opposed, it is worth quoting at length from Bartkus's work regarding the early 1920s in Russia:

> There seems to have been no fewer than fiteen autonomous authorities func-tioning during the early 1920s. At first, local organizations, such as the na-tional councils of the Finns, Poles, Lithuanians, Latvians, Estonians, Ukraini-ans, Georgians, Armenians, Azerbaijanis, Bessarabians, and Cossacks, and the Muslim councils, Kuraltais, of the Bashkiris, Crimean Tatrs, Kazakhs, and Turkestans were established to provide rudimentary government. Be-cause the border regions suffered the indiscriminate ravages perpetrated by various armies, whether foreign ones like those of the Germans and Turks, or of the White Russians and Bolsheviks who were engaged in a bloody civil war, these local organizations provided much needed protection and other basic services. *As the authority of the Provisional Government in Petrograd evaporated, these national councils appropriated for themselves correspond-ingly greater powers for trade, communications, the maintenance of law and order, and defense. Into the political vacuum created by the Bolshevik coup strode these national councils declaring their independence.*[12]

A similar pattern took place in Yugoslavia in the 1990s, with the breakups of the Slovenes, the Croats, and the Kosovo Albanians. Yugoslavia's successor states faced similar problems with Croatia being challenged by Serbs, then Serbia by Kosovo, while Bosnia was crumbling under territorial conflicts among Muslims, Croats, and Serbs.

Separatist conflicts have not been absent from the Middle East and North Africa either. Turkey, Iraq, and Iran all have had to deal with Kurdish irreden-tism. Morocco has resisted emancipation efforts by the Saharaouis for about thirty years. Palestinians have been struggling for an independent state over most of the past half century. In 1994, South Yemen also briefly tried to split from the rest of the reunified country.

Even the well-established democracies of the West have to deal with sep-aratist conflicts. Spain has had a violent movement for the separation of its Basque region and a more peaceful movement for the autonomy of Catalonia. France has endured continued low-intensity separatist violence in the island of Corsica. In the 1980s, it faced separatist conflict in New Caledonia. The UK has waged a struggle against the Catholics of Northern Ireland who want to rejoin the Irish republic. And Cyprus has only recently reduced the tensions among its Turkish and Greek populations over the seizure of northern Cyprus by Turkish minorities supported by Turkish troops. Even Canada has suffered a long, albeit nonviolent, separatist dispute over the fate of its Quebec province, which was only quieted down by referendum in 1995.

In sub-Saharan Africa, however, where there are many more countries, each with many more minorities, Ethiopia is the only one having faced multiple significant separatist movements, namely from Eritreans, Somalis, Afars, and Oromos. Yet, as the only African state not to be a colonial creation, Ethiopia is in fact poorly representative of some of the political dynamics prevailing across the continent. To some extent, a point to which I return at length in Chapter 6, it can be argued that it is itself an absolutist conquest state, which is paying the price of its hegemonic projection by suffering separatist conflicts at its periphery.[13] The secession of Eritrea in 1991 can more accurately be described as an episode of decolonization, as Ethiopia assumed the position of successor state over the region from Italy upon the end of the UN Trusteeship in 1952. In addition, the separatist nature of Ethiopia's minorities must be tempered. According to Christopher Clapham, "Ethiopia . . . has a tradition of statehood, and a profound sense of its own identity that is not merely the property of a single ethnic group. Not only Amharas and Tigrayans, but many Oromos and most of the peoples of south western Ethiopia think of themselves as Ethiopian, and have no secessionist agenda."[14]

Apart from Ethiopia, no African country has faced significant violent separatist action from more than one minority, although most African countries count many different ethnic groups, and not a few of these groups have otherwise arguably developed into articulate "subnationalisms."[15] Of the forty-seven sub-Saharan African countries born of the colonial episode less than fifty years ago, the only ones having endured sustained conflict with significant secessionist overtones since 1990 have been Sudan over its southern region, Senegal over Casamance, and Angola over the enclave of Cabinda.

Looking at ethnic groups rather than countries provides an even more dramatic picture. Of ninety-seven African ethnic groups identified by the Minorities at Risk (MAR) project as "at risk" of discrimination or another form of persecution, only nine (9 percent) have engaged in any level of separatist violence since 1990, despite the general weakening of the state that has unfolded over the same period.[16] In contrast, of the sixty-two minorities in Asia, sixteen (26 percent) have committed to separatist violence. In the Middle East and North Africa, the ratio is four groups out of twenty-nine, or 14 percent. And of the eighty-five minorities in Eastern Europe and the former Soviet Union, fifteen (18 percent) have waged separatist struggles. Although the Dinka of Southern Sudan or the Diola of Casamance get significant media attention for their struggles for autonomy, their salience hides in fact their exceptional status by

African standards. More common is acquiescence to postcolonial national integration, even by groups outside ruling coalitions. Furthermore, although Africa's separatist deficit has been most paradoxical in the current period of apparently widespread reconfigurations of power across the continent and other regions, it actually predates it. In a 1981 paper, Donald Horowitz identified nineteen potentially separatist groups worldwide, based on differentials of economic advancements between groups and their regions. Of these groups, the only six that turned out *not* to be separatist were all African.[17]

Africa's lack of separatism could be understandable if there were evidence of general satisfaction of Africans with their political conditions. Yet, this is not the case. Political violence is actually widespread across the region. At least thirty-five of Africa's ninety-seven minorities at risk have engaged in nonseparatist political violence since 1990. And, as mentioned earlier, thirty-two of its forty-eight countries have suffered at least one minor nonseparatist civil conflict since 1960. In fact, most of Africa's major conflicts have been for the overthrow of governments and control of the state rather than separation from it.

The paradoxical nature of African political violence—its tendency not to challenge the integrity of the weak state but to contribute to its reproduction— might be fruitfully illustrated by looking in more detail at the case of Chad, a particularly arbitrary and dysfunctional African postcolonial state with a long history of civil conflict. Like most other contemporary African states, Chad is a colonial invention, a space of conquests amalgamated in 1900 by the French, who used it mostly as a reservoir of labor for their other colonies and for the development of cotton plantations in the south. In the north, which is mostly desertic, there was only a token French presence. The French did little toward the effective integration of the territory and, at independence in 1960, Chad became the fragile container of a mosaic of different and occasionally polarized communities. Although there are many ethnic groups, the country's main political divisor is the north-south axis. In precolonial times, southern communities had frequently been enslaved by kingdoms from farther north. But the French developed the south as "useful Chad," and the country's first president, François Tombalbaye, was from the south.

The immediate postcolonial hegemony of the south was soon challenged by northern elites. In 1966, the northern-based National Front for the Liberation of Chad (FROLINAT) launched an armed insurgency against the government. In 1975, Tombalbaye was overthrown and killed, and replaced in 1979 by a FROLINAT government under Goukouni Oueddeï. After continued fighting, Oueddeï was chased from power in 1982 by his former ally Hissein Habré, another northerner. Habré ruled until 1990, provoking the death of an estimated 40,000 Chadians, many of whom were southerners. He was eventually overthrown by one of his former lieutenants, Idriss Déby, a Zaghawa from the east. Déby has himself since been the target of multiple insurgencies, the most recent of which in April 2006 and January 2008 were only repelled thanks to French assistance.

The history of Chad is thus characterized by continuous warfare among armed groups from poorly integrated communities. When southern elites were in power, until 1975, northerners refused to accept their dominance and strove to take over. Thereafter, southerners became increasingly marginalized politically and turned into more passive spectators (and victims) of factional conflicts among northern and associated groups. Although Chad has endured through all these conflicts, it is dubious that it has existed as more than a political reference and the prize of insurgencies. It has been described as "aberrant, marginal, a fictive state."[18] Sam Nolutshungu has noted that "both colonial rule and the postcolonial state have offered very little of tangible value to motivate a stronger attachment to a unifying state, which many populations encounter only intermittently and mostly as a restrictive and oppressive force."[19] If not absent or oppressive, the Chadian state has been unstable, incompetent, and unable even to pay its own employees outside of Ndjamena.[20]

And yet, against these overwhelming odds, Chad has endured. To some extent, it owes its survival to repeated French interventions on its behalf. But these interventions have usually taken place against foreign threats, or in defense of existing governments against rebels. They have never occurred in defense of the state of Chad against separatists, for there have been none. Of the several dozen rebel organizations Chad has known since the mid-1960s, not a single one has had a secessionist agenda. When it began its insurgency against the southerners in the 1960s, FROLINAT made it clear that it did not seek secession.[21] One of its tracts in 1971 read: "There will be no Katanga, no Biafra, in Chad. We will mercilessly eliminate any tendencies toward secessionism."[22] Similarly, after years of northern domination, southerners did not voice any separatist desire during Chad's national conference in 1993. Robert Buijtenhuijs notes that, although southerners called for federalism and decentralization, they explicitly ruled out secessions. North-south rivalries are overwhelming, he notes, yet they "do not challenge the Chadian state *per se* . . . which they neither deny nor reject."[23] As Nolutshungu writes, state formation in Chad may be a failure but it has resulted in "the entrenchment of the idea of common belonging among Chadians and a real sense of nationhood." And he adds: Chadians concur "that the state should 'exist.' . . . It is as if no argument of experience, of failure and bloody disintegration, could challenge the presumption that the state that had once been decreed to exist, ought to continue to exist."[24] Such paradoxical resilience begs for an explanation.

Chad is not unique. After seizing control of half the national territory in 2003, Côte d'Ivoire's Forces Nouvelles rebels insisted that their actions "should not be seen as reflecting a will or decision to secede."[25] A couple of years later, despite virulent opposition between the rebels and the government, their spokesman Sidiki Konate reaffirmed that "although the north has cotton, diamonds and peanuts we don't want to secede, we don't want partition . . . we don't want a split."[26] Throughout Africa, Richard Joseph notes, "the more disabled the African state, the more tenacious the commitment to restore it."[27] And yet, the preservation of the state is not prima facie a maximizing strategy for the increasing number of peripheral communities at the margins of the hegemonic bloc that underwrites the continent's postcolonial power configurations. More often than not, these groups have not reaped significant benefits from their integration into the state, and they have sometimes been persecuted at its hands. Often, too, they lie at the territorial edges of weak states and could conceivably make claims for autonomy that central governments would be hard put to challenge. One would expect the wide dispersion of natural resources in Africa to frequently support such exit strategies. Yet, despite some vocal opponents here and there who generally fail to translate their discourses into meaningful political mobilization, very few African marginalized peripheral groups actually promote separatist paths of development.

Why Do People Secede?

It is possible that Africa's relative lack of separatism can be explained within our existing understanding of the determinants of secession.[28] There may be variables that inhibit secessions around the world that could also account for Africa's apparent deficit. I review most theories of separatism here. While a few shed some light on Africa's situation, most reinforce the expectation that African states should see greater levels of separatism.

Economic arguments typically fall in this latter category. For example, several scholars suggest that regional inequalities within a country promote the rise of secessionist sentiments, whether in richer regions that resent subsidizing the rest of the country, or poorer ones that may blame the state for their failure to develop.[29] In either version, this argument leads us to expect more rather than fewer secessions in Africa, where regional inequalities are substantial. Similarly, the availability of natural resources in specific regions is often linked to separatist conflicts.[30] If a region is dependent on the center for its revenues, it has less bargaining power to demand autonomy. If it has its own resources, however, it is more likely to be aggressive about autonomy.[31] Here again, the reliance of many African economies on primary commodities, and the latter's tendency for regional concentration, lead us to expect greater separatism. Another argument, according to which lesser educated citizens are more likely to embrace manufactured (sub)nationalist sentiments, and lesser educated young males more likely to be recruited into secessionist movements for lack of better lifestyle alternatives, also suggests a greater prevalence of separatist conflicts in Africa where secondary school enrollments are low.[32] Finally, some authors argue that poverty and slow growth rates are major secessionist risk factors, for they exacerbate the grievances of various groups and reduce the opportunity costs of warfare.[33] Here again, we would expect Africa's low-income countries to be relatively more prone to separatism than their better-off counterparts elsewhere around the world. In general, thus, economic theories would promote expectations of greater secessionism in Africa. If the continent's separatist deficit is to be explained, we must therefore look at noneconomic arguments.

Cultural theories are only somewhat more enlightening. Quite a few of them also set up expectations of greater African separatism. One argument, for example, holds that the more culturally heterogeneous a country's populations, the more likely they may be to wish for separate paths of self-determination. Africa's broad ethnic diversity should then be associated with separatism. A variation of this argument suggests that territorial concentration affects ethnic groups' desire for a separate destiny.[34] Black minorities dispersed across nations, for example, provide a weak foundation for separatist activism. Kurds concentrated in the northern region of Iraq, on the other hand, have a more intuitive and practical claim to territorial sovereignty. In Africa, although people of different ethnic backgrounds can be dispersed throughout countries, each ethnic group also tends to have its home region.

On the other hand, other cultural theories might better account for Africa's lack of separatism. Some authors suggest that, rather than mere heterogeneity, it is the presence of a dominant cultural group that encourages others to exit.[35] Most African countries, however, count a large number of different ethnic communities and there is not usually one dominant group from whose control others might wish to escape. As such, there may be fewer incentives to secede, and less organizational capacity for doing it. It is also possible that specific groups will only seek separatism when they face eradication or fear cultural annihilation. In general, the weakness of African states may militate against secession in this case, as they may be incapable of fully meting out to their populations the required dose of "unbearable tyranny" or "savage repression."[36]

Finally, it is sometimes argued that ethnic diasporas contribute to secessionist sentiment as they tend to keep grievances alive, offer irredentist support, magnify beliefs in ethnic purity, and provide funding to local organizations.[37] If there is a diaspora element to secessionism, then it might also militate against secessions in Africa. Although many Africans live abroad, not many of them are so economically well off as to financially support political movements in their region. In addition, apart from Eritreans and Somalis, it is unclear whether African diasporas are more likely to represent specific communities or to be broad cross-sections of their country's populations, which would negate their potential effects as minority representatives.

As with cultural explanations, political arguments can enlighten or muddle our understanding of Africa's lack of separatism. Here too, some theories lead to expectations of greater separatism. The continent's weak democratic performance, for example, tends to deprive minorities from voice and protection, and might make it more likely that they would seek an exit option. Ironically, however, democratic transitions can exacerbate existing ethnic tensions and favor state disintegration, as happened in the Soviet Union or Czechoslovakia.[38] Thus, the extent and intensity of political change may matter a great deal.[39] Since many African countries have been engaged in almost continuous political transitions since the early 1990s, we should expect Africa to be among the most separatist of regions. Taking transition to one of its extremes, state collapse should also be associated with secessions. When the central state is so weakened as to be unable to exercise its authority across the territory, its ability to resist and prevent a secessionist drive is greatly reduced. The collapse of the central state, as happened in different forms in the Soviet Union, Yugoslavia, or Somalia, also makes it more likely for peripheral or constituent regions to seek their own path. From this perspective, Africa's secessionist deficit is particularly glaring. Apart from the separation of Somaliland from Somalia, no other region of the continent has seized upon state failure to disengage and build its own state. On a related note, the extent to which a system is prone to political violence in general may also herald a greater separatist propensity. Nonsecessionist conflicts can have secessionist effects, or both types of conflict may result from similar factors.[40] But once again, the secession of Somaliland amid continued clan-based fighting in the rest of Somalia provides the only African example of the parallel dynamics of factional and separatist politics in Africa. Elsewhere on the continent, the general propensity to engage in political violence does not correlate with separatist activism.

Some political theories, however, make greater sense of Africa's secessionist deficit. First, to some extent, the transition argument does explain something in Africa. It is hard to refute that the post-1990 period has been characterized by an increase in separatist activity on the continent. In fact, most of the instances of secessionist conflict in Table 2.1 took place after 1990. The inertia of African authoritarianism in the pre-1990 period may thus have accounted for the scarcity of separatism. The rigidities of the Cold War also probably froze more than one separatist ambition, while the end of the Soviet Union signaled new possibilities for subnationalist movements, at least in Eastern Europe, Central Asia, and the Balkans. Leading events in specific countries and demonstration effects illustrate normative shifts or perceptions of such shifts in the international community. When the principle of self-determination gains popularity over the norm of territorial integrity, the costs of secession may appear reduced to would-be separatists as the likelihood of recognition—the ultimate proof of existence—rises. This may have affected the decision of several African groups to engage, resume, or intensify separatist conflicts in the early 1990s. The support of a neighboring state might also be a crucial factor in determining the odds and success of a secession. The separation of Bangladesh from Pakistan in 1971 provides the textbook case on the effects of a supportive neighbor—India in this case—on the secession of groups or regions.[41] As I will discuss later in this chapter, the fact that the rules of the African Union (AU) prohibit interference in the politics of another African state and violation of colonial boundaries may have reduced opportunities for neighborly support in Africa and, with it, the likelihood of separatism. A final useful political argument relates to the previous existence of a region as a state or distinct administrative unit. Having once been an independent state may facilitate contemporary mobilization toward separatist agendas.[42] Subnational mobilization may also be easier in regions that already have their own administrative existence and apparatus, and where collective action is facilitated by established leadership and a preview of what independence could be. Regional administrative existence may promote the density of social ties through shared regional ethnic institutions, such as schools, newspapers, museums, and so on.[43] This argument might be very relevant to Africa. From the perspective of the modern world system and of international law, precolonial African political systems did not exist, apart from Ethiopia, which was recognized by European powers. Thus, although some regions of Africa experienced statehood in the past, they have no experience of recognized statehood, which reduces their odds of recognition and may hamper their attempts at presenting their followers with a credible vision of their future as states. In addition, the strong historical centralization of the African state limits the extent to which subnational administrative units can become plausible frameworks of subnational mobilization. This variable may thus prove useful in explaining Africa's separatist deficit.

There are finally a few arguments about the extent to which certain underlying structural circumstances may facilitate or impede separatist insurgencies. On the side of facilitation, the age of a country may matter. Intuitively, the younger a country, the less likely it is to have already passed through the growing pains of nation-building and national integration and the more vulnerable it may be to dismemberment.[44] Clearly, African states are very young by world historical standards. This variable should thus make their territorial resilience more paradoxical. A couple of other arguments are more favorable to Africa's lack of separatism. For one, having noncontiguous land masses may put states at greater risk of secessions. Countries whose territories are separated by other countries or by water (e.g., Angola, Comoros, or Pakistan before the secession of Bangladesh) may see their distant component(s) turn more vulnerable to centrifugal forces. There are a few discontinuous states in Africa, but they are the exception. The land mass contiguity of most African states may thus play in their favor. Second, the larger a country and its population, the greater the potential for breakup. Most African states have relatively small populations, which should reduce the odds of secessionism. There are, however, a few very large states on the continent, most of which have been affected by separatism: the DRC, Ethiopia, Nigeria, and Sudan come to mind.

Altogether, theories of separatism offer a mixed bag with respect to Africa's secessionist deficit. Some might partly account for Africa's lesser propensity for secessions. Most, however, only deepen the mystery. Either way, they call for empirical verification.

Estimating Africa's Secessionist Deficit

One way to reliably assess the explanatory power of these theories is to combine them in a general model and observe their effects simultaneously. Multivariate regression analysis is a statistical technique that does just that. It can tell which variables are robustly associated with separatism, positively or negatively. Africa itself can be thought of as one such variable. Every country can be coded as African or not and the effects of that variable on separatism can be estimated. If all the other variables capture what inhibits separatism in Africa, the effects of the Africa variable will not be statistically significant. Whatever distinguishes the continent will have already been captured. If, on the other hand, the Africa variable has its own negative effect on separatism, there still is some unexplained continent-specific condition that is inimical to separatism.[45]

Because some theories deal with features of countries as a whole (e.g., level of development, size), while others relate to regions within countries (e.g., regional income inequalities), I proceeded along two different tracks. First, I created a data set by countries. This approach takes as the unit of analysis the structure against which separatist movements are created. For example, characteristics of Russia would be analyzed, while the dependent variable—the presence of a secessionist conflict—would be triggered by the activities of Chechen rebels. This approach makes it easier to collect data and is well suited to test theories that relate to countries, but it is weaker for testing region-specific theories. Because data by country is available over relatively long periods of time, it is also possible to enter several observations for each country at different time periods. Doing so allows us to control for variables that change over time. The country data set covers all available countries of the world over the period 1960–1999 in five-year intervals (1960–1964, 1965–1969, etc.). The dependent variable is adapted from the Peace Research Institute of Oslo's (PRIO) measure of "domestic conflicts based on territorial incompatibility," which refers to struggles over separatism and autonomy.[46]

I derived another data set from the Minorities at Risk project at the Center for International Development and Conflict Management at the University of Maryland.[47] This project identifies 338 "politically-active communal groups in all countries with a current population of at least 500,000." For each of these groups, it codes numerous cultural, political, economic, demographic, and other characteristics. In this second data set, I used each one of these 338 groups as an observation. Although these are identity groups and not regions, they are proxies for subnational regions, controlling for the extent of their geographical concentration. Using the PRIO data set again, each group was coded as to whether and how intensely it engaged in a separatist conflict over the period 1990–2003 (for which most data was available). Forty-eight groups qualify as separatist with at least minor violence since 1990.[48] In addition, the MAR data set offers a variable measuring the intensity of separatist sentiments for each group. Using both the PRIO-derived variable and the MAR index, I tested the relationship between separatism and group characteristics. I also created a version of the MAR separatism index for the country data set by adding up the separatist scores of all minorities for each country. Some hypotheses were tested in both the country and the group settings, which gave a better assessment of their robustness; others depend on variables only available for one of the data sets. At any rate, I used both conflict and sentiment as dependent variables in each data set.

Tables 2.3 and 2.4 present the findings by countries and minorities, respectively. For each table, I first did a set of regressions by category of explanatory variables. In other words, I first tested the economic theories, then the cultural theories, and so on. Variables that were statistically associated with separatism in each of these specific models were included in the general models shown in the tables. If a variable was not significant in the first sets of regressions, it did not make the cut for the final model. The fact that a variable had a significant impact on separatism in the first sets did not guarantee, however, that it would still do so once all other relevant variables were brought in. Thus, some of the variables in the tables are not statistically significant.

Results of Analysis

Before commenting on the effects of the Africa variable, it is worth briefly discussing the overall results and the general predictive quality of the models. Overall, political theories seem to have greater predictive powers than either the economic or cultural ones. Several theories that are almost considered common wisdom in the literature, such as the linkage between natural resources and separatism, do not appear very robust. In fact, none of the economic variables had any significant impact in any of the regressions. Thus, poverty, lack of education, the presence of natural resources, and economic differentials between a region and the rest of the country do not appear to be reliable triggers of separatist conflict or sentiment.

Among cultural variables, the linguistic diversity of a country is a very significant predictor of separatism. The more heterogeneous a country, the more likely it is to encounter separatist activity. This relationship is not as

Table 2.3 The Causes of Separatism at the Country Level

	Model (1) Conflict	Model (2) Sentiment
Africa	–0.49***	–4.0***
	(6.4)	(3.3)
Latin America	–0.44***	–4.2***
	(8.3)	(4.2)
GDP ($000)	–0.004	0.2
	(1.45)	(0.1)
Linguistic diversity	0.41***	3.6**
	(4.3)	(2.1)
Size of largest group	—	–0.9
		(0.5)
State failure	0.2***	1.9***
	(4.1)	(2.8)
Nonseparatist political violence	0.07***	—
	(3.3)	
Regime transition	–0.05***	—
	(2.8)	
Post–Cold War	0.12**	—
	(2.5)	
Repression	0.38***	2.4
	(3.3)	(1.5)
Population (millions)	0.54**	—
	(2.1)	
Country size (million sq. miles)	—	3.1***
		(2.8)
R^2	0.18	0.45
No. of countries	153	143
No. of observations	932	143

Note: Model (1) is estimated with a Prais-Winsten regression, with heteroskedastic panels-corrected standard errors, 1st-order autocorrelation. It covers the period 1960–1999, in five-year increments. The dependent variable (*terrint*) is a measure of the occurrence and intensity of separatist conflict, on a 0–3 scale. Numbers in parentheses are Z values. Model (2) is estimated with an ordinary least squares regression, with heteroskedasticity-robust standard errors. It covers the period 1990–1995. The dependent variable (*sumsep*) is the country sum of each of its minorities' score on the MAR separatism index. Unlike in Model (1) *Post–Cold War* is not measured in model (2) because this data set has no time dimension. Numbers in parentheses are *t* values. Constants omitted for both models. Variables omitted because of insignificance in all partial models: male secondary education, oil, democracy, country age, and territorial discontinuity. Significance (two tails): * for 10%; ** for 5%; *** for 1%.

clear-cut when looking at the level of minorities, however. None of the indicators of cultural heterogeneity or distance between groups, their regional concentration, their share of the population and the presence of a diaspora seemed to matter in terms of promoting the willingness of a group to engage in separatist conflict. Yet, having a regional base (as opposed to being a dispersed minority) did favor the rise of separatist sentiment. That is the only statistically reliable cultural effect on groups, however, and it would be expected to favor African separatism, since African minorities typically have a region of origin.

Table 2.4   The Causes of Separatism at the Subnational Level

	Model (1) Conflict	Model (2) Sentiment
Africa	–0.39** (2.5)	–0.7*** (3.3)
Latin America	–0.41*** (3.8)	–1.1*** (5.3)
GDP in 1990	–3.5 (0.6)	—
Male secondary education, 1990	–0.001 (0.6)	–0.0 (0.2)
Oil and coal	0.09 (0.7)	0.1 (0.4)
Economic differentials	—	–0.0 (0.9)
Regional base	—	0.6*** (3.4)
Group concentration	0.04 (1.2)	0.1 (0.9)
Belief specificity	0.03 (1.2)	—
Cultural heterogeneity	0.27 (1.4)	0.1 (0.3)
Diaspora	—	0.1 (0.7)
Discrimination, 1990	0.1*** (2.9)	—
State failure, 1990	0.12*** (2.9)	0.1** (2.4)
Lost autonomy	0.14*** (2.9)	0.4*** (6.0)
Autonomous region	0.34** (2.5)	0.2 (1.1)
Friendly neighbor	—	–0.0 (0.7)
Group size	—	0.3 1.1
Country size	–0.03* (1.7)	—
R^2	0.25	0.41
No. of groups	310	288

Note: Ordinary least square regressions, with heteroskedasticity-robust standard errors. In model (1), the dependent variable (*terrint*) is a measure of the occurrence and intensity of separatist conflict, on a scale from 0 to 3, measured for the period 1990–2003. In model (2), the dependent variable (*separatism*) is a measure of the strength of separatist sentiment among subnational groups, on a scale from 0 to 3, for the 1990s. Numbers in parentheses are *t* values. Constants omitted. Variables omitted because of insignificance in all partial models: racial, linguistic and customs specificity, population share, dispersion, democracy, and territorial discontinuity. Significance (two tails): * for 10%; ** for 5%; *** for 1%.

The greater impact of the political variables suggests that the decision to secede, around the world, is first and foremost a decision that derives from a country's political system and from a group's particular political situation. Possibly one of the most powerful findings of Table 2.3 is the systematic and large effect of state failure on both separatist conflict and desire. The more failed the state, the more likely subnational components will want out (and the better they might think their odds are). In addition, the prevalence of nonseparatist political violence usually relates to the likelihood of separatist conflict. Both of these variables, of course, would lead us to expect more separatism in Africa. Regime transitions, however, surprisingly appear to reduce the likelihood of secessions. Finally, the end of the Cold War did indeed encourage separatist insurgencies, as does the level of repression of minorities by a regime.

Turning to specific minorities in Table 2.4, politics continues to be the driving force. Both being discriminated against and living in a failed state are strong predictors of the willingness of a group to engage in secessionist conflict, and the latter also of separatist sentiment in general. And, as predicted, having once had autonomy strongly militates in favor of being separatist, as does the current autonomous status of a minority. Given the lack of historical or contemporary autonomy of many of Africa's regions and minorities, this variable is likely to contribute to Africa's separatist deficit.

Africa and Latin America

Even when accounting for the different theories of separatism, there are fewer secessionist conflicts in Africa than one would expect, as indicated by the significantly negative coefficients of the Africa variables in Tables 2.3 and 2.4. All models systematically overpredict the likelihood of separatism in Africa, even though this region is very well represented in all samples, with more than forty countries and some ninety minorities. Table 2.5 shows the results of an experiment. Running the regressions of Tables 2.3 and 2.4 in all non-African countries, I obtained coefficients of the effects of each specific variable on separatism. I then plugged in these coefficients to generate predicted values of separatism for African and non-African countries, and compared those with the actual values in both parts of the world. While the models were generally a good fit for the rest of the world, Table 2.5 shows that they were way off the mark for Africa, where they predicted levels of separatist sentiment and separatist conflict respectively as much as 4.8 and 2.6 times larger than actual. In other words, there are as yet untheorized reasons for why African countries experience relatively little separatism. Our current understanding of the dynamics of secessions does not allow us to account for Africa's separatist deficit.

Nor does it, however, make sense of Latin America's.[49] In fact, Latin America has not experienced a single separatist conflict since the separation of Panama from Colombia in 1903. This unusual trend begs the same question as

Table 2.5 Actual and Predicted Values of Separatism in Africa

	Actual (%)	Predicted (%)
Proportion of country-years with separatist conflict		
Africa	8	38
Rest of the world	11	14
Proportion of groups with separatist conflict		
Africa	9	21
Rest of the world	15	16
Proportion of countries with separatist sentiment		
Africa	51	87
Rest of the world	48	53
Proportion of groups with separatist sentiment		
Africa	19	49
Rest of the world	36	33

Note: Predicted values are calculated based on logit versions of the models from Tables 2.3 and 2.4, with the dependent variables converted to dummies. The models are first run for all non-African countries. Using the coefficients they generate, predicted values are established for the entire world. Reported here are the predicted and actual values for African countries and non-African countries.

Africa's: Can it be explained through the lens of prevailing theories? The answer, by and large, seems to be that Latin American groups and minorities are not constructed in ways that either promote separatism or make it a thinkable part of the registry of political action. Latin American countries do not typically have regionally based subnational groups that could engage in territorial collective action. Until recently, their political divisions were more based on class than ethnicity.[50] Their indigenous minorities also tend to be heterogeneous communities. In addition, the negative Latin American effect in the group data set might partly be an artifact of the type of data that MAR reports and the type of groups it identifies. Of the thirty-three Latin American groups in the data set (there are ninety African ones), ten are categorized as "ethnoclasses," that is, "ethnically or culturally distinct peoples, usually descended from slaves or immigrants, most of whom occupy a distinct social and economic stratum or niche."[51] The categorization of these groups as classes suggests that the mode of their relationship with the state and with other groups in society is not regional, even if they may occasionally inhabit a particular region. Apart from the "Chinese" of Panama, nine of these ten groups are black minorities (or variations thereof, such as "Black Karibs" in Honduras, "Antillean Blacks" in Costa Rica, or "Afro-Brazilians" in Brazil). The twenty other observations are all "Indigenous Peoples," that is, "conquered descendants of earlier inhabitants of a region who live mainly in conformity with traditional social, economic, and cultural customs that are sharply distinct from those of dominant groups."[52] These indigenous groups will on occasion be regionally concentrated, yet their existence as a group is more often a function of external categorization than internal aggregate identity. For indeed, these "indigenous peoples" often include groups of different regions and/or languages and consequently make poor candidates for collective action. Eleven of them are actually categorized in the plural, as "indigenous peoples," but aggregated as one group each. For Bolivia, Ecuador, and Peru, the data set differentiates between "lowland" and "highland indigenous peoples" but also treats each as a single, supposedly homogeneous group. For all of Latin America, the only indigenous groups that are named are the Amazonian Indians of Brazil, and the Mayans and Zapotecs of Mexico, the latter ones of which actually score some positive value on the MAR separatism index.[53] In conclusion, the preponderance of ethnoclasses and indigenous peoples among Latin America's minorities is partly a substantive reason for why this region has developed less separatism (as most theories of separatism assume that a regionally grounded and distinct community is available to develop separatist sentiments) and partly a methodological problem of mixing Latin American apples with oranges from other parts of the world.

The question of the negative effect on separatism of being an African country or minority is more puzzling. Many of the variables associated with separatism in the statistical models—ethnic heterogeneity, state failure, nonseparatist political violence, and repression of minorities—are prevalent in Africa. What prevents these factors from triggering secessions on the continent? Are there some conditions specific to Africa that act as inhibitors of separatism?

Why Do African States Not Disintegrate?

The most commonly heard argument for the stability of Africa's political geography suggests that the rules of the Organization of African Unity (OAU), which commit member states to respect the territorial integrity of other member states, inhibit territorial change by outlawing it.[54] The principles of noninterference, territorial integrity, and respect of colonial borders were reiterated in the Constitutive Act of the AU in 2000. While these rules do not apply to rebel groups, the argument goes that they make it harder for the latter to obtain support from another state in their separatist struggles, reducing the friendly neighbor effect. For example, they make a case like India's military intervention on behalf of Bangladesh in its struggle against Pakistan legally all but impossible. Some believe that these rules might also lower the probability that a separatist movement would be recognized, without which little can be diplomatically achieved. According to this argument, then, the OAU has set norms that have been more inimical to self-determination than elsewhere.[55]

To some extent, this argument rings true. Yet, it has some serious flaws. First is the question of whether the principle of territorial integrity truly is more salient in Africa than elsewhere. International relations and international law specialists are rather unanimous in asserting the near absolute nature of the principle,[56] while the norm of self-determination is deemed to be everywhere much weaker. It is in fact a rather solid doctrinal and jurisprudential position in international law that the right of self-determination is restricted by the principle of territorial integrity.[57] The 1945 UN Charter makes clear that the right of self-government cannot be equated with a right to secession. Resolution 1514 (1960) of the UN General Assembly makes disruption of territorial integrity incompatible with the UN Charter, a principle restated in the final act of the 1975 Helsinki Conference.[58] Most recently, the European Union (EU) reasserted the doctrine of territorial integrity in the 1990s in response to the Yugoslav crisis, acknowledging the right, under certain normative conditions, of independence to the constitutive republics of the federation—Bosnia-Herzegovina, Croatia, Macedonia, Montenegro, Slovenia, and Serbia—while denying it to its constitutive nations (or ethnic groups). The basic underlying principle was that "the right of self-determination must not involve changes to existing frontiers."[59] One can therefore be rather confident that sanctity of boundaries "in no significant way distinguishes the African position from that universally adopted by states."[60]

Yet, one could argue that, although universal, the principle is stronger even for Africa because of the OAU. Its resolutions have no teeth, however, and make little difference in practice. Many African states make a habit of violating OAU resolutions. OAU norms did not prevent Côte d'Ivoire, Gabon, Tanzania, and Zambia from recognizing Biafra in the late 1960s. In addition, in the 1970s, Libya supported separatist movements in northern Chad; the Chadian government supported separatists in Southern Sudan; the Sudanese government supported separatists in Ethiopia; and Ethiopia and Uganda were helping the Southern Sudanese.[61] Note also that, apart from the Soviet Union and Yugoslavia, the only state in the world that has in fact constitutionally recognized the legality of secession (although largely refraining from applying its own law) is Ethiopia, the seat of the AU. As a result, talking of an effective norm of self-restraint in Africa is somewhat exaggerated. Furthermore, if such a norm exists, what power do African states have to enforce it? Certainly, OAU norms of territorial integrity do not seem to apply to Casamance, where rebels received assistance from Guinea-Bissau and Gambia, or Southern Sudan, as indicated above. Moreover, Africans have tinkered with their borders over time, especially right after independences, showing that the principle of postcolonial integrity is no stronger than elsewhere. Rather than the norm of integrity being stronger in Africa, it might only be more salient because African states are empirically weaker than states elsewhere. Thus there is greater contrast between their weakness and the rigidity of their territorial claims. This makes the rules appear particularly stringent, but they are not more so than elsewhere. Across the world, at any given time, sovereignty can be thought of as in fixed supply. When they decide to engage in separatist rebellion, in Africa as elsewhere, rebels are choosing, for their foreseeable future, a nonsovereign solution to their problems.

The empirical findings about separatist "sentiment" described in the previous section also undermine the argument that Africans are not separatist because their actions would be somehow thwarted by lack of recognition or lack of foreign help. If this were the case, we would expect a lack of separatist insurgencies in the region but not of separatist aspirations. Yet, instead, the data show that Africans are on average less likely than people of other regions even to voice separatist preferences, much less to act upon them. We must therefore find an explanation for both of these dimensions, which a focus on OAU rules of recognition does not provide. At any rate, there is no particular evidence that recognition is less forthcoming in Africa than elsewhere. Lee Seymour has shown that although there have been eighty-four different separatist conflicts around the world since 1975, only five internationally recognized states have been created through violent secession since 1945, one of which—Eritrea—was in Africa.[62] Thus, while the propensity for separatism is lesser in Africa than elsewhere, the odds of recognition are not worse in Africa. In fact, Seymour's data suggest that the broad gains from separatist conflict are greater in Africa than elsewhere.

Another commonly heard argument is that African states have endured because there is no obviously superior arrangement available.[63] For example, it is often argued *a contrario* that there are no clear foundations for separatism in Africa because no region is sufficiently homogeneous to warrant secessionism, thereby justifying the existence of, and attachment to, the postcolonial state as rational by default.[64] Certainly, there are no clear cultural lines of demarcation along which many countries could ever be partitioned. While this is true, there are also usually no clear cultural lines of demarcation between African countries, making this argument a mere matter of inertia. More important, the dearth of homogeneous potential successor states cannot explain the continent's lack of separatism, as secessions are only rarely a matter of cultural unity.[65] Neither Eritrea nor Somaliland—Africa's two somewhat successful secessions—are ethnically or culturally more uniform than Ethiopia or the rest of Somalia. Nor are any of the former Soviet republics that proclaimed their independence in the 1990s ethnically homogeneous.[66] While my findings suggest that the regional concentration of a group does promote separatism, they do not imply any territorial monopoly of this group over its region. There is no reason therefore to expect regions of African countries to be less separatist because of their ethnic heterogeneity. The province of Katanga, in the DRC, is a case in point. Katanga's Lunda were a minority whose party, the Confédération des Associations Tribales du Katanga (Confederation of Tribal Associations of Katanga, CONAKAT), only polled 11 percent of provincial votes in the December 1959 communal elections, but who nevertheless embarked on a secession drive from 1960 to 1963 that, although never recognized, developed a substantial degree of functional effectiveness.[67]

One also occasionally hears the argument that secession-prone regions of Africa no longer display any separatism because they are already de facto run autonomously. National governments have been so weak that there is no need to challenge them and make the split more formal. Local leaders can exert autonomy without rocking the boat of national unity. According to Ian Gorus, discussing the case of Katanga in 2002, "the actors are much more autonomous now. They have been since the weakening of Mobutu. As a result, they do not feel the need to challenge Kinshasa."[68] With this argument, then, weak states should be more likely to see national compliance, and strong ones to face separatist conflicts. Yet, the evidence is rather unequivocal against this proposition. One of the most statistically robust determinants of separatist conflict and sentiment around the world, as shown in Tables 2.3 and 2.4, is state failure. That it is not more so in Africa is paradoxical. In addition, the claims of autonomy of local African elites might be exaggerated. In Katanga, for example, Kinshasa continued to appoint governors throughout the war, and progovernment Zimbabwean forces were deployed in the region from 1998 to 2003. Numerous African regional elites may engage in parallel informal activities for their benefit, but they do not as such acquire autonomy from the center. In fact, they often rely on their official role as state agents to carry out these activities, and one tends to find a surprising local resilience of the weak state in these regions, as illustrated in Chapter 3.[69] In addition, while making a plausible claim with respect to the lack of separatist activism by local elites, this type of argument does not explain the lack of separatist sentiments among regional populations at large.

Another variation of this argument stresses that people escape the state individually. They go into exile, for example. They become refugees. Or they withdraw into subsistence agriculture. This type of individual exit has been shown, since the work of Victor Azarya and Naomi Chazan, to deflate capacity for collective exit or the use of collective voice.[70] Yet again, while certainly contributing to an explanation of the lack of collective separatist *action*, this hypothesis does not properly make sense of the lack of separatist *preferences* among people. Moreover, the suboptimal nature of individual escapes, and the material miseries they imply, might logically be expected to eventually trigger the desire for a more collective response, or at least reduce the opportunity costs of such action.

Faced with all these paradoxes, some have then argued that the lack of African separatism might simply be due to successful national integration, shaped by colonial and postcolonial shared experiences. For Neuberger, the "emotional ethnic ties" of partitioned African groups have weakened in the process of national integration, reducing thereby the demand for irredentism.[71]

Crawford Young, for his part, highlights the depth and territorial specificity of nationalist feelings generated in Africa over the past forty years and through the colonial episode. For him, African nationalism originates in the shared experience of "common colonial subjugation." For this reason, he contends, there has been no real confrontation between territorial nationalism and political ethnicity. Furthermore, the affective ties of territorial nationalism appear impervious to negative popular perceptions of the state and its behavior and have so far shielded states torn by civil strife or prolonged economic crises from disintegrating completely.[72]

If territorial nationalism is the cause of territorial resilience in Africa, however, its own origins in turn remain unclear. Thinking of nationalism as an exogenous variable is not particularly helpful in this case. To say that Africans do not challenge their states because they are nationalist tends to merely rephrase the puzzle of territorial resilience. Moreover, if colonialism really shaped identity through shared misery, how is one to explain the partition of India and other nonterritorial separatisms in postcolonial environments? How does one also account for nationalism in Africa's former French colonies, since the latter were ruled under two distinct administrative entities—Afrique Occidentale Française and Afrique Equatoriale Française—until the late 1950s? And what is one to make of the exclusive character of some of Africa's nationalisms, such as Ivoirité, which purports to exclude large segments of Ivorians from the benefits of belonging to the state? This argument is also hard to reconcile with the salience of subnational conflicts in Africa, which tend to be simultaneous with professions of nationalism. In the DRC, for example, where nationalism is rampant, Katangans have fought Kasaians, Lundas have opposed Lubas, Hemas and Lendus have killed each other in the Ituri province, each region has "autochthonous" populations discriminating against newcomers, and the whole country seems unified in its hatred of its Rwandophone minorities. It remains to be explained why territorial nationalism coexists with political ethnicity in Africans' quest for identity and trumps it when it comes to providing the foundations for statehood.

Finally, inferring from James Fearon and David Laitin, Africa's lesser relative preponderance of separatist violence could be due to the fact that African countries tend to have a plurality of smaller ethnic groups rather than large hegemonic ones. These authors find that having one dominant ethnic group is associated with separatism, as minorities consider it less likely that they could obtain a share of the state, given the existing domination of the majority, and are more likely therefore to pursue a separate path.[73] Since African states are so heterogeneous, their constituent groups may be more likely to fight for control of the state than for escape from it, as they each have a decent chance of grabbing some share of power. This echoes Benyamin Neuberger's argument about the "plural softness" of the African state, a "state of minorities," which does not have the will or capacity to fully enforce itself upon its constituent groups, finding instead ways to accommodate them and give them access to the state.[74] Looking at the data, it is true indeed that the largest ethnic groups in African countries average 41 percent of the population, whereas elsewhere around the world they reach about 73 percent on average. Yet, there is no empirical backing for the claim that the lack of a dominant group reduces separatism. Table 2.4 suggests that there is no effect of group size on separatist conflict or sentiment. Yet, although the issue of group size alone is not relevant, the "plural softness" hypothesis has some merit. I will return to it later as a building block of my own argument.

In conclusion, another theory of the lack of territorial challenge to the postcolonial African state is needed if we are to make sense of Africa's separatist deficit. It is the purpose of this book to offer a new answer. Before that, the next chapter turns to the institutional equivalent of the separatist deficit and describes the perplexing resilience of the authority of otherwise decrepit state institutions in Africa's failed states.

Notes

1. Fearon and Laitin, "Weak States."
2. Figures in this paragraph are based on the data set "Armed Conflicts, 1946–2006, Version 4—2007," an update of the data set described in Gleditsch et al., "Armed Conflict" (www.prio.no/cwp/armedconflict).
3. Deng, "Self-Determination."
4. Throughout this book, I use *separatism* and *secessionism* interchangeably to refer to the desire for one's sovereign independent country.
5. See Chapter 6.
6. See Holsti, *The State*, 150–182.
7. I discuss Latin America in somewhat more detail later in this chapter.
8. The count of forty-nine is a very conservative estimate, aggregating many related conflicts. Under this count, for example, Chad has had only one civil conflict since 1960.
9. Hale, "The Parade of Sovereignties," 31–56.
10. Treisman, "Russia's 'Ethnic Revival.'"
11. Bartkus, *The Dynamic of Secession,* 147.
12. Ibid., 149, emphasis mine.
13. Abbay, "Diversity and State-Building."
14. Clapham, "Ethiopia," 30. To be fair, this is probably also true of some groups in other regions.
15. Forrest, *Subnationalism in Africa.*
16. Minorities at Risk, www.cicdm.umd.edu/inscr/mar.
17. Horowitz, "Patterns of Ethnic Separatism," 171.
18. Nolutshungu, *Limits of Anarchy*, 2.
19. Ibid., 233.
20. ICG, "Tchad," 6–7.
21. Buijtenhuijs, *La conférence*, 58–60.
22. Quoted by ibid., 61.
23. Buijtenhuijs, *La conférence*, 146–147.
24. Nolutshungu, *Limits of Anarchy*, 14, 280–281.

25. EIU, *Country Report: Côte d'Ivoire*, 25.

26. *Africa Research Bulletin*, February 2005, 42(2):16114

27. Joseph, "Nation-State Trajectories," 15.

28. This section summarizes work I carried out with Katharine Boyle. For more detailed findings and for all questions of data, sources, and methodology, see Englebert and Boyle, "The Primacy of Politics."

29. Hechter, "Dynamics of Secession," 275; Hale, "The Parade of Sovereignties," 33; Bookman, *The Economics of Secession*, 44; Horowitz, "Patterns of Ethnic Separatism"; Horowitz, *Ethnic Groups in Conflict*; Collier and Hoeffler, "The Political Economy," 37–59.

30. Ross, "What Do We Know?" 11–12; Le Billon, "Angola's Political Economy."

31. Treisman, "Russia's 'Ethnic Revival,'" 222; Bookman, *The Economics of Secession*, 46; Collier and Hoeffler, "The Political Economy."

32. Collier and Hoeffler, "Greed and Grievance." There is no indication in this argument, however, as to why conflicts promoted by the lack of opportunity for young men should be more about separatism than about control of the government. This variable might thus be equally associated with the prevalence of all conflict in Africa, including nonterritorial ones.

33. Collier and Hoeffler, "The Political Economy," 5.

34. Ibid.

35. Treisman, "Russia's 'Ethnic Revival,'" 231; Hale, "The Parade of Sovereignties"; Laitin, "Secessionist Rebellion," 852; Collier and Hoeffler, "The Political Economy"; Sambanis, "Partition as a Solution," 457.

36. Young, *Politics of Cultural Pluralism*, 460 and 474; see also Bartkus, *The Dynamic of Secession*.

37. See Malkki, *Purity and Exile*.

38. Ayres and Saideman, "Is Separatism as Contagious?" 92–114.

39. Laitin, "Secessionist Rebellion"; Lapidus, "Contested Sovereignty," 11.

40. Horowitz, *Ethnic Groups in Conflict*, 12–13.

41. Young, *Politics of Cultural Pluralism*, 489.

42. Gurr, *Minorities at Risk*.

43. Gorenburg, "Not with One Voice," 115; see also Bookman, "The Economics of Secession," 49.

44. Fearon and Laitin, "Ethnicity, Insurgency, and Civil War," 84.

45. For a more thorough discussion of method, see Englebert and Boyle, "The Primacy of Politics." The data set and codebook are available at www.politics.pomona.edu/penglebert.

46. Gleditsch et al., "Armed Conflict."

47. For details on the project and access to its data, see www.cidcm.umd.edu/inscr/mar/. The limits of the MAR data set did not allow for a replication of the quinquennial approach used with the country set.

48. Using a simple separatist-conflict dummy as dependent variable yielded similar results.

49. Other continent variables did not have any significant impact.

50. On the class argument, see Holsti, *The State*. Deborah Yashar (*Contesting Citizenship*, 54–77) has shown that indigenous identity has increasingly substituted for class identity in several Latin American countries since the 1990s, partly as a function of the loss of regional autonomy of indigenous groups. Although these groups' demands have so far focused on regaining autonomy and recognition of their indigenous status by the state, they may yet evolve toward a more separatist agenda.

51. From www.cidcm.umd.edu/inscr/mar/about/types.htm.

52. Ibid.

53. The three remaining Latin American minorities-at-risk groups are the "East Indians" and "Africans" of Guyana, and the "Jews" of Argentina.

54. OAU Charter, Addis Ababa, May 1963, articles III and IV; Resolution 16(1), First Ordinary Session of the Assembly of Heads of State and Government, Cairo, 1964.

55. Neuberger, "Irredentism and Politics," 107.

56. Bartkus, *The Dynamic of Secession*, 68.

57. See Dugard, "A Legal Basis."

58. Bartkus, *The Dynamic of Secession*.

59. For a good summary of the doctrine articulated by the Badinter Commission, see Rich, "Recognition of States."

60. Emerson, "The Problem of Identity," 300.

61. Connor, "The Politics of Ethno-Nationalism," 15.

62. Seymour, "The Surprising Success."

63. For example, Young, "Nation, Ethnicity, and Citizenship," 245.

64. Horowitz, 'The Cracked Foundations," 5–17.

65. Forrest, *Subnationalism in Africa*.

66. Treisman, "Russia's 'Ethnic Revival,'" 231.

67. Gérard-Libois, *La sécession katangaise,* 41.

68. Ian Gorus, interview, Lubumbashi, April 2002.

69. See also Roitman, *Fiscal Disobedience*.

70. Azarya and Chazan, "Disengagement from the State."

71. Neuberger, "Irredentism and Politics," 105.

72. Young, "Nationalism and Ethnicity."

73. Fearon and Laitin, "Weak States," 10–11.

74. Neuberger, "Irredentism and Politics," 105.

3

The Enduring Authority
of Weak States

Beyond its paradoxical capacity to preserve its territorial integrity, the African state also displays institutional resilience. However failed the state, its agencies and laws retain currency. They maintain their local authority. Even when collapsed, the state does not dissipate or dissolve. Even when the government it-self has become unable to project its power, the state apparatus remains ubiqui-tous across its territory. Even when citizens respond to state failure with oppor-tunistic disengagement and substitution, they cannot fully free themselves from it.

This resilience of the weak state's authority may come as a surprise given its very weakness and the multiplicity of adaptive institutional arrangements devised by Africans to deal with its shortcomings and avoid its exactions. Nonstate associative life is vibrant in Africa, and the state faces competing sources of public authority. Yet, by and large, societal responses to state fail-ure have not prevented the reproduction of state institutions and of their au-thority. The African weak state is formidably resilient. Incapable, deserted, hollowed out, and substituted for, it nevertheless manages to retain a com-manding presence in the lives of Africans. State personnel and agencies still find the power to impose themselves onto people. In addition, nonstate actors tend to acquiesce to the state's continued existence and reproduce its author-ity in their interactions. Even in zones of open insurgency, rebels typically maintain and use the state institutions left behind. They become the state more than they challenge it. Altogether, the authority of the African state appears immune to its incapacity; it transcends its weakness and failure.

Staying Alive: Agencies of the Failed State

Robert Rotberg's claim that state collapse is equivalent to a "vacuum of au-thority," where the state is reduced to "a mere geographical expression, a black hole into which a failed polity has fallen [and where] the forces of entropy have overwhelmed the radiance that hitherto provided some semblance of order and other vital political goods," does not find much support in Africa where state failure does not translate into an institutional vacuum.[1] Michael Bratton's assertion that the weak African state "remains the most prominent landmark on the African institutional landscape" is more accurate.[2] The agencies of the failed state tend to go on and on, and continue to carry authority, however comatose they might be. They may no longer do much for citizens, but they are still there and they continue to make their presence felt. They retain a degree of legal authority, even when they are severed from the center. Thus, while a government might be hard put to project any power outside its capital city, it will not be uncommon for state agencies in remote provinces of the country to continue to exercise local authority.[3] The laws, institutions, and agencies of the state endure; its authority continues to project across the territory, even when not enforced from the center.

Sam Nolutshungu captured this resilience in his study of Chad, an enduring but continuously failed state. Noting the state's material disintegration, he remarked that "there is another sense in which it continued to exist. The state is also an ensemble of competences, legal and ideological . . . and of possibilities of authoritative action, uniquely recognized as such, both domestically and internationally."[4] The puzzling continued "authoritative action" of the local personnel and agencies of the failed state in the DRC is one of the main reasons I initially embarked on this research project. I was surprised as I traveled to Katanga, North Kivu, and Orientale provinces in 2001 and 2002 with the visibly enduring presence of the state in these remote and largely disconnected regions. Unpaid for months if not years, many civil servants continued to report to work, even when their offices had been destroyed or pillaged as in Kisangani, which had suffered three rounds of devastating war. Without any budget to carry out their mission, they continued to go through the motions of their work. Multiple "authorities" persisted in checking one's papers, demanding and issuing authorizations for seemingly anything, and enforcing apparently outdated, irrelevant, or otherwise burdensome regulations. In Katanga, civil society activists complained to me that, although they had taken over responsibility for many services from a truant government, they could not shake off the ability of state agents to impose themselves onto them. "We build private roads, but the state comes and sets up tolls," one of them told me.[5]

Others have noticed the remarkable degree of local physical state presence and authority of the failed Congolese state. A 2006 report on mining in Katanga by Global Witness noted a "bewildering range of officials . . . [at] the entrance point to each mine, at the mineshafts . . . , at the exit point from the mines, along the roads, at checkpoints and at border posts," including representatives of several departments from the Ministry of Mines, the Mining Police, the Ministry of External Trade, the Office des Douanes et Accises (Customs Office, OFIDA), the National Intelligence Agency (ANR), the Lubum-bashi mayor's office, local traditional chiefs (who are state agents in Congo), the state-sponsored Association of Artisan Miners of Katanga, and last but not least, the Office Congolais de Contrôle (Congolese Office of Control, OCC).[6]

Similarly, a 2007 report by the Pole Institute, a North Kivu–based Congolese NGO, highlighted the multitude of state agencies and the continued legal formality of procedures involved in the official weighing of cassiterite exports by trading firms in Goma. These agencies included the official mineral certification body, the OCC, OFIDA, the nontax state revenue collection agency, the Provincial Mining Division, a representative of the governor, the ANR, the immigration control agency, the military intelligence agency, the Mining Police, the presidential guard, and the provincial military police.[7] All these agencies were present at the weighing and many of them later required traders to come to their offices for the formal issuance of certificates. Yet, this was all taking place in a city and region where state agencies long ago stopped providing services such as security, public health, education, and infrastructure.[8] The state was both no longer there and yet still overwhelmingly present.

Such resilience is not unique to Congo. In partitioned Côte d'Ivoire, then largely under the authority of a UN mission, President Laurent Gbagbo stressed in 2006 that "every institution functions," although he noted that "the decisions we take do not manage to reach the entire territory."[9] On the one hand, Gbagbo was delusional, for the state had really collapsed around him. On the other hand, he was right, for its apparatus had endured despite his own personal lack of control over it. Even in zones of conflict in the west of the country, state cocoa marketing agencies continued to function, for example. In the north, rebels maintained and enforced international borders and levied custom duties and taxes. Schools followed the national curriculum and administered state-mandated school tests.[10]

While stressing the "striking" absence of government in rural areas of the Central African Republic, Thomas Bierschenk and Jean-Pierre Olivier de Sardan also note the state's continued local institutional presence and authority as embodied in village and district chiefs. Even when they no longer receive instructions or salaries from the center and must compete with other sources of local authority, these chiefs carry on as local state appendages and are the main perpetuators of the weak state. Most of them, they write, "see themselves first and foremost as representatives of the state in a quite literal interpretation of [the law]. . . . They visually emphasize this by sporting an official medal which symbolically reinforces the official definition of their duty."[11] This is not only true of the Central African Republic. Across the continent, "encapsulated in state bureaucracy by legislation," chiefs reproduce the local authority of the weak state.[12]

Even when nonstate agents organize to substitute for failed state agencies, the latter tend to endure in parallel. In the DRC again, with the formal judiciary ravaged by corrupt practices in the 1990s, many lawyers started resorting to out-of-court settlements, a practice that gave rise to a parallel negotiated legal system. Yet, the latter did not displace the formal judiciary and actually relied on its jurisprudence and other official sources of the law. Moreover, out-of-court settlements were brought to court clerks for authentication.[13] The legal framework of the state also perpetuated itself through the work of the justice and peace commissions developed by the Catholic Church. Although they meant to "circumvent the state as a mediator of societal conflicts," Denis Tull writes that these institutions were "informed by state-formulated facts of offenses as a 'legal' framework. . . . They thus [upheld], in effect, modern state laws and may ultimately [have bolstered] the persistence of statehood."[14]

Social Acquiescence and the Nonstate Reproduction of State Authority

The capacity of the state's agencies and legal structure to endure in decentralized form in times of weakness might partly be a function of the significant degree of acquiescence to these agencies displayed by citizens at large, however cynical they might be about them. Take the example of the traders in the markets of Lubumbashi, Katanga, who are, as in many parts of Africa, overwhelmed with taxes and fees. They pay an initial tax to have access to market space, monthly and annual taxes for the right to maintain a market stall, a tax for water (which they do not get), and a tax for cleaning (which they have to do themselves). They also have to build their own stall and there are no functioning restrooms and virtually no other infrastructure. In other words, they receive nothing in exchange for the multiple extractions to which they are subjected. The revenues from the taxes, collected by the market managers who are appointed by the city, evaporate along the way. The market managers contend they pass on the funds to the commune, which, in turn, reports transferring them to the city, and so on. This is hardly unusual. What is surprising, however, is the apparent acceptance of this arbitrary taxation by the retailers themselves. In a poll of the opinions of traders about these exactions by public authority in several Lubumbashi markets, typical responses included "it is the commune's money," "we do not have a choice," "what are we going to do? It is the state that requires it," "it is not up to us to demand justification," and finally, "*ni bya l'Etat,*" which means "it belongs to the state" or "these are the things of the state" in Swahili.[15]

There is more than fatalism in this acceptance of the arbitrariness of the public domain. The "ni bya l'Etat" expression is actually in part ironic and is often proffered at tax collectors by traders to signify their understanding that this money will actually line their pockets and not accrue to the state. In fact, it seems to be used anytime someone abuses a public good. If a civil servant is told to carefully manage public monies or to take care of the public assets under his control, he might answer "ni bya l'Etat," which signifies that the money or asset in question is now removed from the realm of accountability by virtue of being in the domain of the state. It affirms both his public authority over these assets and his capacity to abuse them.[16] The same expression, in the mouths of his victims, conveys their understanding and general acceptance, however grudgingly, of this state of affairs.

The anecdote from the Lubumbashi markets illustrates what might be a broader trend across the continent, characterized by a reluctance to challenge state institutions or state prerogatives while simultaneously knowing that people in position of state authority abuse it. Data on Nigeria from the Afrobarometer tell a similar story. When asked "how much do you trust the police?" 89 percent of Nigerians responded "not at all" or only "a little." But when asked the extent to which they agreed or disagreed with the statement "the police always have the right to make people obey the law," 78 percent agreed or strongly agreed.[17] Regular police exactions (the official police slogan "Fire for Fire" has been popularly perverted into "Fire for Naira") do not undermine the perceived legality of the police as an official institution.[18] Yet, everybody knows that police are for sale, that they use their official functions for private profit. In Nigeria as in Congo, although there is a clear understanding that the resources extracted or the violence perpetrated in the name of the state actually benefit private individuals and pursuits, the right of these state agents to tax or use force is not questioned.

There is also a tendency for organizations that substitute for the state to fall short of radically challenging it and to end up contributing to its reproduction, willingly or not. It is necessary to stress here the vitality of associative responses to state decay in Africa. The state's institutional resilience does not imply that Africans are not also resilient in the face of adversity. Across Africa, many people organize to mitigate the effects of state weakness on their lives, provide public goods, and establish bonds of social solidarity. There *is* adaptation; there *is* substitution; and there *is* resistance. Michael Bratton noted such vibrancy as early as 1989, stressing the increased instances of refusal to comply with the state since the beginnings of its economic crisis.[19] Since then, much literature on Africa's civil society and on patterns of disengagement or escape has stressed the innovative responses of Africans to state failure.[20] Some have highlighted the numerous associative adaptations to Africa's crisis, and the multiplicity of institutions attempting to exercise public authority across Africa.[21] In numerous instances, these associations have been successful in providing public goods, even complex ones like environmental sustainability.[22] There is also much evidence that Africans have stood up to their governments on many occasions.[23] Commenting on the vagaries of the democratic movement in Cameroon, Célestin Monga has argued that a civil society has been vociferous and has posed effective challenges to the state for a very long time, manifested through informal groups and cultural practices.[24]

Yet, there is an apparent contradiction between the multiplicity of popular social experiments in Africa and the limited extent to which they end up undermining the state, which other authors have also observed. Richard Joseph, for example, has noted the "persistence of the modernist ideal of the nation-state in Africa despite the medievalist reality of multiple, overlapping political forms" on the ground.[25] Writing on Cameroon, Francis Nyamnjoh has found it "curious that opposition parties, the media, the churches, and other associations have failed to capitalize . . . on the widespread inclination at the grassroots towards a more democratic social and political order. . . . The bulk of Cameroonians want a change for the better. . . . What, then, stops them from pursuing their aspirations in an organized and sustained manner, with or without violence?"[26] In his study of coping mechanisms by Kinshasa residents, Theodore Trefon has shown the strength of popular inventions, yet simultaneously made clear the lack of significant political invention: "In marked opposition to their inventiveness for physical, social and cultural survival, the Kinois have proven themselves abysmally inapt with respect to transforming political discourse and political desires into political mobilisation."[27] To some extent, therefore, there may be an exaggerated perception among scholars of the institutional decline of the African state and of the magnitude of the social and political reconfiguration it faces.[28]

In much of Africa, associative life seems to have produced little erosion in the authority of the state, and little improvement in its accountability. Nonstate actors frequently display what Bratton refers to as a "deferential attitude of dependency" vis-à-vis the state.[29] Demands for greater state accountability are few or largely ineffective. In essence, associations do not fully become civil society. Few transformative political coalitions seem to emerge from the spread of associational life, and the state tends to maintain its ways despite associational activism.

Sometimes, nonstate actors experience difficulties in reforming the state because they do not appear to represent a credible alternative to its ways. They might even seem to embrace the logic of the state and mimic its authoritarian or corrupt ways. Augustine Ikelegbe notes that Nigerian civil society, for example, exhibits many organizational weaknesses, including corruption, a willingness to be co-opted, occasional reliance on state financing, and the absence of democratic values in internal structures and operations.[30] In the DRC, the nebula of organizations regrouped under the umbrella network that calls itself "Civil Society" has a structure that broadly imitates that of the state, including a president and multiple administrative branches. As Lund puts it, "the idea of the state is . . . effectively propelled by institutions which challenge the state but depend on the idea of it to do so."[31]

When not copying the state, some nonstate actors use it to establish or support their own authority. As the work of Sally Moore in Tanzania shows, the development or assertion of local authorities and local community organizations often takes place in a competitive environment where disputes are frequent. Groups then often rely on government intervention to resolve these disputes, thereby reproducing state authority in their region, even as they attempt to substitute for it. Thus, organizations in rural communities tend not to mobilize in such a way as to challenge the state, but find it easier to increase their own local influence and power by aligning themselves with whatever is left of it. Implicit and explicit references to the state in local politics, and claims of state recognition in support of local displays of authority, are frequent. Often, local organizations also rely on official legal instruments to assert their local authority.[32]

Christian Lund has found that conflicts between the Mamprusi and the Kusasi of Northern Ghana tend to revolve around state symbols of chiefly authority. One group typically asserts its hegemony over the other by claiming state authority through the display of symbols of sovereign statehood, such as the national flag, official stationery, rubber stamps, and other "administrative regalia."[33] Such practices went on throughout the multiple episodes of state collapse experienced by Ghana in the 1970s and 1980s and promoted the peripheral reproduction of the state even when it had imploded at its core and despite unsettled local political relations. In northern Côte d'Ivoire, the state's helplessness in confronting rising criminality in the early 1990s led to the transformation of traditional hunter associations—*donzo ton*—into "community guardians." Yet, the government was nevertheless able to co-opt the *donzo ton* to make them work on its behalf. Crucial in this co-optation was the *donzo ton*'s own desire to achieve "government recognition of the association as a legitimate private security organization." The government went as far as providing hunter identity cards to "true" *donzo*.[34] In Niger, Lund again shows that, like chieftaincies, hometown associations and vigilante groups embrace "the formal language of the state," reproduce the territorial delimitations of districts, and rely on "ensigns of authority," derived from the police and the prefecture in addition to resorting to other forms of legitimation.[35] In Southern Nigeria, David Pratten and Charles Gore illustrate how organizations such as youth associations, vigilante groups, and area "boys" do "not project a revolutionary anti-state message" and seek in fact the patronage of local politicians.[36] Lund notes that, "in this sense, they may come across as innovative and transforming yet conservative at the same time . . . paradoxically, they become part of what they depict as 'exterior.'"[37]

Finally, nonstate organizations sometime simply refuse to challenge the state. Returning to the example of justice and peace commissions in the DRC, Tull again notes that, while they "are institutional innovations," they

> do *not* want to substitute the state. These organizations are very explicit in that their para-juridical approach does not aim at replacing the state in the long run, for example in order to create an autonomous non-state sphere of collective action, sometimes depicted by observers as the "retraditionalization" of a

society that purportedly turns its back on a state that has deceived its expectations for too long. . . . Time and time again, Kivu residents have affirmed to
this author that they will not allow the state to abdicate its responsibilities . . .
the *idea* of the state and the normative conception and functions underpinning
it are apparently deeply rooted in a society.[38]

Even large-scale organizations with a precolonial past, while largely
resurgent since the 1990s, seem likely to refrain from challenging the state.[39]
The king of the Ashanti may be the head of his own quasi state, yet, as he made
clear to the British Broadcasting Corporation (BBC) in 2005, "Some would
think we are challenging the authority, but we would want to assure them that
we are partners with them."[40] Such an attitude contrasts with the one displayed
by his ancestor before the crystallization of the postcolonial state. In 1958, the
Ashanti king had refused to participate in the ceremonies of independence of
Ghana, complaining that it amounted to usurpation of his own sovereignty. In
Uganda, where the Buganda kingdom has witnessed a remarkable resurgence
since the early 1990s, its main demand has been to be further incorporated into
the state through constitutionally recognized privileges and federalism, rather
than compete with it.[41] In general, "traditional" authority across Africa has
more often partaken in what Richard Sklar has called "mixed government"
than attempted to reaffirm a sense of historical legitimacy in contradistinction
to the postcolonial state.[42]

Practices of passive resistance and substitution to the state both eventually
tend to contribute to its reproduction. Rather than undermining state authority
or promoting more accountable state-society relations, local associative or
"traditional" responses to state decay tend to favor the local reinforcement of
its authority. The equilibrium properties of the weak African state transpire
through this propensity of nonstate actors to reproduce it. For formidable as its
resilience might be, it gets much help from others, including many among its
apparent victims.

Rebels as State Custodians

While regular citizens, civil associations, and traditional chiefs might find it
difficult to break away from the shackles of the state, one would at least expect
rebels, insurgents, and other actors endowed with the tools of political violence
to challenge the states that they fight. Yet, African rebels appear in general as
conservative in matters of state institutions as everyone else. They might take
issue with state authorities, but not with the authority of the state. Separatist or
not, they typically do not embark upon institutional innovation; they rarely implement any substantive political project in the regions they control.

The example of the DRC's Rassemblement Congolais pour la Démocratie (Congolese Rally for Democracy, RCD) is telling. As an insurgent movement, it had effective control of the two Kivus and large swaths of Haut-Congo and Katanga between 1998 and 2005. A large part of its political discourse called for a transformation of the state, particularly the introduction of federalism and the devolution of power and fiscal resources to the local level. Yet, as Denis Tull, who lived for several months in RCD-controlled territory, observed, "rumors suggesting that the rebels have engaged in a bottom-up process of reconstruction of the withering state administration do not stand up to any scrutiny. . . . The RCD has simply taken charge of the administrative apparatus it found in place. . . . [L]egal prescriptions and administrative procedures dating back to Mobutu . . . have been maintained."[43] This was true of the main RCD faction, which was in control in Goma. In the "Grand Nord" region of Kivu, where another faction of the RCD was in control, local rebels enforced the border with Uganda where they taxed cross-border trade, contributing to the maintenance of Congo's territorial integrity. At the Kasidi customs post, rebels staffed OFIDA, the customs agency.[44]

In Côte d'Ivoire, the Forces Nouvelles (New Forces, FN), who controlled the entire northern half of the country from 2003 to 2007 and whose leaders' national identity had been questioned by the regime in power, not only maintained existing state agencies in their region but also celebrated national holidays on their own in the north.[45] Although they announced the creation of new agencies and administrative sectors, these did not usually result in significant changes on the ground. The rebels actually participated in the national government in the south (although they did not often report for duty) while militarily holding the north. The conflict was largely resolved in 2007 when rebel leader Guillaume Soro accepted the country's prime ministership, under the very authority of Laurent Gbagbo, the man he had been fighting since 2003.

In Southern Sudan, too, the civil administration of the Sudan People's Liberation Movement (SPLM), after more than twenty years of significant territorial control, remained at best skeletal and well inferior in practice to what it was said to be on paper, before the apparent end of the conflict in 2005. For sure, the SPLM had some level of "a functioning civil administration throughout SPLA [Sudan People's Liberation Army]–controlled territory," particularly a court system based on customary courts, which might have compared favorably with what the Sudanese government had previously provided.[46] Yet, Ken Crossley has argued that the SPLM gave little more than theoretical support to its own legal structures and that its bureaucratic structure "exists largely in name only." Crossley also contends that the SPLM leadership showed little interest in creating a civil administration.[47] Adam Branch and Zachariah Mampilly write that, despite some limited achievements, "the construction of a representative, inclusive, and autonomous civil authority has not been essential, nor has the SPLA made a significant effort to build such a local government."[48] In a later work, Mampilly contrasts the limited institutional achievements of the SPLM with the much further-reaching reforms of the Tamil Tigers in Sri Lanka.[49]

Finally, even the few separatist insurgencies among Africa's rebellions also reproduce the postcolonial state to the extent that they usually call for the independence of their region on the grounds of past colonial existence. Separatist movements in Eritrea, Somaliland, and Western Sahara, and to a lesser extent in Southern Sudan and Casamance, have all had for a primary goal the restoration of a colonial space and have typically sought control of an administratively defined region rather than an ethnic one. They may be radical in the extent to which they call for new states, but they are conservative in the extent to which they base these calls on past colonial existence, which is the foundation of nearly all African states. They do not challenge the African state system; they want to partake in it.

Why Does the Authority of Africa's Weak States Endure?

Whether it be the multiplicity of local agencies on the ground, the passive acquiescence of citizens, the tendency for nonstate actors to invoke the state, the collaboration of chiefs, or the mimesis of rebels, the equilibrium properties of Africa's weak and failed states fly in the face of expectations. In broad theoretical terms, we would expect the inefficiencies of African states to give rise to other institutional arrangements. In a book entitled *The Sovereign State and Its Competitors*, Hendrik Spruyt showed how material changes, anchored in demographics and trade, gave the territorial state a comparative advantage in Western Europe around the eleventh century over alternative forms of collective action.[50] While his book made a compelling argument about the competitiveness of the state, it also implied that changes in the material conditions that were favorable to states could lead them to lose this competitive edge to other forms of organization. For all practical purposes, sovereign territorial states have largely demonstrated their incompetence in sub-Saharan Africa. They have lost their institutional comparative advantage. As instruments of collective action, they are at best dysfunctional, inefficient, and suboptimal. Yet, as illustrated in this section, they do not generally seem to be threatened by institutional competitors. On the contrary, although many alternative institutions rise to organize public life at the local level, provide basic services, foster community, and guarantee people a modicum of safety, the limited extent to which these alternative institutions have actually reconfigured power and challenged state authority has been astonishing. Africa defies predictions that the "the crumbling of one form of political order can reveal or give rise to the emergence of new or incipient kinds of political order."[51] What explains

Africa's institutional inertia and the maintenance of the hegemony of its failed states over other forms of social organization and challenge?

A first level of answer might deal with the fact that there has not been much time yet to properly assess the long-run evolution of the African state. Some of what appears today as aimless institutional noise might well be the precursor of greater and more fundamental changes to come. After all, Spruyt documents an evolution that took three centuries, while African states have only been independent for a few decades. While this is possible, two elements militate against such an interpretation of institutional resilience. The first is that contemporary African political actors tend to show lesser propensity for institutional innovation than they did in the latter years of colonization or in the early years of independence. Right before the waves of independence, there were several attempts at innovation throughout the continent, including federation and the creation of intercolonial political parties, like the Rassemblement Démocratique Africain in 1946, which united politicians throughout Francophone West and Equatorial Africa. The development of the Rwenzururu Kingdom in parallel to the Ugandan state also dates back to the early 1960s. These and other innovations were what Basil Davidson rightly calls "political initiatives of foresight and imagination."[52] They contrast with the relative lack of political imagination that prevails fifty years later.

The second is that rapid, discontinuous change does happen in history, particularly when states are weak. With the monarchy in deep decay, the French General Estates led to the revolution of 1789, which ushered in massive political transformation, both in the system of rule and the foundations of political legitimacy. In comparison, the African national conferences of the 1990s, albeit patterned after the general estates, did not bring about similarly significant changes in the nature of power in Africa, despite some other considerable achievements.[53] When the burden of taxation without representation became unbearable, the colonists in America rose in revolt against the British Crown and invented their own political system, also laying down alternative principles of political legitimacy. In Africa, potential holders of alternative legitimacy—be they chiefs, churches, or civil society activists—tend not to rise in defiance of the state's endless extractions and predation. When the Soviet Union faltered in 1989, many of its constituent republics were quick to unilaterally proclaim their sovereignty. In Africa, it is exceptionally rare for subnational units to do so, even when beyond the repressive reach of the state (Biafra, Eritrea, and Somaliland appear to be the only instances).

A second argument might invoke reasonableness. It is not necessarily the vocation of every organization to displace the state, and economic or public-good substitution may often be all that is reasonably needed. From this perspective, much is happening on the ground as people organize to mitigate the negative effects of state failure, including through the private provision of education, health care, and some other public goods. It might also be unrealistic to expect nonstate actors to become "new sites of potential sovereignty" in a world dominated by states.[54] As Kingston has noted, "given the entrenchment of the state system in the twentieth century, it is now extremely difficult for such political entities to make the transition to statehood."[55]

While much of that is indeed reasonable, one would at least expect non-state actors in Africa to contribute to reforming the state, that is, change the way power operates. With the state weakened and associative life strong, one could expect the state to surrender some ground to nonstate actors, and the latter to exert greater leverage on the former. Robert Putnam has shown, for example, how civic associations in northern Italy contribute to accountable state institutions.[56] The rich literature on nonstate institutions in Africa, which posits disengagement or engagement as the two prevalent modes of political action, also seems to assume that, if Africans do not build alternative autonomous institutions of their own, they will at least promote a reform of existing ones.[57] Yet, African state actors somehow remain immune to the consequences of widespread domestic institutional developments. Their authority seems to suffer no challenge. As for nonstate institutions, they neither fully disengage nor promote state reform, but rather cohabit with the state in what Achille Mbembe has referred to as an arrangement of "conviviality."[58] In doing so, nonstate actors, far from normative expectations of their reformist impulse, actually reinforce the equilibrium nature of Africa's weak states. Adaptation and reaction to state failure do not lead to state reconstruction.

Pushing the argument of reasonableness further, one might also ask what can realistically be expected in terms of institutional innovation from poor people focused on day-to-day survival. It is true that poverty can be an impediment to social change. Yet, it must be borne in mind that change is usually initiated by elites, who retain a capacity for agency in times of crisis. Chiefs, regional politicians, civil society activists, opponents, or rebel leaders are not dissuaded from action by their supporters' dire material conditions. In the case of rebels, at least, it is in fact equally likely that the poverty of their supporters will facilitate their enlistment in the rebellion. Paul Collier and Anke Hoeffler have provided ample evidence that the lesser the level of education of young men, the more likely they are to join rebellions.[59] Whether this is a matter of opportunity cost or grievance does not affect the overall pattern. Poor or angry, a gun is not a bad thing to have. Moreover, the paradox is not so much that there is no political mobilization at all in Africa, which poverty might have explained, as the fact that its agenda is not typically focused on reforming the state. Recall from Chapter 2 that while the propensity for political violence is great in Africa and people are willing to mobilize for conflict, they just tend not to do so for transformative political agendas.

Even if fully aggrieved by state failure and aware of the necessity for change, it might nevertheless be rational for many not to challenge the state. In his seminal work on *Exit, Voice and Loyalty*, Albert Hirschman suggested that one can sometimes be dissuaded from leaving a transaction or a political situation because one would still suffer from its poor quality, from its negative externalities. For example, if public schools in my neighborhood were bad and I decided to pull my children out and send them to a private school, I would not contribute to improving the quality of public schools. As a result, I would still suffer from their negative impact on things such as local social capital and property prices. Thus, I might consider that I am better off leaving my children in and trying to mitigate their poor education by helping them at home with their school work.[60] A similar logic might dissuade potential state challengers in Africa from actually challenging their states. Anyone thinking of starting, say, their own commune in the margins of the state, would be well aware not only of the continuation of a deteriorating environment around them (such as bad roads, health care, and the general lack of public safety), but also of the continued capacity of state actors to be a nuisance to them. Any rebels wishing to build up their own institutions would still be confronted with the effects of the remaining dysfunctional institutions of the state in the areas they control. The followers of any chief wishing to establish his political authority in the face of an illegitimate state would still have to cope with ineffective bureaucracies whenever they need essential documents for travel or education.

While such circumstances would indeed reduce one's propensity for disengagement, we would still expect those who fail to exit to help reform the system. If I left my children in public schools, I might consider volunteering in the classroom or joining the parent-teacher association. In Africa, the puzzle of institutional inertia includes both the lack of exit and the lack of voice, the lack of alternative to the state and the lack of reform of the state. While Hirschman gets us on the right track, his analytical tool still falls short of capturing the comprehensive resilience of Africa's weak states.

Third, we should bear in mind that there are some significant exceptions to the general picture of state resilience and social acquiescence painted in this chapter. Some countries have witnessed cases of more or less far-reaching institutional innovation, such as the largely autonomous Rwenzururu Kingdom of Uganda in the 1960s and Somaliland since 1991.[61] Some local groups have risen to challenge the political legitimacy of the state, such as Bundu dia Kongo for the autonomy of Bas-Congo in the DRC after 2000, and, to a lesser extent, Buganda in Uganda after 1990. Some rebels have offered alternative modes of governance to that of the state they were fighting, like the National Resistance Army/Movement (NRA/M), also in Uganda, in the 1980s and after. I will come back to these in Chapter 6. At this point, however, while these cases serve as reminders that my generalizations about institutional inertia miss some significant variations, it must be stressed that they remain exceptions. For as salient and informative as they can be, they are rare. Given the failures of the African state, the puzzle is that there are not more such radical initiatives. In part, their scarcity can be attributed to the continued repressive capacity of the weak state, as illustrated by the violent destruction of Bundu dia Kongo by Congolese authorities in 2007 and 2008. Yet, proximity to Kinshasa made this repression possible. In most cases, weak governments have a hard time deploying repression across large territories.

Finally, one could argue that weak African states endure because they have engineered legitimacy for themselves over time, irrespective of their lack of capacity. Joel Migdal suggests that "certain areas of state-society interaction can create meaning for people in society, and that meaning, in turn, can naturalize the state. . . . People . . . cannot imagine their lives without it."[62] Public "rituals and ceremonies" provide one place where such naturalization of the state occurs, for they "connect the sacred to the notion of the nation and the mundane institutions of the state."[63] For anyone familiar with the propensity of African leaders to stage public ceremonies and other dramatizations of their power, this argument certainly resonates. Alternative elites, not tapped into the sacralized structures of state power, might find it more difficult to convince potential supporters to follow them. Yet, one should probably not take for granted the ease with which this argument assumes that people can be fooled all of the time. While there is plenty of evidence for the attachment of Africans to state structures, imputing it to their failure to imagine alternative scenarios is a bit akin to not explaining it at all: it's all in their head. While there are cultural elements to state acceptance, there must also be some rationality to the endurance of failed institutions. Actors who appear to be on the losing end of inertia must somehow also benefit from it. For sure, the assumption of Africans' participation in universal human rationality might be my own bias. Yet, it is one that I embrace without reservations, for it forces us both to treat Africans as equals and to maintain a certain explanatory discipline, which can otherwise too easily be evaded with unfalsifiable arguments about meaningful irrationality. To be clear, I do not disagree that the ritualization of praxis can create meaning that favors institutional stability. But I think such an argument must be embedded within a foundation of rational behavior to account for this very praxis.

In conclusion, there is no fully satisfying explanation for the enduring authority of weak and failed African states. Particularly puzzling is the widespread decentralization of this authority. States can crumble at their core, yet their agencies and personnel continue to project their authority at the local level, and, in general, citizens continue to acquiesce to it. How can the authority of the state survive the erosion of its governing capacity? What is it about the weak African state that allows local actors to continue to derive authority from it? Why do Africans tend to reproduce the state even as they seek to avoid it? Why are remnants of dysfunctional state institutions so appealing to rebels that they maintain them in the territories they control?

Notes

1. Rotberg, "Failed States," 9.
2. Bratton, "Beyond the State," 410.
3. Herbst, *States and Power.*
4. Nolutshungu, *Limits of Anarchy*, 272.
5. Fidèle Banza, personal interview, Lubumbashi, April 2002.
6. Global Witness, *Digging in Corruption*, 14 and 19.
7. Pole Institute, "Rules for Sale," 30–31.
8. See Seay, "Authority at 'Twilight.'"
9. Christopher, "Laurent Gbagbo" (translation mine).
10. Amuri and Gourdon, "Etude diagnostic des organisations." See also Airault, "Où va l'argent du cacao?"
11. Bierschenk and Olivier de Sardan, "Local Powers," 445.
12. Van Rouveroy van Nieuwaal, "Chieftaincy in Africa," 23. See also Mamdani, *Citizens and Subjects.*
13. Interview with Jean-Claude Muyambo, chair of Katanga Bar Association, Lubumbashi, April 2002.
14. Tull, *The Reconfiguration,* 227–228.
15. GANVE, "La participation nationale."
16. E-mail exchange with Reubens Mulenga, University of Lubumbashi, 1 June 2005.
17. Available from http://afrobarometer.org/results/nig00final-28apr04.xls.
18. Naira, the Nigerian currency. I am grateful to Katharine Boyle for bringing this point to my attention.
19. Bratton, "Beyond the State."
20. Azarya and Chazan, "Disengagement from the State"; Baker, *Escape from the State*; Bratton, "Peasant-State Relations."
21. Tostensen, Tvedten, and Vaa, *Associational Life*; Lund, "Twilight Institutions."
22. See, for example, Horning, "Madagascar's Biodiversity Conservation Challenge."
23. See Bratton and van de Walle's emphasis on the role of protest in *Democratic Experiments in Africa.*
24. Monga, "Anthropology of Anger."
25. Joseph, "Nation-State Trajectories," 14.
26. Nyamnjoh, "Cameroon: A Country United."
27. Trefon, "The Political Economy."
28. See, for example, Laakso and Olukoshi, "The Crisis"; Baker, *Escape from the State*; and Forrest, *Subnationalism in Africa.*
29. Bratton, "Beyond the State," 415.
30. Ikelegbe, "The Perverse Manifestation," 6.
31. Lund, "Twilight Institutions," 689.
32. Moore, "Post-Socialist Micro-Politics."
33. Lund, "Bawku Is Still Volatile," 605.
34. Basset, "Dangerous Pursuits," 9, 15.
35. Lund, "Precarious Democratization," 865–866.
36. Pratten and Gore, "The Politics of Plunder," 232.
37. Lund, "Twilight Institutions," 688.
38. Tull, *The Reconfiguration,* 227–228.

39. Although I treat this topic here rather briefly, I presented substantial evidence in support of my claims in Englebert, "Patterns and Theories."

40. BBC News, "Yes, It's Good."

41. Englebert, "Born-Again Buganda."

42. Sklar, "African Polities."

43. Tull, "The Limits," 5–6.

44. Pole Institute, "Rules for Sale," 36.

45. EIU, *Country Report: Côte D'Ivoire,* 13.

46. Johnson, "The Sudan People's Liberation Army," 65; and Johnson, *The Root Causes,* 105.

47. Crossley, "Why Not to State-Build," 143 and 145.

48. Branch and Mampilly, "Winning the War," 10.

49. Mampilly, "The Paradox of Plenty."

50. Spruyt, *The Sovereign State.*

51. Kingston, "States-Within-States," 1.

52. Davidson, *The Black Man's Burden,* 184.

53. For more details on these conferences, see Chapter 4.

54. Roitman, *Fiscal Disobedience,* 21.

55. Kingston, "States-Within-States," 6.

56. Putnam, *Making Democracy Work.*

57. Azarya and Chazan, "Disengagement from the State"; Harbeson, Rothchild, and Chazan, *Civil Society in Africa*; Bratton, "Peasant-State Relations."

58. Mbembe, *On the Postcolony.*

59. See, for example, Collier and Hoeffler, "Greed and Grievance."

60. Hirschman, *Exit, Voice and Loyalty,* 98–103.

61. On Rwenzururu, see Kasfir, "Cultural Sub-Nationalism." On Somaliland, see Bryden, "State-Within-a-Failed-State."

62. Migdal, *The State in Society,* 137.

63. Ibid., 158.

Part 2
Sovereignty

Why do African peripheral elites tend to refrain from secessionism?
Why do the members of Africa's oppressed or marginalized minorities not develop greater separatist aspirations? How do the decrepit and dysfunctional agencies of Africa's weak states retain authority? Why do many Africans seem to acquiesce to the abuses of states that provide them with few benefits? Why are nonstate actors, including rebels, inclined to reproduce the institutions and practices of these failed states?

Chapter 4 offers a theoretical framework for answering these questions. Its essential component is that, even when their financial resources dry up, states can still generate allegiance because their institutions and offices, widely distributed across their territories, continue to be the repositories of sovereignty. Domestically, state sovereignty manifests itself through legal command, that is, the monopolistic capacity of the state to order people around through the law. Local elites can acquire parcels of the state's sovereign powers by associating with its local offices, which they in turn can use to extract their own resources locally or to exert local domination. The exogenous origins of African sovereignty, deriving from diplomatic recognition rather than effective state-building, allow this power to endure even when the state is deeply decayed. The private extractive benefits associated with sovereign legal command are such that they typically dwarf alternative modes of accumulation and advancement, and bias political action away from challenges to the state and toward reproduction of its institutions, laws, and practices, even for peripheral and apparently victimized actors. In short, sovereignty provides holders of state office (at any level of the state) an *internationally* derived *legal* foundation, which is largely constitutive of the *domestic* authority of the state and of their subsequent claims for domination and extraction over their fellow citizens.

Chapter 5 provides illustrations of the sovereign bias in African politics by looking at groups that choose to remain loyalists and to refrain from nonsovereign institution-building in their region, although they harbor many of the conditions that might otherwise be associated with secessionism. It focuses mainly on the strategies of the elites of four minorities and regions. These are, in sequence of increasing complexity, Barotseland in Zambia, the Anglophones of Cameroon, the Rwandophones of the Kivu regions of the DRC, and the Biafra and Delta regions of Nigeria. Each of these cases illustrates some different dimensions of the exchange of national submission for regional domination and extraction by local elites.

Chapter 6, in turn, looks at variations across the continent in the strategies of local elites vis-à-vis the state. It relates regions and time periods that have witnessed separatist conflicts to variations or perceived variations in the international supply and relative domestic benefits of sovereignty. Cases include the Casamance region of Senegal, the Tuaregs of Mali and Niger, Southern Sudan, Eritrea, Somaliland, and Ethiopian separatist movements. It also discusses the relative intensity of African separatism in the 1960s and early 1990s.

4

The Domestic Currency
of International Sovereignty

The capacity of African rulers to privately appropriate the resources of the state or to use it as an instrument of private predation is a well-established element in the logic of its survival and reproduction. Personal rule, neopatrimonialism, prebendalism, and the "politics of the belly" are all predicated on the private appropriation (and parallel redistribution) of the resources of the state and its citizens by rulers.[1] The existence of parallel private government in Africa has progressively led to the fiscal bankruptcy of its states, as it undermined their capacity for productive activities and generated exponentially growing demands for redistribution. Combined with increased (albeit discontinuous) outside pressure for economic and political liberalization, their fiscal crisis has considerably weakened the majority of African states and led quite a few to actual failure. Yet, the private benefits that continue to accrue to them in situations of failure have made African rulers willing to live with it, while some have even thrived on its apparent chaos and on maximization of unaccountable governance.[2] Because of the benefits of weak statehood, we now understand why African national elites may have few incentives to rebuild their states and embrace better governance. Although state failure may represent an extreme situation where the control of rulers is actually jeopardized, generally weak and broadly unaccountable states represent significant political assets.

While the behavior of the rulers of weak and failed states makes rational sense, it is much harder to understand why the regional elites of marginalized, peripheral, oppressed, neglected, or dispossessed groups do not challenge these states more forcefully. And why do parallel and nonstate political, economic, and cultural actors, who often preside over vibrant unregulated flows where most of Africa's economic and social dynamism resides today, not rise as alternative sources of power and institutional development? The instrumentalization of state weakness alone cannot answer these questions, for if only state weakness mattered, many groups would set up their own weak state. To create a weak and dysfunctional state should not be too onerous indeed. Many African warlords have demonstrated sufficient capacity for force and territorial control that they could turn their fiefdoms into states, appoint some institutions and create some offices, and begin enjoying the returns of weak statehood. Yet, as illustrated earlier, institutional innovation is rare in Africa. The question then becomes: What is it that makes existing state institutions transformable into private resources for both rulers and peripheral actors, and that can apparently not be replicated through separatist or nonstate strategies of political action?

It is my contention that a good part of the answer has to do with sovereignty. I refer here to "international legal sovereignty" or the international recognition of a state by its peers and its formal status in international law, with its attendant theoretical attributes of equality with other states, nonintervention, self-determination, and territorial integrity.[3] Membership in the UN is evidence of this status. The notion of sovereignty that I invoke here is therefore that which prevails in the study of international relations where it denotes the idea that "final authority over most if not all social, economic, and political matters should rest with those in control of the territorial units that make up the system."[4] In this sense, a state is sovereign when its monopoly of control over its territory and population is recognized as such by others irrespective of its domestic qualities.

Yet, while using the concept of *international* sovereignty as it applies in international relations, I am actually interested in its *domestic* currency, or the manner in which it is used in political and economic relations *within* African states. Others before me have discussed the role of international recognition in the domestic politics of Africa. Robert Jackson and Carl Rosberg contrasted the concept of "juridical" sovereignty to that of "empirical" sovereignty in order to highlight the fact that African states derive their sovereignty from international recognition more than from effective rule over their territories and populations.[5] Jackson later elaborated on the concept, relating it to the idea of "negative sovereignty," or sovereignty awarded as a category to postcolonies without evidence of their capacity to rule themselves. Specifically, he traced the sources of African negative sovereignty to the international legal apparatus of decolonization, developed first and foremost within the UN, and to the normative implications of the ideology of development, according to which former colonies have the right to exist as states before they may be able to do so on their own and even have a right to be assisted in becoming empirical states.[6]

The significance of these authors' insight on the sources of African state sovereignty cannot be overemphasized. Jackson and Rosberg's concept of juridical statehood stresses that the properties of the African state "can only be defined in international terms" and that its internationally acquired "juridical attributes . . . serve as a test of government's claim to be a state."[7] At a time when many

African states lack the capacity to project their power across their territories, it bears stressing that they exist today as sovereign entities only because they were once colonized. Past existence as a colony is indeed the unique principle guiding contemporary recognition as a sovereign entity in Africa. This principle was enshrined in UN General Assembly Resolution 1514 (XV) of 1960, which provided sovereignty to former colonies and outlawed their territorial reconfiguration, making postcolonies the monopolistic units of self-determination in Africa. Although this resolution was of general application, its timing coincided with the first wave of African independences and it was aimed at the continent. As a result, the international recognition and guarantee of their existence provides African states with their sovereignty rather than any particular action of their own. As Jackson summed it up, "To be a sovereign state today one needs only to have been a formal colony yesterday."[8] African statehood is postcolonial and entirely supported and legitimated by international law and diplomacy.[9] Rather than claiming international recognition based on their domestic performance, African regimes are fonder of reaffirming the international recognition of their status to their domestic populations. This is in part why visits of African heads of state abroad and their meetings with other heads of state tend to receive such disproportionate coverage in African media, with speeches before the UN General Assembly all-time favorites.

While I use a similar definition of sovereignty as Jackson and Rosberg's and embrace their finding of the external nature of state sovereignty in Africa, their main arguments as to its domestic effects differ significantly from mine. According to them, rulers use the international recognition of their statehood, and the benefits of attendant norms of noninterference and territorial integrity, to gain a significant advantage over their nonsovereign opposition. African rulers, they argue, rely on the guarantees of their borders and the shielding of domestic affairs afforded them by international sovereignty to repress their domestic opponents or co-opt them with the resources of foreign aid. Africa's weak states persist then because their rulers use sovereignty to stave off domestic challenges. Christopher Clapham too argues that African states' survival is predicated on their use of international financial patronage and rules of nonintervention to defeat internal opponents. Sovereignty, he finds, is part of a pattern of using foreign policy in order to control opposition at home.[10]

Although one would be hard put to find issue with these theories, my argument differs to the extent that I ask a rather different question. Going beyond the capacity of rulers to repress domestic challenges (which African sovereigns share with others elsewhere), I ask why there are in fact so few challenges, especially at a time when the already limited empirical sovereignty of African states has further eroded and the principle of noninterference has become so contested in international law. My question addresses therefore the behavior of nonrulers more than that of rulers, focusing principally on the attitude of second-tier state actors and nonstate actors and on their lack of challenge of the state rather than on the latter's capacity to resist them. Yet, despite the evolving nature of the question, the answer remains sovereignty.

Sovereignty and Legal Command

Even when the state is no longer capable of performing its public functions, like providing health and education services, adopting basic development policies, or maintaining infrastructures, it still retains a residual of command. In other words, the institutions and officers of the failed state continue to carry some authority. This authority is derived mainly from the fact that the state is law. For, even without capacity, state agencies enforce themselves upon people by law. Making laws and being the law is a privilege of the prince. It arises from the recognized quality of statehood, and is one of sovereignty's attributes. In other contexts, sovereignty and statehood can derive from social contracting, historical domination, or democratic acquiescence. In most African countries, where historical legitimacy is tenuous, the means of violence widely available outside the state, and democracy limited, it is international recognition that provides states with their sovereign authority to rule, that is, to make enforceable rules. Hence, *it is international sovereignty that confers institutions, agencies, and officers of the African state the main source of their domestic command.* Because African state sovereignty is juridical, African state power is *de iure*. Because the state is defined by its legality rather than its effectiveness, this power of command survives its failure or the erosion of its effective capacity. Imbued with the enduring legal nature of state command, appendages of the weak state continue to exert significant control across distant parts of their territories, even if the central government itself is unable to "broadcast" its own power to these regions.[11] This juridical nature of state power, acquired from the international juridical nature of sovereignty, accounts in part for the prevailing legalism in African politics. The near obsessive use of official stamps by people in positions of authority (and those who emulate them) illustrates the legal nature of power in Africa and means to symbolically convey to the administered the sovereign connection of the administrators.

It should be stressed here that what endures of African statehood in times of weakness or failure is legal *command*, that is, the capacity to control, dominate, extract, or dictate through the law. These are the functions of the state that are least dependent on domestic institutional effectiveness and most on sovereign status. In contrast, the state's capacity to provide security, order, and public services, not to mention implement coherent policies and initiate social transformation, will have dissipated as it weakened. Sovereignty is indeed broadly irrelevant to the question of what states can do for you, but critical to what they can do to you. For sovereignty is concerned more with "the location of ultimate authority" than with the duties that may come with it.[12]

The essential point so far is thus the lawmaking ability of the state. By laws, one must understand public rules in a general sense and not only the output of formally legislating bodies such as parliaments and national assemblies. In fact, one of the favorite tools of rule-making in Africa is the decree. In the DRC, even mining concessions are awarded to companies by presidential decrees (and can be withdrawn in the same manner).[13] These have the advantages, for the ruler, of rapidity and lack of oversight. Rules are not only made at the top, however; they involve many levels of the state. Provincial, communal, and other local authorities are also endowed with parcels of the rule-making sovereign prerogative because they are parts of the state. In addition, they and local representatives of the national state, like security forces or customs agencies, are also often tasked with locally implementing the law.

This latter point is particularly important and merits further attention in the overall argument. In order to comprehend the behavior of regional and nonstate elites as well as commoners, one ought to understand the widespread distribution throughout society and territory of the rule-making and rule-implementing functions of the state. Across African states, sovereign roles are parceled out down to the lowest and most local levels of officialdom. As Patrick Chabal and Jean-Pascal Daloz remind us, "most political actors are simultaneously dominant and dominated."[14] This reciprocal domination is usually exercised through legal command and involves many actors not directly associated with central state power who nevertheless benefit from some form of access to local appendages of the state.

Studies of African administrative and judicial systems have painted a picture of the extensive decentralization of legal command. In the DRC, the national hierarchy of command includes ministers, secretaries-general, directors, division chiefs, and bureau chiefs. It continues at the provincial and urban levels with chiefs of provincial divisions, provincial bureau chiefs, section and cell chiefs, chiefs of urban services, chiefs of sections and cells, and chiefs of subsections and subcells. Communal administrations add layers. In Lubumbashi, for example, city officials include the mayor, burgmeisters, chiefs of neighborhoods (*quartiers*), chiefs of cells, and street chiefs. Each *street* thus has a chief who is in some measure an agent of the state.[15] Of course, there are also innumerable people in nonchiefly positions at all these levels, who carry authority over regular citizens, including clerks, advisers, assistants, secretaries, and more. In each case, the major function of these administrative layers is command, the ordering around of people. Similarly, in his study of the Niger justice system, Mahaman Tidjani Alou mentions that

> The operation of the legal system involves a large number of actors. . . . Judges . . . are assisted by administrative staff, in particular the court clerks and the secretaries who work in the offices of the clerk of the court and the public prosecutor. The clerks . . . , whose diverse functions effectively involve

them in areas beyond the purely legal sphere, play an important role in facilitating access to the judge, the secretaries perform a vital role in the drawing
up of official documents. . . . The police and gendarmerie also perform legal
duties and are, therefore, involved in the delivery of justice, mainly through
the investigations they conduct under the auspices of the judges.[16]

In Uganda, as of 2007, there were 80 districts and 900 subcounties, each a
manifestation of the sovereign state endowed with a local government, altogether accounting for more than 580,000 elected and nonelected positions of
legal command widely distributed across the country.[17]

One can pause here and wonder how legal command can be such a powerful tool of control and domination in Africa where states are so weak that
they would be hard put to enforce obedience with the law. For sure, sovereignty has been defined as producing "*habitual* obedience," but we know that
laws may not always be obeyed, especially when there is little credible sanction of force accompanying them.[18] They may also be resisted as unfair or discriminatory, especially in Africa's arbitrary environments. There are several
reasons, however, why compliance with the law in Africa is more widespread
than one would otherwise expect and why it also matters surprisingly less than
one would think for the continuation of legal state domination.

First, the pervasiveness of regulation in Africa cannot be overstated.
African societies are highly legalized, and survival is not infrequently predicated upon following procedures.[19] There appears to be, for example, an endless series of circumstances when one will need a birth certificate or some evidence of nationality, including enrollment in school, matrimony, voter
registration, or starting a business. These documents will have to be obtained
at some agencies of the state and produced to some other agencies as evidence
of one's status. If nothing else, the ubiquity of police and military roadblocks
puts a significant premium on the necessity of official documents. In the DRC,
Theodore Trefon's detailed urban anthropological work confirms that "every
Congolese . . . is condemned . . . to clash with the exigencies of civil servants
from which it is impossible to escape."[20] As a testimony to the importance of
legal documents, many of the difficulties that prevented a settlement of the
conflict in Côte d'Ivoire between 2003 and 2007 revolved around the conditions for the acquisition of certificates of nationality by northerners.

Second, one may find an advantage to the law and use it to ascertain
claims toward others, as with property rights or affirmative action, for example. People who are victimized by the law may also be able to victimize or exploit others through the law. Once laws are accepted in one branch of life, so
they tend to be in all of them. People's pursuit of certainty and security, cou-
pled with local individual and group strategies of domination, promote the
sanctity of the legal, formal state realm.

Third, one can generally minimize trouble by following the law, which provides a structure of relative certainty, however arbitrary it might be, that is par-

ticularly needed in weak and failed states where people are otherwise vulnerable. As such, laws are largely self-enforcing. Stories about the prevalence of informality and of the illicit in Africa should not overlook the broad compliance with the law generated by the desire to avoid trouble or even by fear. As Tidjani again writes in the context of Niger, "the law is perceived as terrifying."[21]

Finally, it may hardly matter after all whether or not the law is obeyed, for even the avoidance of the law by citizens gives power to its enforcers. Although many people do indeed follow the law, it is also true, as Achille Mbembe and Janet Roitman observe, that "every law enacted is submerged by an ensemble of techniques of avoidance, circumvention and envelopment which, in the end, neutralize and invert the legislation."[22] Yet, these techniques do not neutralize the law enforcers, predicated as they usually are on their collaboration (if not initiative). As Giorgio Blundo remarks, "opportunities for enrichment will depend on the capacity [of civil servants] . . . to brandish the administrative norm while hinting at the ways to bypass it."[23] In the DRC, one can either try to have all the required documents for driving around town or purchase a "certificate of loss of documents" at the police station, an "authentic false document," as Trefon puts it.[24] Similarly, when going through customs, you may declare half the value of your goods, pay tax on that half, and share the other half of the tax due with the customs agent afterward.[25] Thus, one often needs the state to bypass it.

Returning to the argument, although the right to make laws belongs to sovereign authorities, nothing in practice could prevent rebels from issuing their own rules. And, of course, some of them do. In Congo, the RCD issued decrees. In Uganda, the National Revolutionary Council of Yoweri Museveni established rules and structures of governance in the territories it controlled between 1981 and 1986.[26] Yet, rebels will impose their rules only if they can demonstrate credible force or popular legitimacy (nonsovereign sources of command) in the areas they control, whereas sovereign governments can make enforceable laws without effective control. The state is thus imbued with a domestic agency that is unrelated to its might. As if by magic (but in fact by law), international sovereignty is converted into domestic authority. Even though African states do not have a Weberian monopoly of force, they do have a monopoly of statehood, and that is the one that really matters in a world of "negative sovereignty."

What are, specifically, the powers of legal command with which international sovereignty endows state institutions and agents? And how is their implementation decentralized and widely distributed?

Declaration

One of the most basic and yet most awesome powers of the law is to name things in or out of existence. *Saying* the rule is the essence of rule-making (and, hence, of ruling), and the privilege of the state. The declaratory power of the law allows the state to define itself (as in the constitution) and define membership in itself (e.g., through nationality laws). As such, it can include and exclude, make national or foreign. It is through the power of the law, for example, that Ivorian authorities declared Allassane Ouattara to be a foreigner and made him ineligible for presidential elections, even though he had served as prime minister under the late president Félix Houphouët-Boigny.[27] Similarly, in 1972, a law gave the Zairean nationality to some 300,000 Kivu residents of Rwandan origins, only to be reverted by another law in 1981, which stripped them of the nationality and threw these populations into great political precariousness.[28] The state can also endow things—rather than people—with its nationality, as Liberia does to ships with its "flag of convenience." Many ships around the world sail under the Liberian flag, including Carnival Cruise Lines and 35 percent of all oil tankers (including those of Mobil and Chevron).[29]

Through legal declaration the state also identifies and authenticates. For example, it issues (or not) identity cards and birth certificates to its citizens, which they will need in order to demonstrate their citizenship and avail themselves of their rights. In the 1960s, when the Rwandan populations of eastern Congo were already in political limbo regarding their status, local authorities occasionally seized their ID cards, leaving them without evidence of their juridical status.[30] The importance of having identity documents in countries where harassment by security forces is a near constant was illustrated by the remarkable enthusiasm of the Congolese for registering to vote in 2005 after it was announced that voter cards would count as identity documents. While more than 25 million adult citizens registered (approximately 50 percent of the country's estimated population), only about 17 million actually voted in the legislative and presidential elections of July 2006. The state may also certify the authenticity or origins of people and things, as some African states have committed to do with diamonds under the Kimberley certification process to verify that the gems did not originate in conflict zones.[31]

Even "traditional" authority often owes its existence or continuance to the state's powers of declaration, as chiefs are frequently appointed or endorsed by the state, a practice that dates back to colonial times. The institution of chieftaincy has also frequently been abolished by law, as in Uganda in the 1960s or in Burkina Faso in the 1980s. In Zaire too, customary rule was abolished by law between 1973 and 1976, and chiefs became a mere extension of the state's administrative apparatus.[32] Sovereign power thus has a significant edge over "traditional" sources of power, even if the latter are likely to claim greater historical legitimacy.

The declaratory power of the sovereign is maybe nowhere more obvious than in the judicial system where judges literally say the law. However corrupt and inefficient some judges and their clerical staff may be (see discussion later in this chapter), there are fewer less ambiguous instances of the social needs for the continuation of their task. People may react to the decay of judicial systems by increasingly resorting to private arbitrations and out-of-court settlements,[33] yet their need for official documents as evidence in support of their claims preserves the demand for these state-sanctioned official legal services.

The state also decrees the currency and—at least in the days before World Bank–sponsored market reforms—the rate at which the currency is to be exchanged for that of other countries. Once the currency is created, the state also determines the amount of it in supply. Because many African countries have their currencies printed abroad by commercial enterprises, there is no need for effective capacity in order to control this dimension of monetary policy. The practice of seignorage, or the financing of fiscal deficits by monetary expansion, even temporarily allows the state to create wealth, usually in the form of civil servants' salaries, before inflation undoes the magic.

It is in the DRC, once again, that one can find one of the most extreme and outrageous usages of sovereign monetary declaration. In 1993, after a bout of hyperinflation, a monetary reform created the *new zaire* which was worth 3 million of the old *zaire* currency. The contract was awarded to a company that had the notes printed in Argentina and Brazil. It received instructions from the Zairean government to print two or three sets of certain series for a total equivalent to $30–40 million.[34] As Béatrice Hibou puts it, Mobutu Sese Seko really "organized the smuggling of officially sanctioned counterfeit banknotes." He was later "able to choose whether to change some of these banknotes into dollars or to use them for paying the army."[35] Kenya's Daniel arap Moi apparently once did something similar.

Although the above examples focus on the declaratory powers of the state's highest authorities, this prerogative too is decentralized. Trefon notes, for instance, that the governor's office of Katanga "arbitrarily fixed the price of cement" in 2005. And when setting up a new church in the DRC, one must go to the local office of the ministry of justice to get a "declaration of existence" for $25.[36] In Niger, prison sentences can be reduced for medical reasons—but the medical condition must be authenticated by the state. This creates a market: "the detainee has to 'buy' a medical certificate attesting that he is suffering from one of the serious illnesses regarded as grounds for appeal for an amnesty (AIDS, tuberculosis, leprosy)."[37]

All this you can do as a sovereign, and only as a sovereign can you do it without effective actual existence. And what sovereignty does, only sovereignty can undo. This is why rebels who may enjoy large territorial control over parts of the country keep on fighting until they gain (partial) control of the state apparatus and the tools of sovereignty. After the Sovereign National Conference of Zaire reiterated in 1993 the citizenship demotion of the Kivu populations of Rwandan origins, the latter finally resorted to violence and contributed to the creation of the Alliance des Forces Démocratiques pour la Libération du Congo-Zaire (Alliance of Democratic Forces for the Liberation of Congo-Zaire, AFDL) in 1996 and of the RCD in 1998, the goal of which was to seize power in Kinshasa in order to force their reintegration into the state, which was done through the nationality law of 2005, adopted by a transition parliament that included RCD representatives. Similarly, the refusal to grant some northerners identity cards and to let them register as voters in Côte d'Ivoire eventually led to the launch of the FN insurgency, the purpose of which was the legal reinsertion of the Northern "Dioulas" into the Ivorian polity and the adoption of a new constitution no longer banning their leader, Allassane Ouattara, from running for president based on his alleged alien status. The goal of these groups is to regain control of, or participation in, the lawmaking process and undo their legal marginalization. It is not surprising therefore that when the state adopts certain laws to discriminate against specific groups, the latter tend not to reject the authority of the state to have passed such laws, because they too benefit or hope to benefit from their association with the sovereign lawmaking state. What they do instead is fight their way back into the state—through conflict and subsequent power-sharing agreements—in an attempt to rewrite the law in a manner more beneficial to them. Hence, Africa's sovereignty regime promotes conflicts for control of the state but not for challenge of it.

Regulation and Control

Legal command also involves regulation and control of many dimensions of social life. The provision of security and police services, however privatized they have become in many African countries, is an essential part of this function. Even in very weak African states, the extent to which security and police functions endure, and are even apparently multiplied, is quite surprising. In the DRC, these functions are widely distributed among several agencies including the national police, the presidential guard, the military, the ANR, and multiple ministry-specific and province-specific police forces. The level of detail with which they purport to control one's activities stands in remarkable contrast with their apparent complete failure to actually provide any security. When I was doing research in Katanga in 2002, I had to obtain an authorization from the ANR to travel, on a weekend and for personal reasons, from Lubumbashi to Likasi, about 100 miles away. The formal request for authorization, on official University of Lubumbashi letterhead with the stamp of the office of the university president, had to justify my status, my connection to the university, and the motive of my trip. Once on the road, however, I never ran into any police or ANR presence.

Of course, all research activity—and probably other business activities involving travel—typically requires formal authorizations in Africa. Once one has successfully gone through the formal procedures of accreditation as a researcher, one still frequently needs authorizations to move around the country, which may come as "orders of mission," a typical form of legal command more often associated with the military or the bureaucracy. These orders are obtained from the appropriate authority in the capital and duly stamped. They request safe passage from the local security agencies one might encounter along the way and authenticate one's status and research agenda. Traveling with a colleague from Dolisie to Mossendjo in southern Republic of Congo in 2001, our orders of mission, which we obtained in Brazzaville, were inspected and stamped at a roadblock on our way out of Dolisie, then at the entrance of Makabana, upon leaving Makabana, upon reaching Mossendjo, and again in reverse sequence when we returned. Once, upon arriving in Goma by air from Kinshasa during the war in 2001, I was held for some time at the airport because of my failure to produce an order of mission. I was perplexed that rebel authorities cared for an order of mission from the government they were fighting and whose legitimacy they were challenging, and I kept arguing that I was not on a mission from the government, so how could I produce such a document? For her part, the airport security agent was equally perplexed by my attempt at free movement without some authorization from someone.

The resilience of the weak state's regulating functions is visible in many other dimensions beyond pure policing. It should be stressed again, however, that what usually remains in the weakest states is the command part of regulation, not necessarily its substance in terms of its initial purpose, such as public health, trade policy, or standards and measures. Recall, from Chapter 3, the findings of Global Witness on the "bewildering range of officials" at the entrance points of Katanga's mines.[38] For a state believed to have collapsed, this multiplicity of agencies represented a remarkable degree of state physical presence. Yet, these agencies hardly provided any services.

There is not either any specific public service performed by the requirements of regulation imposed upon virtually all economic activity in the DRC. One cannot find another purpose than extraction for the annual US$20 "carbonization license" that charcoal makers must purchase in Lubumbashi, or the monthly transportation tax and annual bicycle tax that is payable by those who bring the charcoal to market. Neither businesses nor the public benefit from the multitude of inspecting state agencies that descend upon them with great regularity. A baker, for example, must face the "service of economic affairs," which controls prices and commercial documents; the "service of industry," which does exactly the same thing; and the "environment" and "public hygiene" services, which assess the enterprise's cleanliness and authorize operations. Although their visits are scheduled for twice a year, they sometimes take place as often as every week.[39]

The Office Congolais de Contrôle (Congolese Office of Control, OCC) deserves additional scrutiny. Its name alone suggests omnipotent command, while simultaneously remaining silent on what it is supposed to control and what the purpose of its controlling mission may be. For sure, similar agencies exist elsewhere; California, for example, has an elected state controller's office that

accounts for and controls disbursements of state funds. Yet, for anyone familiar with the dysfunctional nature of public institutions in Congo, the juxtaposi-
tion of "Congolese" and "Control" is replete with Kafkaesque promise. The
OCC was created as an agency of the Ministry of External Trade for the control of the quality and quantity of Congolese exports. Its brief increased over
time to include the control of the quality, quantity, price, and conformity of "all
merchandises and products" (whether for export, import, or restricted to the domestic economy), technical controls of "all machinery and labor," and the
"management and exploitation of silos, general stores and customs entrepôts,"
while also granting it the freedom to undertake "all operations relating directly
or indirectly to its legal activity."[40] Given the derelict nature of the state bureaucracy in Congo, the extent of informalization of economic activity, and the
prevalence of smuggling, it is doubtful that the OCC still performs most of
these controls in terms of public service. Yet, it is noteworthy that its existence
endures and that it continues to exercise its power of legal command over Congolese citizens, with a decentralized presence in the field all the more remarkable given the otherwise failed nature of the Congolese state. In a survey of
Congolese companies, 67 percent declared being at the receiving end of a relation of control or authority rather than collaboration with the OCC, while 56
percent were dissatisfied or very dissatisfied with the nature of its services.[41]

Although the country's endless supply of material and my own research
bias lead me to frequently cite examples from the DRC, the regulation and control functions of sovereign command are common features throughout Africa,
even in states that benefit from more favorable reputations. Recounting a trip
from Malanville to Cotonou, in Benin, Nassirou Bako Arifari reveals that "by
the time we [reached] Cotonou we [had] passed a total of sixteen control—or,
to be more precise, extortion—points along the 750km route." Once in Cotonou, "the officer whose job it is to weigh the vehicles [on the bascule bridge at
the entrance of town] charges the driver 700 francs, without actually weighing
the vehicle." Similarly, "having a second-hand car released from the port of
Cotonou involves passing through seventeen successive points of corruption,
ten of which are located within the customs system."[42]

The extent to which weak African states continue to be able to "regulate"
economic activity is visible in the degree to which African governments are
considered "business friendly" by the World Bank's International Finance
Corporation (IFC). In its annual report on "Doing Business" around the world,
the IFC ranks 175 countries in terms of how easy it is to do such things as start
a business, employ workers, enforce contracts, deal with licenses, record property, or trade across borders. Given its probusiness bias, the IFC's measure-
ments actually capture the lightness of the regulatory burden. Of the 175 countries in the 2007 edition of this survey, African countries averaged a rank of
131, as against 73 for non-African ones.[43] The DRC was ranked 175.

Nonsovereign actors may regulate activity in the territories under their control, but they cannot match the sovereign propensity and ability for regulatory proliferation. Furthermore, they need effective control in order to regulate, and hence they cannot distribute this power to their supporters. The state, in contrast, can create agencies almost at will and endow them with almost limitless competence, as hinted by the case of the OCC. This capacity to regulate and control social and economic intercourse is a crucial element of legal command. Even when the regulation function per se ceases to be implemented, their legal status ensures that the agencies of regulation and control endure together with their power of command over citizens and transactions.

Appropriation

Finally, command involves the right to appropriate resources from people and territory, whether through transfer of the ownership of assets or taxation of income and transactions. One of the most frequent expressions of the appropriative power of command in Africa is the vesting of all land ownership in the state. Most African states have passed laws making the state the sole or residual owner of land and land resources, from mineral deposits to timber. As Catherine Boone points out,

> Legally . . . African peasants have never really been freeholders. . . . This means that across most of rural Africa the most basic institution of a market society—private property in the means of production—does not exist, and *central state agents exercise direct or indirect political control over access to livelihoods for the vast majority of the population.*

Thus the lack of commoditization of land in Africa creates a premium to legal command as a mode of allocation. For, even though state capacity has eroded, "state actors can still deliver and enforce rural property rights."[44]

Legal control of the land has allowed sovereign governments to reduce traditional chiefs into a position of dependency toward the state. It has also made it possible for them to market their territories in exchange for hard currencies. Some West African governments, for example, have offered the use of their land for the dumping of European toxic waste in exchange for hard currencies, a practice that forced the Ivorian government to resign en masse in 2006 after several individuals died from exposure.

In addition, sovereignty confers the power to legally seize assets in the form of nationalization. The right to nationalize is a well-established sovereign prerogative, whose legitimating principle usually comes from the fact that the government is deemed to represent the people and therefore the assets are acquired by the people as a whole, supposedly for some greater good. Yet, in practice, there is of course no such requirement of representation. Most African governments nationalized their mining industry and their few manufacturing enterprises starting in the 1960s, although some of these have been reversed since the 1990s. Possibly the most astounding and politically successful manipulation of the sovereign legal privilege to appropriate may have been Mobutu's "Zaireanization" policy of 1974. At the stroke of a pen, he promulgated decree Ordinance-Law 74-019 on 11 January 1974, whereby the assets of foreigners were transferred to some Congolese citizens, namely cronies of his regime.[45] Although the state did not directly appropriate these assets as it would in a nationalization exercise, it used its sovereign right of appropriation to transfer them from foreign owners to Congolese owners, essentially turning theft into policy.

Beyond the appropriation of assets, the state can also, in a more routine way, extract part of the income of its citizens or of the value of their transactions in the form of taxes, tariffs, and other fiscal levies. Taxation is of course one of the most legitimate, basic, and exclusive powers of the prince. One may resist the state's powers of taxation; fiscal evasion is universal. Nevertheless, disobedience does not usually imply that this right is not recognized to the state. In part because many Africans are poor and work outside the formal sector, income taxes do not represent a large proportion of the revenues of African governments. Taxes on international trade, on the other hand, represent about 25–30 percent of their domestic revenues.[46] These taxes are particularly sovereign in nature, relying as they do on prerogatives associated with legal control of borders, customs, and territory. Some African countries have developed a comparative advantage in acting as intermediaries in the trade of other nations. These "entrepôt" states, which include Benin, Burundi, Equatorial Guinea, Gambia, Somalia, and Togo, import goods at very low tariffs before reexporting them to their final destination, extracting income from their trade diversion. Much of the cargo arriving in the port of Benin, for example, is reexported to Nigeria.[47]

Beyond income and trade taxes, the bread and butter of appropriation by state agents takes place through miscellaneous taxes, fees, and tolls imposed, formally or not, on all sorts of human activity. The city and commune of Lubumbashi combine to generate no less than twenty-six taxes and levies, not including those invented by their agents in the field.[48] In Chad, those in charge of the local *préfectures* in the south systematically embarked upon the taxing of livestock movement among local herders, in animal heads, after 1982. *N'djamena Hebdo* reported that "over time, the levied heads of livestock . . . turned these administrative and military authorities into large livestock owners."[49] In Zimbabwe, police and paramilitary squads seized foreign notes from tourists and money changers in 2003, officially "to buy fuel for farm vehicles."[50] Of course, throughout much of the continent, African citizens are also often made to pay private taxes at roadblocks or when stopped by people in uniform.

Other collective actors, like rebel groups or chieftaincies, may also be able to tax people, but they cannot do so legally and must resort to force or popular legitimacy in order to manage levies on the income and assets of people in the regions they control. The Kingdom of Buganda, for example, regularly receives tribute from its subjects on a voluntary basis (which may be fostered by a dose of social pressure), but it is explicitly not allowed by the Ugandan Constitution to raise taxes, as it is only a "cultural" institution and therefore forbidden to partake in the sovereign right of appropriation.[51] Local districts, on the other hand, which are decentralized expressions of the sovereign state, do have fiscal powers. It is the Ugandan Constitution that distributes the legal right to tax, an attribute of the sovereign state.

Still, the sovereign nature of the right to tax warrants further inspection, for it is not as clear-cut as that of the other sovereign prerogatives. While declaration, regulation, and control are unequivocally sovereign monopolies, the power of extraction seems somewhat more available to nonstate actors. The Congolese rebel organization RCD, for example, raised its own taxes in the areas it controlled between 1998 and 2003, in addition to servicing established Congolese taxes. It also set up its own monopsony for the purchase of colombo-tantalite (coltan), the Société Minière des Grands Lacs (Great Lakes Mining Society, SOMIGL), which alone was allowed to market coltan from diggers, in exchange for a monthly tax of $1 million. Other Congolese rebel groups raised taxes, too. The Front Nationaliste et Intégrationiste in the Ituri region of Congo reportedly taxed Anglo Gold Ashanti freight landing fees at Mongbwalu in 2004 and 2005.[52] It also collected customs fees at the land border with Uganda. Furthermore, there is plenty of evidence that the Ivorian FN developed an extensive taxing structure in the territory they controlled between 2003 and 2007. Although their administration of the north was haphazard, the FN had a new tax agency by September 2003, the Direction de la Mobilisation des Ressources (Direction for Resource Mobilization, DIRMOB), later renamed La Centrale, suggesting that sovereignty is not the only foundation of the power of appropriation.

Yet, many of these rebel taxes remain predicated on physical control or on claims to sovereignty by the rebels. In general, they take place at specific physical locations, like ports of entry, where control can be more easily exercised. Unlike that of the state, the power of appropriation of these rebels is thus not transferable. The FN, for example, mostly relied on roadblocks to generate tax revenue, charging between CFAF400 (francs issued by African Financial Community, US$0.80) for private vehicles and CFAF70,000 (US$140) for loaded trucks and buses along the main north-south road that stretches under their control from Bouaké to the border with Burkina.[53] However, when it comes to taxes on trade, it is partly true that the sovereign is also limited to spaces where it can exert physical control. The main difference is that the state is the default authority at these ports of entry in the absence of forceful competitors.

In addition, rebels make great use of the local remnants of sovereign state institutions in their strategies of extraction. The RCD, for example, mainly collected taxes through existing regional state agencies, free-riding on their enduring sovereign nature. As Tull notes, it "claimed to administer its territories in accord with Congolese law," hoping thereby to claim some of its sovereignty.[54] The RCD collected official Congolese taxes in addition to its own, as well as the custom duties along the border with Uganda, Rwanda, and Burundi. It also seized some of the revenues generated by Kivu's public enterprises and parastatals. This is also true of the Ituri rebels, who used the Congolese border as a resource. As a result, although the Congolese state was no longer capable of any agency in Ituri, its powers of command were maintained by rebels who kept the expression (and, for many locals, the oppression) of Congolese statehood alive.

The FN also partly relied on sovereign power. For one, they were part of the national government. They also maintained several local state agencies. When one entered Bouaké coming from the north in 2006, the main roadblock had a sign that read "*Halte—Police Des Drogues*" (Stop—Drug Police). Also, the FN's repeated claims that they did not want to secede, their celebration of national holidays, and their singing of the national anthem at official functions reinforced their claim to sovereign authority.

One possible difference between the power of appropriation of the sovereign and its competitors, in the end, is that the latter may experience a capacity for extraction more limited to their physical presence or to the highest level of the rebellion, which can appropriate specific institutional resources like marketing boards. Sovereign power, on the other hand, may be more easily distributed at the local level, delegated to secondary authorities, as it necessitates less force to be enforceable. In other words, it may be easier for individual state officials, like custom agents, policemen, or civil servants, to claim extractive power from their association with the state than to do so from association with rebel structures.

As a final dimension of appropriation, it is also normally a prerogative of the sovereign to decide on the allocation of its revenues from taxes, profits, and royalties. In practice, this prerogative has eroded in Africa since the 1980s as conditional lending has forced many governments to commit to certain spending constraints. More recently, the practice of "shared sovereignty" between donors and very weak or failed states appears to have created a further setback for the sovereign appropriative command. In Liberia, all candidates in the postconflict elections of 2005 had to agree to a future oversight of their government spending by international civil servants delegated from donor countries (although the subsequent government of Ellen Johnson-Sirleaf seemed to emancipate itself from this constraint). In Chad, the facilitation of the financing of the oil pipeline to the Cameroonian coast was made possible by the World Bank in exchange for establishing limits on how the revenues from oil could be spent.[55]

Yet, as the work of Nicolas van de Walle has made amply clear, respect by African governments of conditionality should not be overstated.[56] In addition, events in Chad in 2006 all but debunked the myth of shared sovereignty and demonstrated the enduring power of sovereign lawmaking in failing states. The original agreement between the World Bank and the government over the allocation of revenues from the oil pipeline had stipulated that the majority of the funds were to go to development projects overseen by a committee composed of religious, community, and political leaders. In effect, the bank was using its financial leverage to give nonstate actors a voice in the allocation of funds derived from the exploitation of natural resources. But all it took from President Idriss Déby in January 2006 to make this deal unravel was a unilateral law redefining the allocation of these resources and relaxing the government's spending restrictions.[57] In doing so, the Chadian government not only reasserted its authority vis-à-vis the World Bank but also vis-à-vis its own civil society now marginalized in this issue as in others, sharply reminding it of the lack of avenues of political control outside the state.[58]

The Question of Causality:
Evidence from the Sovereign National Conferences

The argument so far has hinged upon two related claims. One is that the power of the African state is mostly the power of the law, which is not dependent upon effective institutional capacity or physical control. The second is that legal authority is conferred to the state by the international recognition of its sovereignty. The previous section has tried to establish each claim separately, relying on historical evidence and the work of others to assert the exogenous origins of African state sovereignty (i.e., the concepts of "negative sovereignty" and "juridical statehood") and providing examples of the command performance of the law in Africa through its powers of declaration, regulation, control, and appropriation. Before turning to the ways in which legal command can be converted to serve individual strategies of domination, accumulation, and survival, it still behooves us to establish causality between sovereignty and command.

How can we tell that the command authority of state institutions derives mainly from their sovereignty? Usually, this cannot be directly observed. People do not typically justify their obedience to the state with any explicit reference to its sovereignty. There were, however, several instances in a handful of French-speaking African countries in the early 1990s of practical and explicit political struggles over the control of sovereignty, which very clearly indicated both its widely accepted nature as the ultimate provider of public authority and its exogeneity. These instances took place at the so-called national conferences, which were convened as part of local attempts at democratization in Benin, Chad, Congo-Brazzaville, Gabon, Mali, Niger, Togo, and Zaire, and where opposition groups attempted to wrestle sovereignty away from the existing organs of the state. Even when incumbents successfully prevented such conferences from happening, as in Burkina Faso and Cameroon (and later in Nigeria), the reason for their resistance was the fear that they would successfully proclaim themselves sovereign. The label "sovereign national conference," which several of these conferences gave themselves, demonstrates that political reformers in these countries did not believe they could achieve significant change without first formally wrestling away sovereignty from the state. For their decisions to be enforceable, they had to take over sovereignty. In doing so, they attempted to make themselves, rather than the government, the beneficiaries of the international recognition of the state and of its attendant powers of legal command, which would make their decisions irresistible. The vehemence with which heads of state typically fought back confirms the importance of controlling sovereignty.

The first—and by far the most successful—national conference took place in Benin in February 1990. At the time, the regime of President Mathieu Kérékou was on its knees, having had to abandon its official Marxist-Leninist ideology in the wake of the Soviet collapse, and facing a financial crisis of hitherto unmatched proportions. Begging to France for fiscal support to pay civil servants, the Beninese government was encouraged to organize some sort of national convention in order to open up the system and usher in democratic reforms.[59] The "National Conference of the Live Forces of the Nation" was thus convened by President Kérékou in Cotonou on 19 February and assembled some 524 delegates and organizations. Its most important tasks were to prepare the draft of a new constitution and discuss new economic policies to exit the crisis. While the regime had hoped that the conference would facilitate an orderly transition and restore Benin's international credibility in the new post–Cold War environment, it rapidly got out of government control. Following a rare revolutionary impulse, the conference approved by show of hands on the second day an addition to its internal bylaws that proclaimed "its sovereignty and the supremacy of its decisions."[60]

Much upheaval ensued, with the government representatives fighting this proclamation tooth and nails. They argued, Fabien Eboussi-Boulaga recalls, that "legality was on their side. They were the flag bearers of the state, they were covered by its symbols and brandished its internationally recognized attributes to the face of the world."[61] Declaring sovereignty, however, reassured the reformers that the conference's decisions would be enforceable upon all, particularly the government. Eventually, the conference's sovereignty was once again reaffirmed at its closing by a vote of 370 against the 17 delegates of the government.

The conference participants felt strongly that sovereignty was the key to a real power grab. Yet, despite its bold posturing, the conference was in fact unable to become sovereign without government approval. Kérékou showed up to address the delegates the last day and was at first defiant, denying their right to make decisions regarding the political system. It was only after an interruption in his speech for a long private conversation with the conference's president, Catholic bishop Isidore De Souza, in which he was probably offered some form of pardon for crimes committed in office, that Kérékou reappeared in the middle of night and merely declared to the delegates that he would not oppose the continuation of their work, an implicit admission of their decision.

The conference was thus able to strip Mathieu Kérékou, whose regime was by then exceedingly weak, of much of its presidential prerogatives, and to usher in a new system. In fact, it abolished existing institutions of the state, including the presidency and the government. Fully aware that it had to wrestle the ultimate foundation of power from President Kérékou if it was to get a chance to democratize the country, it literally hijacked sovereignty from state institutions in what was then very perceptively referred to as a "civilian coup."[62] Kérékou was allowed to stay in power as a figurehead only, while all executive authority was given to a conference-elected prime minister—Nicéphore Soglo—until the elections of 1991 (at which Soglo became president).

In addition to demonstrating the central nature of sovereignty to political power in Benin, this case also shows that sovereignty was in fact *not* up for grabs by the conference. Despite trying on several occasions, it was unable to become sovereign until the president agreed to it.[63] It should be pointed out, in this respect, that it was still felt necessary for the president to issue decrees after the conference endorsing its decisions and "legally [conferring] sovereignty upon the interim regime."[64] The fact that the conference could not become sovereign without government assent is a direct consequence of the fact that sovereignty is legally given to the state from outside through recognition of the government. There is therefore no possibility to claim it domestically. The authors of a successful military coup would inherit sovereignty with the state, but otherwise, sovereignty is safely lodged with the government, which alone among domestic actors can choose to relinquish it. If the foundations of sovereignty were domestic, such as representation or morality, the conference could have plausibly claimed them. But sovereign legality belonged exclusively to the government and could not be stolen, as it was held outside the field of contentious politics.

Two more conferences saw relatively successful declarations of sovereignty followed by regime change. In the Republic of Congo, the 1991 national conference passed a resolution declaring that it had sovereign power and that its decisions would be binding to all.[65] The government opposed it but could not prevent it. The conference abrogated the constitution and national assembly and dissolved several other state institutions. It created a Supreme Council of the Republic to act as transition parliament and restored the flag and national anthem of the 1960s. Deprived of the usual presidential prerogatives to manipulate political processes, President Denis Sassou-Nguesso lost the elections of 1992.[66]

In Niger, too, the 1991 conference declared itself sovereign and abolished the constitution, dissolved the national assembly and the government, and suspended the chief of staff of the armed forces, "effectively [taking] over the authority of the state."[67] Upon the completion of its work, it also appointed a High Council of the Republic, as transition parliament, on the Beninese and Congolese models. In Niger as in Congo, the effectiveness of the conference's claim to sovereignty was a function of the surrender of government forces.

By then, however, other African governments had begun to learn their lesson and would be careful not to put themselves in similar positions. In Gabon the conference was unable to declare itself sovereign. No significant reform ensued and Omar Bongo remains president to this day, strong in part because of his French connections and apparently grooming his son for eventual succession. In Togo, the government also successfully resisted calls for the conference's sovereignty, and President Gnassingbé Eyadéma remained in power until his death in 2005. The 1991 conference did at first pass "Act Number One," in which it suspended the previous constitution, declared itself sovereign, and proclaimed the "binding character of its decisions."[68] Yet, the government subsequently suspended its participation because the conference had "exceeded its recognized position . . . and its competence in declaring itself sovereign."[69] When government delegates later returned to the conference, they did so with the explicit rejection of its sovereignty and the reservation of their right to reject any of its decisions. Because of its failure to assert its sovereignty, the Togolese national conference was never able to properly usher in democratic reforms and wrestle control of the state away from Eyadéma. The following decade was marked by social conflict, violence, and continued authoritarianism. The Togolese example highlights the impossibility to seize sovereignty without government willingness to surrender what it acquired without rather than within. In Act Number One, the delegates invoked numerous alternative legitimating principles, including their alleged representative nature and the disqualifying abuses of the state, making a broad moral claim to sovereignty, only to be denied by the refusal and walkout of government delegates.

Chad provides a more nuanced version of the same scenario. President Idriss Déby managed to cede sovereignty to the national conference in 1993 while limiting the scope of this cession and preserving the enforceable power of the presidency and the state. The compromise between the opposition and progovernment delegates was that the conference would be sovereign for the future (e.g., for drafting a new constitution) but would not be able to dissolve current state institutions or undermine the office of the presidency. The conference's Act One captures this compromise and perfectly states the powers of sovereignty, as well as the continued association of the presidency with it:

> Article 1: The National Conference of Chad is sovereign. It freely debates and takes decisions that are imperative and *exécutoires* by the organs of the transition.
> Article 2: The president of the Republic is the guarantor of national sovereignty.
> Article 3: The institutions set up by the national Charter [Chad's equivalent of a constitution] remain *en vigueur* until the establishment of the transition institutions.[70]

In his opening speech, President Déby had articulated the nature of sovereignty and the necessity for his regime to keep it within the state: "The structures of the state, by remaining valid for the duration of the conference, will guarantee the state's perennial nature [*pérénité*], the continuation of the administration, public order and national sovereignty."[71] The resulting Act One, as Buijtenhuijs thoughtfully remarked, conveyed the notion that the conference was "sovereign for tomorrow, but not for today."[72] While it avoided a dramatic confrontation à la Togo, this compromise nevertheless turned out to be equally catastrophic for reformers in the long run. The Superior Council of the Transition (CST), which was to manage the one-year transition until the next elections and be sovereign and independent from the president, was unable to impose its control over the agencies of the state, particularly the armed forces, and to stop Déby from asserting presidential prerogatives from which he had formally been stripped, such as the sacking of ministers. Eventually, a mere six months after the end of the national conference, the president managed to create a majority among the CST to dismiss the transition government. He eventually won the elections of 1996 and subsequent ones, and the national conference failed to achieve a bona fide transition to democratic rule.[73]

The systematic push by reformers at national conferences to grab sovereignty confirms its monopolistic nature as the source of command. Sovereignty alone makes decisions legal and binding, and it exists only outside the political arena. The challenge for national conferences became therefore to veil themselves in it. Yet, because African sovereignty is exogenously granted upon the state, this was impossible without the government relinquishing it (or outside countries reassigning it). Only weak governments in Benin, Congo-Brazzaville, and Niger let go of their sovereign claim. Even then, however, they made sure sovereignty was imparted to transitional institutions by their own decrees rather than directly by the national conferences, something the latter did not object to. The sovereignty of the state itself was thus never contested, nor was it displaced.

"Sovereign" national conferences only managed to force governments to use their sovereignty in the ways they dictated. These included new constitutions and the creation of new state institutions, first among which were numerous "High Councils of the Republic" or similarly named transition legislative bodies, and new governments. The creation of new institutions by successful sovereign national conferences and the subsequent effectiveness of these new institutions' power provide evidence that the source of authority of state institutions is their sovereignty. Sovereign command originates in the domestically enforceable nature of internationally acquired sovereignty.

The Exchange Value of Legal Command

While state weakness and fiscal bankruptcy undermine the continuation of patron-client co-optation, sovereignty maintains the command value of state office, allowing those in positions of formal authority to carry on instrumentalizing their access to the state by converting their command into domination and resources. In other words, by guaranteeing the residual *command* value of state institutions, sovereignty also guarantees their *exchange* value, irrespective of the degree of state weakness. Sovereignty is the gold standard that underwrites the convertibility of state institutions in the market for domination and extraction. As a result, state institutions appeal to rulers and opponents alike, uniting them in their embrace of the state while pitting them against each other in their competition for it.

Not only does sovereignty maintain the state's exchange value, but it does so, like an overvalued currency, at an artificially high level, unwarranted by the state's weakness. Without sovereignty, the largely incapable institutions of weak states would be mostly devoid of command and thus broadly worthless in terms of personal power and private appropriation. As a result, they would most likely confront institutional competition. But sovereignty shields them from such competition and confers upon them monopoly rents, offering those associated with them benefits above and beyond their social utility. State agents are thereby able to extract a sovereign surplus from their fellow citizens.

The exchange of sovereign command for domination and resources is available at all levels of state power and even, to some extent, to people outside state power. For those in positions of relative political authority or aspiring to such status, sovereign command is essentially exchanged for domination. In these instances, local representatives of the state trade their national submission for access to sovereignty in order to reinforce, exert, or establish their domination over local populations. For many others in the employ of the state, sovereign command is exchanged for income, whether as a matter of mere survival for the majority, or of accumulation for some. Finally, for some outside the state, intermediation—or the facilitation of the daily negotiation of state arbitrariness by others—provides an important and surprisingly widespread resource.

Prebends

In situations of state failure, there will typically no longer be any significant resources to be distributed from the center to the periphery. Even in the many cases that would not qualify as outright failure, the fiscal shrinkage of the state and the conditionalities of donors, particularly since the early 1980s, have significantly reduced the amount of resources available for neopatrimonial redistribution. The resilience of sovereign command, however, allows holders of state power at the center and the periphery to continue parlaying their authority into prebends, whereby they themselves raise the resources they wish to appropriate. Richard Joseph identified as early as the 1980s the essential role of prebends in African politics. The prebend is by and large "an office of state," which can be acquired as a reward or through purchase and which, it is understood, the holder will use for the private appropriation of the rents that it entails.[74] From a prebendal perspective, state institutions and agencies retain their appeal for local elites even after the state is bankrupt or even if they are outside the main patron-client networks, because they can use the authority of these agencies—derived from state sovereignty and hence relatively constant—to dominate local populations and/or extract resources from them. The state no longer needs to buy regional compliance with clientelistic transfers to regions and their elites. Instead, local regional elites will maintain their association with the failed state to retain their sovereign prebends. Data showing how public service employment remains high despite the collapse in public service salaries illustrate the continued advantages of public positions in times of state fiscal bankruptcy and provide evidence of prebendal appeal. In the DRC, public salaries fell in real terms from an index value of 100 in 1970 to about 20 in 1990, while private salaries rose above 100. Yet, public employment rose over the same period from about 200,000 to more than 300,000.[75]

Joseph put a greater emphasis on the redistributive element in prebends and their compatibility with patron-client relations. Writing before the fiscal collapse of the state, he saw prebendalism as affording local patrons the state-derived resources they needed to buy local clients. From the perspective of the postfiscal collapse era, however, the crucial mechanism of prebendalism is its capacity to provide local patrons with parcels of state authority that they use in maintaining their local domination over people and resources, extracting from them rather than from the center. Tull identified this type of prebendalism in Zaire: "Contrary to the leaders at the apex engaged in the large scale plundering of public resources, local agents did not squeeze the state. Rather they used the (state) authority conferred upon them to extract resources from 'those in contextually inferior positions.' Not unlike in the international sovereignty game, the theoretical *attributes* of the state served as a resource, not the empirical proof of the state as such."[76]

To some extent, the production or reproduction of the local elites' status as elites, or of the economic inequality from which they benefit, is contingent on their sovereign connection, which induces the local reproduction of the state in its very failure. While visiting rebel-held Kisangani in 2001, I was told by Congolese civil servants that they continued to go to the office each day before heading off to their fields *"pour rester matriculés,"* that is, to remain officially registered as state agents. To some extent, this was no doubt part of a strategy to retain a claim to their salary should arrears be paid one day after reunification. But it was also part of maintaining their formal association to the sovereign state, even if by then it had all but collapsed, because it supported their claim to the attendant privileges of extraction from others. As Denis Tull again noted in the context of Goma during the war, "opportunities for predation are perhaps the main reason for the astonishing fact that local officials still go to their offices."[77]

Sovereign prebends can either be parlayed into domination—the acquisition or reinforcement of one's elite status over local populations—or directly exchanged for income. Prebendal domination by regional elites is the explanation I advance for the deficit of separatism in Africa. I only provide a brief discussion of it in the following section, as Chapter 5 is entirely dedicated to this topic. Direct income extraction is a more universal strategy that deals with nonelites too and contributes to the generalized nature of acquiescence with the failed predatory state. Together with intermediation, I provide more examples of this latter dimension here because I do not systematically return to it later.

Prebendal domination. In their quests for local hegemony, status, and class consolidation, regional leaders benefit from partaking in the command authority of the state, as it provides them with a unique tool to exert their local domination over people. Recognition of their local status by the state provides such leaders with an edge over local rivals by limiting political competition. The state may also confer upon them powers of declaration, control, regulation, and appropriation over local people and resources, such as the allocation of land, from which they can derive additional leverage in their relations with others. Local elites can thus be expected to seek access to sovereign state institutions such as provincial governments, regional bureaucratic agencies, parastatals, or recognized chiefdoms, in order to strengthen their local position.

Such use of legal command by local elites in their local relations of power by and large reproduces at the domestic level the strategies of extraversion that African rulers use internationally. According to Jean-François Bayart, African elites extract a rent, in terms of domestic domination and economic accumulation, from their relation of dependence with the rest of the world. Bayart suggests that historical examples of this process include slavery, some dimensions of the colonial relationship, the Cold War, structural adjustment programs, and recent civil conflicts. In each case, African elites have utilized their country's overall relationship of dependence vis-à-vis the rest of the world to pursue and consolidate domestic strategies of authority and representation.[78] To some extent, the use of state prebends for local domination multiplies this strategy down the hierarchy of elites. Regional leaders use their subaltern position in the state—from which they may no longer even accrue any salary or budgetary transfer—to consolidate their local ascendancy. They convert national submission into local domination. They do so by using legal command, that is, their legal association to sovereignty and its attendant capacity to produce legal authority. As a result, although their region may be neglected or even repressed by the state, they find a class advantage in locally maintaining the structures of the national state. This is a direct consequence of the political nature of class domination in Africa, or the fact that class relations on the continent articulate around control of power rather than control of economic production.[79]

Localized conflicts, which may appear based on primordial identity dynamics, are not infrequently the expression of competition between the elites of different groups for access to the tools of sovereign domination. Take the case of the Mamprusi and the Kusasi of northern Ghana. According to Christian Lund, divisions between these two groups revolve essentially around appointments to the chieftaincy, the delimitation of administrative districts, and access to land.[80] Over the past decades, these groups have endured significant conflict to have one of theirs accede to the chieftaincy, or to have a chieftaincy of their own. Because in Ghana, as in many other African countries, the government appoints lesser chiefs to office, these local disputes have articulated around the recognition of each group's claims by the state. As a result, Lund argues, "ethnicised political competition can be seen, at least partly, as an attempt by various groups to solicit the recognition of rights and status by national and other levels of government." It is thus mostly the declaratory power of the state that local elites seek here in their local struggles for domination: "Common for most political activities [in the region] is that they are directed towards the *state as the source of distinction, i.e., the institution that can qualify claims as rights or discard them as illegitimate*."[81] This explains how, for a while after the fall of Nkrumah, two local competing chiefs would "claim authority" by displaying symbols of sovereign statehood, such as flying the national flag at their house. And, in 1983, a raid by the Kusasi against the Mamprusi president of the local Traditional Council focused on the destruction of state symbols of authority such as "official documents, stationery and rubber stamps, as well as registers and court books, . . . all items that signify central state recognition of the Traditional Council's public authority," which Lund labels "administrative regalia."[82]

What may appear therefore at first as some case of local ethnic conflict is in fact a conflict about local access to sovereign power, or "the invigorating authorisation and recognition of the state to operate with validity," in order to ascertain a local dominant position.[83] Lund's original study also explicitly articulates the class nature of these local struggles over sovereign command. When one group has its representative in power, it appears to rise as the dominant class, leaving the unrepresented group as the commoners and occasionally using the chiefly status to make claims to land ownership against members of the other group.

Northern Ghana provides but one instance of a very widespread pattern of local sovereign hegemonic domination in Africa. It is particularly interesting because it relates to the manner in which "traditional" institutions use or attempt to use powers derived from legal command in order to strengthen their locally dominant status, and sheds light therefore on the paradoxical compliance of traditional chiefs, which I had raised in Chapter 3. After all, chiefs represent a "natural" alternative to weak states and their authority is widely believed to originate elsewhere, in precolonial history. Yet, as this case suggests (like the case of Barotseland in the next chapter, where domination is exercised *within* a single group), chiefs are chiefs and might thus be concerned first and foremost with their powers over their own people or over local competitors rather than with the representation of their people. As such, they are not shy to comply with the state in exchange for parcels of legal command that they can expend on their subjects.

Prebendal extraction. In one of his classic speeches, Mobutu once observed that "everything is sold, everything is bought in our country. And in this traffic, the possession of an ordinary parcel of public power constitutes a veritable currency of exchange [for] the illicit acquisition of money or of a material or moral value, or moreover, the evasion of all sorts of obligations."[84] What Mobutu put his finger on was the exchange value of sovereign power through prebendal extraction. It is a widespread practice in Africa. Strategies of both accumulation and survival are often predicated upon gaining access to parcels of sovereign authority in order to extract resources from others. In fact, positions of authority are often understood first and foremost for their benefits and extractive value. Referring to Cameroon, Francis Nyamnjoh stresses that "every presidential decree of appointment concludes with an emphasis on the benefits of the position to the individual concerned, but hardly ever with the responsibilities that go with the office (*'l'intéressé aura droit aux avantages et prérogatives liés a la fonction'*)."[85] Achille Mbembe refers to this system as "private indirect government":

> Functions supposed to be public, and obligations that flow from sovereignty, are increasingly performed . . . for private ends. Soldiers and policemen live off the inhabitants; officials supposed to perform administrative tasks sell the public service required and pocket what they get. . . . Traffic in public author-

ity . . . is such that everyone collects a tax from his or her subordinates and from the customers of the public service. . . . Relations of subjection . . . are formed through tolls, extortion and exactions [which] are, in turn, linked to a particular conception of *commandement.*[86]

Mbembe does not articulate the sovereign origins of *"commandement,"* but he identifies its systemic nature with great perceptiveness. All three categories of legal command contribute to income-generating prebends. As custodian of the legal and a paramount expression of the sovereign power of declaration, the judicial system typically presents fertile ground for the exchange of command. Citing a government report, Kenya's *Daily Nation* revealed in 2003 the existence of a rising scale of payments that affected about half of Kenya's judges, with the cost of a favorable judgment rising with the seniority of the judge and the severity of the case. While a magistrate's decision could be bought for US$50 to $1,900, it cost between US$636 and $20,356 for favorable sentencing at the High Court level and US$19,800 at the Appeal's Court.[87] In the DRC, many judges can be similarly bought. If one cannot afford a judge, it is sometimes possible to pay a clerk of the court to type a modified version of the judgment.[88] In Niger, where bribing judges is also common practice, a user of the court of Kandi reports that "in the courts, the person who has spent the most money is right; there is no justice, it's like a public auction."[89]

Sovereign declaration is not limited to the judiciary. In the DRC, four companies are "officially approved" by the government for testing the mineral content and radioactivity of copper and cobalt shipments in Katanga. Ironically, however, these tests are redone once out of the country, usually in South Africa, because analysis carried out in the DRC is not considered reliable.[90] The purpose of the tests is thus internal. Congolese authorities use their sovereign right of declaration and regulation to create enforceable domestic institutions, which are converted to additional layers of resource extraction. In fact, rumor tellingly has it that one of these testing companies, Labo Lubumbashi, does not even have a laboratory to test minerals, providing quick attestations in exchange for payment of the fee. These attestations can then be used when stopped by military and custom authorities inside Congo. But they are useless abroad. They only serve for the domestic exchange of sovereign command.

In many parts of the continent, the need for identification cards also represents a formidable local opportunity for extraction. A former volunteer for Catholic Relief Services recalls this meeting with pygmies in northern Republic of Congo:

I asked if any of them had identity cards. Everyone shook their heads. Not a single person had an official document despite this being a basic citizen's right. "Everything here costs money," said the elder. "Birth certificates too. We don't have money to pay for these papers. But then the police come and hassle us and cause problems. If they stop us at road blocks then they fine us or beat us because we can't show our ID."[91]

Thus, local state agents can charge for the provision of required documents, a power derived from the sovereign authority to authenticate, and police the lack of obedience to these requirements. There is little Africans can do against the enforcement by police of their country's laws.

Opportunities for income also accrue from the state's powers of regulation and control. In some cases, like traditional prebends, official local positions of public control are priced as a function of the income that can be expected from them. The same humanitarian worker in Congo-Brazzaville also recalls this story about police in the timber-rich region near Cameroon: "The chief of police charges each of his deputies 200,000CFA [$400] a month to keep their positions." The deputies then erect roadblocks by the sawmill and wait for the workers to go home, at which point they fine them, "saying it is illegal to be out after ten thirty at night."[92] Hence, the deputies use their legal power of control, based on some labor regulation, to extract resources from people associated with the production of a natural commodity. The revenue from the natural resource is thus realized via sovereign command, likely reinforcing the attachment to the state of resource-rich regions. This is a very valuable prebend, but it is extremely local as it must be realized on the road at a specific time after the workers leave their evening shift. In order to get his cut from this prebend, the police chief uses his higher hierarchical position in the sovereign chain of command to charge his deputies for use of this rent. In this case, this parcel of state sovereignty is valued at an astounding US$400 a month, or about a third of the country's per capita GDP. This is the exchange rate of the deputies' authority, and it provides an example of the degree of economic extraction that takes place in the margins of formal taxation in Africa.

The pricing of positions of sovereign extraction is common throughout Africa. Giorgio Blundo and Jean-Pierre Olivier de Sardan remark that "an appointment to an 'interesting' post which offers regular access to illicit benefits may give rise to the monthly payment of *enveloppes* (bribes) to the sponsor by the recipient."[93] These payments very much illustrate the rental nature of the sovereign position—people literally pay rent to occupy these functions. In the DRC, too, as state agents receive funds from their position, they are expected to send a percentage of that back up the hierarchy or they will be affected to less rewarding positions.[94] Hibou notes that, in Cameroon, "civil servants must pay to receive their salaries, and even a minister must pay for access to the budget allocated to his department."[95] In Nigeria, it is also frequent for the victim to have to pay the police to investigate a crime.

The subversion of rules by state agents for revenue extraction is particularly popular because the implementation of state regulations is, with taxation, one of the most decentralized forms of sovereign command. Earlier in this book, I quoted from a Global Witness report about the massive presence of local state agencies controlling and regulating the artisan mining sector in Katanga. The prebendal purpose of their existence should now become clear. The rest of the quotation reads as follows:

> A bewildering range of officials are preying on miners, négociants, transporters and traders, and demanding sums which, once totaled, represent a significant amount of money. Those who work in the sector have little choice in the matter: their ability to work, to buy and to sell is dependent on paying these bribes. . . . These sums of money, commonly referred to as "per diems," are handed over in cash to officials from the various government departments and usually go straight into their pockets.[96]

Particularly interesting here is the notion that people "have little choice in the matter" of paying the fees. This is not so much because of their fear of violence, but because these are all sovereign agencies, which can legally harass local economic operators: "You can't refuse. If you don't pay, they arrest you and make you pay double."[97]

When one faces arrest, evasion of the law is not much of an option. But even when rules are not obeyed, their enforcers will find prebendal opportunities. In fact, state agents will often seek the violation of a regulation in order to create an opportunity for financial sanction: "The driver will never have all the documents demanded by the officer. They start by requesting the insurance certificate, registration papers, driving license, certificate of technical inspection, logbook, and so forth. If all these are in order, they may then ask to see the first-aid kit, the fire extinguisher, and so on" until the victimized individual is finally found not to be in compliance and some penalty can be immediately assessed.[98]

It is, however, with the sovereign right of *public* appropriation that opportunities for *private* appropriation are logically maximized. In countries characterized by personal rule, any appropriation by the state can easily become private. The degree of extraction that takes place in Africa under this sovereign prerogative is remarkably heavy. Taxes on personal income may contribute very little to national budgets, but taxes on the daily activities of people are a big and sometimes the essential part of the private income of state agents. Although taxes are often imposed at the center, they are usually collected locally by regional actors representing the state. There are also multitudes of local taxes assessed and raised by local authorities, not to mention fraudulent duties levied by individual state agents. Altogether, Africans typically face a wide array of fees, administrative levies, licenses, permits, and other taxes, all of which represent very significant income flows to the holders of sovereign power. Recall the example of the market traders of Lubumbashi from Chapter 3. In addition to their personal income tax, they had to pay a tax to have access to market space, monthly and annual taxes for the right to maintain a market stall, a tax for nonexistent water, and a tax for nonexistent cleaning. In northern Cameroon, motorbike taxi operators are similarly burdened by the requirements of an *impôt libératoire*—literally, a tax that frees you to operate a business—a driver's license, vehicle registration, vehicle insurance, vehicle inspection sticker, permit to carry passengers, parking permit, customs receipt for the imported vehicle, and the requirement that the motorbike be painted yellow and that a helmet and gloves be worn.[99] Such level of taxation of relatively low-income individuals by and large guarantees their disobedience, offering police a legitimate reason to stop them, and opening the door for negotiation. Hence, to return to an argument made earlier, whether people obey the law or not has little effect on it retaining its exchange value, since the opportunities for fiscal evasion can also be the object of exchange. According to the International Crisis Group (ICG), the area of North Kivu in the DRC "that lies within the [government's] military control produces around $1.1m a month in declared revenue, mostly from taxes on imports and exports, especially of fuel. While 85 per cent is supposed to go to the Central Bank in Kinshasa, much is embezzled at the source. Provincial officials often grant waivers to traders to import and export goods without paying customs duties and receive generous kickbacks in return."[100] In Katanga, too, tax evasion is routinely parlayed into private appropriation by local authorities. At the border with Zambia, the taxes of different government departments can be jointly negotiated for a flat fee of US$3,000–$5,000 per mineral-carrying truck in addition to a 1 percent exit tax on the declared value of the goods. If one chooses rail transport instead, a fee of $50 per metric ton of cargo (with one train car weighing about 40 tons) will cover "fees to EMAK [the Association of Artisan Miners of Katanga], the mayor's office, the ANR, the Police des Mines, the Commerce Extérieur and the Service des Mines." Some trading companies pay quasi "monthly salaries to senior officials at OFIDA, ANR and other government departments to secure their cooperation."[101]

In Senegal, too, village chiefs or other local administrators regularly hijack the revenue from the "rural tax." Local Senegalese state agents are so overwhelmed by their opportunities for tax extraction that they seek voluntary help, which pays itself in exchange. For example, the eighteen tax collectors in Kaolack, a city of 200,000 inhabitants, rely on "a cohort of informal collectors." In Pikine, there are thirty-one official and ninety-five voluntary ("*bénévoles*") collectors. The volunteer, a sort of tax farmer, is actually recognized by the administration but receives no official salary: "He must then organize 'arrangements' with local businesses." And, of course, he will have to pass along part of their payment to his hierarchical superiors.[102]

Finally, it is worth noting the vocabulary of sovereign extraction. In Katanga, the fees paid to the many local "regulating" agents are referred to as "per diems" or "visas," both of which convey to the victims the official nature of the power brought to bear upon them.[103] Simultaneously, however, the concept of per diem suggests the idea of a payment to an official, on account of his official status, but for his private sustenance, perfectly capturing the nature of the transaction.

Intermediation

For those who do not have access to any public institution or status, the benefits of sovereignty can also be exploited through intermediation between the state and people. Intermediation is a common entrepreneurial activity in countries characterized by bureaucratic arbitrariness and predation. The goal of the intermediary is to offer her customers an escape from sovereign command or a reduction in the transaction costs of dealing with state authority and capture thereby a portion of the sovereign rent. Intermediaries may arise through personal connections to people in positions of authority or the comparative advantage of their social or geographical position.

In the DRC, not surprisingly, intermediation occupies a large segment of informal economic activity. The fact that it is a parasitic endeavor, centered on the facilitation of relations between the sovereign and individuals, is well expressed in the term that frequently describes it there: *protocole*. When arriving at N'djili International Airport in Kinshasa, for example, one can be rapidly overwhelmed by the large amount of uniformed and nonuniformed people on the tarmac and in the terminal, all of whom seem to claim some official function and make demands on the freshly disembarked traveler. These typically include requests to take possession of one's passport and ticket, and the necessity to abide by some health or administrative regulations. Evidence of the purpose of one's visit must be presented as well as a credible address of residence while in the country. One's luggage must also be searched. These administrative barriers, carried out by a multitude of poorly identified agents and pseudo-agents of the state, all of which are more or less arbitrary and many of which are abused by those who manage them, can make life difficult and lead to someone being stranded at the airport or having one's luggage inspected in such detail and by so many people that belongings may go missing. In order to avoid such stressful interactions, one can secure the services of a *protocole*, an individual who will negotiate safe exit from the terminal for one and one's property in exchange for a fee. On my trips to Kinshasa between 2000 and 2005, I typically paid $50 for this service, including transportation to the center of town. Papa M. waited for me on the tarmac, where he took my passport, international vaccination certificate, and baggage claim before I faithfully followed him through the maze of the airport, which he negotiated with ease and rapidity. I rarely saw him exchange money with anyone. In general, successive "officials" whisked us through upon seeing him or after exchanging a few apparently good-humored sentences in Lingala. With him, my luggage was never inspected. In contrast, when I once arrived on my own at Lubumbashi Airport, my suitcase was searched by four or five people at the same time with hands digging in from all directions until I forcefully closed it and, as vigorously as I could, called for someone to get my greeter on the other side of the terminal.

Although officials will sometimes offer their services to facilitate safe passage from themselves and their colleagues, Papa M. is not a civil servant, soldier, or security agent. He is a private Kinshasa driver who has made a business of owning a minivan. Statuswise, he is a private citizen, who has developed an expertise (apparently through practice in the service of international humanitarian and development workers) at negotiating the arbitrariness of the state at N'djili Airport. No doubt at some point he is expected to find the time to redistribute some of his earnings with these officials at the airport who let us through, while keeping the rest as his income. Sometimes he also offers transportation to town for some armed man, maybe as barter. Analytically, what matters is that his *protocole* business allows Papa M. to share in the rents from the sovereign monopoly of border control, even though he is not himself an agent of the sovereign state. The arbitrariness of the state creates opportunities for entrepreneurial and connected individuals like Papa M. to make a profit. As a result, they too derive short-term advantages from the state and are unlikely to challenge it. In the longer run, if state agents were less predatory and created expectations of safer arrivals for international travelers, tourism may well pick up in the country and passenger volume increase, bringing Papa M.'s transportation business greater opportunities and income. But he is not himself able to bring this change about, as it involves difficult issues of collective action, reputation, and credible commitment. Unable to contribute to reaching a higher equilibrium, Papa M. and his peers in the *protocole* business contribute to the reproduction of Congo's dysfunctional and predatory state.

The *protocole* business is in no way restricted to the airport, but has spun a national industry of facilitation of interactions with state agents. For example, the University of Lubumbashi (and probably other ones, too) has a Direction du Protocole, whose entire purpose seems to be to mediate relations between the university (and its guests) and local branches of the state, particularly the security agencies, which charge fees for the granting of permissions to do miscellaneous things, such as being in town. Global Witness also reports that intermediation activities are widespread in the mining sector in Katanga. In order to deal with official roadblocks and border authorities, "private individuals, some of whom are well-known in the mining sector as intermediaries or unofficial agents for companies, operate at the border and intervene whenever a problem arises."[104] And, in Congo's maze of arbitrariness and entrepreneurship, *un problème* always seems to arise. That intermediation is a direct result of attempts to cope with sovereign command is well illustrated by the activities of the "maneuvering mamas" of the river port of Kinshasa.[105] According to Anastase Bilakila, there are about thirty such women who wait at the port terminal for larger ships to arrive from up-country. Upon receiving the signal of an incoming ship, they board their motorboats and make a dash for the ship, which they come up to while it is still sailing. They then directly purchase the goods from the ship's passengers, who may be farmers or traders. In their negotiation over the price of the goods (most of which are foodstuff), they warn the passengers that the port is a hostile environment where they are likely to become victims of officials or impostors alike should they try to unload their merchandises themselves. Having convinced the newcomers to sell them their goods, they later resell them to market retailers. According to Bilakila,

> the traders coming from upcountry depend on the maneuvering mamas because they generally do not have sufficient cash to pay the taxes and other real or false administrative charges. Indeed the river ports are crowded with a multitude of police services, coast guards, soldiers, custom agents, public health agents, etc. who will all try to extract a few francs from them. Between these agents of the state and the maneuvering mamas, the traders see the latter as a lesser evil.[106]

Stories like these are reproduced throughout the country. A large number of intermediaries make a living or find the means of survival by acting as facilitators and suppliers of the material tools necessary to the realization of the command relationship. These include roadside stands that provide the ubiquitous stamps to make documents (look) official or the photocopying of these documents as part of all the required paper work, miscellaneous handlers, and so forth.

Intermediation is far from limited to the DRC, however, and is a relatively widespread occupation across much of Africa. Dickson Eyoh describes the "private administration," that is, the "hordes of document merchants and providers of clerical services found in front of ministerial and other government buildings," that supplies intermediation services in Cameroon.[107] Daniel Smith notes that many Nigerians "find navigating government bureaucracies frustrating and people frequently rely on the aid of intermediaries. Indeed, at almost every major bureaucracy that provides essential services, one finds a small army of intermediaries to expedite one's business." These intermediaries "can be either employees of the bureaucracy or private entrepreneurs who have developed connections in the office." These people "add yet another layer of interests invested in preserving practices of corruption" and, I would add, in preserving the state.[108] Similarly, Blundo imputes the "omnipresence of administrative brokers" in Senegal to the "opaque" nature and "exceedingly large discretionary powers" of public administration. "Armed with a briefcase and rubber stamps of occasionally dubious origins, the broker . . . stakes out the entrance of the justice palace or of the administrative building to intercept the user upon his arrival. He offers him either to facilitate acquisition of an act delivered by public authority, or to speed up some procedure."[109] Tidjani Alou shows the systemic banality of these intermediary transactions. He tells the story of a rural man in Niger who came to town to get a certificate of nationality for his daughter to register for her first-year school entrance examination. As the man looks for the relevant office at the Niamey courthouse, "he is approached by an affable smiling gentleman who volunteers to show him the way to the department that deals with issuing certificates of nationality . . . the stranger introduces him to a middle-aged woman . . . she works in this department." Quoting a judge in Niamey, "when [these intermediaries] see a defendant arriving at or leaving the judge's office, they ask him what he's doing in the courts. He tells them that he's come to see the judge: then the intermediary may say 'but he's my cousin, I know him, if you give me 100,000 CFA francs, I'll go and see him.'"[110]

Although there will be plenty of fraudsters among them, most of these brokers play a legitimate, though not necessarily licit, facilitating role between the administration and the citizen. Intermediation extends the benefits of command to nonstate agents, increasing the number of its beneficiaries and acting as a multiplier of sovereignty. It also makes the system more bearable, manageable, and negotiable to the majority of users, thereby promoting acquiescence to it.

Resilience Revisited

Why do Africa's weak states endure? Given a fixed international supply of sovereignty, African regional elites, like their counterparts elsewhere, face a choice between sovereign and nonsovereign action. They can be expected to capitalize on local grievances and promote secessions or nonstate institutional developments if the potential rewards of such disengagement, in the absence of international recognition, outweigh the potential rewards associated with control or partial control of institutions of the sovereign national state, however decayed. The decision is thus between exit and sharing a possibly small part of sovereignty through a local provincial position or some other delegation of state authority. If elites and individuals can do better in terms of domination and income from staying associated with the sovereign state, we can expect them to reproduce state institutions in their daily actions, ceteris paribus. If, on the contrary, their political and material interests are more likely to be promoted by disengagement from the state, then we might expect them to pursue such a more defiant path, ceteris paribus.

African state sovereignty is exogenous and juridical. It proceeds from the act of international recognition and is unrelated to the empirical effectiveness of the state. While sovereign states everywhere are endowed with the power to rule by the law, this power in Africa is disconnected from social contracting, historical legitimacy, social homogeneity, endogenous class domination, or other domestic foundations. As long as international recognition endures, the state maintains its power of legal command, even if the rest of its apparatus crumbles. Exogenous juridical sovereignty disconnects command from capacity. The residual existence of the weak state becomes largely limited to this power of legal command, a power that is widely distributed throughout the territory and the population.

Legal command can be instrumentalized. Its powers of domination and extraction can be converted into a material resource. Because legal command endures even when the state is failed, its exchange value in terms of domination and extraction also endures, even if the state is fiscally bankrupt and unable to reproduce through the redistribution of financial resources. Most Africans have few alternative options for material advancement. Despite several decades of adjustment, the share of the private sector in the economies of Africa remains small. In addition, existing private activity is often small-scale, parasitic, and state-dependent. Given their lack of alternatives and the lasting powers of command in times of state weakness, many Africans associated with the state instrumentalize sovereignty. In their instrumentalization of sovereignty, African state actors and social intermediaries reproduce the weak state, even though they may be politically severed or disconnected from its center, which they may even oppose. The state endures as the collective outcome of these myriads of individual strategies, repeatedly propped up, as it were, by the utility individuals derive from its power of legal command. Hence, the relative returns of legal command in Africa, derived from its exogenous nature and from the comparative lack of other opportunities, bias the incentives of African elites and others associated with the state away from challenging the state and toward its reproduction through sovereign-based political action.

A few points deserve some elaboration. First is the extent to which it is state sovereignty rather than state weakness that gets instrumentalized in the politics of weak states. What people instrumentalize is sovereign command, the last remaining effective dimension of state power, the last strength of the state, not its weakness. When states are weak, failed, or collapsed, the reason they remain tools of domination and predation is their sovereign nature. The legality of the state, acquired from its international sovereignty, provides resilience to its failed institutions and allows for the continuation of their conversion into private resources. Without their sovereignty, this would not be possible. If state institutions also lost their power of command, they would no longer have domestic currency.

There is no doubt, however, that for sovereign institutions to be instrumentalized, there must be some lack of accountability. If only to the extent that it favors impunity, state weakness promotes thus instrumentalization. But weakness is not necessary. The reason it receives such analytical attention is that it highlights the paradoxical nature of institutional resilience. "How can such weak states endure?" one is compelled to ask upon seeing the likes of

Chad. We expect weakness to make exit more likely, because it makes it easier and more rational. When weak institutions reproduce instead, we conclude that it is because their weakness offers such a resource to political actors. While this is not inaccurate, it is missing the element of sovereignty. Weak institutions could not be instrumentalized if they were not sovereign, if they did not maintain their power of legal command in times of failure. It is international sovereignty that gives national and local state institutions the legal and political foundation to make their decisions enforceable (or *exécutoires* as the French would say more descriptively) over citizens and local resources, even when otherwise incapable to perform their functions.

Thus I propose to strengthen the instrumentalization paradigm and make it more relevant to policy reform by understanding the extent to which it is linked to the sovereignty of institutions and positions of authority. In a time of state failure, sovereignty is a necessary condition for instrumentalization, which may not have been equally true when allegiance was bought by the distribution of fiscal resources from the center. Because the drying up of the state's fiscal resources at the center has increased the value of being able to acquire resources locally, it has also magnified the value of local prebends of command, making the sovereign connection more important than ever and reinforcing the reproduction of the weakest and most peripheral of institutions.

A second concluding point is the extensive nature of sovereign welfare in Africa. There is very little opposition to negative sovereignty, despite its promotion of weak states, because the benefits from sovereignty are widely distributed throughout society, even among those not directly associated with central state power. Reproduction of local state institutions and occupation of its local offices present local elites and anyone associated with state power with their share of the rents of sovereignty. Although they may not be involved in the production of sovereign command, which typically takes place through policy-making and lawmaking, they benefit from it because they are the ultimate *local representatives* of sovereignty. They are the ones with the sovereignty-derived rights to collect local taxes, adjudicate local disputes, control local borders, regulate local activities, require local licenses, allocate local resources, and the like. This they can do whether people obey the laws and policies of the state or try to evade them, since they are also often needed to facilitate such evasion. Either way, their association with the sovereign state reinforces their local domination and capacity for accumulation and reduces the likelihood that they will challenge it.

The actions of intermediaries who mediate the relationship between the state and citizens, exploiting income opportunities derived from the arbitrariness of local sovereign command, further contribute to its universality. Although they may often appear as powerless outsiders to local state agencies and occasionally as their victims, they also have a short-term interest in its sovereign reproduction and, absent better opportunities for survival, are also likely to continue embracing failed state institutions. These mechanisms together ensure that weak states go on reproducing themselves largely unchallenged despite failing to provide many of the most basic functions that are expected of states, not least the security of the human person and of property.

Finally, the extent to which international sovereignty is converted into a domestic resource via legal command has been insufficiently appreciated. The scholarship on Africa's "resource curse," which highlights how economic reliance on primary commodities undermines development and promotes conflict, has failed to identify sovereignty itself as a material resource.[111] In the *Bottom Billion*, Paul Collier laments the landlocked nature of many African states without identifying that their existence, however unconducive to development, is a resource that many cannot afford to forgo. Although the availability of natural resources may sustain fighters, many of Africa's ongoing conflicts are not so much waged over the control of natural resources than over the control of the tools of sovereignty. Hence the overwhelming tendency of these conflicts to be nonseparatist.

Notes

1. See Médard, "The Underdeveloped State"; Sandbrook, "Patrons, Clients, and Factions"; Jackson and Rosberg, "Personal Rule"; Joseph, *Democracy*; van de Walle, "Neopatrimonialism and Democracy"; and Bayart, *The State in Africa.*

2. See Reno, 'The Changing Nature"; Chabal and Daloz, *Africa Works*; Bayart, Ellis, and Hibou, *The Criminalization of the State.*

3. Krasner, *Sovereignty.*

4. Murphy, "The Sovereign State System," 82.

5. Jackson and Rosberg, "Why Africa's Weak States Persist."

6. Jackson, *Quasi-States.*

7. Jackson and Rosberg, "Why Africa's Weak States Persist," 12 and 13.

8. Jackson, *Quasi-States*, 17. See also Herbst, "The Creation and Maintenance."

9. For a contrary point of view, see Young, "The End."

10. Clapham, *Africa and the International System*, particularly chapter 3. See also Clapham, "The Challenge to the State"; and Clapham, "Degrees of Statehood."

11. Herbst, *States and Power.*

12. Boli, "Sovereignty." See also Biersteker and Weber, "The Social Construction."

13. Kennes, "The Mining Sector," 164.

14. Chabal and Daloz, *Africa Works*, 28.

15. Trefon, *Parcours administratifs*, 143–147.

16. Tidjani Alou, "Corruption in the Legal System," 142 and 174.

17. Lambright, "Silence from Below?" 178–179.

18. Austin, *The Province of Jurisprudence,* 194.

19. For a take on the legal nature of African politics, see Comaroff and Comaroff, "Law and Disorder."

20. Trefon, *Parcours administratifs*, 21–22 (translation mine).

21. Tidjani Alou, "Corruption in the Legal System," 157.

22. Mbembe and Roitman, "Figures of the Subject," 340.

23. Blundo, "Négocier l'Etat au quotidien," 87.

24. Trefon, *Parcours administratifs*, 39.

25. Ibid., 71.

26. See Weinstein, *Inside Rebellion*, 175–178.

27. See Akindes, "The Roots"; see also Banégas and Losch, "La Côte d'Ivoire."

28. Willame, *Banyarwanda et Banyamulenge*, 53 and 57.

29. Information on Liberia's flag of convenience is derived from Hoyos, "Shipping"; and Vines, "Vessel Operations."

30. Willame, *Banyarwanda et Banyamulenge*, 84.

31. See www.kimberleyprocess.com; Wallis, "Africa's Conflict Diamonds"; and Innocenti, "Diluted Deals."

32. Tull, *The Reconfiguration*, 76–77.

33. Interview with Jean-Claude Muyambo, Bar Association, Lubumbashi, April 2002.

34. De Herdt and Marysse, *L'économie informelle au Zaire*.

35. Hibou, "The Social Capital," 108.

36. Trefon, *Parcours administratifs*, 67 and 117.

37. Tidjani, "Corruption in the Legal System," 155.

38. Global Witness, *Digging in Corruption*, 14 and 19.

39. Trefon, *Parcours administratifs*, 58–59.

40. Mbalanda, "La gestion des rumeurs," 44.

41. Ibid., 72–73.

42. Arifari, "We Don't Eat the Papers," 180, 190, 199.

43. Available from www.doingbusiness.org/CustomQuery/ViewCustomReport .aspx?excel=true.

44. Boone, "Africa's New Territorial Politics," 63, 69 (emphasis mine).

45. See Young and Turner, *The Rise and Decline*, chapter 11, 326–362; V. S. Naipaul's *A Bend in the River* (New York: Vintage, 1989) offers a fictionalized rendition of this episode.

46. World Bank, *Word Development Indicators*.

47. Hibou, "The Social Capital," 80.

48. Trefon, *Parcours administratifs*, 149–150.

49. Cited by Buijtenhuijs, *La conférence nationale*, 138.

50. Wines, "We Welcome You to Lush Zimbabwe."

51. See Englebert, "Born-Again Buganda."

52. *Financial Times*, 2 June 2005, 7.

53. Airault, "La Vie au Nord."

54. Tull, *The Reconfiguration,* 133.

55. Krasner, "Sharing Sovereignty."

56. Van de Walle, *African Economies*.

57. Cummins, "Exxon Oil-Funded Model."

58. See also *Africa Confidential*, 22 September 2006, 47(19):4.

59. Note, however, that there was only a brief window of time during which the French government put significant pressure on its African client-states for democratization. By the Franco-African summit of 1991, France's demands for democratization had been considerably toned down.

60. Eboussi-Boulaga, *Les conférences nationales*, 72.

61. Ibid., 73.

62. Ibid., 79.

63. On this, see also Nzouankeu, "The Role of the National Conference," 45.

64. Heilbrunn, "Social Origins," 278.

65. *Africa Contemporary Record, 1990–1992* (New York: Holmes and Meier, 1998), B210.

66. Like Kérékou, however, Sassou would return to office later in the decade, but while Kérékou would be reelected in 1996 in a dramatic show of popular political impotence, Sassou retook power by force, with Angolan support, in October 1997.

67. *Africa Contemporary Record, 1990–1992* (New York: Holmes and Meier, 1998), B109.

68. Ibid., B170.

69. Government communiqué, quoted by Heilbrunn, "Social Origins," 290.

70. Translated from the text reproduced in Buijtenhuijs, *La conférence nationale*, 64. Certain words lose some of their essence in translation. While *exécutoire* is enforceable—to be executed—*en vigueur*'s translation as "applicable" loses the vigor component that nicely captures the life force of sovereign institutions.

71. Quoted in ibid., 61.

72. Ibid., 64.

73. See Buijtenhuijs's "postscript" in *La conférence nationale*, 201–210. There was also a national conference in Zaire, which failed to effectively become sovereign, and one in Mali, which followed a regime transition and sided with the government. In 2005, there was also a political struggle in Nigeria over the holding of a national conference, which President Obasanjo successfully resisted.

74. Joseph, *Democracy and Prebendal Politics*, 56 and 65.

75. De Herdt and Marysse, *L'économie informelle au Zaire*, 56 and 60.

76. Tull, *The Reconfiguration*, 66, quoting Schatzberg, *The Dialectics of Oppression*, 56.

77. Tull, *The Reconfiguration*, 135.

78. Bayart, "Africa in the World."

79. Sklar, "The Nature of Class."

80. Lund, "Bawku Is Still Volatile."

81. Ibid., 588 and 589 (emphasis mine).

82. Ibid., 605.

83. Ibid., 604.

84. In a 1977 speech, quoted by Schatzberg, *Political Legitimacy*, 172.

85. Nyamnjoh, "Cameroon: A Country United,"106.

86. Mbembe, *On the Postcolony*, 80 and 84. See Mbembe and Roitman, "Figures of the Subject," especially: "By the discretionary path of 'nomination' and 'the decree,' the autocrat can . . . cede a portion of this anonymous domain [of the state] to the obliged subjects. Nomination to a position of responsibility or command, that is, control of a part of the apparatus of authorizations and formalities, is lived as an allocation in kind from which one can, by being astute, organize levies and parallel fiscal mechanisms" (347).

87. "'Price List' for Kenya's Judges," BBC News, 3 October 2003, news.bbc.co .uk/go/pr/fr/-/1/hi/world/Africa/3161034.stm.

88. Personal interview, Jean-Claude Muyambo, Bar Association, Lubumbashi, April 2002.

89. Tidjani, "Corruption in the Legal System," 147.

90. Global Witness, *Digging in Corruption,* 48.

91. Knight, *Brazzaville Charms*, 208.

92. Ibid., 200.

93. Blundo and Olivier de Sardan, *Everyday Corruption,* 73.

94. Trefon, *Parcours administratifs,* 36.

95. Hibou, "The Social Capital," 100.

96. Global Witness, *Digging in Corruption*, 14.

97. Ibid., 15.

98. Arifari. "We Don't Eat the Papers," 196.

99. Roitman, *Fiscal Disobedience*, 182–183.

100. ICG, "Congo's Transition Is Failing," 13.

101. Global Witness, *Digging in Corruption*, 16.

102. Blundo, "Négocier l'Etat," 86.

103. Global Witness, *Digging in Corruption*, 14 and 15.

104. Ibid., 18.

105. Bilakila, "La 'coop' a Kinshasa."

106. Ibid., 39.

107. Eyoh, "Conflicting Narratives," 272.

108. Smith, *A Culture of Corruption,* 60.

109. Blundo, "Négocier l'Etat au quotidien, " 82.

110. Tidjani, "Corruption in the Legal System," 138.

111. For the best-known exemplar, see Collier and Hoeffler, "Greed and Grievance," and Collier, *The Bottom Billion,* particularly chapter 3.

5

The Calculus
of Compliance

Regional elites are biased in their outlook and actions by the avail-
ability of sovereign command and the scarcity of alternative means of advancement. When they have access to instruments of legal command, they are
more likely to use them in establishing or reproducing their local domination
than they are to pursue the collective interests of their region toward the central state. They will tend to trade national submission for local domination.
Thus, the availability of local benefits from command reduces the odds that regional elites will be political entrepreneurs, institution or state builders, or that
they will stand up to the state. It makes it less likely that they will seek to aggregate and represent regional interests vis-à-vis a central authority. It limits
their urge to challenge state authority. It will make them become, or seek to
become, the state.

This chapter looks at four groups or regions that have been kept largely
outside the neopatrimonial state-building networks and harbor substantial
grievances vis-à-vis the states that neglect, ignore, or repress them, yet have
not developed significant secessionist or authority challenges to the state. I
show how their elites seek to benefit from sovereign legal command in their
local struggles for domination or quests for material advancement. By presenting analytical narratives of their stories, I illustrate the extent to which the use
of tools of sovereign command in local dynamics of social competition, domination, or predation contributes to the reproduction of weak states.

My argument contrasts with the more conventional neopatrimonial explanation for state unity in Africa, according to which regional elites remain part
of the state in exchange for material benefits from the center, which they are
in turn expected to distribute locally. The validity of this more conventional
approach is not in question here, and evidence for it is readily observable. In
this chapter, I point this logic out when it takes place, as with the reliance of
Nigeria's regional elites on the redistribution of oil revenues. But my argument

goes further by stressing that compliance continues when resources from the center dry up, and that such compliance can be expected even from groups without direct access to state resources. I look at regions or groups that have fallen out (or have been kept out) of the redistribution of state revenues and that harbor grievances toward the center—hence they have some good reasons to go and few to stay. I argue that these regions' elites stay because the local domination they can exercise through legal command—which allows them to extract resources locally— provides them with greater relative payoffs than alternative strategies. Thus, they endeavor to maintain or demand instruments of domination connected to state sovereignty.

The cases in this chapter illustrate the argument through a multiplicity of circumstances. They include groups in countries of Belgian, British, and French colonial descent. They look at different types of elites, including traditional authorities, provincial administrators, civil servants, economically dominant minorities, educated youth, and rebel entrepreneurs. They affect areas of ethnic and linguistic homogeneity and others that are mosaics of heterogeneity. They deal with regions devoid of significant natural resources and others replete with them, both mineral and agricultural. They include areas at war and at peace. And they tell of actors driven by unmitigated greed and others by sheer survival. Despite these differences, one cannot but be amazed by the similarities of behavior among these elites brought about by the returns to legal command. Similarly, national submission is always the price of the local sovereign strategy, while its systematic consequences are the reproduction and exoneration of the state.

Regional elites might seek legal command to affirm their authority within their own group or establish it over other groups and their elites. The power of the Barotse Royal Establishment (BRE) over the people of the Western Province of Zambia is very much a matter of in-group command-mediated class domination. Although this domination is largely executed through control of land, it is possible because of the legal distribution of sovereign authority to the BRE. Class domination in Africa is not only a traditional affair, however. Anglophone Cameroon provides an example of the use of legal command by a broader set of regional elites to establish or restore their state-derived class benefits and regional domination. These two cases suggest that sovereign command is frequently exercised *within* a specific group. Rather than representing their group toward the state, regional elites use state power to retain or regain their status within the group. Local inequality is heightened and the state goes unchallenged.

The last two cases focus on the exercise of legal command *between* groups, which is more likely in ethnically heterogeneous environments. Here, local elites use legal command to fight with other groups for dominant local position. In the Kivu provinces of the DRC, Rwandophones have historically sought Congolese citizenship in order to gain access to positions of customary or administrative authority—both of which are regulated by the law—to appropriate land for which they compete with other groups. In Nigeria, ethnic minorities compete with each other for access to statehood and the attendant opportunities for oil revenues and legal command. As a result the Nigerian federation has grown from three states in 1960 to thirty-six since 1996. In both of these cases, the recourse to legal command magnifies local conflict while reproducing the national state.

Of course, there are variations in the calculus of compliance of elites in each region. Specifically, there are some groups or individuals in Barotseland, Anglophone Cameroon, and Nigeria who are more vocal than others in expressing separatist preferences. In general, these variations are a function of the difficulties some of these elites might experience in accessing the tools of legal command or of the availability of alternative means of advancement. In Barotseland, we find that sidelined members of the royal family are more separatist. In Cameroon, it is students with little prospect of state employment. In Nigeria, it is groups that steal oil from pipelines and are thus in need of territorial control. Diasporas also appear to play a similar role, as members of the minority abroad will typically benefit from alternative economic opportunities from the state. The limited separatist movements of Barotseland, Anglophone Cameroon, and particularly Biafra all have significant such diaspora elements.

A Republican King in Zambia

In Barotseland, a kingdom relies on legal command to reinforce its privileges and prerogatives over its subjects as a "traditional" system.[1] The BRE uses a language of tradition and historical legitimacy, but its behavior betrays a desire to be the local embodiment of the sovereign postcolonial state. Barotseland illustrates the sovereign logic of in-group domination and the extent to which control over a natural resource like land is itself a function of access to sovereignty.

Barotseland is a precolonial political entity that was largely consolidated by its status as protectorate under British colonization. Later incorporated as part of Zambia, its insertion in the postcolonial mold has been replete with difficulties. Barotseland is peripheral and distinct from the rest of Zambia in many ways. It is physically remote, lying about 600 kilometers west of Lusaka in what is today the Western Province. It is ethnically different, mainly composed of Lozi, who have a well-developed cultural and political identity dating back to around 1700. To this day, Barotseland maintains a political system that begins with the king (the Litunga) and includes the royal council, district chiefs and their councils, counties, and villages. Kingdom authorities adjudicate land disputes, matrimonial matters, and problems of witchcraft.[2] It is also historically unique. As a British protectorate, Barotseland experienced greater autonomy and a milder form of colonialism than the rest of Northern Rhodesia with which it was administratively associated.[3] In 1961, the BRE even unsuccessfully sent representatives to Britain to seek separate independence. To this day, the BRE is of the opinion that its integration into Zambia was the consequence of an international treaty, the Barotseland Agreement (BLA) of 1964, which was wrongfully abrogated by the Zambian constitution.[4] Finally, Barotseland is also economically different. The poorest province of Zambia, its 620,000 people eke out a living from subsistence farming and cattle ranching.[5] There is little formal employment and people blame the state for underinvesting in their region and keeping them away from profitable state employment.

Barotseland has also been kept outside ruling coalitions, both under single-party rule and since the democratic reforms of the early 1990s. As a result, it has developed a significant degree of grievance toward the Zambian state, as suggested by interviews carried out by Daniel Posner. Asked "Who do you blame for the problems facing your local community?" 45 percent of Mongu respondents answered the government and 32 percent the presidency, the highest combined percentage in the country. Of Lozi respondents, 72 percent also said "many nations" when asked whether they thought Zambia was "one nation or is it really many nations." This compared with 78.5 percent of respondents saying one nation among the Bemba ethnic group, which is close to central power. And while 69 percent of nationwide respondents thought their area did not get its fair share of government services, the proportion rose to 83 percent in Mongu. Also, regarding government appointments, 48 percent of national respondents expressed discontent, as against 82 percent of the Lozi.[6]

And yet, Barotseland by and large accepts its Zambian identity. A majority of its population has voted for non-Lozi parties since the democratization of the early 1990s. In the 1999 national elections, a party that supported a separatist agenda failed to win a single seat in the Western Province. The MAR project reports "a lack of commitment to Lozi organizations" within the region.[7] Posner also indicates that 74 percent of Lozi respondents considered themselves Zambians before being Lozi. To be sure, separatism has not altogether been absent from Lozi political discourse. Yet, no group to this day has taken arms in support of it, and Barotse elites, embodied in the BRE, have generally rejected secession as a political objective.[8] Instead, one of the BRE's main demands has been for a constitutional recognition of its status as part of Zambia.

The Barotseland Agreement: Sharing Legal Command

The colonies of Barotseland and Northern Rhodesia became independent together as Zambia in 1964. The willingness of Barotseland to merge with Northern Rhodesia was conditioned upon the continued recognition of the kingship's status and prerogatives, which had been formalized and enshrined under the British Protectorate. Litunga Mwanawina Lewanika III signed the Barotseland Agreement in 1964, a quasi treaty between him, Northern Rhodesia's then prime minister Kenneth Kaunda, and the British government, which provided the legal basis for the integration of Barotseland within Zambia. In exchange for Barotseland's acceptance that Northern Rhodesia "should proceed to independence as one country and all its peoples should be one nation," the Litunga obtained a very significant amount of *legal* recognition of his powers within his region and over his subjects.[9] The BLA froze the existence of Barotseland as a political system, stating that it would continue to be recognized "as such" by the Zambian government. In other words, the government of Zambia authenticated Barotseland, providing it with the sanction of its sovereignty (in presence of the colonial overlord—the ultimate guarantor of African sovereignty). The extent to which this provision legally codified alleged tradition makes it worth quoting in full, as it suggests the greater benefits to the kingdom of sovereign rather than customary recognition: "The Government of the Republic of Zambia will accord recognition as such to the person who is for the time being the Litunga of Barotseland under the customary law of Barotseland."[10]

More important, the BLA delegated substantial elements of sovereign powers to the Litunga and the BRE, which was to remain "the *principal local authority* [my emphasis] for the government and administration of Barotseland," being empowered to make laws for the region in several essential matters, including as relates to local courts, taxation, government, land, forest, fishing, hunting, game preservation, the reservation of trees for canoes (a crucial resource in the floodplains), and the "supply of beer" (a crucial resource everywhere). This constituted an extensive degree of federal delegation, with the nuance that the BLA recognized the authority of a political elite over its region, rather than the autonomy of the region. While some of the usual co-optation also took place, the extent to which the BLA predicated the insertion of Barotseland into Zambia upon the delegation of legal command to local authorities is worthy of consideration.

The BLA would not withstand the nation-building pressure that swept postcolonial Africa from the mid-1960s onward, however. The adoption of a more centralized constitution in 1969 provided the context for President Kaunda's rescinding of the BLA and downgrading of Barotseland to a mere province. There was some vocal opposition by BRE elites against the dissolution, which contributed to the development of a sense of regional grievance, compounding as it did Barotseland's marginalization from the copper-dominated Zambian economy. Yet, no particular antigovernment mobilization or credible movement toward separation followed. To some extent, this acceptance reflected the participation of some Lozi royals to the national fusion of elites.[11] Yet, these individuals were not central characters of the Barotse system, and the king himself was kept largely outside the reciprocal assimilation until the appointment of Litunga Ilute Yeta IV to the Central Committee of the ruling party in 1988. The repressive capacity of the Kaunda regime certainly provided another reason for the lack of Lozi resistance at the time. Yet, to a large extent, it was the continuation of the BRE's prerogatives in the province during the following two decades that favored the grudging acceptance of their new status by BRE elites. For sure, the removal of the legal basis of their powers caused them certain grief, but the limited substitution of centralized state authority over their fief allowed for their continued effective control of important resources such as land, timber, game, courts, and, by extension, people. The Litunga continued to be recognized by the state as a paramount chief and was thus able to maintain most of his "traditional" powers over locals. The BRE had been hit a blow but it had not crumbled, and no need was seen for a more radical response.

With democratization in the 1990s, however, the opportunity arose for the BRE to articulate its demands, which focused almost entirely on the restoration of the BLA, that is, the reinstatement and clarification of the legal foundation of its insertion into Zambia and of the legal foundation of its local powers. Yet, the Movement for Multiparty Democracy (MMD) of President Frederick Chiluba, who succeeded Kenneth Kaunda in 1991, turned out equally unsympathetic to the BRE's agenda. Over the subsequent years, the BRE lobbied with the Chiluba administration for the restoration of the BLA and practiced a certain degree of political brinkmanship, while systematically rejecting the secessionist option. In 1994, for example, Litunga Ilute Yeta reiterated that "We shall not secede from Zambia" while simultaneously expressing his grievance at the government for its "perpetual enslavement" of his region.[12]

The relation between the BRE and the government deteriorated in 1995, however, after the Chiluba administration passed a new Land Act, which vested the allocation of public lands into the presidency, a typical instance of sovereign appropriation by legal command. There is little freehold land tenure in Barotseland. In contrast, the Litunga is the custodian of land, which he allocates to individuals for housing and farming. An annex to the BLA had stipulated that, although the government of Zambia could use land in the region for public purpose, "the Litunga should continue to have the greatest measure of responsibility for administering land matters in Barotseland."[13] Despite the formal repeal of this power implied with the abrogation of the BLA in 1969, the Litunga had continued to enjoy a large control over land in Barotseland, in part due to the fact that he was still recognized as a traditional authority, which implied local land prerogatives.[14] But it now looked like this would no longer be the case. The Land Act was thus seen as undermining one of the most fundamental powers of the king. There was fear that the new system would convert customary land into leasehold with the president alone habilitated to issue title. Under such conditions, association with the sovereign state lost much of its appeal. While legal ambiguity had been reluctantly tolerable, the centralization of sovereign command by the government in Lusaka annulled the union. Thus, in early November of 1995, the BRE made its strongest-ever public pronouncement on the issue of national integration in the "Resolutions of the Barotse National Conference," held at Lealui.[15] Signed by the Ngambela (the BRE's prime minister), the resolutions stressed Barotse's dejection at the government's refusal to recognize the BLA, accused it of deceit and of "total abrogation of the rights of the people of Barotseland," before resolving that the recognition of the BLA by the government "must be incorporated in the constitution." Notice thus that the BRE did not react to the curtailment of its local authority by challenging the authority and legitimacy of the government in its region, but by demanding its own further legal integration into the state, which would preserve the constitutional (and thus sovereign) foundations of its local powers. Nevertheless, the document added that "if the government continues to be obstinate, the people of the Barotse shall have the right to self-determination by reverting to the original status of Barotseland before 1964," which is the closest thing to a threat of secessionism that the BRE ever uttered.[16]

It would also be the last such threat. Although the government did not bulge with respect to the BLA, the implementation of the Land Act remained superficial and, as in 1969, did not significantly undermine the effective local powers of the Litunga, by and large allowing for the preservation of the BLA by default.[17] While the BRE did not demure from its demands for the restoration of BLA (with the Litunga even taking a trip to London in 1997 to seek British support on the issue), it did not either again challenge the state head-on. The troubles that subsequently engulfed the Chiluba administration, which was accused of widespread corruption, undermined its capacity to implement policies and reduced its will to confront the BRE. The election of Levy Mwanawasa in 2000 further contributed to the restoration of somewhat more cordial relations between the two parties.

Resisting Hegemonic Erosion

The visitor to Barotseland cannot but remark on the degree of preservation of its "traditional" political structure by the kingdom. The BRE retains considerable power throughout the province, particularly in matters of land and natural resources. The capacity of the BRE to exert this local hegemony is a crucial factor in understanding its attitude vis-à-vis national integration. As long as national integration does not threaten its local hegemony, the BRE is unlikely to demand a separate political trajectory from Zambia. If the state does not impede upon its local powers, it will not oppose the state. If it finds that association with the state can reinforce its local powers, then it will actively discourage separatist tendencies in its region. This is why the BRE's demands have historically been limited to the restoration of the BLA. The insistence of the BRE on the BLA is not so much a matter of asserting its region's particularism vis-à-vis the state as it is a means to increase its legal powers over its own people. Indeed, by formalizing its local prerogatives as deriving from an agreement with the sovereign internationally recognized state, the BLA crystallizes the BRE's powers, conferring upon them the seal of the law and stifling the rise of potential challengers. Hence, while it eschews the responsibilities of sovereign statehood (and can blame others for its province's failures), the Lozi leadership benefits from resources associated with the sovereignty of Zambia. The only two times the BRE called for separatism were in the early 1960s, when postcolonial norms of sovereignty were not yet well established, and in 1995, when President Chiluba tried to undermine their local hegemony by passing the Land Act, which removed the power of land allocation from the Litunga.[18] As a former member of the royal council puts it, "with our land no longer ours, we got angry."[19]

The power of giving land to people is a crucial element of the BRE's capacity to maintain its local hegemony.[20] In an era of modernization, and with potential competition from migrants and market forces, such hegemony cannot merely rely on tradition. It is the legalization of its prerogatives by the state that provides the BRE with the sanction of sovereign force. It substitutes legal command for an eroding traditional command. This is why the BRE insists on the restoration of the BLA. For the government, however, the current ambiguous situation, in which laws depriving the BRE of its powers are not being implemented, is a superior outcome as it maintains the vulnerability of the BRE and provides for greater central control over local resources. Although not ideal, this half autonomy remains better for the BRE than the uncertainties and responsibilities of separatism. Under the current system, the BRE can extract resources from multiple sources derived from legal command. Its extraction of tribute from Barotse subjects is linked to its judiciary powers, expressed in the Barotse Native Courts, which have remained in existence after the abrogation of the BLA. The BRE also owns several markets in the Western Province from which it collects taxes from traders. There is also anecdotal evidence that it benefits from the logging and sale of timber from the Western Province. Finally, its effective control over local land has allowed the BRE to enter into contracts with third parties for the management of land-based projects. In 2003, for example, it was revealed in Zambian media that the BRE had concluded lease contracts with a South African firm for the management of the two national parks of the Western Province, Liuwa Plain National Park, and Sioma National Park.[21] There was resentment that the BRE did not represent the interests of the Lozi people in these negotiations, which appeared to have taken on a mostly private nature. According to Princess Nakatindi Wina, a Lozi member of parliament and opponent of the BRE, the latter charged K140,000 (about US$50) for access to a workshop in Limulunga in May 2003 to discuss the matter, and forced local chiefs to acquiesce, essentially preventing any popular input in the process.[22]

Despite these opportunities for income and accumulation, the current situation clearly represents a suboptimal outcome for the kingdom, compared to the period when the Litunga enjoyed the legal power of taxation over his subjects. The political behavior of the BRE can thus be understood as a strategy to safeguard and expand its local dominant status and its access to local opportunities for income. Restoration of the BLA would allow the kingdom to not only resume taxation but also regain legal control over all local markets, game, fishing, hunting, local government, and so on. Thus, the language of the BRE is one of autonomy, one of grievance vis-à-vis Zambia for its neglect of the region. But the reality of its demands is about the restoration of its legal power over its people.

At any rate, the continuation of the BRE's local hegemony depends on the reproduction of the Zambian state, to which the BRE locally contributes. The distribution of sovereign powers to the BRE by Zambia helps stifle the rise of local institutional alternatives and facilitates the Litunga's control over his own people and local resources. In the words of anti-BRE politician Sikota Wina, "the BRE is opposed to new ideas. It is a stronghold against the Western Province. There is no encouragement of investments, even by successful Lozi, because it would weaken the power of the Litunga."[23] The BRE retards development by preventing the rise of alternative economic powers based on private enterprise and freed from land relations.

Variations in Compliance

Although no Lozi group has engaged in violent political action in support of secession of the Western Province, there has been a fair amount of separatist agitation in the region since the early 1990s. Most of it has been the work of Lozi elites who did not belong in the BRE, though many of them actually were of royal lineage and may well have harbored ambitions for the Litungaship. Akashambatwa Mbikusita-Lewanika ("Aka") provides such an example. A son of the late Litunga Lewanika, he unsuccessfully competed for the position upon the death of Ilute Yeta IV in 2000. A founding member of the MMD, he created his own party, Agenda for Zambia, in 1996, which promoted a separatist platform, before rejoining the MMD after the election of Levy Mwanawasa to the presidency in 2000 and then becoming party spokesperson, after which he publicly renounced secession. Prince Imasiku Mutangelwa is another case in point. After a life mostly spent abroad, he returned to Zambia in 1991 and founded the Barotse Cultural Association (BCA) in 1992, which he hoped would be the instrument of a political and cultural renewal of the province. Having run into the resistance of the BRE, he set up the Barotse Patriotic Front (BPF) in 1996, probably the most radical of the Lozi movements, which threatened military conflict in 1998 if Zambia did not grant Barotseland secession.[24] He was put under house arrest in 1999.

What characterizes these and a few other similar Lozi elites is the extent to which they are or have been separatist while also being opposed to the current Litunga. Thus, their anti-Zambian stance appears to be an expression of their opposition to the Litungaship, itself a consequence of being barred from access to the limited opportunities for legal command that the Litungaship affords. Mutangelwa did not resort to separatist action until after seeing his reformist efforts turned down by the BRE: "We wanted to modernize Barotseland. . . . The BPF was born of our frustrations with the compromises of the BRE."[25] Aka positioned himself throughout the 1990s as a credible successor to Litunga Ilute Yeta by embracing a separatist rhetoric. But after Lubosi Imwiko II became Litunga in 2000, he joined the ruling party.

One puzzle remains: Why do Lozi commoners also appear to embrace Zambia given that its reproduction seems to have come at a great cost to their province? Fear of repression may be part of the answer. In the 1960s and 1970s, Lozi activists were frequently put in jail. Nowadays, too, some fear retaliation if they speak against Zambia or the BRE. According to a former member of the royal council, challenging national unity could result in one being "denounced by the Litunga to the central government as anti-government."[26] The prevailing poverty in the Western Province, as well as the dependence of the few Lozi businesses on government contracts, may well reinforce cultural inhibitions. Another reason is the extent to which commoners themselves need the reproduction of legal command. In the absence of well-specified alternatives, Lozi subjects still need the Litungaship for access to land (and subsistence agriculture), for settlement of their disputes, for recognition of their family status, and so on. Thus, the BRE's remaining legal prerogatives make it exceedingly difficult for commoners to bypass the kingdom. The reproduction of the BRE structures down to the smaller villages also guarantees the widespread distribution of its legal command and the constitution of a sufficient critical mass favorable to its maintenance.

Thus, a complex national logic, based largely on the local use by the Barotse elite of some benefits of state sovereignty, trumps the political expression of regional particularism in the Western Province. For the BRE, it makes sense to avoid responsibility for public policy while continuing to accrue benefits from a traditional status recognized and reproduced by the state. In reality, they have few credible choices in terms of self-determination. They would stand little chance of recognition were they actually to go their separate ways, unless they could claim postcolonial status on their own. They have tried that approach to no avail on a few occasions, as when the Litunga traveled to the UK in 1997 to seek support for the restoration of the BLA, and when a petition was presented to the African Union meeting in Lusaka in 2001, demanding a mission to establish the status of the region under the Barotseland Agreement of 1964, which was presented as a treaty between governments.[27] For grassroots residents of the Western Province, it may also make sense not to challenge a state that still monopolizes the provision of development to their region.

Conclusion

The fusion-of-elite model stresses the extent to which elites from different walks of life, such as traditional and state elites, form an alliance around the state to create a nationally dominant social class. There is little doubt as to the broad validity of this model. Yet, in the case of Barotseland, the logic appears reversed. Instead of a quasi-consociationalism, whereby established subnational elites accept the state by partaking in it, threatened elites hang on to the state to regain or maintain their local elite status—even though state policies might be at the root of their predicament. While the state is reproduced in each case, its reproduction might entail greater inequality and "decentralized despotism" in the latter case.[28] While fusion-of-elites models stress the class *formation* effect of the clientelistic state, the sovereign model reveals class *relations,* that is, the sovereignty-mediated domination exercised on populations at the local level.

Barotseland corresponds broadly to what Jean-François Bayart has termed a process of "conservative modernization," that is, the usage of the postcolonial state by some established aristocracy to consolidate its local hegemony.[29] It suggests that local control of state sovereignty is an essential tool of such strategy. As a result, these aristocracies either do not develop or repress separatist tendencies. By and large, the strategies of local domination of these traditional elites undermine their group's agency vis-à-vis the central state; the sovereign loyalty of the regional leadership precludes group exit. This condition allows the central state to continue its policies of neglect, exclusion, or repression without substantial sanction from local populations or leadership. State accountability is one of the main victims of this arrangement.

The Anglophones of *La République du Cameroun*

A traditional political structure like Barotseland invites an analysis centered on the class interests of its aristocracy because of their historical salience and contemporary visibility. After all, there is a king and one can expect that he will wish to remain so. Yet, the logic of the exchange of national submission for local in-group domination is not the monopoly of customary authorities. The Anglophone minority of Cameroon provides an example of its broader relevance. There, the "modern" elites of a marginalized region refuse to challenge the state that discriminates against them. Instead, they demand the increased decentralization of its sovereignty so as to occupy its local offices and reverse the erosion of their local elite status by their Francophone competitors.

This command-based class dimension is often overlooked because of the dominant focus of Cameroonian political discourse and scholarship on identity, which tends to gloss over in-group differentiation. Yet, focusing also on local legal command opportunities unearths more plausible motives for the continuation of political allegiance despite regional marginalization in a time of fiscal contraction, state retrenchment, and increased political liberties.

Grievances and the Limits of Accommodation

It was the Germans who created the colony of Kamerun, only to lose it at the end of World War I when the British and French partitioned it among themselves. The British appropriated two discontinuous sections of the western region, which they renamed Southern and Northern Cameroons, and administered them jointly with Nigeria. The French secured control over the majority of the colony and kept it as a unit of Afrique Equatoriale Française. Although at first a League of Nations Mandate and then a UN Trust Territory, French Cameroon followed the path to independence of most other French colonies, first as a territory in the French Union of 1958 and then as a sovereign country in 1960.[30] In the British Cameroons, a referendum was organized by the UN in 1961 offering local populations a choice between joining Nigeria or Cameroon. The Northern Cameroons chose Nigeria, while southerners, concerned at potential Igbo domination of their region, preferred to cast their lot with *La République du Cameroun.*

The merging of the Southern Cameroons with Cameroun proved to be a biased affair. While the new country became officially bilingual and federal, the Anglophone region would be the *parent pauvre* of the union.[31] With only one-tenth of the territory and a quarter of the population, it has not had an equal say in the matters of the nation. More important, it had to abandon significant elements of its Common Law foundations in order to merge with the more French Napoleonic–inspired institutions and legal system of Cameroun. Similar radical changes took place with respect to the education system, administrative practices, and the currency. Because of its limited demographic weight and the Francophone bias in higher education, Anglophone Cameroon was also unable to provide sufficient numbers of educated elites to make bilingualism a reality across the country, with the consequence that, not only have there always been more Francophones among national government figures, but there have also been many Francophones in positions of state authority in the two English-speaking provinces. In addition, Anglophone political parties were subsumed into the French-dominated single party in 1966. Finally, in 1972, President Ahmadou Ahidjo terminated the federation and created a unitary state wherein the Anglophone region was divided in two, with each sub-region downgraded to provincial status.

Anglophones have had further ground for grievance. Local populations frequently express a sense of spoliation at the fact that 40 percent of the country's export revenues derive from the oil that is mostly located offshore from their region. This sentiment is compounded by the fact that Cameroon's oil has historically been exploited by France's Elf Aquitaine, which has served as a crucial tool over the years in the relationship between Paris and Francophone African heads of state.[32] Cameroon's only refinery, located in Limbe near the South West provincial capital of Buea, is headed and staffed mostly by Francophones.[33] South West Anglophones thus frequently complain that their region has failed to benefit from its oil wealth (as well as from the full revenues from its palm oil, cocoa, rubber, tea, and bananas, which are shipped out through the port of Douala in the Francophone Littoral Province), and they fear the economic takeover of their region by Francophone interests. In addition to their sense of economic exploitation, they also nurture resentment at their perceived difficulties in getting high-ranking jobs in government and in obtaining development projects and infrastructure for their region. Until 1993, for example, Yaoundé, the French-speaking capital, hosted the only university in the country, where most courses were given in French.[34] Also, as of 2005, there were only seven Anglophone ministers out of a sixty-strong government.

Cultural grievances have compounded the Anglophones' sense of material injustice. The reservation of seven-eighths of public broadcast time on state media to French programming, inscriptions in French on the national currency, the practice of using bold lettering on official documents for French text and regular print for English, and the showing of French-language movies in movie theaters in the Anglophone region have all contributed to the impression that French is being imposed on the Anglophones.[35]

Finally, the Anglophones have, together with the residents of the West Province, been the main victims of the Biya regime's manipulation of the country's democratic opening since 1990. The pressure for democratization arose first in the North West where the creation of the Social Democratic Front (SDF) in 1990 was met with ruthless government repression. Subsequently, it was widely believed that the SDF's candidate to the 1992 presidential elections, John Fru Ndi, lost to Paul Biya only because of massive fraud. Over the ensuing years, political mobilization for democracy and in support of Anglophone grievances has been systematically repressed by Biya's security forces.

Curiously, however, despite all this, the Anglophone region has not developed any significant large-scale separatist tendency or movement. On the contrary, a very large majority of Anglophone elites, both in the South West and North West provinces, have come out in favor of national unity, limiting their demands to one form or another of federalism and regional autonomy. For sure, there has been occasional separatist agitation, but these instances have remained few and have not crossed a low threshold of mobilization or violence.

There are few obvious reasons as to why Anglophone Cameroonians have shied away from more radical demands. The fact that the South West and North West provinces are not ethnically homogeneous (being broadly divided between "coastal" and "grassfield" peoples) is not per se an obstacle to secessionist agitation, as illustrated by numerous other multiethnic separatist regions.[36] There is no doubt, however, that the regime of President Paul Biya, in power since 1983, has made generous use of both repression and co-optation in its attempt to keep Cameroon together. Biya has not hesitated to violently repress any incipient separatist movement and opponents have been killed, detained, and exiled. Government repression intensified particularly after 1997 when a more youthful and radical branch of Anglophone activists, based within the student movement and apparently more willing than its predecessors to resort to violence toward separatism, gained ascendancy. Dozens of these agitators were then arrested and much of the remaining leadership of this movement has since been in exile. Yet, while the government's response has certainly played a role, all separatist movements around the world can expect a fair amount of repression, and there are many instances where fear of government violence has not been a deterrent. As such, government repression does not by itself explain the lack of a credible separatist movement in western Cameroon. It does illustrate, however, that Cameroon is not quite as helpless as some other African countries when it comes to the capacity of its government to wield force, despite its serious shortcomings in other dimensions of governance.

In addition to the physical intimidation of would-be separatists, the Biya regime has also made much use of the co-optation of Anglophone elites through ministerial and other sinecures. The appointment of Anglophone prime ministers following the increased voicing of Anglophone grievances in the early 1990s illustrates this approach. Prime Minister Ephraim Inoni, from the South West Province, articulated the exchange properties of his appointment to his provincial supporters in 2005. After listing the expected government investments in the region as "the fruits of the province's privileged position in government," he reminded locals of expectations that they should express their gratitude in the forthcoming 2007 municipal and legislative elections: "to whom much is given, much is expected."[37] Other compliant South West elites also received administrative appointments and material favors.

In some respects, therefore, in addition to its enduring capacity for organized repression, Cameroon has remained a case of neopatrimonial accommodation through redistribution of state resources. As in many other African states, however, the regime's capacity and need to maintain its co-optation strategies has eroded. First, although Cameroon has not experienced an economic crisis to the extent undergone by some of its economically more vulnerable counterparts, it has nevertheless faced serious fiscal tightening since the early 1990s, when the government reduced public salaries by up to 70 percent, which no doubt indented the patronage appeal of the state. The limited weight of oil in its economy (6 percent of GDP and 20 percent of government revenue) also reduced the positive impact of higher oil prices on its budget after 2000 and prevented a loosening of the public purse similar to that experienced in Nigeria during Olusegun Obasanjo's second term. As deftly remarked by Piet Konings, given the limits to the availability of purely redistributive prebends, many are called but few are chosen at the neopatrimonial game.[38]

The weakening of the redistributive system of political compliance induced by economic tightening has been further compounded by the very partial democratization of the regime after 1990. Indeed, the extent to which democratization only requires a minimum winning coalition for the government to be able to rule, as opposed to the promotion of national consensus by the single-party system, favors the exclusion of certain groups and regions from the redistribution of state resources. In other words, democratization reduces the number of mouths to feed for the incumbent regime. Because opposition to the Biya regime from 1990 onward centered greatly on the SDF based in Bamenda in the North West Province (and on neighboring Bamiléké elites from the Western Province), these regions were relatively sacrificed in the redistribution exercise. As a result, Anglophone elites should have had greater relative incentives to challenge Cameroon. Most of them, however, did not.

The Anglophone Elites' Pursuit of Local Legal Command

In order to understand the objectives of Anglophone elites, it is important to understand the nature of their predicament. Linguistic and legal discrimination not only affects their capacity to share the state at the center but also in their own region, as it weakens their qualifications as elites. Dickson Eyoh stresses that "daily encounters with bureaucratic authority in local worlds have made ubiquitous the feelings of the loss of power over Anglophone space. . . . By dint of demography, Francophones have been numerically preponderant in the civil administration and security agencies." Eyoh conducted a survey in 1995 in the Anglophone town of Kumba in the North West Province. There, he recalls, "my discussants were, without exception, quick to comment that *all senior civil administrators* (senior divisional officer and his deputies) and head of security agencies assigned to the administrative division to which the town belongs, *were Francophones.*"[39] The adoption of single-party rule in 1966 also undermined Anglophone elites' *local* power by removing paths to political advancement other than through the Rassemblement Démocratique du Peuple Camerounais (Democratic Rally of the Cameroonian People, RDPC) ruling party, where Francophones have historically been in control. The conversion to a unitary republic in 1972 compounded their political precariousness, as it removed the availability of local institutions. As Eyoh put it, "the burden of administrative centralization has become associated with the act of 'chasing dossiers'; the presumption and reality that obtaining the most elementary services from the state (employment, clarification of transfer notices, regularization of salaries and so on) required the compilation of masses of documents and the chasing of one's file through the *capital*'s bureaucratic maze."[40] Anglophone citizens therefore find themselves compelled to deal with Francophone authorities, denying local elites opportunities for legal command of their own. Given the extractive and corrupt nature of the state, this centralization creates a sense of opportunity deprivation for those caught between the Francophone bias in the staffing of state agencies at the national and local level, and the scarcity of institutions of political control locally available to them.

In view of their loss of local hegemony, the demands of Anglophone elites have focused on the (re)creation of sovereign institutions of control for their region, behind a discourse that stresses its marginalization within the country. The existence and availability of such local sovereign institutions is predicated upon the continued existence of the state itself, which alone is empowered with sovereignty and with the authority to delegate it to regional agencies. Hence, Anglophone elites have used a language of regional grievance but have not challenged the state itself or their eventual integration in it for fear of losing this sovereign connection. Regional grievances have not resulted in separatist action but have supported quests for local domination. Political discourse has polarized Anglophones and Francophones, but its outcome has been at least in part the reinforcement of inequality within the Anglophone region.

Demands for autonomy and federalism embody both the idea of a remedy to regional grievances and the creation of opportunities for local command. According to Eyoh, all Anglophone movements have shared as a "common objective the decentralization of administrative and political power."[41] These demands were first voiced in November 1991 at a government-sponsored Tripartite Conference by four Anglophone delegates who called for a return to the federal arrangement of 1961. Three of them—Sam Ekontang Elad, Simon Munzu, and Benjamin Itoe—hailed from the South West, and one—Carlson Anyangwe—from the North West. In response to the regime's subsequent ignoring of their demand, they went on to convene an All Anglophone Conference (AAC) in Buea in March 1993, which was attended by some 5,000 delegates. The subsequent Buea Declaration listed Anglophone grievances and spoke of "insurmountable dichotomy" with the rest of the country, yet limited its demands to the restoration of a two-state federal system. An Anglophone Standing Committee charged with drafting a constitution submitted its draft in May. It provided for two states, each including provinces and communities endowed with considerable autonomy and with multiple executive, legislative, and judiciary institutions.[42]

The main Anglophone political party, the SDF, also supported federalism from its inception in 1990. The organization by the SDF and some other opposition parties of the *villes mortes* (ghost cities) campaign of general strikes from

April 1991 to January 1992 was in support of convening a Sovereign National Conference through which they hoped to promote a federal revision of the constitution.[43] At its national convention in 1992, the SDF offered a program that included "devolution of power" and "decentralization."[44] Other early profederalist organizations included interest groups that are dependent on access to the state or on recognition by the state, such as the Teachers Association of Cameroon, the Confederation of Anglophone Parents-Teachers Association of Cameroon, and the Cameroon Anglophone Students Association.[45] These groups are put at a disadvantage by a unitary French-dominated state to the extent that it devalues the returns to English-speaking education. One of the earliest demands by Anglophones was in fact to have an independent examination board for their region in order to be able to locally validate educational degrees.[46] Such delegation of sovereign authority is particularly important to the extent that one essential value of education in Africa is the entitlement of holders of formal degrees to access to public service, which requires that the diploma be sanctioned by the state.[47] Having one's own instrument of educational authentication was thus a crucial step for promoting access to the state for Anglophones, and being able to do so in English restored some advantage to them.

Divisions among South West and North West Anglophone politicians can be understood in the context of their respective pursuit of sovereign power. It is commonly argued that Biya has divided Anglophone elites to better rule them.[48] While there has certainly been a heavy dose of such manipulations since the early 1990s, these local elites have not been passive recipients of such policies. To some extent, South-Westerners have used the national government in order to resist the perceived local hegemony of the North-Westerners, which they have feared since the days preceding the merging of 1961. At the time, North West elites under the leadership of John Ngu Foncha promoted unification with French Cameroon, while southerners, represented by Emmanuel Endeley, favored remaining with Nigeria. These divisions reflected as much the internal politics of the region as they did actual sentiments vis-à-vis either Cameroon or Nigeria. Historically, the North West elites dominated the South West region. Having a more developed system of chieftaincies, they were able to at least partly extend their hegemony over the more acephalous southern societies. The northerners reinforced their ascendancy in the late 1950s, managing to take the best jobs and best lands in the South West.[49] The South West's preference for Nigeria probably followed a similar logic to the North West's aversion to it. For southerners, being merged into Nigeria would make a less significant and powerful group of the northerners, while for the latter, Cameroon offered the hope of a more substantive national role.

As a result of their historical relations and of their differential integration into the state, the elites of each region have developed different strategies since 1990. Yet, they have done so in the pursuit of similar goals. The northerners have demanded a return to the earlier two-region federal arrangement, in which the odds are good that they would dominate the west. Southerners, on the other hand, have feared this potential domination, especially after the SDF quickly expanded its influence to their region in the early 1990s.[50] Instead, they have demanded increased autonomy within the existing ten-province system, while at the same time offering themselves with greater abandon to the bounties of co-optation at the center. The systematic appointment of a national prime minister from the South West since 1996 illustrates the second half of this logic, as does the argument of one of them, Chief Ephraim Inondi, that "a man of sense does not go hunting little bush rodents when his age-mates are after big game."[51] It should not detract, however, from the fact that, even among South-Westerners, the pursuit of sovereign power has trumped other strategies for advancement. I have not found any evidence, for example, that South-Westerners have made any demand for some form of derivation of oil revenue as exists in Nigeria, which would have been consistent with a rent-based understanding of regional compliance. To some extent, this may be explained by the much more limited impact of oil on Cameroon's national budget compared to Nigeria. In Cameroon, oil revenues account for about 20 percent of government revenue, whereas taxes, including value-added taxes and other levies collected by local councils, contribute as much as 69 percent.[52] Yet, the lack of an oil-based strategy is also symptomatic of the preference of local politicians for access to state institutions and the attendant opportunities for local control and domination.

The South West Elites' Association (SWELA) illustrates this preference. Founded in 1991, its aims were originally to "distance itself from the view of Anglophones as a homogeneous community" and to call for "regional development and semi-autonomy" on the basis of a ten-state federation, free from "exploitative" and "domineering" northerners.[53] SWELA chose a strategy of compliance with the Biya regime in exchange for access to local dominant positions and an endorsement of their semiautonomy agenda by the government. Key appointments to positions of authority in their province ensued.[54] Other South West elites, particularly university students, have followed a similar path. Across the country, there are numerous student associations that profess their support for the regime, including President Biya's Youth (PRESBY); the Association des Camerounais Biyaristes (Association of Cameroonians for Biya, ACB); the Movement for Youth of the Presidential Majority; Jeunesse Active pour Chantal Biya (Active Youth for Chantal Biya, the president's wife); and the remarkably explicit and flexible Youth for the Support of Those in Power (YOSUPO).[55] The basic logic of these groups is clientelistic as they offer their allegiance in exchange for some benefits. Few of these students, who are still relatively junior in the elite pecking order, can make a credible claim to straightforward public-employment sinecures, however. Nevertheless, the leaders of these groups use their association with the state to generate quasi-legal command for themselves, which they use toward extracting resources from fellow citizens at the local level. For example, in 2000, the South

West regional secretary of PRESBY alleged that its regional coordinator "was in the habit of extorting money from young people who wanted to migrate to Europe and the United States in search of greener pastures, promising that he would use his influence to obtain visas for them." After he became regional coordinator himself, he followed a similar path: "Exploiting his supposed connections with the regime, he extorted money from the various parastatals in the South West province as well as from state employees by either threatening them with punitive transfers or by promising them promotions."[56] Notice the use of legal command in the nature of administrative transfers or promotions. These student elites are neither asking, nor are they receiving, income from the center. Instead, they parlay their tenuous connection to the state into the local exercise of command and extraction.

In the end, Anglophone elites remain attached to Cameroon as part of a strategy to decentralize the tools of sovereignty to their region and regain command capacity *among Anglophone populations,* that is, in order to remain leaders among their people. As a second layer, their conflict has led northerners and southerners to develop competing strategies for seeking such autonomy, with many South West elites pursuing a more decentralized version of the federal goal than their North West counterparts in order to resist the perceived hegemony of the latter among the Anglophones. Thus, while both North West and South West elites use the language of Anglophone grievance vis-à-vis the Francophones to justify their demands, these are very much about local domination, for which they compete with each other.

Variations in Compliance

The government's systematic ignorance or rebuke of the federal demand after 1990 led some Anglophones to adopt a more radical position. After the government rejected the recommendations of the 1993 Buea conference, a group called the Cameroon Anglophone Movement declared itself in favor of total independence. Following this, a Second All Anglophone Conference (AAC II), convened in Bamenda in the North West Province in 1994, threatened to "proclaim the revival of the independence and sovereignty of the Anglophone territory."[57] The Southern Cameroons National Council (SCNC) was created in the wake of the Bamenda conference to back up demands of autonomy for the region. While the SCNC is often referred to as a separatist organization, it has not resorted to violence in the pursuit of its agenda and has not attempted to establish effective territorial control, making it very clear from the beginning that it would pursue its goal in nonviolent fashion through peaceful negotiations with the government, although such negotiations have never been forthcoming. The organization lost much of its steam after the resignation of its original leader in 1996, the exile of another two, and the appointment of a moderate retired ambassador as its new president.[58]

For the threat of separatism to be credible, however, especially without the use of force, the Anglophone elites who proffered it had to present a plausible source of their future sovereignty, an international juridical foundation to their future statehood. Well aware of the external origins of their region's institutional existence, some Anglophone leaders historically associated with the surrender of the sovereignty of the Southern Cameroons and connected to the SCNC, embarked on a journey to the UK and the UN in August 1995 in an attempt at recovering their sovereignty. Their delegation traveled to New York "to request the UN Security Council to set the [1961] plebiscite aside as illegal and return the former West Cameroon to the status of a mandated territory."[59] In part, their legal argument revolved around the fact that the 1961 plebiscite had been nullified as the former southern portion of British Cameroons had not been given equal status with the Republic of Cameroon due to Francophone domination.

What is particularly instructive about this episode is its incarnation of the perception that African sovereignty starts at the UN, a point clearly magnified in this case by the region's former status as a UN Trusteeship. For, indeed, the pilgrimage to New York was one to the God who grants sovereignty to Africans—it was a tribute to juridical statehood. The delegation toured the western region upon its return and displayed a large UN flag at rallies, "claiming it had received it from the United Nations to show that the Southern Cameroons was still a UN trust territory and that independence was only a matter of time."[60] Rather than providing evidence of their separatism, the UN episode illustrates the sovereign structuring of the SCNC's efforts. For, indeed, the appeal to the UN is ultimately a *legal* strategy, derived from the SCNC leadership's unwillingness to embark upon nonsovereign action. The SCNC seeks first recognition, then separatism.[61] It does not first try to establish local control, then lobby for recognition. This diplomatic campaign proved futile, however, as no international encouragement or recognition actually came of it, a failure that undermined the SCNC's separatist agenda and contributed to the decline of the organization's vitality. The SCNC has since continued to seek some form of UN recognition, petitioning, for example, the UN Human Rights Committee in 2006 regarding the "brutal occupation and the colonization of the Southern Cameroons by the Republic of Cameroon."[62]

The SCNC has since been plagued with numerous factional struggles and government repression, although it has not altogether lost its momentum. Most notable among its activities was the takeover of a radio station in Buea in December 1999, during which a retired judge declared the independence of the "Federal and Democratic Republic of Southern Cameroons." He and his accomplices were later arrested, and he was detained for two years before leaving for Nigeria. While there, he assumed the title of president of Southern Cameroons and formed a government in exile in 2001. That same year, marches were organized commemorating the 1961 agreement that led to the incorporation of Southern Cameroons. Some SCNC leaders were arrested, three demonstrators were killed by the police, and the SCNC was banned. It has nevertheless remained active and the object of government repression. Twenty of its members were arrested in late 2006 and detained for several months after attempting to hold a press conference. In an absurd display of sovereign legal command, the government arrested them because of their banned status. In the words of an official spokesman, "any meeting they have cannot be validated by the authorities and it is therefore illegal. . . . When the members of the SCNC have a meeting it is normal to arrest them. They aren't arrested in an arbitrary manner because they are doing something illegal."[63]

Although these events have brought the SCNC some continued salience, their significance can easily be overstated. Very few people have in fact continued to be involved in SCNC activities, although that is certainly in part due to government repression. A 2004 conference in Bamenda to reunite the different SCNC factions brought together no more than fifty people.[64] The exile in Nigeria of its main leader also effectively deprives him of any possible access to legal command (as does his status as a retired judge), favoring thereby his adoption of a more radical stance, such as illustrated by the appointment of a government, and so on. It is actually often the case that exiled leaders adopt a more radical discourse than their counterparts who have remained within the country. Some of it is no doubt endogenous, as they probably had to seek exile—unlike their counterparts—because of their greater radicalism. On the other hand, their exile also promotes the adoption or continuation of a more radical discourse both as a means to maintain relevance and because of the decreased opportunity costs of doing so in terms of access to sovereign resources, which no longer is an option. Because of their greater freedom of expression and/or greater access to means of communication, however, these exiled elites tend to speak more loudly than their more compliant peers at home. As such, they also tend to introduce a bias in our perception of separatist activism, as we are more easily aware of their grievances and positions. In a place like Anglophone Cameroon, however, the exiled leaders of the SCNC represent a minority current. Their separatist sentiments may be shared by many, but their willingness to act outside the structures of sovereign statehood is not.

Finally, one must mention the Southern Cameroons Youth League (SCYL), which was founded in May 1995 in order "to reinforce the role of the educated Anglophone youth in the Anglophone struggle."[65] As a student association, it introduced a generational dimension in the Anglophone question. In sharp contrast to the SCNC, most of whose leaders were of already advanced age, SCYL opted for the armed struggle to bring about the independence of the Southern Cameroons. Yet, it proved equally unsuccessful. Its chairman, Ebenezer Akwanga, and much of its leadership were arrested in March 1997 after a failed attempt to steal explosives. A couple of violent incidents followed against "military and civil establishments" in the North West, but the government's massive repression quenched their desire for further action.[66] Many individuals associated with the Anglophone cause went into hiding after these events. Those arrested were brought before a military tribunal in 1999 in a trial condemned as political by Amnesty International. Much of the remaining SCYL leadership then chose the path of exile and they have since traded insurgency politics for more symbolic and Internet-based tools of struggle. Its secretary-general lives in Germany.

Although it failed to develop a proper insurgency, SCYL nevertheless displayed a more radical propensity than other Anglophone organizations. It is in fact the only Anglophone group to have manifested any amount of political violence. To some extent, the variation in outlook between SCYL and more conservative Anglophone elites relates to their opportunities for access to sovereignty. As Anglophone students—twice disadvantaged as westerners and as youth—the members of SCYL have few plausible routes of access to sovereign benefits, which increases the relative returns of defiance. Their elders are monopolizing the struggle for local sovereign institutions and are the self-designated recipients of the anticipated benefits of federalism. With freezes in public service hiring (and its Francophone bias), these students have had little to expect from either unitarism or federalism, and have therefore embraced a more radical agenda. They have maintained this radicalism, now expressed nonviolently over the Internet, as a luxury afforded by the exile of their leadership and possibly as a necessity for the refugee status that gives this exiled leadership access to the means of survival.

Variations in national compliance among Anglophone Cameroonians should not be overstated. SCNC and SCYL are minority movements. Most Anglophone political organizations, starting with the SDF and SWELA, promote Cameroonian national unity. As Konings and Nyamnjoh note, "the Anglophone secessionist demand . . . faces far more resistance than federalist demands in the Anglophone community itself."[67] In addition, the SCNC endorses a sovereign path to self-determination, putting recognition ahead of separation. Only SCYL and a few other marginal organizations can truly be thought of as secessionist. Without further empirical verification, the divergences among these movements appear by and large consistent with variations in individual positions regarding access to sovereignty. These Anglophone elites, which are or were once well established as regional elites, tend to seek the preservation or restoration of their locally dominant position by promoting the local reproduction or the creation of structures of sovereign statehood. Some of those who see themselves as their successors, like most students, adopt a similar position and are likely to concentrate their demands upon the sovereign authentication of their degrees as means of access. A minority of well-connected ones may more wholeheartedly embrace the regime in exchange for immediate predatory prebends. Yet, one would also expect that some less well connected Anglophone students or exiled leaders would consider their low odds of eventual sovereign access (especially after others have already staked claims to the few existing opportunities) and decide they have little to lose from taking on a more defiant approach to the state. I do not mean to collapse all variations in nationalist or separatist outlook among Anglophone Cameroonians to questions of personal interest and to trivialize actions that certainly also follow different and sometimes more altruistic or ideological motivations. Yet, ceteris paribus, people will seek access to the opportunities provided by sovereignty in Cameroon as elsewhere in Africa, because these are usually superior to other available alternatives. When these opportunities are not available, there is likely to be more variance in terms of compliance with the state.

Conclusion

The case of Anglophone Cameroon is well summarized by Nyamnjoh's statement that the "power elite becomes obsessed with maximizing power at ethnic or regional levels, while *treating the centre as sacrosanct.*"[68] This is no mere coincidence and certainly no paradox, as local power is maximized by embracing sovereign state structures. The *national* reproduction of Cameroon is thus guaranteed by *local* strategies of power maximization, even though these are couched in a language of grievance and a behavior of polarization toward the center.

As with Barotseland, the strategies of sovereign embrace by Anglophone elites contribute to the production of state-derived inequality in their region. It is in fact the fear of being on the losing side of this inequality that divides the elites of the South West and North West provinces. This division brings about an interesting question regarding the level of aggregation of collective action among Anglophones. In a continent where one usually expects ethnicity to be the prime level of subnational political action, the salience of a colonial language as the prime marker of identity is at first puzzling. What makes local elites invoke their Anglophone status as opposed to their ethnic status, as was the case with Barotseland, for example? One might argue that the salience of linguistic differences in Cameroon illustrates the resilience of colonial identities. This may well be partly true. However, I think, along with Daniel Posner, that people choose the level of identity that best serves their interest among a repertoire of identity options.[69] Anglophone western Cameroonians are no more a natural political community than the North West and West provinces together or ethnic groups within them would be. Yet, promoting Anglophone identity provides a foundation for claims to occupy power within this administratively defined region. The fact that sovereign institutions are defined by their colonial origins determines the level of aggregation of collective action. There is thus no paradox to either Anglophone identity or Cameroonian national sentiment. Attachment to Cameroon guarantees the source of sovereignty, while promotion of Anglophone identity offers an avenue for the takeover of existing institutions that have been internationally defined as attached to the sovereign state. Within this Anglophone identity, it also makes sense for South West elites to promote their "coastal" identity, which corresponds to the administrative boundaries of their province and justifies the claims to office of their elites in their avoidance of North West hegemony.

All for Congo (Congo for Nobody) in the Kivus

The North and South Kivu provinces of the DRC represent a complex case in the dynamics of African state reproduction because of the multiplicity of actors, motives, identities, and resources. It is not my purpose to provide an exhaustive account of Kivu politics, which is beyond my knowledge. What I wish to show is the crucial role that sovereign command has played in the conflict *between* communities in the region, and the extent to which its use by the local protagonists has encouraged them not to challenge either the Congolese state or the nature of their insertion in it, even though these two variables are related to their predicament. Specifically, the opportunities provided to Kivutian groups in their local struggles by tools of sovereign state power, such as manipulations of the law and citizenship, creation and deletion of regional administrative units, and local political and administrative appointments, have sidelined the use of alternative means to settle or mediate claims to land and security. This bias has promoted the simultaneous reproduction of the conflict and of a dysfunctional Congolese state, while largely exonerating the latter from its responsibility in the region's violent crisis.

Although most communities in the Kivus seem to have resorted at one time or another to sovereign tools of domination over other communities, I focus mostly on the Rwandophones, composed of Congolese of Hutu and Tutsi ethnicity who arrived in the region in successive waves since the nineteenth century.[70] Highly dependent on land for agriculture and livestock, they have at times enjoyed and at times suffered from an ambiguous and fluid status in Congolese law. Since the early 1990s, they—and particularly the South Kivu Tutsi known as the Banyamulenge—have been the targets of repeated attempts at denying their citizenship rights, depriving them of land, expelling them from the region, and physically exterminating them. Yet, despite this persecution, a near-unanimous belief in their treasonous and irredentist nature, and the presence of an ambiguously supportive regime in neighboring Rwanda, the Rwandophones have systematically chosen allegiance to Congo as part of their strategy of survival and advancement. Faced with the need to control land and security, they have fought to maintain their membership in the

Congolese polity as the prime vector for national and local state power and for the recognition of their property rights.

With its opportunities for authentication, appropriation, and control, legal command has given the Rwandophones greater immediate returns than other possible strategies, including exile or social contracting with other regional groupings, although these have also at times been attempted, if only at the margins. Legal command, however, is a tool of domination and not of negotiation, settlement, concession, or reciprocity. The properties of legal command predispose local actors to attempt to win the conflict rather than to settle it. It biases their choices away from establishing credible mechanisms of local cohabitation. In doing so, it ends up reproducing the conflict and shielding the state from its effective responsibility in their shared misery, alienation, and insecurity.

Vulnerability

The Rwandophones of North and South Kivu probably number less than one million altogether. North Kivu's total population is around five million. The Nande are the largest group in that province and reside mainly in the north. The Rwandophones are maybe the second largest group, possibly numbering between 500,000 and 700,000 combined Hutu and Tutsi, or 10 to 14 percent of the North Kivu population, although some authors estimate that their proportion is as high as 25 percent.[71] Hutus comprise the great majority of them. In general, the Rwandophones of North Kivu live in Goma and in the neighboring territories of Masisi and Rutshuru, where they probably form a majority. There are also some around Walikale. The Hunde are the ethnic group whose geographical distribution most closely matches that of the Rwandophones, and it is with them that they have most often come in competition in North Kivu. Other groups of significance in the province include the Bashi, the Tembo, and the Nyanga.

The origins of the Rwandophones in North Kivu are multiple. Some are the descendants of a Rwandan lineage that probably settled around the mid-nineteenth century. Many more belong to families that arrived between the 1930s and 1950s as part of a Belgian colonial policy of immigration to relieve famine in Rwanda and provide labor for local colonial plantations. Still others, mainly Tutsi, came as refugees from violent persecution in Rwanda in 1959–1963 and again in the 1970s. Since the early 1990s, the main social divide in the region has been either between all Rwandophones and local "autochthonous" populations (such as the Nande and Hunde), or between self-identified "Bantu" groups, composed of these autochthonous groups and the Hutus on the one hand, and the Tutsi, perceived as "Nilotic" invaders, on the other.

Around three million people live in South Kivu. Rwandophones are a much smaller minority there, numbering probably no more than 100,000 Hutu and Tutsi, or 3 percent of the population. The relative weight of the Tutsi is greater than in North Kivu, however. The International Crisis Group estimates the South Kivu Tutsi (Banyamulenge) at up to 40,000 and the Hutu at about 50,000.[72] Other authors also place the total Banyamulenge population at 20,000 to 50,000.[73] Historically located around the village of Mulenge in the heights above the Ruzizi plain north of the town of Uvira, the Banyamulenge live mostly in the administrative divisions ("territories") of Fizi, Uvira, and Mwenga, where they are minorities and are traditionally pastoralists, although many of their children have followed formal education and engage now in professional activities, civil service, and the armed forces.

Like their counterparts in North Kivu, the Banyamulenge are also composed of people of distinct origins, some again tracing their ancestry to settlers from Rwanda in the mid-nineteenth century, others having arrived more recently as a result of anti-Tutsi violence in Rwanda right before and after independence.[74] Other important communities of South Kivu include the Vira, the Bembe, the Fulero, the Tembo, and the Shi.

In North and South Kivu, relations between Rwandophones and self-described local autochthonous populations (and, sometimes, among the latter too) have been difficult since the colonial era, with tensions usually deriving from the dependence of local communities on land for agriculture and livestock. Because of the crucial role that local chiefs play in allocating land, competition for control of chieftaincies has become a by-product of the land question. When the first Rwandophones arrived in South Kivu in the nineteenth century, they typically obtained land and grazing rights from local chiefs in exchange for payment. They remained under the authority of these chiefs except for a brief period between 1906 and 1933 when the Belgians granted them their own chieftaincy.[75] In North Kivu, Banyarwanda also initially obtained land from Hunde chiefs in exchange for payments, but they eventually earned their own districts in Rutshuru and Masisi, where they appointed Rwandophone chiefs.[76] Unlike in South Kivu, these chieftaincies endured. Thus, Rwandophone migration to North Kivu was accompanied by the creation of local administrative and power structures, which dramatically changed the relation between local populations and migrants.

After a few conflict-ridden years at the beginning of independence, the Rwandophones—particularly Tutsi—made great political and economic strides during the first half of the Mobutu regime. Several of them were appointed to important positions in the Mobutu administration, in part because their vulnerability made them less of a threat than elites from other ethnic groups. Barthelemy Bisengimana served as chief of staff of the president from 1969 to 1977, and Cyprien Rwakabuba in the political bureau of the single party, its central committee, and in parliament.[77] Several Tutsi were also appointed to positions in the provincial administrations from the late 1960s onward, which reduced their need for local territorial chieftaincies.[78] Some Rwandophones used these connections with the regime to acquire land outside of traditional channels. This became a particularly salient strategy after the adoption of a new land law in 1973, which vested all ownership of the land in the state and facilitated expropriations. The law also provided the legal foundation for autochthonous chiefs to sell their community-owned land to outsiders—frequently Rwandophones. The results of these reforms carried the seeds of future polarization between communities as they increased both ownership of Kivu land by Rwandophones and economic differences between ethnic groups. The Zaireanization of 1974, whereby Mobutu appropriated the assets of foreigners to redistribute them to regime cronies, further benefited some Rwandophones. In Masisi, for example, it resulted in their ownership of more than 45 percent of all available land.[79] Some estimate the total land acquired by mostly Tutsi Rwandophones under the Mobutu regime to have been as high as 80 percent in Masisi and Rutshuru.[80]

The Rwandophones' fortunes would soon turn, however. Although a 1972 law had given citizenship to those who had been in Congo since 1950, all Rwandophones were legally stripped of their citizenship in 1981, apparently as a consequence of their declining influence in the Mobutu administration. As with most Congolese laws, however, its haphazard implementation did not immediately undo the material gains of many Rwandophones, but it did increase the precariousness of their situation. When the Mobutu regime began to crumble in the early 1990s, the fate of the Rwandophones quickly worsened in parallel with the state's capacity for maintaining order and security. They and other populations also fell victim to Mobutu's fomenting of local conflicts across the country to reward local allies and maintain his overall control in a time of rapidly diminishing resources and authority. Moreover, with the approaching possibility of elections—and, hence, of redistribution of access to state power—ethnic-based mobilization increased across the country; in the Kivus it predictably took place along the axis of "autochthonous" populations against Banyarwanda "outsiders." As a result, violence rose and the Rwandophones who had benefited from their connection to state power became a prime target of it. Anti-Rwandophone violence erupted in 1993 in Walikale and Masisi, leading to the death of several thousand Banyarwanda. The arrival of mostly Hutu refugees in North Kivu in the wake of the Rwandan genocide after April 1994 compounded the crisis, adding to it the political salience of the Hutu-Tutsi cleavage. The International Crisis Group reports that, after this inflow of refugees, "almost without exception, Tutsi in Masisi and Goma sold their land and cattle and left for Rwanda."[81]

In South Kivu, the Banyamulenge remained sheltered from violence a while longer. Many of their youth, however, identified with the Tutsi diaspora living in Uganda and joined the Rwandan Patriotic Front (RPF) insurgency against the Hutu-dominated Rwandan government in 1991, leading many Congolese to question their loyalty to Congo. The situation rapidly deteriorated for the Banyamulenge after 1995. First, the High Council of the Republic, which served then as parliament, declared all Banyamulenge to be Rwandan immigrants and refugees, irrespective of their date of arrival.[82] Then, in 1996, 800 to 3,000 Banyamulenge infiltrated South Kivu from Rwanda at Kigali's bidding and attacked Rwandan Hutu refugee camps, forcing their residents to flee back into Rwanda.[83] The deputy-governor of South Kivu then asked all Banyamulenge to leave the country "within six days or be attacked and killed."[84]

This period marked the beginning of the direct involvement of the Tutsi-dominated Rwandan government into Kivu politics and created a de facto alliance between Rwandan and Congolese Tutsi. Yet, the two should not be equated. For sure, when the AFDL rebellion began in August 1996, it was as a Rwandan invention. But the decision by the Banyamulenge to fight in 1996 was directed first and foremost against the attempts by local Congolese—not Hutu refugees—to dispossess them.

The AFDL insurgency led to the overthrow of the Mobutu regime in May 1997 and his replacement with Laurent-Désiré Kabila. In the first year of his rule, he was surrounded by Rwandan security officers and Congolese Rwandophone Tutsi advisers who had recovered, through the war, the kind of positions and influence they had enjoyed at times with Mobutu. In North Kivu, many Tutsi refugees returned to their homes in Masisi and Rutshuru.[85] Yet, strong anti-Rwandan sentiments from the rest of the Congolese population and Kabila's increased unpopularity led him to expel the Rwandan soldiers and sack the Tutsi faction of his regime in August 1998. This decision was followed in short order by a new Rwandan-sponsored Tutsi insurrection in the Kivus and the formation of the RCD.[86] Failure by the Rwandan army to capture Kinshasa led to a prolonged war that saw the RCD—and the Rwandophone component of its leadership—in effective control of the Kivu provinces from 1998 to about 2005.

The peace agreement of 2003 led to the formation of a transition government under Joseph Kabila (the son of Laurent-Désiré, who had been assassinated in 2001), with vice presidencies for the leaders of the main rebel groups. Azaryas Ruberwa, the RCD's Munyamulenge chair, became vice president in charge of security and defense. Despite ongoing violence, elections were held throughout the country in 2006. Ruberwa ran for president and obtained 1.69 percent of the votes. The two Kivu regions voted overwhelmingly for Joseph Kabila, who won the nationwide elections. In March 2007, the Kivu provincial assemblies elected two non-Rwandophone governors.

The Rwandophones' Avoidance of Separatism

Although Congo's Rwandophones were comfortably ensconced in the benefits of statehood between 1965 and 1980, it is puzzling that they did not thereafter develop a secessionist profile in view of the multiple exactions they suffered at the hands of Congo and of the deep distrust, and even hatred, that many Congolese profess toward them. Although they controlled large segments of territory in the east for more than five years after 1998 and enjoyed the support of a Rwandan government that sometimes professed irredentist desires, they never adopted the secessionist agenda that the Congolese unanimously seem to impute them. And, although the democratic transition of 2003–2006 resulted in their exclusion from positions of authority both in Kinshasa and in the Kivus, they did not defect. On the contrary, despite ongoing violence, many displaced Rwandophones have returned to their villages, particularly in North Kivu.

It is worth digging a little deeper into the evidence of the Rwandophones' lack of secessionist ambitions, since the belief in their desire to steal the Kivus or part thereof is so widespread, even among some Western scholars.[87] When I was doing interviews in North Kivu in 2001, I was told repeatedly of such fears, including the alleged existence of a US-backed plan for the cession of Kivu to Rwanda or the creation of a Kivu buffer zone separated from Congo. These representations seemed to belong to what Stephen Jackson eloquently describes as "conspiracy theories of domination by shadowy elites from neighbouring Rwanda, pulling the strings of Congolese 'puppets' in the present war to construct an ethnically-based '*Empire Hima-Tutsi*' in the heart of the DRC."[88] Such perceptions are also true in the rest of the country. All over Congo, even among sophisticated intellectuals, one encounters anti-Rwandophone sentiments that feed off a fear of Tutsi imperial ambitions and discredited theories of their alleged "Nilotic"—rather than Bantu—nature.[89] Everywhere, rumors circulate that RCD authorities and Rwanda are intent on setting up an independent state in the east or annexing the Kivus. Stanislas Bucyalimwe Mararo writes of "the process of annexation of Kivu, a project which has not yet been abandoned by Rwanda and all the external lobbies which work to support Rwandan policy of partitioning the DRC."[90] As a keen observer of the Kivu scene puts it, "virtually all Congolese in the east believe that Rwanda intends to annex Kivu to create a separate 'Hutuland' and 'Tutsiland'—these ideas have been circulating in Kivu with paranoiac reverberation since the 1960s."[91]

The idea of Hutuland often seems to refer to the fear that the Rwandan government wants to appropriate the Kivus in order to create a homeland for its Hutu population and thereby get rid of them in Rwanda. The Rwandan government's facilitation of policies of resettlement of former displaced Hutus in North Kivu has provided fodder for this view. After 1993, Tutsis have also been singled out as wanting to install a "Republic of the Volcanoes" as part of the creation of a "Hamitic" empire in Central Africa.[92] The notion of Tutsiland refers to these fears that the Rwandan Tutsi regime would ally with Congolese Tutsi in order to create a Tutsi empire in the region (which in some versions also includes the Tutsi of Burundi and even the related Hima Ankole of Uganda).

The Rwandan government has at times encouraged such expectations by making dubious claims of Rwandan historical control over the region. Rwandan president Pasteur Bizimungu displayed a map of Rwanda including parts of Kivu in October 1996 and claimed that Rwanda used to reach into Congo. And, after being deprived of the Congolese nationality by a 1991 law, a group called "People of Rwandan Origins in Zaire" wrote a letter to the UN Secretary-General requesting authorization to create a separate and independent state in North Kivu.[93] Nothing came of it. Despite their salience, these are exceptions that contrast with the long pattern of nonsecessionist and nonirredentist behavior by Congolese Rwandophones and the Rwandan government.

Had Rwanda wished to take over the Kivus, it might have been relatively easy to do so. Under the RCD between 1998 and 2003, the Rwandophones could have conceivably created a Central Kivu province, uniting Masisi and Rutshuru in the north with the regions around Mulenge in the south, and merging it with Rwanda. They might have been a majority of the population in such a redefined region. At any rate, being a minority is rarely an obstacle to secessionist movements and it was not an obstacle to the Rwandophones controlling both Kivus, the Oriental province, and large chunks of Katanga from 1998 to 2003.

Not only were Rwandophones capable of realizing separatist ambitions had they had them, but they also would have had some reasons and material opportunities to do so. If nothing else, the degree of racism against them throughout Congo might have pushed them over the edge. In a 2002 public opinion survey jointly run in Kinshasa, Kikwit, and Lubumbashi-Mbuji-Mayi, respectively, 83 percent, 82 percent, and 54 percent of respondents declared that Tutsi, Hutu, and Banyamulenge living in Congo were not Congolese.[94] In the words of Bishop Ngabu of Goma (a Rwandophone himself), "the non-acceptance of Banyarwanda as Congolese is a cancer for Congo."[95] Their deprivation of citizenship would also have provided a logical incentive.[96] Finally, the sheer volume of collective violence visited upon them since the early 1990s (without discounting that meted out by them) would have made many another people seek the protection of their own homeland. In terms of material incentives, the Kivus enjoy favorable dispositions for would-be separatists. They are very peripheral to the rest of Congo and as much part of the Grands Lacs region. They are disconnected from the national economy, with their trade massively turned east across Africa and all the way to Asia.[97] They are also rich in mineral and agricultural resources and would make a viable state.

And yet, despite expectations, grievances, and opportunities, the Rwandophones did not turn secessionist and Rwanda did not act upon any irredentist impulse. Instead, Rwanda sent its troops all the way to Kinshasa both in 1996 and 1998 in order to overthrow Mobutu and then Kabila. When the latter attempt failed, the RCD took over the institutions of the Congolese state in the provinces under its control and began negotiating the reinsertion of their community in Congo. As shown in Chapter 3, they maintained Congolese law, appointed governors in the existing provinces, and tried to create new Congolese administrative divisions in the south to give the Banyamulenge their own territory. Thus, they chose to work with Congo rather than emancipating from it. Even Mararo, who otherwise suspects them of separatism, concedes that "no action toward a complete restructuring of the organization of territorial administration was undertaken" by either the AFDL or RCD.[98]

When I interviewed Azarias Ruberwa, the RCD secretary-general, in Goma in 2001, I was surprised by his professed attachment to Congo. Despite evidence to the contrary, he affirmed that the territorial integrity of Congo allowed the country to "remain a power [*une puissance*] in Africa." Upon my objections that the country was a weak collection of polarized communities, he responded: "Let's create a Congolese nation because it does not exist yet."[99] Some of that was no doubt tactical lip service, but his subsequent behavior and that of his movement backed his assertions. In the words of another Western scholar in the region at the time, "patriotism, unity, and nationality are essential components of everyday discourse in Kivu" irrespective of ethnic communities.[100]

The Necessity of Congo

The Rwandophones avoid separatism because they instrumentalize sovereign legal command for access to land. There are by and large two ways of claiming rights to land in the region, and both necessitate working within the Congolese sovereign framework. The first is the pursuit of "native authority."[101] In this instance, access to land is predicated upon control of local chieftaincies, which are legally entitled to allocate it to people in their jurisdictions. However, in order to make a claim to these chieftaincies, which are agencies of the state, one must first have secured Congolese nationality. By law, the acquisition of Congolese nationality requires in turn that one belongs to a "tribe" or an ethnic group recognized as historically (i.e., colonially) Congolese.[102] The second option involves engaging in "civic politics." Here, traditional chieftaincies are bypassed and access to land is obtained through control of political and administrative power in national or local branches of the state. Once again, these positions are only available to nationals, requiring that one first establish nationality, along the same tribal pattern.

The conflict between the Rwandophones and other Congolese groups has thus generally focused on manipulations of the conditions to acquire nationality and of appointments to customary and administrative positions of authority. Both of these approaches are dependent on the sovereign powers of authentication, appropriation, regulation, and control. As a result, Rwandophones and their enemies have all needed the reproduction of Congo for their local struggles, the reproduction of its sovereignty for their access to land. Congo has come out reinforced rather than challenged. Yet, its reproduction has taken place in a manner that has simultaneously produced local disunity. Because the acquisition of Congolese nationality is based on the recognition of the Congolese status of one's ethnic group, unity-enhancing claims to nationality produce disunity-enhancing local conflicts about the genuineness of such claims among groups. Pressures generated by individual access to land result in ethnic confrontations based on claims of autochthony and allochthony, which collectivize and multiply the potential for violence, all the while reproducing the very state that created the laws and adopted the policies at the root of local grievances.

The pursuit of customary chieftaincies has been the Rwandophones' most enduring approach. Typically, members of the community and new settlers request the usage of land from the local chief. The chief assigns plots to families in exchange for tribute. This form of allocation was maintained and reinforced in the postcolonial era when chieftaincies increasingly became extensions of state administration, which frequently appointed them. The three smallest units of Congolese territorial administration—the *localité,* the *groupement,* and the *collectivité*—are in fact managed by chiefs. Chiefs of *collectivités*—the level usually referred to as chieftaincies—have particularly important land prerogatives. In the Kivus, these chiefs are called Bami. Control of chieftaincies must thus be understood as control of a sovereign tool of command over land, the region's scarcest resource.

As a result, local competition for land in the Kivus has often translated into competition for control of these chieftaincies. Since these were historically in the hands of "autochthonous" populations, the Rwandophones have "persistently [called] for a Native Authority of their own."[103] They have typically chosen one of two ways to go about this quest. One way has been to authoritatively remove "autochthonous" chiefs in existing chieftaincies and replace them with Rwandophones. Grassroots attempts to implement this option in the early 1990s, when Hutu leaders tried to forcibly remove Hunde chiefs in Masisi and replace them with Hutu authorities, led to retaliatory violence by Hunde gangs against Rwandophone populations.[104] Once the RCD was in control of the region after 1998, it returned to this approach. Claiming to represent Congolese sovereignty in the region, the RCD forcibly removed several Hunde chiefs in Rutshuru and Masisi and appointed Rwandophones in their stead.[105] Several non-Rwandophone chiefs were also killed in the Kivus under both the AFDL and the RCD.[106]

The other way to seize control of chieftaincies has been to promote the creation of new chieftaincies by higher levels of state authority. This approach has a long history in the region, dating back to the creation of Rwandophone chieftaincies by the Belgians. Apart from Rutshuru, however, the Rwandophones lost all their chieftaincies after independence. Their lack of control over local state authorities until the 1990s prevented them from reestablishing these chieftaincies or creating new ones. With the AFDL in power after 1997, the Banyamulenge of South Kivu called again for a territory of their own, to be protected by their own troops and located along the border with Burundi in the Ruzizi plains.[107] The insurgency of August 1998 put these plans on hold until 1999, when the RCD, acting as the Congolese sovereign over that region, carved the new *territoire* of Minembwe from the existing *territoires* of Fizi, Mwenga, and Uvira. The *territoire* is the level of administration between the *collectivité* and the province.

It is interesting that the RCD Banyamulenge still found it necessary to create a *territoire* for their ethnic kin in South Kivu even though they were already in complete military control of the region, suggesting their understanding that forceful control by itself would not provide them greater safety in the long run. What could really help them was the creation of a sovereign arrangement that could survive the end of the conflict. Hence, the creation of Minembwe as a new decentralized administrative unit of the Congolese state. But the RCD could not claim the authority to gerrymander South Kivu if it could not make a plausible claim to representing legitimate sovereign statehood in the region. Thus it was essential for the RCD to act according to Congolese law and within the institutional parameters of the preexisting Congolese state. This necessity contributed to their lack of challenge of the Congolese state.

In the end, however, this too proved unsuccessful as the Kabila transition government rejected Minembwe after 2003. An endorsement would have given the Banyamulenge their own electoral district and the guarantee of at least one deputy. Despite Ruberwa's threat to defect from the coalition, the Minembwe experiment was thus brought to an end, once again by sovereign fiat, and the Banyamulenge were left without the local sovereign structures that they had been craving for decades.[108]

The historical difficulties of the Rwandophones with chieftaincies have made the pursuit of "civic politics" at the provincial level a popular alternative, although one also plagued with hurdles and competition with members of "autochthonous" groups. The Rwandophones' experience with provincial politics began with failure as "autochthonous" representatives from Beni, Lubero, and Masisi managed to obtain the splitting of the Kivu province in 1962 into three smaller provinces: North Kivu, Central Kivu, and Maniema.[109] The creation of North Kivu produced a province with a majority Nande population, whereas all groups had previously been minorities in the larger Kivu province. Thus the Rwandophones were crowded out of administrative power in the new province—undermining their quest for civic citizenship.[110] "Autochthonous" populations of Nande, Hunde, and others subsequently used their control of North Kivu Province to push back the rights of Rwandophones, reappointing, for example, Hunde chiefs in districts where they had been displaced during the colonial era. After its takeover in 1998, the RCD proceeded to revert this situation by appointing numerous Rwandophones to positions of provincial authority in North and South Kivu. According to the International Crisis Group, Hutus ended up occupying as much as 80 percent of administrative posts in Rutshuru, Masisi, and Goma.[111] The legality of such appointments of Rwandophones in the civil administration necessitated, however, that the RCD wear the veil of Congolese sovereignty, providing a rationale for the maintenance of Congolese law in the areas under its control.

The Rwandophones' preference for federalism—the most clearly articulated part of the RCD's political agenda—proceeds from a similar pursuit of local autonomous sovereign institutions. In the words of Ruberwa, "we want local autonomy, we want federalism. . . . We want a united Congo. . . . What we do want is to change the mode of management in Congo and have more autonomy for the provinces. . . . Yes to the unity of Congo but never to unitarism."[112] The RCD actually undertook a certain measure of federalism in the territory under its control with the formation in 2001 of provincial assemblies in the east, but these had largely faded by 2003.[113] Yet, by promoting the decentralization of some powers and fiscal resources to the provinces, the Rwandophones hoped to promote an institutional evolution that would guarantee the existence of levels of authority where they would be significant actors. The RCD was more successful in this respect than with either chief replacements or chieftaincy creation. In fact, although the 2005 constitution rejected federalism, it adopted what the Congolese refer to as a "highly decentralized unitary state" and endowed the existing eleven provinces (then intended to rise to twenty-five by 2009) with jurisdiction, among other things, in matters of land titles, establishment and residency of foreigners, and the application of customary law, thus providing a role for the province over traditional authorities. It also calls for the retrocession of 40 percent of central government revenue to the provinces. Although it would be hard for the Rwandophones to form a majority in the North Kivu or South Kivu provincial assemblies, they may conceivably have more voice there than in national institutions by belonging to coalitions. They can also resume their earlier pursuit of civil service employment in the provincial bureaucracies, from which they could derive significant practical powers of execution and legal command.

The pursuit of civic politics has also extended to the Rwandophones' regional patron, the Rwandan government, as illustrated by its sponsoring of the political career of Eugène Serufuli Ngayabaseka, a Congolese Hutu from North Kivu. In 1998, Serufuli founded an NGO called Tous pour la Paix et le Développement (All for Peace and Development, TPD), whose major activity was the repatriation to North Kivu of Congolese Rwandophone refugees from Rwanda, for which it received financial support from Kigali.[114] Serufuli joined the board of the RCD in 1998 and was appointed governor of North Kivu in 2000. His appointment facilitated the TPD's efforts to repatriate Congolese Hutu refugees.

Serufuli's trajectory illustrates Rwanda's preference for Congolese sovereign institutions. While TPD was originally an NGO, Rwanda promoted the rise of Serufuli to provincial governor, where he was better able to implement the type of repatriation policies that it desired. These policies involved the authoritative reallocation of land to despoiled Hutus. In its pursuit, Serufuli allegedly replaced "all the administrative and traditional authorities with some reliable members of the TPD."[115] Thus, as an agent of Rwanda, Serufuli gained control over the local Congolese state.[116] This conformed with Rwanda's strategy to control the local representation of the sovereign Congolese state so as to have the authority to reallocate land and other resources to returning refugees. In pursuit of its economic and security objectives in the Kivus, Rwanda thus promoted the reproduction rather than the dismemberment of a sovereign Congo. Luca Jourdan appropriately refers to this instrumentalization of Congolese sovereignty by Rwanda via Serufuli as "indirect rule."[117]

Whether one chooses the chieftaincy or civil tracks, Congolese citizenship is a prerequisite for access to legal command. One cannot normally be a chief or a civil servant without being first Congolese. And one cannot appoint chiefs and civil servants, or create chieftaincies and administrative divisions, without being first Congolese. Acceding to or securing Congolese nationality has thus historically been the Rwandophones' first political priority. Denying them this status has, conversely, been their opponents' main political weapon. As a result, the legal rules for the acquisition of Congolese sovereignty have been particularly unstable.

In the 1964 constitution, citizenship was limited to "any person whose at least one ancestor is or was member of a tribe or of part of a tribe established on the territory of Congo before 18 October 1908," the date of creation of the Belgian Congo. This appeared to exclude migrant Banyarwanda from the 1930s and later refugees. Yet, the Rwandophones' material opportunities and political influence improved after Mobutu's takeover. A 1972 law gave Zairean nationality to all people from "Ruanda-Urundi" established in Kivu before 1 January 1950, and having since resided there continually. However, under pressure from the other Kivutian communities who had seen large chunks of their land appropriated by Banyarwanda over the previous decade, Mobutu turned up the heat on his erstwhile allies and promulgated a new nationality law in 1981. Now any person was deemed Zairean "whose at least one ancestor is or was member of a tribe established on the territory of the republic in its limits as of 1 August 1885," that is, in the early phase of the Leopoldian regime. Others were foreigners and had to make an explicit and individual request of naturalization.[118] Confusion continued in practice, however, as it was hard, with subsequent marriages, to determine who had ancestors in the territory before or after 1885. Meanwhile, well-placed businessmen and influential politicians obtained naturalization for themselves.

In 1991, the National Sovereign Conference (CNS) brought to the fore the broad current of public opinion against the Rwandophones and refused to admit delegates representing "foreigners," preventing the presence of Rwandophones among the North Kivu delegation. This ban was partly due to the lobbying of Nande, Hunde, and Nyanga representatives, who seized upon this new legal tool of exclusion.[119] The legal status of the Rwandophones would not again be discussed until the nationality law adopted by the transition parliament in November 2004. This time, having secured their participation in the transition system, the Rwandophones were able to obtain more generous terms of inclusion. According to the 2004 law, "every person belonging to ethnic groups or nationalities whose members or territory constituted what became the Congo . . . at independence" is Congolese. Moreover, a child "is Congolese by birth . . . whose parent—mother or father—is Congolese."[120] Taken together, these two articles first recognize citizenship to all the Rwandophones who migrated to Congo during the entire colonial period and their descendants. Second, it provides an opportunity for citizenship for the children of couples where only one of the parents qualifies under the general stipulation. This includes the numerous families formed between descendants of early migrants and of more recent refugees.

Although the fortunes of the Rwandophones wax and wane throughout these laws, the tribal or ethnic source of Congolese citizenship is a constant. The law does not confer citizenship to people who resided in its territory at some point up to independence. Instead, it confers it to people who belong to groups that did. This is an odd formulation.[121] It makes Congolese nationality both colonial and ethnic. One of its implications is the possibility to reject individuals en bloc. If one can demonstrate that a group was not present in today's Congolese territory at a specific date, its descendants have no claim to citizenship. Thus it encourages autochthony-allochthony distinctions. Another consequence is that it reinforces ethnic identification, making it a matter of legal benefits. To be a Congolese national, one must first be a Congolese tribal. The law does not, however, specify a list of these ethnicities and nationalities, maintaining a level of uncertainty that may well again prove problematic for the Rwandophones.

We can now revisit the observation made in Chapter 3 that the RCD did not provide any significant legal or institutional innovation in the region it controlled between 1998 and 2005. This inertia appeared particularly puzzling in view of its leadership's avowed intentions to reform the state. To some extent, it was a function of its poor relations with most local communities and of its own factionalism.[122] But the above discussion should by now have made it clear that there was more to it than that. The necessity to occupy sovereign positions in order to control the allocation of land contributed to the RCD's decision to administer the territories under its control "in accord with Congolese law," maintaining prewar legal codes, administrative structures, and bureaucratic procedures.[123] Given their goals of obtaining recognition of the Rwandophones as legitimate Congolese and securing their access to and ownership of land, there was little incentive for the RCD to promote new unrecognized administrative structures and challenge existing laws. Eager to design a solution to their problem that would endure after the war, they worked within the law, claiming a piece of sovereign power and reproducing the institutions of the Congolese state.

The Rwandophones' strategy of relying on legal command in their local struggles also led them to seek participation in national governments in order to directly affect these laws. Under Mobutu, this approach was embodied in Bisengimana's influence as the president's chief of staff. With the AFDL, Rwandophones had direct access to the center of power as cabinet members. Under the transition, the RCD managed to participate in a power-sharing government and transition parliament that produced the 2004 nationality law. In each case, participation in power at the center was antithetical to challenging the existence or the territorial reach of Congo as a state.

Conclusion

Explanations for the conflict in eastern Congo are often couched in terms of land and ethnicity. While these dimensions do matter, the extent to which they are mediated by sovereign command is usually unexplored. Access to land is predicated upon control of the law or positions of legal authority. These positions necessitate citizenship, which is defined in ethnic and colonial terms. There are two main consequences to this sovereign bias in local politics. First, it reinforces the existence of Congo in its postcolonial design, despite the repeated failure of the Congolese state to provide peace, security, and development to the communities of the Kivus. Second it structures local political and economic life along ethnic lines. Kivutians articulate collective interests at the ethnic level in order to compete for ethnically defined local positions of sovereignty. Their joint predicament at the hands of Congo translates into conflict among themselves for the preservation of Congo.

"To Keep Nigeria One Is a Task That Must Be Done"

Any self-respecting study of the scarcity of secessionism in Africa must sooner or later come to grips with Nigeria.[124] I focus here on the two regions most likely to challenge the country's territorial integrity: Biafra and the Niger Delta. Although the availability of oil affects the calculus of Nigeria's actors, sovereignty plays a crucial role in structuring access to oil revenues, particularly through the pursuit of federated statehood by local elites. In addition, competition *between* local communities for access to oil revenues and the daily survival strategies of people who lack such access also rely on legal command.

There appear to be good reasons for expectations of Nigeria's demise and dismemberment. With more than 130 million people divided into about 300 ethnic groups, 36 states, and 776 local government authorities (LGAs), a profound Christian-Muslim schism, strong precolonial histories and identities, regionally located natural resources, an inefficient and corrupt government, and an entitlement-based concept of citizenship that promotes ethnic competition and polarization, it is puzzling that Nigeria has not entirely come apart at the seams. Although the possibility of disintegration cannot be ruled out, very few if any of Nigeria's political elites, within or outside the state apparatus, have so far credibly challenged its existence as a sovereign state. As its 1999 constitution puts it, Nigeria appears as "one indivisible and indissoluble sovereign state." For a state that has broadly failed in its attempts to bring about development, accountability, or public goods in general, the extent of its success in keeping the country one is noteworthy.

There appears to be a rather intuitive and obvious explanation for Nigeria's resilience, which differs from this book's argument. Nigeria has oil. Lots of it. Nigeria has been Africa's main oil exporter since 1979.[125] Oil contributes 76 percent of government revenue, 95 percent of exports, and one-third of GDP.[126] The federal government redistributes a significant portion of oil revenues to the states and local governments, which have become wholly dependent on these funds. On average, internally generated revenues represent less than 20 percent and 10 percent, respectively, of all state and LGA revenues.[127] As a result, one can understand the attachment of both federal and regional elites to Nigeria if only as a cash cow. The Northern region, for example, although excluded from power at the center between 1999 and 2007, had no serious incentive for secession in view of its dependence on the redistribution to states of the revenues from oil. Were the northern states to secede, it is hard to see how they could avoid the fate of neighboring poverty-plagued Niger. The same applies to Yorubaland in the west. The radical wing of the Oodua People's Congress has at times called for a Yoruba nation and postured in defiance to the federation, yet it has fallen short of promoting secession. The creation of an independent Yorubaland seems indeed of limited appeal in contrast to a federal system with continued accrual of oil revenue. Even when their elites are out of power at the center, Nigeria's regions continue to benefit from their association with the state through the redistribution of the rents from oil. As a result, their allegiance is hardly paradoxical.

For important as oil is, however, it is not the whole story of Nigeria's territorial preservation. The real puzzle lies in the allegiance of Nigeria's Eastern region, particularly the Niger Delta and the formerly separatist Igboland or Biafra. The elites of the Igbo, Ijaw, Ogoni, Itsekeri, and other groups of the "South East" and "South South" regions have almost always been out of power at the center. Meanwhile, revenues from the oil that lies underneath their soil have funded the exponential growth of the federal system from which they have been largely excluded.[128] The share of oil revenues that accrues to their states has fallen from 50 percent in 1960 to 13 percent since 1999 (after having plummeted as low as 1.5 percent in the 1980s). There are also few visible benefits from oil in these regions, which remain among the poorest of the country and those with the least infrastructure and social services. Desolation and degradation, on the other hand, are clearly visible. That this desolation has come at the hands of state-controlled activity is well known to locals and the root of their resentment at the government. Despite all this (and despite the potential mobilizing effects of the historical precedent of the Igbo secession of 1967), separatist discourse remains marginal in both regions. For sure, some Igbo groups have agitated since 1999 for a new Biafra and there is significant Ijaw activism for self-determination, yet, these movements do not appear to represent a majority opinion and their objectives are far from being unambiguously separatist.

Moreover, while an oil-based theory of Nigerian unity makes some sense for the top elites who partake in its rents, it does not account for the acquiescence of smaller elites and nonelites deprived of such access. Although states are awash in oil dollars, civil servants often go unpaid for months at a time. Furthermore, as Daniel Smith has recently shown, Nigerian politicians increasingly tend to "eat alone"; they no longer honor the redistributive duties of patron-client relations.[129] Thus, despite the abundance of resource at the center, there are many groups and individuals who fail to benefit from oil rents. What determines their acquiescence?

In this section, I investigate why the grievances of Igboland and the Delta have not taken a more separatist turn. I argue that the sovereign appropriation of the oil sector has forced local demands into a national framework. I recognize, however, that there are variations in the acquiescence of Eastern populations, which I discuss with particular reference to the Movement for the Actualization of the Sovereign State of Biafra (MASSOB), the Niger Delta People's Volunteer Force (NDPVF), and the Movement for the Emancipation of the Niger Delta (MEND). I show that these variations relate to differences in access to local sovereign prebends and in the availability of alternative opportunities for advancement. Finally, I address the importance of sovereign command and intermediation in the strategies of survival and advancement of those who find themselves outside networks of power.

Eastern Compliance: The Sovereign Structuring of Oil

There is a relative salience of separatist discourse in Eastern Nigeria. John Paden notes that talking of the "partition option is no longer taboo" in the east.[130] And the International Crisis Group comments that "support for an armed separatist insurgency has grown" in the Delta region.[131] Yet, by and large, the political climate there as elsewhere is nonseparatist. A survey by

Scott Pegg of a small nonrandom sample of Delta residents found that 72 percent believed that the end point of self-determination is to remain part of Nigeria.[132] In neighboring Igboland, Smith writes that "many Igbos do not support the idea of secession" and, while they "generally believe that the interests of their region have been neglected since the civil war . . . the number of people willing to face violence, imprisonment, or death in the name of the revival of Biafra remain few."[133]

To some extent, the small size of some local ethnic groups, like the Ogoni or the Itsekeri (each about 500,000), may partly explain their avoidance of separatism. But there is no irrevocable reason why these groups could not coalesce in support of a broader regional claim for sovereignty. In addition, larger groups like the Igbo and Ijaw have enough demographic weight to lead a credible claim to statehood. Separatist prudence might also proceed from the fact that, weak as it is, Nigeria remains an intimidating military power with the capacity and reach to quell most insurgencies. Yet, expected military superiority of national government forces is a near constant in separatist decisions around the world. One would never argue that the Chechens or the Sarahawis embarked upon secession confident that they could defeat Russia or Morocco on the battlegrounds. In addition, political violence by nonseparatist vigilantes is relatively common in Nigeria and seems unaffected by the unequal balance of power. At any rate, the cohesiveness of a state military response should not be overestimated. It might be easier for Nigeria to project military power in places like Liberia and Sierra Leone, which is politically neutral and financially rewarding, than at home.

Why is the Eastern region not separatist, then? The answer to this question is complex and multidimensional. Yet, a significant part of it has to do with the extent to which sovereign mechanisms structure the oil industry and the redistribution of its revenues to regional elites, biasing their actions toward the embrace of Nigeria and reducing the relative appeal of separatist strategies. Although one often hears of the actions of Shell, Mobil, Exxon, and other international oil companies in Nigeria, such emphasis hides the degree to which the Nigerian state has extended its sovereign might over the oil industry and shares it with regional state authorities. Since the Petroleum Act of 1969, the state owns all oil and gas anywhere in the country. By the Land Use Decree of 1978, it also has the right to appropriate all land. Both of these texts, incorporated in the 1999 constitution, are pure legal sovereign appropriation and resemble those in many other African countries. The states of the federation are closely involved in the implementation of this sovereign appropriation, as state governors can "revoke a right of occupancy for 'overriding public interests' including mining purposes and the installation of pipelines" or "acquire any land on behalf of private or public oil companies."[134]

Oil revenues accrue to Nigeria through sovereign taxation and royalty payments. In addition, nearly all companies operate as joint ventures under majority state ownership, with profits shared between multinationals and the government.[135] Shell Nigeria, for example, actually is the Shell Petroleum Development Company, a Nigerian state-majority-ownership company, whose operations are carried out by the private partner. The joint-venture agreements "make no provision for direct participation or ownership of communities near the areas of operation."[136] With taxes, royalties, and shared ownership, the government collected 95 percent of the profits from oil as of May 2006 with prices at US$70 a barrel.[137]

The state also provides the central mechanism in the distribution of oil revenues, which are collected by federal authorities and pooled monthly into a Federation Account, from which they are allocated between the three levels of government. Approximately 50 percent of the funds go to the federal government, 25 percent to states, and 20 percent to LGAs. In addition, all states are entitled to a specific proportion of the revenues collected in their area. While this so-called derivation payment applies to all regions, it is for all practical purposes an additional transfer to the oil-producing states. In 1960, each state retained 50 percent of the tax revenues derived from its territory. Since 1999, the amount stands at 13 percent.[138] Derivation highlights the centrality of the state. Resources are extracted and appropriated along a sovereign path, then redistributed along a parallel sovereign path.

Because these transfers together constitute by far the main source of income of states and LGAs, they define the terms of the political debate. Demand for statehood and access to its offices have become effective local means to benefit from oil. Biafra and Delta residents and politicians may be suspicious of their marginalization in national politics, yet they find an interest in accessing local parcels of sovereignty in their own strategies of accumulation and survival. They favor a language of grievance vis-à-vis Nigeria to justify their demands for more states and more revenues, but doing so does not undermine Nigeria per se. On the contrary, for local states to be effective tools of accumulation, Nigeria—which imparts sovereignty—must be preserved.

Demand for statehood has been a constant among ethnic communities in the south and in the east. Calls for self-determination and community "ownership" of natural resources have been made largely in support of demands for statehood and additional federal income, rather than separation.[139] As Brennan Kraxberger makes clear, "local groups have sought statehood to obtain better access to oil money *controlled by the centre.* . . . New states have not been expected to supply their own budgets, stimulating demands for more."[140] Nationally, the number of states has risen from three in 1960 to thirty-six since 1996.[141] And the number of LGAs has gone from 301 in 1976 to 776 in 1996.[142] Most new states seem to have resulted from demands by regional elites who perceived themselves as marginalized and devoid of access to the rents from oil. Paden notes that "much of the pressure for new states has come from southern minorities. . . . In the 1996 review of claims to new states, there were a total of 72 requests for new states, 2,369 claims for local councils."[143] With the federal government resisting the creation of new units, some governors have taken it upon themselves to increase the number of LGAs in their jurisdictions. In Bayelsa, for example, the governor added twenty-four LGAs to the existing eight in 2000. According to the International Crisis Group, "proliferation of local government units is a serious national problem."[144]

The Ijaw lobbied for years for the creation of Bayelsa State, which happened in 1996. Although they used a discourse of environmental degradation and marginalization of the Ijaw people in support of their demand, the leader of the movement for Bayelsa State, Chief Alfred Diete-Spiff, was in fact the former governor of Rivers State, from which Bayelsa was carved, and thus a person directly implicated in the environmental degradation and marginalization of the region.[145] Exclusion of Diete-Spiff from control of Rivers State may have resulted in his demand for the creation of an Ijaw state. Ogoni elites have also lobbied for statehood but have not so far been successful.[146]

Discourses of community grievances and calls for regional autonomy have also supported demands for greater revenue for existing states. Since the return to democracy in 1999, southern states have repeatedly called for an increase in derivation to 25 percent. Southern elites have done relatively well out of this strategy. Despite the prevailing discourse of grievance and marginalization, the average annual allocation to "South South" states over the 1999–2002 period was about US$500 million. This compared with US$240 million for the South East, which includes Biafra, and an average of about US$240–270 million for the other big six regions.[147] Coastal states also benefited from the 2002 decision to impute offshore oil to them for revenue derivation purposes.[148]

Nonstate elites in the Delta region have also been able to benefit from connection to Nigerian sovereignty by claiming recognition as "host communities." According to the host community system, "communities deemed by the government and [oil] companies to be 'owners' of land on which oil infrastructure is based are considered eligible for oil company benefits." This system "*recognizes* [my emphasis] individuals or communities which own land on which companies have terminals, flow stations, pipelines and other physical assets." Itsekeri and Ijaw elites have made generous use of this provision and reaped equally generous benefits from it. Sovereign authentication of these communities as traditional "owners" of the land (the Itsekeri even resorted to colonial legal texts to show their ownership over the town of Warri) is likely to reduce their incentives to challenge the state that authenticated them.[149]

Requests for statehood, local government, or host community status are sovereign moves, that is, moves whose goal is to partake in the benefits of Nigeria's sovereignty. The elites of regions that appear as victims of Nigerian national integration promote association with the state and thus perpetuate it. Nigeria endures as a result of their action. But since state demands are supposed to represent collective interests, they are couched in terms of communal grievances and also promote the crystallization and polarization of local identities. Thus national unity and local disunity are simultaneously engendered by sovereignty.

In comparison, secessionism has little to offer Delta and Biafra elites. If they were to seek independence, they could not obtain recognition. Without it, they could not credibly pass legislation to give themselves similar powers of command. Particularly, they would face legal hurdles in claiming ownership of oil operations. Altogether, the odds of doing better than under Nigerian sovereignty would be low. Hence, the sovereign structuring of oil limits the plausible options of eastern elites, biasing their demands toward local statehood and increased derivation, and away from independence.

The fixed supply of international sovereignty conditions Nigeria's equilibrium. My argument is not that Biafra and Delta residents do not want an independent state. Rather, it is that they operate under an overarching constraint that makes it rational for them to pursue a share of Nigerian sovereignty instead of their own independence. This constraint is the scarcity of sovereignty. Daniel Smith illustrates, for example, the emotional attachment to the idea of Biafra among Igbo market men. Reading their comments, one gets the feeling that Biafra would be their preferred path. Their attachment to Nigeria appears reasonable rather than affective. Their awareness of the extent to which international sovereignty constrains their option is remarkable. They ask Smith, "Would America support an independent Biafra?" And, referring to the longevity of the leader of the 1967 Biafra secession, Odumegwu Ojukwu, they ask, "Is it true . . . that if the leader of an independence movement survives for thirty years after the start of that rebellion that the United Nations will automatically *recognize* [my emphasis] that people?"[150] In similar fashion, the ICG quotes a seventy-year-old former speechwriter for Biafra leaders: "I no longer believe in separatist movements," he says, "and I am now a loyal Nigerian nationalist. But Biafra is always somewhere in the back of my mind."[151] This disconnect between regionalist sentiment and national attachment is a consequence of the instrumentalization of sovereignty.

Variations in Compliance

Both the Delta and Biafra harbor separatist groups. If local elites embrace Nigeria out of their understanding that sovereignty structures their opportunities for advancement and accumulation, why do some groups choose instead the path of defiance?

In the Delta, sovereignty is not the only way to access the benefits from oil; one can also steal it.[152] Because many wells are onshore and there is a wide network of pipelines and pumping stations across the region, Nigerian oil is surprisingly lootable. The practice of "bunkering," whereby pipelines are tapped and the crude is smuggled by barges to tankers at sea, is by some estimates a US$2 billion a year business, accounting for up to one-third of the country's entire production.[153] Bunkering does not require sovereignty. What it does require, however, is a measure of territorial control for access to the pipelines and the creeks. While the practice is clearly illegal, it is less illicit when coated in a language of minority resource control and self-determination, which the need to control territory lends itself to. Thus, bunkering groups are more likely to challenge state sovereignty and to promote a separatist discourse, as has been the case for Alhaji Mujahid Dokubo-Asari's NDPVF and the MEND. The leaders of these groups were not initially local established elites in positions of state or traditional authority with access to sovereign benefits. Their lack of such access combined with the opportunities provided by bunkering account in large part for their more radical attitude. That it is mostly an attitude and a discourse, however, is suggested by the lack of effective separatist insurgency of these groups.

With about nine million people, the Ijaws are present in several states, including Ondo, Edo, Delta, Akwa Ibom, Rivers, and Bayelsa (where they are a majority). Their militants have been responsible for most activism in the Delta region since 1998, when some 5,000 youths held an "All Ijaw Conference." The conference refused to recognize "undemocratic decrees" like the Land Use and Petroleum decrees and called for the "immediate withdrawal" of "military forces of occupation and repression." Yet, its practical demands were more subdued and included holding a "sovereign" national conference to form a Nigerian federation of ethnic nationalities, while "agree[ing] to remain within Nigeria."[154]

The conference also set up an Ijaw Youth Council (IYC), one of whose leaders was Dokubo-Asari, a man in his mid-thirties who had spent much of his life abroad.[155] After factional infighting within the IYC, Dokubo-Asari developed the NDPVF in 2003, a militia that engaged in oil theft and in battles with other militias for the control of areas noted for oil theft potential.[156] The NDPVF progressively radicalized and launched attacks on oil installations after 2003, which contributed to destabilizing oil prices.[157] Dokubo-Asari and the leader of a rival faction, Ateke Tom, were given amnesty in 2004 in apparent exchange for ceasing their operations. Dokubo-Asari allegedly returned home a richer man.[158] Yet, he continued to threaten violent action unless "complete control" of Delta oil revenue was given to Delta residents or, rather, "to their state and local governments."[159] He was arrested and charged with treason in September 2005. MEND surfaced after Dokubo-Asari's incarceration, apparently organized by his supporters, mostly young unemployed men. MEND's actions have marked an increase in violence and radicalism. Yet, their demands have focused mostly on compensation for environmental damages, greater derivation, and the channeling of money "through foundations controlled by communities rather than through corrupt state and local governments."[160]

Both the NDPVF and MEND have been prime actors in the bunkering business, from which they get their financing.[161] Bunkering is a nonsovereign activity and represents a significant alternative path of survival and accumulation. Control of territory for bunkering purposes has led to numerous gang fights involving the NDPVF and MEND.[162] Much of the NDPVF's violence in 2003–2004 was for control of riverine villages with access to pipelines in Rivers State. Dokubo-Asari himself admitted doing well out of the business.[163] He even claimed to have a small refinery. From 2003 to 2005 he controlled the town of Tombia in Rivers and had access to the pipelines that go through the area. Despite their involvement in violence, neither the NDPVF nor MEND actually launched a secessionist movement. Thus, while reports on the region often stress the importance of bunkering in providing finances to these groups, one can also conceive of these groups as providing a structure and a rationale for bunkering and for the necessity of territorial control that comes with it. Self-determination justifies bunkering or, in Dokubo-Asari's words, "depriving from our oppressors what is ours."[164] If this is the case, the defiance of these groups (composed of younger, less-integrated elites) toward the Nigerian state can be better understood as the pursuit of illegal nonsovereign economic opportunities in an industry dominated by sovereignty, rather than as an expression of a political struggle for emancipation.

In contrast to the Delta, bunkering opportunities do not exist in Biafra, which is further inland and has considerably less oil. Yet, separatist attitudes are made possible there by the availability of alternatives to sovereignty, including reliance on a significant Igbo diaspora and on the relative strength of private enterprise and small manufacturing in the region, both of which reduce the necessity to rely on the state. As in the Delta, however, the actual secessionist objectives of Biafra activists can easily be overstated.

MASSOB, created in 1999 by Ralph Uwazurike, calls for a Biafra Republic. It has a website, two radio stations, and a cabinet "appointed" by Uwazurike in 2004.[165] Despite its threats to restore Biafra, MASSOB's activism has been somewhat low-key and its demands subdued. MASSOB has been a nonviolent movement despite occasional skirmishes with regional militias like the Bakassi Boys. Its main achievements have been the organization of marches, rallies, and a general strike in August 2004. It also boycotted the 2006 census. Its leaders have threatened in their speeches to restore Biafra, but have only taken symbolic actions to this effect. For sure, some of MASSOB's moderation can be explained by the vigorous repression it has suffered at the hands of the federal government. Hundreds of its members and supporters have been arrested and detained, and dozens have been killed. Uwazurike himself was charged with treason and apparently went into hiding. However, MASSOB's agenda is to seek change through nonviolent sovereignty-endorsing ways. Like other groups, its main demand is for the convening of a sovereign national conference to preside over the peaceful dissolution of

Nigeria. Its name is particularly interesting in this respect, calling as it does for the "actualization" of Biafra's sovereignty. This approach appears to presume that the Igbo nation is sovereign but in need of some sort of trigger mechanism (presumably recognition granted by a Nigerian sovereign conference) to become effective. Thus, MASSOB wants to use Nigeria's sovereignty to pronounce Nigeria dead—which is secessionist in intent but respectful of legal command in means.

MASSOB's softer approach can be partly explained by the nature of nonsovereign opportunities available to the Igbo. First, Biafra separatism appears to be greatly driven by the Igbo diaspora, which is emancipated from sovereignty but also without a comparative advantage in local violence. Uwazurike has recognized that MASSOB gets its funding from Igbo abroad, and he has been accused by some of having enriched himself in the process. As Smith puts it, "a good deal of the most visible pro-Biafra propaganda is produced by [Igbo] living abroad," while many Igbo on the ground do not support the idea of secession. The "Voice of Biafra International" radio station and "Biafra House," a cultural center, are based in Washington, DC.[166] Uwazurike too is a product of the diaspora, having studied political science at the University of Bombay in India, where he spent ten years and was president of the Nigerian Students Organization.

Another reason why Igbo are simultaneously less likely to pursue sovereign opportunities and to embark on violent defiance is their reliance—somewhat uncharacteristically for Africa—on small manufacturing and commerce. There are numerous small- and medium-scale industries operating in Igbo states in the manufacturing of commodities such as shoes, shirts, motor parts, toilet paper, printing, meat processing, metal and plastics, brewing, and even handguns.[167] In fact, Eastern Nigeria has been one of the main areas of Chinese foreign direct investment in Africa outside of the usual stable countries such as South Africa or Mauritius.[168] These activities relieve Igbo entrepreneurs from having to derive income from sovereignty but also mitigate their propensity for upheaval, as they would disproportionately suffer from chaos and economic disruption. Thus, the region's economic outlook supports cultural defiance but not actual separatist activism. This is partly why the Igbo establishment is not sympathetic to MASSOB. During MASSOB's call for a general strike in August 2004, the local governors urged people to go out and work, and Governor Orji Uzor Kalu, of Abia State, accused MASSOB of attempting to destabilize Nigeria.[169] As R. T. Akinyele writes, "several Igbo organizations, including the *Ohaneze*, the umbrella union of Igbo people, were quick to remind Uwazurike that the dream of Biafra died in 1970" and "eastern legislators and all the governors from the south-east zone, whose states fall within the proposed Biafra, quickly distanced themselves from the scheme."[170] In fact, General Ojukwu is the only domestic Igbo elite to openly support MASSOB. Even he, however, seems to be hedging his bet as he also ran for president of Nigeria in 2003. Igbo economic elites and state authorities are thus reluctant to challenge Nigeria. Most of MASSOB's supporters are unemployed youth and "poor men in urban areas," or people without access to sovereignty and without alternatives that require law and order.[171]

Although alternative sources of economic opportunities in the Delta and Biafra occasionally promote defiance to the federal government, they do not generally lead to challenges to Nigeria per se. In both regions, supporters of separatism are mostly young unemployed men without direct access to sovereign benefits. Established chiefs, economic elites, and state authorities typically do not endorse their actions.[172]

Beyond Petroleum: Command and Intermediation as Popular Resources

Why the majority of Nigerians who live in Igboland and the Delta do not provide more fodder for secessionist entrepreneurs remains to be explained. The redistribution of oil rents from the central state to local authorities translates in fact into very few benefits for local populations. Although Delta states receive 25 percent of federal revenues for 15 percent of Nigeria's population, Ijaw poverty rates remain among the highest and education levels among the lowest. The ICG notes that "since 1995 . . . federal government allocations to Niger Delta states have grown several fold, although the bulk of this money is believed to have benefited a small elite."[173] One of the main causes of poverty in these two regions is the failure of local authorities to redistribute the oil manna. In general, local state elites appropriate resources, which they may redistribute to allies through public contracts, but less frequently to people through social programs. In Rivers State, for example, US$84 million of the US$1.2 billion 2006 budget was for the governor's discretionary spending, US$60,000 a day was allocated to official transport and travel, and US$100,000 a day for the governor's "grants and donations." As for the State Assembly, it reserved US$5.4 million for its own travel budget and US$2.8 million for entertainment.[174] According to *Africa Confidential*, every state governor has a lodge in Lagos and Abuja, "each one furnished extravagantly at public expense. There are similar lavish dwellings in each state capital. The money is spent on the trappings of power, with little left for the job of government itself."[175] Meanwhile, many state civil servants in the east go unpaid for months at a time. Why do local populations not more forcibly challenge this unjust order?

In Nigeria as elsewhere, the broad decentralization of the command benefits of sovereign institutions helps account for the resilience and popular acceptance of the state. Throughout Biafra and the Niger Delta, there are many people in lesser positions of sovereign authority who rely on it to extract resources from fellow citizens. Like elites, they do not have an incentive to undermine

Nigeria. They constitute, to some extent, the underlying social networks (the public opinion) that favor the reproduction of Nigeria.

As in African states with fewer natural resources, prebendal domination is a crucial tool of survival and advancement in the lower tiers of Nigerian officialdom. The recent work of Daniel Smith on corruption in Igboland suggests the extent to which sovereign command, exercised here by Igbos on Igbos, can produce compliance among an otherwise politically repressed and marginalized group. Examples include the endless police checkpoints where drivers automatically make payments to policemen. These checkpoints rely on legal requirements: "In addition to the actual vehicle registration certificate, Nigerian drivers are expected to carry several other official documents, including one that verifies that the police have determined the vehicle is not stolen. Without all the proper documents, one is likely to be delayed at police checkpoints with demands for money. Each of these documents has its own bureaucracy and officials who need to be 'settled'"—Nigeria's term for bribery.[176] A 2007 article in *Vanity Fair* noted similar practices in the Delta with between twenty and thirty police checkpoints between Warri and Port Harcourt (a distance of about 100 miles) "where drivers simply hand cash out the window in order to pass."[177] These practices are not the monopoly of police. In Nigeria, too, "people commonly pay extra money for basic services such as the issuance of licenses, passports, and birth certificates. . . . Everything from obtaining birth and death certificates, to registering a company, to applying for a passport, to renewing a motor vehicle registration normally requires some sort of payment in addition to the official fee."[178] And, writing about Biafra, Johannes Harnischfeger comments that "anyone with sufficient money and influence can make use of state institutions to harm his opponents, whether in land or business disputes or in personal vendettas."[179] Finally, for those not directly associated with the state, intermediation remains an opportunity. Smith again notes that "many Nigerians find navigating government bureaucracies frustrating and people frequently rely on the aid of intermediaries."[180]

Patterns

The main demand of the Barotse Royal Establishment is for the restoration of the Bartoseland Agreement of 1964, an essentially federal clause of the constitution. Federalism, with two or ten states, is also the focus of the political struggle of Cameroon's Anglophones. In the DRC's Kivu provinces, access to—and creation of—local chieftaincies is the essential mode of decentralization of sovereignty. And, of course, unbridled federalism is the essential demand of Nigeria's local elites. Hence, one of the main paths of regional access to legal command is to call for autonomy, decentralization, or federalism, all of which allow local elites to inherit sovereign powers and build or reinforce their local hegemony. The goal is to obtain access to local sovereign institutions of the state and use them in relations of extraction or domination within or between local groups. Regional elites support the reproduction of the national state in exchange for access to dominant local state positions. Local dynamics of power and material advancement trump national dynamics of group inequality.

Of particular interest is the level at which demands for decentralized sovereignty aggregate. By and large, the manner in which sovereignty is distributed at the subnational level determines the level of identity that people and elites are likely to privilege in their political behavior. In Barotseland, what appears as Lozi ethnic collective action is actually much more dependent on the region's past colonial specificity, its former legal status as quasi sovereign, and its current existence as a province. In western Cameroon, in contrast, Anglophone status is privileged over ethnicity or other forms of identity because it matches the contours of once-sovereign institutions and of existing provinces. It is doubtful that Anglophones would coalesce as a minority if they did not share a colonial past or if existing Cameroonian provinces cut across linguistic communities. One should not therefore see a contrast between the organization of collective action along "ethnic" lines in Barotseland and "colonial linguistic" lines in Cameroon. For, in fact, in both cases, local actors choose colonially inherited institutional expressions of identity. The apparently ethnic nature of local conflicts in the Kivus follows a similar logic. Administrative chieftaincies in the region have been defined in ethnic terms since colonial times. Because of their plausible colonial institutional existence, ethnic groups represent credible levels of aggregation of political action and thus micro-ethnicities provide the foundation for identity aggregation, leading to massive local polarization as a side effect of claims to sovereign access. Irrespective of the level of collective action promoted by local elites, however, the sovereign logic of their action, and the subsequent reproduction of the state, is similar across the cases.

The extent to which conflicts over natural resources are mediated through sovereignty is also worth noting. Access to land is crucial to most peripheral communities in Africa. But the path to such access is overwhelmingly defined by sovereign prerogatives of appropriation and of authentication of participants through citizenship criteria. This is also true with oil in Nigeria. One often thinks of the politics of oil in the region as if oil was physically available. But, with the exception of bunkering, oil revenues can only be appropriated via sovereign paths. Thus, decentralized natural resources may well foster state reproduction more than separatism.

Finally, this chapter has also illustrated what factors account for variations in elite compliance with the state, an exercise continued in the next chapter. By and large, established elites are likely to seek to maintain the state, as are those with no better opportunity than sovereignty, even if their access to sovereignty is limited and its rewards few and small. In contrast, those with no local status as elite or no plausible access to sovereignty, and thus with little to lose, may very well choose to embark upon a more defiant path, especially if encouraged by the availability of nonsovereign economic opportunities, such as oil bunkering in Nigeria. The opportunity to rely on a diaspora (as exists for the Igbos) and the exiled condition of specific elites (whose own survival as refugees correlates with their rejection of the sovereign state) also contribute to defiance by offering paths of advancement alternative to sovereign command.

Altogether, the nature of African sovereignty, its relative material appeal compared to other opportunities for advancement, and its capacity to endure irrespective of effective conditions on the ground, bias regional elites away from challenging the state and from constructive political entrepreneurship. Local elites become more likely to adopt patterns of extraversion and derive authority from their connection to sovereignty rather than to build local relations of accountability and local foundations of political legitimacy. In this respect, the African sovereignty regime impedes state-building.

Notes

1. Segments of this case study were originally published as Englebert, "Compliance and Defiance."

2. Interview with Mukela Manyando, Ngambela (Prime Minister) of Barotseland, Limulunga, July 2003.

3. Caplan, *The Elites of Barotseland*, 38–73; Hall, *Zambia*, 54–86.

4. Barotse National Conference, "Resolutions."

5. "Doing God's Work in Zambia." *Boston Globe Magazine*, 8 June 2003, http://search.boston.com/globe/magazine/2003/0608/bishop.htm.

6. Posner, "Zambian Political Attitudes Questionnaire," 1996. Methodological details of this survey are presented in Appendix B of Posner, *Institutions and Ethnic Politics*.

7. Minorities at Risk, "The Lozi."

8. I overlook the pro-separatist attitude of Litunga Mwanawina Lewanika III, who wanted Barotseland to secede in 1961 as Zambia approached independence. Nothing came of it, and the Barotse leadership, even then, declined to forcibly challenge its region's integration into Zambia.

9. *The Barotseland Agreement 1964*, 14.

10. Ibid., 15.

11. Pitch, *Inside Zambia—and Out*, 151.

12. "Lozi Leader Warns President Chiluba: We Could Break Up with Zambia," *The Post* (Zambia), 3 April 1994.

13. *The Barotseland Agreement 1964*, 18.

14. Interview with Masheke Iliamupu, professor at University of Zambia, Mongu, Limulunga, July 2003.

15. Lealui, which lies in the floodplains a few miles from Mongu, is the official residence of the Litunga and seat of the kingdom when the plains are not flooded. Dur-

ing the rainy season, the kingdom's capital moves to Limulunga (in the Kuomboka ceremony), which is equally close to Mongu but above the plains.

16. Office of the Ngambela, "Resolutions of the People."

17. Interview with Masheke Iliamupu.

18. See Chapter 6 for an in-depth discussion of variations over time of international norms of sovereignty.

19. Anonymous interview, Mongu, July 2003.

20. Rotberg, "What Future for Barotseland," 22.

21. "Barotse Royal Establishment Press Release," *The Post* (Zambia), 9 July 2003; and "The Great Betrayal," *The Post* (Zambia), 10 July 2003.

22. Interview with Princess Nakatandi Wina, Lusaka, July 2003.

23. Interview with Sikota Wina, Lusaka, July 2003.

24. Interview with Imasiku Mutangelwa, Lusaka, July 2003.

25. Ibid.

26. Anonymous former *induna* (member of the royal council) interview, 2003.

27. "Lozis take," *The Post* (Zambia).

28. The expression "decentralized despotism" is from Mamdani, *Citizens and Subjects*.

29. Bayart, *The State in Africa*. Prima facie, the argument made about Barotseland here might also apply to the Buganda, Ashanti, and Zulu kingdoms.

30. See Le Vine, *The Cameroons*.

31. On the federal arrangement, see Le Vine, *The Cameroon Federal Republic*.

32. See Verschave, *La Françafrique*.

33. Konings and Nyamnjoh, "The Anglophone Problem."

34. Konings, "Anglophone University Students."

35. Personal communication with Maggie Fick.

36. On the ethnic differences between North West and South West, see Nyamnjoh, "Cameroon: A Country United."

37. "Cameroon: Major Investments for the South West," *Cameroon Tribune*, 4 April 2005.

38. Konings, "Anglophone University Students," 15.

39. Eyoh, "Conflicting Narratives," 266 (emphasis mine).

40. Ibid., 265 (emphasis mine).

41. Ibid., 260.

42. Konings and Nyamnjoh, "The Anglophone Problem," 219.

43. See Englebert, "Cameroon: Background to a Crisis."

44. Konings and Nyamnjoh, "The Anglophone Problem," 216. At first in favor of a two-state federal system, the SDF later promoted the adoption of a four-state system in deference to the preferences of its Francophone members.

45. Ibid., 217.

46. Nyamnjoh, "Cameroon: A Country United," 104.

47. Although many African states have dropped the automatic guarantee of public employment to university graduates since the 1980s, degrees are still a necessary condition to compete for these jobs.

48. See, for example, Nyamnjoh, "Cameroon: A Country United," 106; Konings and Nyamnjoh, *Negotiating an Anglophone Identity*.

49. Konings and Nyamnjoh, "The Anglophone Problem," 211–212.

50. Ibid., 215. In the 1992 presidential elections, John Fru Ndi polled 86.3 percent in the North West and 51.6 percent in the South West.

51. "Cameroon: Major Investments for the South West," *Cameroon Tribune*, 4 April 2005.

52. These figures are based on 2005 data, as reported by EIU, *Country Report: Cameroon*, 17.

53. Nyamnjoh and Rowlands, "Elite Associations."

54. Konings and Nyamnjoh, "The Anglophone Problem," 225; see also Nyamnjoh and Rowlands, "Elite Associations," 329.

55. Konings, "Anglophone University Students," 15.

56. Ibid., 15.

57. Cited in ibid., 6. Note the use of the term *revival,* which appeals to the notion that Southern Cameroons already had sovereignty in the past. This is the familiar post-colonial argument, further discussed in Chapter 6, which is cognizant of the historical and external origins of sovereignty in Africa.

58. Konings, "Anglophone University Students," 11.

59. Nyamnjoh and Rowlands, "Elite Associations," 323.

60. Konings, "Anglophone University Students," 6.

61. This is an approach it also followed with the Commonwealth of Nations, repeatedly but unsuccessfully seeking throughout much of the 1990s to be recognized by this organization and to deny recognition to the Cameroonian government (see Konings and Nyamnjoh, *Negotiating an Anglophone Identity*, 96–99).

62. "Cameroon: Pro-Independence Group Silenced," United Nations Integrated Regional Information Network (IRIN), 19 February 2007 (received as e-mail from IRIN@irinnews.org). The SCNC also obtained hearings at the African Commission on Human and People's Rights in Banjul between 2003 and 2005. After being submitted in 2003, the case was deemed admissible in 2004. Hearings on the merit were held in 2005. A decision was expected by 2009 (e-mail, Nico Fru Awason, 24 April 2007; e-mail, Robert Eno, 20 March 2009).

63. UN IRIN, "Cameroon: Pro-Independence."

64. "Conference to Unite SCNC Factions Flops," *The Post* (Cameroon), 17 December 2004.

65. Konings, "Anglophone University Students," 10.

66. Ibid., 11.

67. Konings and Nyamnjoh, *Negotiating an Anglophone Identity*, 21.

68. Nyamnjoh, "Cameroon: A Country United," 109 (emphasis mine).

69. Posner, *Institutions and Ethnic Politics.*

70. I use the term *Rwandophone* to refer to all Kinyarwanda-speaking people of both Kivu provinces, Hutu and Tutsi. The Rwandophones of North Kivu are often labeled *Banyarwanda*. In South Kivu, the Tutsi are often called *Banyamulenge,* although this term, which had little currency before the 1980s, was originally restricted to those among them who had settled long ago.

71. Pabanel, "La question de la nationalité," 36. It is harder to give credence, however, to the International Crisis Group's contention that they may represent 40 percent of North Kivu (ICG, "Congo's Elections," 19).

72. ICG, "Congo's Elections," 19–20.

73. Reintjens and Marysse, "Conflicts aux Kivus," 6.

74. For more details about the historical settlement of Rwandophones in the region, see Willame, *Banyarwanda et Banyamulenge*; Vlassenroet, "Citizenship, Identity Formation, and Conflict," 502.

75. Vlassenroet, "Citizenship, Identity Formation, and Conflict," 502.

76. Willame, *Banyarwanda et Banyamulenge,* 42.

77. Ibid., 53. Mararo, "La guerre des chiffres," 14. Rwakabuba retained his positions into the 1990s.

78. For the case of South Kivu, see Willame, *Banyarwanda et Banyamulenge*, 82.

79. Ibid., 55.

80. Autesserre, "Local Violence, National Peace?"

81. ICG, "Congo's Transition Is Failing," 9.

82. Willame, *Banyarwanda et Banyamulenge*, 89.

83. Ibid., 93.

84. Tull, "The Dynamics of Transnational Violence," 6.

85. ICG, "Congo's Transition Is Failing," 9.

86. The RCD actually progressively splintered into several factions, including the RCD-Goma, RCD-Kisangani, and RCD-National. The RCD-Goma remained the largest and most powerful and is the one I refer to with the acronym RCD. Although the RCD leadership never entirely consisted of Tutsi, they were the dominant group.

87. For example, Forrest. *Subnationalism in Africa,* 61. See also their classification by Minorities at Risk as "latent separatist" (www.cidcm.umd.edu/mar/data.asp).

88. Jackson, "'Our Riches.'"

89. See also Clark, "Explaining Ugandan Intervention."

90. Mararo, "L'administration AFDL/RCD au Kivu," 192, 196, and 204.

91. E-mail message to the author from Western scholar studying the Kivus, 2001.

92. Willame, *Banyarwanda et Banyamulenge*, 69.

93. Ibid., 58. This is reminiscent of the actions of Cameroon's Anglophones and reveals both the unwillingness of these elites to work within a nonsovereign environment and their understanding that African sovereignty comes from UN recognition rather than from empirical existence.

94. BERCI, "Le rapport préliminaire," 23.

95. Interview, Goma, November 2001.

96. In this respect, it may be worth noting that many Congolese seem unfazed by the apparent contradiction between denying Rwandophones their nationality and then fearing their alleged separatist intentions.

97. Jackson, "Our Riches," 9.

98. Mararo, "L'administration AFDL/RCD au Kivu," 179.

99. Interview, Goma, November 2001.

100. Anonymous e-mail, October 2001.

101. I borrow the expressions "native authority" and "civil politics" from Mamdani, *When Victims Become Killers.*

102. I return to this in Chapter 7.

103. Mamdani, *When Victims Become Killers*, 238.

104. Personal interview with Bishop Ngabu, Goma, November 2001.

105. ICG, "The Congo's Transition Is Failing," 9.

106. Tull, "The Dynamics of Transnational Violence"; Mararo, "L'administration AFDL/RCD au Kivu," 184–185.

107. Mararo, "L'administration AFDL/RCD au Kivu," 182; Willame, *Banyarwanda et Banyamulenge*, 97.

108. ICG, "Congo's Elections," 19–20. The continuation of ethnic violence in the Kivus is partly linked to this failure of the postconflict settlement to provide an institutional solution to the Rwandophone problem.

109. Tegera, "Nord-Kivu," 9.

110. Willame, *Banyarwanda et Banyamulenge*, 48.

111. ICG, "Congo's Elections," 9.

112. Personal interview, Goma, 2001.

113. Tull, "The Dynamics of Transnational Violence," 143.

114. Jourdan, "New Forms of Political Order," 7.

115. Ibid., 7.

116. On Serufuli, see also ICG, "The Congo's Elections," 9–10.

117. Jourdan, "New Forms of Political Order," 5.

118. Willame, *Banyarwanda et Banyamulenge*, 57.

119. ICG, "Congo's Elections," 9.

120. "Loi No 04/024 du 12 novembre 2004 relative a la nationalité congolaise, articles 6 and 7," 3.

121. Some other African countries have a similar tribal approach to nationality, as discussed in Chapter 7.

122. Mampilly, "Stationary Bandits."

123. Tull, *The Reconfiguration*, 135.

124. This title was the federal government's slogan in its war against the secessionist Biafra republic from 1967 to 1970 (quoted by Nugent, *Africa Since Independence*, 71).

125. Frynas and Paulo, "A New Scramble," 234.

126. ICG, "Fuelling the Niger Delta Crisis," 10.

127. Suberu, "Democratizing Nigeria's Federal Experiment," 67.

128. This is especially true for the "South South" and Delta regions, where most of the oil is located. There is significantly less oil in Igboland.

129. Smith, *A Culture of Corruption.*

130. Paden, "Unity with Diversity," 18.

131. ICG, "The Swamps of Insurgency," 23.

132. Pegg, "What They Really Want."

133. Smith, *A Culture of Corruption*, 194–197.

134. Frynas, "Corporate and State Responses," 30.

135. ICG, "Nigeria's Faltering Federal Experiment," 5.

136. ICG, "Fuelling the Niger Delta Crisis," 24.

137. Ibid., 23.

138. Frynas, "Corporate and State Responses," 38.

139. See Suberu, "Democratizing Nigeria's Federal Experiment," 65.

140. Kraxberger, "The Geography of Regime Survival," 417 (emphasis mine).

141. Alapiki, "State Creation in Nigeria," 50.

142. Frynas, "Corporate and State Responses," 33.

143. Paden, "Unity with Diversity," 23.

144. ICG, "The Swamps of Insurgency," 24.

145. Alapiki, "State Creation in Nigeria," 60.

146. Frynas, "Corporate and State Responses," 37; ICG, "The Swamps of Insurgency," 4.

147. Paden, "Unity with Diversity," 30. Exchange rate conversions mine.

148. Sklar, "Unity or Regionalism," 45.

149. ICG, "The Swamps of Insurgency," 13–15. See also ICG, "Fuelling the Niger Delta Crisis," 2.

150. Smith, *A Culture of Corruption*, 202–203.

151. ICG, "Nigeria's Faltering Federal Experiment," 16.

152. Of course, this is partly a function of one's point of view. For some, the thief is Nigeria.

153. *Africa Confidential*, 20 January 2006, 47(2):1–2, and 25 June 2004, 45(13):5. Other sources estimate the losses at closer to 10 percent of output.

154. "Kaiama Declaration by Ijaw Youths."

155. ICG, "Fuelling the Niger Delta Crisis," 4, and *Africa Confidential*, 10 September 2004, 45(18):1.

156. ICG, "Fuelling the Niger Delta Crisis," 4.

157. *Financial Times*, 29 September 2004, 6.

158. ICG, "Fuelling the Niger Delta Crisis," 5.

159. *Africa Confidential*, 1 April 2005, 46(7):4.

160. ICG, "Fuelling the Niger Delta Crisis," 5.

161. *Africa Confidential*, 23 July 2004, 45(15):4.

162. ICG, "Nigeria's Faltering Federal Experiment," 7.

163. *Africa Confidential*, 1 April 2005, 46(7):5.

164. Ibid.

165. See www.biafraland.com/massob.htm.

166. Smith, *A Culture of Corruption*, 194 and 195.

167. *Africa Confidential*, 9 August 2002, 43(16):6; Brautigam, "Substituting for the State."

168. Deborah Brautigam, personal communication; see also Brautigam, "Chinese Business."

169. *The News* (Nigeria), 30 August 2004. Some suspect, however, that governors are more supportive in private than they are in public.

170. Akinyele, "Ethnic Militancy," 633–634.

171. Smith, *A Culture of Corruption*, 197–198.

172. The same is true among the Ogoni where traditional chiefs have dissociated themselves from the activities of the Movement for the Survival of the Ogoni People. See Obi, "Global, State, and Local Intersections," 184.

173. ICG, "The Swamps of Insurgency," 12.

174. *Africa Confidential*, 21 July 2006, 47(15):7.

175. *Africa Confidential*, 28 May 2004, 45(11):7.

176. Smith, *A Culture of Corruption*, 58, 61.

177. Junger, "Blood Oil."

178. Smith, *A Culture of Corruption*, 17–18, 56; see also ICG, "Fuelling the Niger Delta Crisis," 17.

179. Harnischfeger, "The Bakassi Boys," 28.

180. Smith, *A Culture of Corruption*, 60.

6

Separatist Illusions and Sovereignty Variations

State sovereignty is a significant resource for Africans, for which many are willing to surrender claims of self-determination. As a result, the weak state endures. Yet, the fact remains that there *are* separatist movements and insurgencies in Africa. How can the argument be reconciled with this apparently contradictory evidence? In this chapter, I argue that all instances of African separatism belong to one of three categories. First are what I call cases of self-indetermination, where a separatist group is well identified as a cultural region or minority but its discourse supports demands for local access to sovereign state institutions. In other words, these separatists fight for the acquisition and control of local sovereign state institutions, the opposite of secessionism. Next are cases of selfless-determination, where a usually heterogeneous coalition seeks independence for a territory on the grounds that it was once a colony. These separatists demand postcolonial recognition; they seek juridical statehood. Finally, the supply or relative benefits of sovereignty vary across places and times, with the result that the calculus of compliance occasionally no longer falls squarely on the side of sovereignty. There are two subsets to this latter category. First is the highly idiosyncratic case of Ethiopia, the lone continental exception to juridical sovereignty. Ethiopia's unique history and its own colonial propensity toward peripheral groups limit the availability of sovereign legal command for some of its regional elites and increase the relative returns of separatism. Second, there are times where separatism becomes more attractive because of the apparent uncertainty or weakening of international rules of recognition. This was partly the case in the 1960s, when the principle of postcolonial recognition was not yet fully crystallized, and in the early 1990s, when the collapse of the Soviet Union and Yugoslavia sent Africans a largely misleading signal about the possibility of new norms of recognition.

Self-Indetermination: Separatists for National Unity

For regional elites to have access to legal command, they need local sovereign institutions. When these institutions are lacking, an effective way to obtain them is to make demands for local autonomy. Should the state be unresponsive, conflict might ensue. Local actors in these conflicts stress their cultural differences and their persecution by the central government in support of their demands for autonomy, and appear secessionist. This is largely illusory, however, as their main interest is to partake in the bounties of sovereignty rather than to challenge it.

Groups from regions where the central government exerts direct authority are most likely to make demands for autonomy and decentralized institutions. Such direct rule, referred to by Catherine Boone as "administrative occupation," typically happens in regions that lack strong local hierarchies, as is the case with lineage societies.[1] The social promotion of new elites in these societies finds itself hampered by this administrative occupation from the center: there are no desirable chiefly positions to vie for and administrative positions are under the control of outsiders. Thus, local scenarios of upward political mobility or "social revolution"[2] translate into opposition to the central government and frequently develop a separatist discourse. Yet, the goal is not necessarily to engage in local state-building but to become the local dominant class, which more often than not necessitates the preservation of the postcolonial state, alone empowered to decentralize its sovereign command.

State Institutions for Class Formation in Casamance

Casamance, the southernmost region of Senegal, is squeezed between Gambia and Guinea-Bissau and isolated from the rest of the country.[3] It has an ambiguously distinct colonial past, having been administered separately from the rest of Senegal from 1854 to 1939, under direct authority of the governor of French West Africa, and only integrated with it toward the end of the colonial period.[4] It is largely composed of Diolas, a lineage society with little historical exposure to Islam and to the marabout hierarchies that prevail in much of Senegal. Economically, it is largely outside the state-sponsored mechanisms of distribution of wealth. Its 800,000 inhabitants benefit little from the region's tourism industry, and many saw their land expropriated to the benefit of Wolof migrants in the early 1980s. Residents blame the state for underinvesting in their region and keeping them away from state employment.

It comes as no surprise therefore that Casamance has been the stage of a violent separatist rebellion waged since 1982 by the Mouvement des Forces Démocratiques de Casamance (Movement of Democratic Forces of Casamance, MFDC). It is often argued that the conflict began as a consequence of land expropriations by northerners; the change of president from Léopold Senghor (a

Serer, culturally closer to the Diolas) to Abdou Diouf (a Wolof); economic dis-affection of the region; and an increased sense of local identity paradoxically de-rived from education, migration, tourism, and the discourse of the Catholic Church.[5] That the leader of the MFDC—Augustin Diamacoune Senghor—was a Catholic priest in a Muslim country has been seen as evidence of the region's cultural alienation and desire for self-determination.

Yet, an analysis of the dynamics of the conflict and of the actions and de-mands of the MFDC leaders suggests more ambiguous and less radical goals. After a few years of relatively subdued violence, the conflict picked up inten-sity in 1990 following a large MFDC offensive. When a cease-fire was con-cluded in 1991, it led to a split in the MFDC leadership. The head of its armed wing, Sidy Badji, a French army veteran, renounced the pursuit of indepen-dence and settled down with his supporters near the Gambia. There they have since engaged in informal economic activities, including smuggling. Mean-while, a "Southern Front" emerged, which refused to recognize the cease-fire. Its leaders were Léopold Sagna, a former Senegalese soldier, and Salif Sadio, a school dropout. Diamacoune aligned with the Southern Front.

Despite occasional cease-fires, the Southern Front sustained the conflict over the ensuing years and followed a strategy of occupying economically ad-vantageous areas and spreading violence across the region. After a large army operation, however, Diamacoune made clear in 1998 that he was ready to give up independence demands in exchange for better economic and social devel-opment in Casamance. A 1999 MFDC summit in Banjul, Gambia, for the first time refrained from demanding independence. A provisional peace agreement was signed after the election of Abdoulaye Wade to the Senegalese presidency in March 2000, in which the MFDC moved further away from separatist de-mands and asked for more investment and support from Dakar. In 2003, Dia-macoune again asked his men to renounce their demand for independence.[6]

In retrospect, the rebels' rapid disengagement from the original objective of independence and their lack of unity around this goal has been one of the most notable elements of Casamance's insurgency. For sure, at least some of the members of the MFDC actually desired independence for their region for at least some of the time since 1982. Yet, the movement's official demands and the actions of its militants and fighters on the ground increasingly strayed from this objective. The year 1993 may have marked a turning point in this respect. That year, the MFDC requested the arbitration of a French archivist to estab-lish whether Casamance had been ruled as a distinct colony, hoping to be able to invoke the principle of postcolonial sovereignty in its claim for indepen-dence. In December, the arbitrator decided against them. This ruling signifi-cantly undermined the movement's independence agenda. Thereafter, it no longer called for independence, and the rhythm of its cease-fires with the gov-ernment accelerated. The MFDC's Banjul platform of 1999 characterized this evolution. Although it called for special elections within ten years to establish an assembly that would vote on independence, the short-term demands focused on self-governance through the creation of a Casamance government, parliament, and judiciary, as well as "any other necessary institution" and its own budgetary powers.[7]

The evolution away from independence did not necessarily reflect inconsistency, however. If the MFDC's goal was to obtain control of local sovereign institutions, their original and subsequent positions are not contradictory.[8] That this was at least part of the original intent is well illustrated by Vincent Foucher, who notes that after the first cease-fire in 1991, "ardent discussions were held [among MFDC supporters] on the justifications for independence and what would happen after it was obtained: the imagined redistribution of state jobs . . . became a major topic of discussion."[9] Before exploring this argument in further detail, it is necessary to understand who the MFDC leadership was.

The position of political elites in Casamance contrasts greatly with the rest of Senegal. There is no tradition of centralized rule and very little hierarchy in political relations altogether, even at the local level, where the "main authority figures are the patriarchs" who "do not control access to land or labor" but act instead as "intermediaries for the spirit shrines that are the centerpiece in customary modes of regulating land, agricultural production, social life, and community space."[10] Because of this lack of local hierarchical social organization, the Senegalese state was unable to apply its fusion-of-elites policy in Casamance, despite its successes in the Wolof groundnut basin. Instead, it resorted to administrative occupation, appointing nonlocal civil servants and administrators, including governors from the Senegalese military, and posting educated Casamançais cadres outside their region of origin. Furthermore, the few Diola "big men" who were appointed to the national government lacked local roots. In the words of a local lawyer, "Casamançais found that their cultural differences translated into ostracism from state management."[11] This policy essentially deprived rising modern Casamance elites from access to the material benefits of sovereignty. Quoting again from Boone's excellent work, the problem of local Casamance elites became that they had "few points of access to administrative and patronage resources."[12] This problem was compounded by the fact that local elites did not control access to land and labor and were thus even more dependent upon administrative offices. Without such opportunities, rebellion is a rational strategy, either to create one's own sovereignty or to shape a local political elite capable of being a counterpart to the government and receive sovereignty benefits. From this perspective, the Casamance war was as much about the formation of a local dominant political class as it was about the assertion of cultural identity.

Casamance separatist leaders thus are not local authority figures pushing for cultural recognition. They are, by and large, modernized, educated would-be elites who have been kept off local positions of administrative authority by Dakar's policy of direct rule in the region and whose social status is frequently a function of their education or migration experience.[13] They have relatively tenuous links with their region. Of the five top leaders of the movement, four spent a considerable part of their life away from Casamance and acquired social status through education or military careers.[14] Sidy Badji fought with the French army in Indochina, Algeria, and Morocco, then worked in Dakar before returning to Casamance. Diamacoune was ordained a priest in 1956 (and by joining the church also joined the strongest social hierarchy in Casamance), then went to study theology in Belgium, before returning to Ziguinchor and becoming active as a teacher and youth organizer. Léopold Sagna was a soldier and quit the Senegalese army in 1980 with corporal ranking. Only Salif Sadio (who is younger) is truly a local, with less education than the others. Foucher calls our attention to the extent to which education played a role in shaping local preferences. The Diola, he notes, had the highest level of primary education in Senegal. By the late 1970s, there was a "large set of youth with education but without future. . . . Young Diola were faced with increasing difficulties with getting into the civil service and the army, where their elders had earlier secured attractive positions." These educated people then developed an interest in the culture and history of their region.[15]

Separatist demands arose as a result of the desire of local cultural activists and educated elites to rise as local political elites and to take control of the local domestic appendages of international sovereignty, with or without Senegal. It may be hard to impute such motives ex post facto to these leaders but the evolution of the conflict suggests that Casamançais separatism has been more about state-derived class formation within Casamance than about subnational assertion.

Other authors have already pointed out the fact that the conflict was more about association than separatism.[16] My argument builds on theirs, but goes further: MFDC elites were not only trying to negotiate their integration into Senegal, but more so their local hegemony within Senegal. As mentioned earlier, there is a traditional vacuum of political elites in Casamance. Before the conflict, there was not either a strong entrepreneurial class, as the business sector (mostly tourism) was largely in the hands of French operators. As a result, social promotion had largely been defined since the end period of colonialism through education and access to civil service.[17] As the state descended into fiscal crisis in the late 1970s, however, these opportunities contracted and modernized Casamance elites were left struggling for access. With opportunities for employment within the state ever more remote, the desire to invest in local public institutions may have grown. But Dakar's administrative occupation deprived Casamançais of such local access. Separatist warfare provided at least a means to revoke Dakar's direct rule and promote the rise of local institutions with their attendant opportunities for legal command.

This interpretation is consistent with several patterns of MFDC elite behavior. It accounts for the erosion over time of the proindependence content of their demands. It sheds light as to why the MFDC did not build institutions in liberated territories, as one would expect from a separatist movement.[18] Finally, it also brings context to the practice of the Senegalese state to provide financial transfers to MFDC leaders who stop fighting or abandon separatist claims.[19] This may appear at first as a simple case of co-optation, but there is more to it. MFDC leaders use these transfers to reinforce their local power. By having access to state resources and redistributing them, they make the case for their legitimacy and potential as local elites. Lacking other social foundations, they establish their local political hegemony by demonstrating their counterpart status to the state. They acquired this status by fighting, then negotiating the terms of their renunciation to violence. Separatist posturing becomes an equilibrium as it guarantees the flow of resources, which enhance the separatists' local control. Credibility as a local patron is derived from a recognition by Dakar of one's status as separatist leader. The conflict becomes a way to achieve elite status and benefit from sovereignty.

Although local grievances did exist, they were not a sufficient condition for separatist conflict until they got instrumentalized by elites. Deprived of the benefits of sovereignty, these elites challenged national integration so as to renegotiate the terms of their access to statehood. What appears as a secessionist conflict, opposing the central government's hold on a region, was more subtly some sort of local class conflict, whereby an elite-in-formation struggled to establish its local domination through legal command.

The Tuareg: Rebellion for Decentralization

The Tuareg are a Berber-related minority of about 1.5 million people who live in a vast Saharan region straddling southern Algeria, northern Burkina Faso, northern Mali, central Niger, and southwestern Libya.[20] In both Mali and Niger, where they represent no more than 10 percent of the population, they inhabit distant arid areas that lack physical and social infrastructure. Pastoralists, their livestock have been decimated by successive droughts, and they have had to fight the settlement of more sedentary groups of farmers along the few local waterways. Their traditional nomadic lifestyles and reliance on long-distance trade have also been perturbed by postcolonial borders. By and large, over the last century, theirs has been a history of decline, immiseration, and marginalization.

The Tuareg are culturally distinct from other groups in the region. While there is no strong evidence for the existence of a precolonial Tuareg "nation,"[21] there is a shared sense of cultural identity among all the Tuareg "tribes" of the Sahara. Neglected if not repressed by successive regimes in Bamako and Niamey, the Tuareg have also developed an acute sense of grievance toward their respective governments.

As in Casamance, then, it is not surprising that the Tuareg of both countries eventually rebelled. Yet, also as in Casamance, labeling their rebellion "separatist" would be misleading. Instead, the rebels' agenda was to become a local state bourgeoisie, to unseat the domination of the traditional Tuareg aristocracy and of centralized bureaucrats, and to multiply and take over the local levers of the state. There were generational and class elements to this agenda as the rebels were opposed to their elders within the Tuareg social hierarchy. But the rebellion also signified an attempt at domination *between* groups, as the rebels' demands largely excluded local non-Tuareg groups. In general, in both countries, the rebellions can be understood as state-mediated strategies of local domination by modernized "social cadets." By fighting the state, the rebels obtained recognition by the state of their status as local elite. Armed with this recognition, they demanded parcels of legal command under the veil of autonomy. They became part of the state and consolidated their elite status. Hence, the state endured, its local domination reinforced by institutional multiplication.

In Mali, where the rebellion began in 1990, most of the conflict was characterized until 1995 by relatively low-intensity skirmishes and irregular rebel attacks on local military or government outposts. The rebels and their leaders were quite young, at most in their early thirties. Many of them had originally been recruited into Libya's "Islamic legions" while in exile following the droughts of the 1970s and 1980s. Upon their return they had failed to find employment. Unwilling to do pastoral jobs, they lacked alternatives. They were unwilling to work with traditional chiefs who controlled local positions of authority, because they were marginalized by them and resented the extent to which the chiefs "had been given privileges by the regime," at least in terms of local administration, and were believed to have appropriated much of the drought-related food aid.[22] They were later joined by young unemployed intellectuals who shared their distrust of traditional powers. These men were not only kept at bay by their chiefs, but failed to find employment in the provincial administrations, which were mostly staffed by southerners or sedentary northerners like the Songhai.[23]

A crucial goal of the rebels was thus to replace the chiefs. Yet, while they were mostly opposed to their own local leadership, they turned their weapons against the Malian state. In their attempt to dislodge the chiefs, the young rebels had to make themselves a credible substitute. Thus, they fought the state to obtain concessions from it and become the locally dominant group—a scenario again akin to Bayart's "social revolution." Attacking the chiefs (which happened rarely) would have made criminals out of them; attacking the state allowed them to claim representation of Tuareg grievances and make a claim for local sovereign access.

This is not to imply that, as with Casamance, there were not at times genuine hopes for independence among the rebels. Some wanted the creation of a "free Tuareg state"[24] and others did call for the secession of northern Mali and the "establishment of a Tuareg and Maure state."[25] In 1994, one group threatened to declare an independent Azawad (the Tuareg name for their region).

Yet, there was little of substance beyond such posturing, which lacked popular support. The real demands of the rebels surfaced instead in their negotiations with the government, which led to the signing of the Tamanrasset Accord in 1991 and the National Pact in 1992 and focused on regional autonomy, jobs in the national government, and regional economic development (which are code words for resource transfers to the region). Tuareg complaints included lack of representation, lack of decentralization, authoritarian and military rule in their region, and abuses by civil servants from the south.[26] Later on, the rebels added demands for the integration of rebels into the army.[27]

The autonomy provisions of the Tamanrasset Accord did offer the rebels significant opportunities for patronage and legal command. Their region was granted "particular status" and was allocated almost half the funds from the national investment program. Moreover, the agreement provided for "local assemblies with legislative and executive branches that will regulate all economic, social and cultural issues" specific to these regions.[28] The accord's implementation unraveled, however, as the regime of Moussa Traoré was overthrown in March 1991. Yet, the National Pact, reached in negotiations with the new regime in April 1992, covered essentially similar ground.[29] It confirmed the "particular status" of the north and provided for multiple layers of local assemblies responsible for agriculture, livestock, water, urbanism, housing, environment, industry, transport, communication, health, education, culture, and tourism. It also called for the integration of the rebel leaders in the military and administration. Both agreements thus stressed the creation of local sovereign institutions endowed with legal command and of prebendal administrative and military positions. And both of these demands promoted the rise of rebels and their leaders as a local elite.

Application of the pact was very slow, however, and deeply deficient, whether as a result of the government's unusually weak capacity or lack of goodwill. The 1992 constitution, for example, did not include the north's "particular status." Partly as a result, scattered violence continued. Over the subsequent years, however, the administration progressively put in place a decentralization reform for the whole country, which culminated in the organization of local elections in 682 communes in 1999.[30] The communal councils have widespread responsibility including that of collecting taxes and making budgets for health, education, and some local infrastructure. Moreover, they have the authority to "act in cooperation" with development agencies in their region.[31] This is particularly important in Tuareg country where there are so few local resources. The government is unable to transfer significant resources to the region, and the value of prebends is limited by the prevailing poverty and the lack of any significant surplus to appropriate. Having the authority to deal with foreign NGOs as public authority (a delegated sovereign prerogative) thus offers opportunities for access to financial flows. The administrative levels above the communes are the circles and the regions. Each circle and region also has councils and executives, all of which together represent a significant number of positions with sovereign authority.

The rebellion also represented an attempt by Tuareg to gain and consolidate ascendancy over other groups in the region. Historically, relations between the predominantly light-skinned Tuareg and the sedentary black populations of the north—principally the Songhai and Peuhl—have been tense as they compete for scarce resources. The Tuareg also once held the local black populations as slaves. After the rebels obtained institutional concessions from the government, relations between the groups worsened as non-Tuareg felt excluded from the north's special status and from the new opportunities for employment.[32] A local militia, Ganda Koy ("Masters of the Land"), emerged in 1994, as a group representing the interests of the sedentary black populations, who are a majority in the region. There were many clashes between Ganda Koy and the rebels over the following couple of years, with the former often doing the government's bidding.

Although the conflict largely subsided after 1996, there have been occasional upsurges in violence since then. While they might be depicted as separatist in the media, each one of them has usually involved demands for the implementation of earlier government concessions. In May 2006, for example, Tuareg rebels seized the towns of Kidal and Meneka and stole all weapons from local army bases before retreating in the neighboring mountains. Their leader, Lieutenant Colonel Hassan Fagaga, was an officer who had been integrated in the national army as a result of the 1990s insurgency. He demanded "an improvement in living and working conditions for the ex-rebels who had been integrated into the army" and a better implementation of the National Pact.[33]

The conflict in Niger followed a similar logic. Here too, droughts and lack of economic development, compounded in this case by discriminatory policies toward nomads, were the principal reasons behind the rebellion, whose goal was also the acquisition of regional autonomy.[34] As in Mali, many of Niger's Tuaregs had escaped the country during the droughts, seeking refuge in Algeria and Libya. In early 1990, between 18,000 and 25,000 of them returned, prompted by their host country.[35] The first rebel attack took place in May of that year, against the prison and police station of Tchin Tabaraden. Massive government reprisals and repression of Tuaregs ensued, with casualties estimated at 600–700 by humanitarian organizations.[36]

The rebels were civil servants, secondary-school students, former petty officers and gendarmes who deserted or were fired, and "*ishomars*" (*chômeurs*)—idle unemployed youth.[37] Their secessionist credentials were questionable, although their demands were somewhat more radical than in Mali. In 1992, they announced that they were not seeking independence but rather the establishment of a federal system, in which each ethnic group would have its own administrative entity and regional autonomy. Other demands included economic development and increased political representation. Nevertheless, the degree to which the Nigerien rebels were hoping for autonomy dwarfed the aspirations of their Malian counterparts. In 1994, a rebel faction called for "revolution" in the name of a "Tuareg nation"[38] and demanded that a Tuareg administrative region (to comprise two-thirds of Niger!) be created; that each regional administrative echelon have its assembly; that only Tuareg populations be allowed to vote and run for office in the region; that 75 percent of its jobs be reserved for Tuareg (100 percent for development project chiefs); that 40 percent of security forces and 50 percent of top military staff be Tuareg; and that 25 percent of the government's investment budget and 100 percent of taxes from mining companies operating in the area be allocated to the region.[39] Not surprisingly, these demands were rejected.

Peace agreements concluded in Ouagadougou in 1994 and 1995 offered the Tuareg much more limited concessions. They set up "territorial collectivities" with elected assemblies and presidents. These assemblies were given the power to manage their own budgets, economic development projects (here also, an essential local resource and source of employment), and social and cultural affairs.[40] They also provided for the reintegration of former civil servants, the readmission of former students, the creation of special army units in the north to include demobilized rebels, and the integration of remaining fighters into the army. The government also promised a more proactive employment policy in the region and agreed to transfer to the territorial collectivities parts of the proceeds from mining in the area.

That the conflict subsided in the following years suggests that the government met the Tuareg's reservation price, that is, public employment, opportunities for local legal command, and transfer of resources. The remaining violence was in fact associated with the slow pace of the implementation of the accords. Still, Tuareg began populating local positions of authority (the first Tuareg prefect of Agades was appointed in 1996).[41] In 1997, a rebel leader, Rissa Ag Boula, was appointed minister. By 1999, 1,600 Tuareg fighters had been integrated into the army.[42]

In both Mali and Niger, it is misleading to think of the rebellions as self-determination movements. Secessionist desires are muted. Rebels, who are marginalized youth in an already marginalized region, want resources and the tools to generate them. These tools are those of legal command, in order to extract revenues within their own region and from their own people, as well as from foreign donors who represent a steadier source of funds than the government. Sovereign extraction necessitates the creation of local sovereign institutions, however, and thus maintenance of the state, which deflates whatever secessionist hope some of them may have once entertained.

The Tuareg case also illustrates that the logic of sovereign domination and predation is not necessarily one of accumulation, but often operates at a very basic level of survival. The Tuareg rebels do not rise from these insurgencies as formidable local hegemons. They merely trade complete misery and destitution for relative poverty. Apart from the occasional minister, most of them gain very minor positions in local councils, or as poorly equipped and only occasionally paid soldiers and civil servants. This might be the politics of the belly, but these bellies remain skinny. Yet, they have found some means of survival; they have instrumentalized sovereignty to improve their lot at the expense of others in their region.

New Sudan Is Still Sudan

The logic of the war that the Southern Sudanese have waged against their government since the 1950s is a lot more complex and multilayered than the Casamance and Tuareg insurgencies. For sure, it contains more genuinely separatist elements and rationales beyond the pursuit of sovereign prebends by southern elites. Profound differences centered on race, religion, history, and resources separate the north from the south and create overlapping cleavages that may have pushed southerners beyond a threshold of defiance to the state. If nothing else, the lasting nature of the conflict—from 1955 to 1973, then again from 1983 to 2005—suggests the depth of the grievances.

Yet, important as they are, these elements do not erase the presence of a sovereign prebendal logic and the extent to which some southern elites have also fought for and negotiated the acquisition of local sovereign institutions and rents. Part of the logic of the conflict seems to be about some southern elites' attempts to turn Sudan into a normal African postcolonial state and participate in it. Sudan is rather unique, indeed, among African postcolonial states. The self-identification of the Khartoum regime as Arab and Islamic and its subsequent attempts at Arabicizing and Islamicizing the rest of the country have led the state to be hijacked and ideologized, giving it a non-negotiable identity that supersedes juridical statehood. Ahmad Sikainga calls the Khartoum government's definition of citizenship based on an Arab-Islamic framework "one of the most conspicuous features of the post-colonial Sudanese state," implemented through "the relentless efforts of the northern elite to impose their model on the non-Arab and non-Muslim groups in the country."[43] As a result, it has been hard for southern elites—typically black and Christian—to plausibly act as local agents of the state. With legal command unavailable, they have rebelled, first and foremost to demand separation but also to change the nature of Sudan into a more conventionally neutral African state—"New Sudan"—and obtain sovereign autonomy in the south. Yet, New Sudan is still part of Sudan. Its existence necessitates that of Sudan whose sovereignty it shares.

The history of Sudan, from precolonial times, has not been charitable to the south and its populations. Khartoum was first colonized by the Egyptians (who were then a province of the Ottoman Empire) in the 1830s; Southern Sudan was also under their authority, although its integration was broadly limited to the supply of slaves. The 1885 Mahdist insurgency kicked out the

Egyptians, only to be followed twelve years later by the more robust British colonial invasion.[44] When establishing the colony of Sudan, the British reached out to a greater territorial domain than had ever been under Khartoum's authority, resulting in a heterogeneous colony with ambiguous political relations among its constituent members.[45] The southern part of the country was administered separately by the British until 1947, at which point it was amalgamated with the rest of the colony. Even after the territories were merged, the British implemented a "Southern Policy" that promoted English and Christianity in the region, increasing its distinctiveness from the northern rulers.[46] Yet, when Sudan became independent in 1956, it was in its post-1947 configuration with northerners firmly in the driver's seat.

Northern elites who are Muslim and conceive of themselves as Arab quickly seized control of the state and endeavored to change the country in their image. Southerners were deprived of access to state office, even at the local level. By the time of independence already, only 4 of 500 senior administrative posts were staffed by southerners.[47] Arabic language was imposed in the administration and, by the 1960s, the rulers began advocating for an Islamic state.[48] The government opposed southern autonomy, fearing that it would interfere with efforts to Islamicize the country.

The first southern rebellion, known as Anya-Nya, began almost simultaneously with independence in response to these exclusionary policies and spread across the south after 1963. After nine years of conflict, the Addis Ababa Agreement of 1972 between government and rebels underlined the willingness of the rebels to consider a nonseparatist solution to their predicament. The southerners tried to solve their security dilemma by fighting for a change in the nature of Sudanese statehood. They demanded integration in the state and regional autonomy instead of independence. The agreement gave the south local taxation powers and set up local sovereign institutions such as a High Executive Council and a southern regional assembly.[49] In addition, it provided for the integration of rebels into the national army (albeit deploying them locally).

This arrangement broke down when the north once again attempted to redefine statehood in a manner that made no place for southern elites and deprived them of access to sovereignty. From the late 1970s onward, a process of Islamic radicalization took place in Khartoum, which led to the dissolution of the southern region and the application of sharia law to the south in 1983. In addition, the Khartoum government began granting oil concessions in the south to Chevron and Total in the late 1970s, without including southern leaders in the negotiations. The south, under the Addis Ababa Agreement, was to be allowed taxation rights over activity in the region, but northern policymakers worked to sideline them from authority over oil extraction and production. Attempts were also made to redraw provincial boundaries to incorporate oil-bearing areas into the north.[50] In 1980, Sudanese president Gaafar Mohamed

Nimeiri dismissed the southern president of the High Executive Council because of his autonomist positions.[51]

Frustrated, the southerners returned to war in 1983. The rebellion's leader was John Garang, a US-educated Dinka military officer, who merged several factions into the Sudan People's Liberation Army. Although much of the rank and file and a good part of the SPLA leadership were at heart secessionists, the SPLA never officially embraced secession. This was partly for tactical reasons, as SPLA leaders were aware of the difficulties of garnering diplomatic and military support for such endeavors. Yet, this approach was also consistent with the objectives of John Garang and some other leaders to seek regional autonomy in order to escape the northern domination and rule their own region. Thus, the southern rebels at least in part fought to restore or establish inclusiveness, to normalize the Sudanese state and convert it into a "normal" African postcolonial state where all groups have the same opportunities in principle of local access to sovereignty.

The SPLA developed a rhetoric that called for a "New Sudan" where citizens would not be discriminated against based on religion or race, and all regions would be able to participate in government. The movement also called for self-determination for all groups, but Garang himself remained explicit in his rejection of secession. He remained focused on a united Sudan and protested attempts by the government to classify the SPLA grievances as southern rather than national problems. In a 1989 statement, Garang sought "to assure the Sudanese people that the Movement is totally against separation."[52] By emphasizing New Sudan, Garang suggested that if the northern opposition (and eventually the northern government) worked with the SPLA, he could deliver southern support for a unified country. This is not to deny that there was a significant secessionist component to the SPLA ideology. In fact, Francis Deng suggests the movement had "a multifaceted policy that does not exclude and probably even prefers separation as the ultimate goal."[53] Yet, the movement used the term *self-determination* ambiguously and was willing to work within the national context.[54]

SPLA demands and actions illustrate its desire for inclusion, sovereign institutions, and resources. Its original 1983 manifesto called for an end to Khartoum's interference in selecting southern leaders; lamented the "unconstitutional" dissolution of the southern regional assembly and executive; denounced attempts to redraw the border between the north and the south; contested the planned piping and refining of southern oil outside the region; generally accused the government of neglecting the south's economic development; and complained of its insufficient efforts to integrate and provide for the Anya-Nya fighters in the national army. The SPLA further laid out its objectives in the Koka Dam Declaration of 1986, in which it asked the government "to discuss the basic problems of Sudan and not the so-called problem of Southern Sudan."[55] Finally, as discussed earlier, the very behavior of the

SPLA in "liberated" territories did not indicate any significant state-building intention. More often than not, the provision of public services was left to non-governmental organizations and foreign donors. Zachariah Mampilly, who has compared rebel governance in Southern Sudan, Eastern Congo, and Sri Lanka, acknowledges the limited institutional achievements of the SPLA in contrast to the Tamil Tigers' embryonic state.[56] On paper, the SPLA had elaborate structures, including governors, county secretaries, town mayors, tax and criminal codes, a school curriculum, an AIDS policy, and "commissions and commissioners for everything."[57] In practice, however, UN humanitarian assistance was responsible for providing food and medicine to millions of southerners. The SPLA funneled most humanitarian aid through its own structures, allowing it to claim that it had begun to build up a civilian administration, yet, as Ken Crossley explains, "though perhaps impressive on paper, the SPLM/A on the ground has a bureaucracy that implements few to no relevant programs or services. Officials formulate policies and demand recognition but, for all intents and purposes, govern nothing and have nothing with which to govern."[58] In the end, instead of building institutions, the SPLA demanded them.

The Comprehensive Peace Agreement (CPA) of 2005 may have changed the terms of the SPLA's calculus, as it offered the possibility of separate sovereignty for the south. The CPA's main emphasis remained on a united Sudan, with a focus on power-sharing, military integration, the de-Islamicization of the south, the establishment of autonomous southern institutions, and the fair sharing of oil revenues. Yet, it also provided for a referendum on secession in 2011.[59] On the one hand, this provision highlights the more genuine separatist nature of the SPLA insurgency compared to Casamance or the Tuareg. On the other, the referendum remains consistent with a broad strategy of national integration, for it provides the southern leaders with a credible threat to back up their New Sudan demands. If Khartoum reneges on its commitments under the CPA, then southern elites can be expected to lobby for secession on the referendum. If they receive a fair share of the state, they might campaign against secession in 2011. The fact that Garang was in favor of national unity probably facilitated the government's agreement to the idea of the referendum.[60]

Patterns

Two patterns emerge from the comparison of the above three cases. First, some separatist movements are vectors for the formation or replacement of regional elites. Aspiring regional leaders organize separatist rebellions to challenge the state and obtain recognition as a local counterpart or interlocutor, in competition with existing local authority. What appears like a challenge against the state is also a challenge against the local dominant group. Thus separatist goals are rapidly converted into demands for state institutions and resources, all of which serve to strengthen the new elites vis-à-vis previous dominant authorities. This dynamic can take place within a group, between groups, or both.

Second, although they have chiefs, the Diola of Casamance, Tuareg of Mali and Niger, and the Dinka and Nuer of Southern Sudan are lineage or clan societies. Thus, the three cases relate to groups where political authority exists at a relatively disaggregated level. The propensity of such groups to engage in separatist activities might reflect instances of what Bayart has labeled "social revolutions," the displacement of traditional elites by more modernized social cadets. Such revolutions are more likely to happen, Bayart notes, in lineage societies where "conceptualisation of the dominant group considered likely to reproduce itself in the modern state [has] been problematic."[61] Separatist insurgencies might provide local cadets with the opportunities to undermine their elders and become the local dominant class and counterpart to the state.

Selfless-Determination:
In Search of Postcolonial Identity

Some of Africa's secessionist movements make a historical claim to a separate colonial existence from the state to which they now belong. To some extent, these movements attempt to use the norm of recognition of postcolonial sovereignty in their favor. While international law is generally opposed to the recognition of new states through secession, it considers decolonization an acceptable form of self-determination.[62] Both the UN and the OAU enshrined this principle, with the explicit stipulation that colonies have a right to sovereign independence within their intangible colonial boundaries only.[63] This principle provides the essence of African juridical statehood. Jackson calls it the "victory of categorical self-determination," with which the "self" became "ex-colonial 'jurisdictions'" in an act of decolonization as "enclosure."[64] It has also promoted the perception that an ambiguous colonial status raises the odds of recognition for some regions, encouraging local elites to make a claim for separate sovereignty. Eritrea illustrates this type of secession. In its war against the Ethiopian government, the Eritrean People's Liberation Front (EPLF) articulated Eritrea's separate status under Italian colonial rule. The historical validity of this argument eventually guaranteed their success and recognition by the international community.

Although Eritrea stands alone as a successful case of secession in Africa, several other movements have used claims of distinct colonial existence to legitimate separatist claims. In Somalia, the northern secessionist territory that emerged in 1991 as the Somaliland Republic traces its claim to sovereignty to the fact that it was once a British colony whereas the south was administered by Italy. The Front for the Liberation of the Enclave of Cabinda has noted that the Portuguese administered Cabinda separately from the rest of Angola until it was formally incorporated in 1956. To some extent, Western Sahara's war against Morocco derives from the same principle, since it was a colony of Spain. Its history accounts for the support of a majority of OAU governments for the Sahrawi.

Although their cases are weaker, Southern Sudan, the Casamance, and Congo's Katanga Province have at times made similar claims. It is indeed part of the SPLA's argument that the three southern provinces of Sudan were administered by the British separately from the rest of the country, and that the options of annexation by another East African colony or of outright independence were considered by the British.[65] Recall also that the MFDC argued unsuccessfully that historical differences in colonial administration justified their claim for separate independence from Senegal.[66] And, although it was largely an affair of traditional Lunda chiefs and Belgian settlers, the Katanga secession of 1960–1963 also partly relied on the claim that the province had been integrated late to Congo and for the most part separately administered by Belgium.[67]

In all these cases, regional political elites embark upon separatist strategies based on the claim that their region should legally qualify for postcolonial sovereignty. Note that this is a distinct undertaking from local state-building. These elites do not build states from the bottom up. Rather, they identify—correctly or not—an opportunity to acquire juridical sovereignty and make a claim for it. They seek to appropriate for themselves what they perceive to be a latent unit of international sovereignty. This approach differs from endogenous state-building by its extraversion, its soliciting of existence from the international system.

The success of Eritrea's struggle in 1991 sent the signal to other movements that claims of colonial specificity do indeed raise the odds of recognition. Somaliland has yet to be formally recognized by any government, but has received increasing signs of sympathy from other regimes and benefits from elements of partial recognition from some countries, particularly Ethiopia. Cabinda has had less success, largely because of the more ambiguous validity of its claims and because the oil it harbors has stifled the willingness of Angolans and Westerners to consider its arguments. In the case of Western Sahara, however, recognition by many African governments and the willingness of the UN to organize a referendum on independence would not have been achieved without a postcolonial claim.

Resorting to the postcolonial claim may also have some significant internal political benefits. Writing about the Russian Federation, Dmitry Gorenburg argues that institutional remnants from the Soviet republics facilitated ethnic mobilization for autonomy as they made it more credible to the local populations.[68] Henry Hale's evidence that already autonomous Soviet regions were more likely to demand sovereignty supports this argument.[69] In Africa, postcolonial claims facilitate mobilization by offering local populations and competing elites the promise of a future neutral state, of a juridical shell that all will have an equal claim to inhabit. The universal appropriable nature of the promised state is essential to political mobilization. Hence the relative frequency of African insurgencies based on administrative territories and divisions rather than on ethnicity.[70] Past administrative structures are more apt at mobilizing supporters than bonds of ethnicity because they offer the prize of a more universally generous institutional outcome. The very pluralist nature of the postcolonial state facilitates mobilization. The next few pages offer more detailed accounts of how this logic contributed to separatism in Eritrea and Somaliland.

Eritrea

Eritrea was established as an Italian colony in 1889 and fell under British military administration in 1941. Over the subsequent years, the British, the UN, Italy, and Ethiopia were divided as to what to do with it. Options included keeping it under British administration, turning it into a UN trust territory, returning it to Italian rule, and merging it in federation with Ethiopia, which claimed historical control over some of its regions.[71] After much debate, the UN approved the creation of the Ethiopian-Eritrean Federation in 1952. Yet, the following decade saw the progressive dismantlement of the federal arrangement and the exclusion of Eritreans from the instruments of self-rule. By 1956, the Eritrean assembly and constitutions had been suspended. Amharic was imposed as the sole language of the state and schools, and Ethiopian civil servants and teachers were dispatched to Eritrea. The Eritrean flag was discarded in 1958, followed the next year by the imposition of the Ethiopian penal code. The Eritrean government was downgraded to an administrative unit in 1960.[72] Eventually, in 1962, Ethiopia altogether abolished the federal system and proclaimed Eritrea to be its fourteenth province. Over the next thirty years, several movements waged a relentless war of independence from Ethiopia, which cost the lives of more than 60,000 fighters and culminated with the rebels' capture of Asmara in 1991 and the near unanimous approval of a referendum on independence in April 1993.

Why did the Eritreans, facing similar institutional demotion and alienation as Barotseland or Anglophone Cameroonians, turn to a full-fledged secessionist conflict rather than merely seeking control of the local appendages of Ethiopian sovereign statehood? And why did they pursue sovereignty along the lines of the former Italian colony rather than on the basis of their religious communities or ethnic nationalities? To a large extent, the iron military discipline that characterized the insurgency, its successful construction of a nationalist ideology, and its ability to harness the resources of the Eritrean diaspora underwrote the considerable popular mobilization for secession. Yet, two other factors also help to answer these questions. First, the largely (though not exclusively) Amharic Christian nature of the Ethiopian empire made it occasionally difficult for Eritrean elites, particularly Muslim ones, to be local agents of the state and exercise local sovereign command. Second, once they turned to insurgency, Eritrean postcolonial multiethnic and multireligious statehood alone held the promise of a state that could be internationally recognized and appropriable by all. As a result, the insurgency gained wide support and became increasingly successful after it settled its pluralist nature and established its goal of postcolonial statehood.

Like most African countries, Eritrea is ethnically heterogeneous, with about nine significant ethnic groups, some of which straddle the borders with Ethiopia, Djibouti, and Sudan. It is also rather religiously polarized, with more or less half the country's three million people Sunni Muslim and the other half Orthodox Coptic Christian. The Highland provinces, which are mostly Christian and populated by Tigrinya (also present in Ethiopia), have historical connections with Ethiopia, whose rule they were under at times. The areas populated by Muslims have a greater proportion of Tigrai people and have been historically under the influence of outside Muslim rulers like the Ottoman and Egyptian empires.[73]

Ethiopia, in contrast, is a very ancient state, largely centered on an Amharic ethnic core and a political culture embedded in Orthodox Coptic Christianity. Upon taking over in 1952, Ethiopia attempted to swallow and assimilate Eritrea, and to "impose a single Ethiopian identity." Only three senior federation officials were Muslim, as against ninety-six Amharic ones.[74] At the same time, religious affiliation was paramount "as a principle of social order that defined individual and group access to economic and political resources."[75] Ethiopian rule over Eritrea must thus be understood as a period of hegemonic crowding out of many Eritrean elites, particularly Muslim ones who had almost no point of access to statehood. The fact that access to positions of statehood in Eritrea was conditioned by Ethiopian-ness precluded local strategies of access to sovereignty, at least for people who did not belong to Highland groups with a closer historical connection to Ethiopia, and made separation more attractive.

Under British administration and early on under the federation, there was acceptance of Ethiopian sovereignty by some Eritrean elites. A Unionist Party, largely composed of Christian Tigrinya, favored Ethiopian rule, even after the breakdown of federalism in 1962, based on their Christian bonds with the empire. This shared identity made highlanders credible local representatives of the Ethiopian state and gave them access to its institutions. Unity was thus a rational position for them. Among the Muslim intelligentsia, however, "alienation and disaffection" were more prevalent.[76] It is not surprising, then, that Eritrean separatism begins as a matter of Muslim communities and elites. The first group to oppose union with Ethiopia and demand independence, already under British rule, was the Muslim League. Similarly, the first group to engage in political violence in 1961, the Eritrean Liberation Front (ELF), was established by Muslim elites who countered Pan-Ethiopianism with Pan-Islamism.[77] For them, the nonappropriable nature of the Ethiopian state was an essential trigger.

From 1970 onward, particularly following the creation of the EPLF, Christians began to join the leadership of the secessionist movement, including Issayas Afeworki, who would later be president. To some extent, the willingness of some Muslim leaders to associate with Christians proceeded from the limited success of the Pan-Islamic approach and its foreign policy expression of Pan-Arabism, which undermined Eritrea's claim for independence with Western powers and African states alike. For the Christians, abandoning collaboration with Ethiopia might have had a double motivation. First, Ethiopia's rule over Eritrea was based in part on collaboration with traditional authorities, which stifled opportunities for new, younger, and modernized elites, particularly those returning, like Afeworki, from studies abroad.[78] More important, however, the increased dispatching of civil and military authorities from Addis Ababa to Eritrea fostered the alienation of all, Muslims and Christians.

For about a decade, the Muslim ELF and the pluralist EPLF coexisted and occasionally clashed with each other. By 1981, however, the EPLF had established itself as the main liberation movement. To this transformation of the rebellion into a more secular movement corresponded a change in ideological emphasis away from Pan-Arabism and toward the creation of a pluralist postcolonial Eritrea.[79] From the early 1980s onward, the EPLF increasingly appeared to stress the principle of postcolonial statehood as justification for independence. The movement argued that "Eritrea is not part of Ethiopia and we are not Ethiopians. We are an African country colonized by another." As a result, the EPLF claimed, their "case was a just struggle conducted against coercive incorporation and not a case of secession."[80]

To a large extent, such a focus was necessary as postcolonial Eritrea offered a neutral institutional environment over which both Christians and Muslims could agree. This change of emphasis also corresponded to better odds of recognition. By making their struggle one for decolonization, they placed it within the accepted parameters of self-determination. By stressing the Arab nature of the rebels, Ethiopia had succeeded for some time in presenting itself as the stalwart of postcolonial territorial integrity and the rebels as secessionists intent on Balkanizing the country. But as the regime in Ethiopia progressively crumbled under the assaults of multiple insurgencies and the Eritrean rebels provided a unified decolonization narrative of their struggle, more and more countries became sympathetic to their claim. It should still be noted, however, that Eritrean independence would not have been so readily recognized in 1993 had the Transitional Government of Ethiopia (TGE) not first acceded to it. There was a remarkable coincidence as the EPLF seized Asmara, the Eritrean capital, on 24 May 1991, while the TGE overthrew the Mengistu regime in Ethiopia on 28 May and immediately endorsed Eritrean self-determination. Together with the decolonization claim, this endorsement made it easier for outsiders to recognize Eritrean independence.

The Eritrean assumption of postcolonial sovereignty also carried substantial domestic benefits, as it highlighted the cultural pluralism of the postcolony in contrast to the earlier emphasis on religion.[81] While religious identity is liable to characterize the state in exclusionary terms, the acknowledgment and celebration of ethnic pluralism offer the prospect of a state that is appropriable by all. Postcolonial statehood, still based on juridical sovereignty despite thirty years of warfare, offered a guarantee of such pluralism. Thus it provided one of the foundations for the mobilization of Eritreans. It fostered expectations of access to the state, denied under Ethiopian rule.

There is no doubt, however, that the Eritrean separatist calculus was also facilitated by the country's large diaspora whose resources and ideologies affected the costs and benefits of unrecognized insurgency. Many of Eritrea's liberation movements were actually established by members of its diaspora, principally in Egypt and Sudan. The EPLF had a strong organizational presence among Eritreans in Europe and the United States. These individuals provided significant income to the insurgency (and continue to be taxed by independent Eritrea).[82] By providing income to the rebels, the Eritrean diaspora compensated them for the foregone income of sovereign participation and raised the relative returns of insurgency over compliance.

Somaliland

The northern outer layer of the Horn of Africa became the British Somaliland Protectorate in 1886, while its southern counterpart was colonized by the Italians and named Somalia. Both colonies, like parts of Eritrea, Ethiopia, Kenya, and all of Djibouti, were populated by Somalis, but they were not politically unified, falling under the authority of different clans. The Issaq clan dominates in Somaliland. In Somalia, the main clans are the Darod, Hawiye, and Reewin.

Cultural similarities and Somali nationalism were such, however, that the two colonies decided to unite as one country—the Republic of Somalia—after independence, with a view toward eventually swallowing up the Somali regions of Kenya, Ethiopia (Ogaden), and Djibouti. As usual with such territorial mergers, one region gained ascendancy while the other found itself at the losing end of national integration. In this case, the south dominated. "Right at the outset," as Hussein Adam puts it, "proportional balance was ignored. The south provided the capital city, the anthem, the flag and the constitution. The parliament elected a southern president who nominated a southern prime minister. His cabinet included four northern ministers out of fourteen."[83] The northern resentment generated by the southern power grab provoked the defeat of the 1961 referendum on the union in Somaliland. The Somali National League, the main political party in the north, boycotted the referendum.[84] The union was nevertheless approved nationally because of southern votes and likely fraud.[85]

Northern military officers were particularly disgruntled at their subaltern position in the unified hierarchy. Somaliland lieutenants attempted a coup in Hargeysa in December 1961 but failed. Northern politicians, meanwhile, were more likely to play the co-optation game. In 1964, Mohammed Ibrahim Egal formed the Somali National Congress with southern politicians in an attempt to unseat the ruling southern Somali Youth League (SYL). Having failed to do so, he joined the SYL after the 1964 elections. He campaigned for southerner Ali Shermarke in the 1967 presidential elections and was appointed prime minister by the latter after his election.

Shermarke was assassinated in 1969 and succeeded by southern Major General Mohammed Siad Barre. Egal was jailed and remained imprisoned almost without discontinuity until 1982. Adam describes Barre's rule over Somaliland as "semi-colonial oppression" in which the Issaq were singled out for persecution.[86] Barre ruled with a mix of pseudosocialist ideology and patronage among southern clans, from which the Issaq remained excluded.[87] Following the failed invasion of the Ogaden region of Ethiopia by Barre in 1977–1978, the Somali government encouraged many Ogadeni refugees to settle in the north and take over Issaq businesses. Barre also appointed southerners to positions of authority in the north.

In 1981, Issaq exiles in London set up the Somali National Movement (SNM) with the goal of overthrowing Siad Barre. The movement soon moved to Ethiopia, from which it operated until 1988, when it entered Somaliland.[88] Attacks by the SNM against government and army facilities in Somaliland were met with brutal repression by the Barre regime, including aerial bombings of cities, which resulted in an estimated 20,000 casualties and possibly one million refugees.[89] The memory of these lethal attacks has provided ferment for northern identity.

The Barre regime fell in January 1991. In May the SNM's central committee convened a meeting with traditional clan elders in Burao, which unilaterally declared the independence of the Republic of Somaliland.[90] A Council of Elders subsequently established a presidency and a bicameral legislative system, and elected Egal president in 1993. He was reelected by parliament in 1997, when a "Conference of Somaliland Communities" adopted a constitution that provided for the election of the president by free universal suffrage. The new constitution was approved in 2001 by 97 percent of voters in a referendum that was widely perceived as a plebiscite on the question of independence.[91] Article 1 of the constitution stated that "the country . . . gained its independence from the United Kingdom . . . on 26th of June 1960 . . . and . . . joined Somalia on the 1st of July 1960 . . . then regained its independence by the Declaration of the Conference on Somaliland Communities held in Burao [in] May 1991 and shall hereby . . . become a sovereign and independent country known as the 'Republic of Somaliland.'"[92]

Two-thirds of eligible voters participated in the referendum. Among the populations of eastern Somaliland, where members of the Harti subclan of the Darod predominate, there was much less enthusiasm for independence and many abstained from voting.[93] Egal died in 2002 and was replaced by Vice

President Dahir Rayale Kahin. Presidential and legislative elections were finally organized in 2003 and saw a victory of Rayale by a mere 80 votes out of nearly 500,000.

Why did the SNM choose the path of secession, instead of sticking to its original intent to take over power in Mogadishu and share in Somalia's recognized sovereignty? Why did its leaders not resume the politics of co-optation that had prevailed in the 1960s? To some extent, a falling-out between the three main insurgencies fighting Barre, after his removal in early 1991, prevented the establishment of a new social contract for a unified Somalia. In addition, Barre's policies of exclusion and repression of the Issaq, particularly extreme after 1988, created an insurmountable gap. From the earlier stages of his administration, the clan elders of Somaliland had been kept outside the networks of patronage centered in the south. Northerners were also largely excluded from business and public opportunities in their region, while the country was being "darodized."[94] Even after the fall of Barre, exclusion of the SNM from the new government in Mogadishu made it give up on its plans for Somali federalism.[95] Moreover, as with Eritrea, the presence of a significant Issaq diaspora abroad affected the rebels' cost-benefit structure. Not only was the SNM launched by Issaq expatriates in London, but throughout its struggle it has relied on funds from Issaq communities in the Gulf, Arab countries, East Africa, and the West.[96] The fact that Issaq had always constituted the largest segment of the Somali diaspora in Western Europe facilitated the launch of the secession.[97] It has also no doubt contributed to the survival of Somaliland since 1991 in the absence of many other significant resources.

While these elements certainly played an essential role, we can make additional sense of Somaliland's decision by focusing on its postcolonial nature and on the conditions in Somalia as of 1991. Three dimensions are particularly salient and affected the comparative benefits of compliance and secession for the Somalilanders. First, the utter collapse of Somalia through gang and militia warfare in the wake of Barre's overthrow presented a rather unique situation. Although Somalia retained sovereignty, there were few actual sovereign institutions to inhabit, and prevailing violence made any use of the state physically risky. Without a functioning core in Mogadishu, claims to represent the state in Somaliland were at best tenuous, largely precluding the possibility of association of Somaliland elites with the sovereign Somali state. Thus, SNM leaders shelved their earlier preference for federalism. To some extent, the existence of Somaliland, however abstract and historical, might have provided a more plausible institutional resource to local elites.

Second, by resurrecting the postcolony of Somaliland, the SNM elites were entertaining reasonable hopes of international recognition. The SNM's declaration of independence occurred in the same month as Eritrea's, which was immediately endorsed by Ethiopia. The appointment of Egal as president of Somaliland in 1993, an affirmation of its claim to sovereignty, took place the same year as the Eritrean referendum that ushered in its international recognition. In the transforming international environment of the early 1990s, Somaliland's declaration did not necessarily appear a lost cause. The postcolonial nature of Somaliland is crucial in this respect. To merit recognition and juridical statehood, it had to make a claim about its colonial origins. Its brief international recognition as a postcolonial sovereign country before joining Somalia in June 1960 provided legal fodder for this claim. Somaliland, the SNM argued, was not secessionist and its unilateral declaration of independence was in keeping with the principles of the UN and OAU, as it respected borders inherited from colonization.

With hindsight, this approach has been less than successful. As of 2009, not a single country has recognized Somaliland. Yet, it has not been a complete failure either. Somaliland elites have had opportunities over the years to demonstrate at home an increasing degree of international recognition. Its president has been on official visits to Ethiopia, Senegal, and Ghana. In 2006, President Rayale visited the UK as a guest of the British government. Relations are close with Ethiopia, where Egal had received state honors, and where Somaliland holds its foreign reserves.[98] Ethiopian Airlines has a connection to Hargeysa and the Ethiopian authorities accept Somaliland travel documents.[99] In 2005, the AU sent a fact-finding mission to Somaliland, whose government later applied for admission. Altogether, there is increasing international sympathy for Somaliland's claims, especially as the rest of Somalia continues to be mired in violence. Its postcolonial claim may still prove a fruitful path to sovereignty.

Finally, the postcolony might have presented Somaliland's Issaq with a neutral juridical arena, after decades of exclusion at the hands of southerners, capable of accommodating traditional and rebel elites, as well as other clans. Like in Eritrea, the choice of Somaliland as the platform for independence by the Issaq-dominated SNM sent a signal to all local elites and communities of the future inclusiveness of the state, its availability to entertain all claims of appropriation. Clan elders, particularly, sought a return to some form of sovereign recognition, which they had enjoyed under British rule but had lost under the repressive Barre regime. The exiled SNM leaders' need for domestic legitimacy encouraged them to associate elders with their project. It was thus a "conference of Somaliland communities" that restored the country's independence in 1991, illustrating the pluralist claim of the new state, and leading eventually to what I. M. Lewis refers to as clan elders' leadership in the new republic.[100]

Postcolonial statehood also suited Somaliland's clan diversity. With Somalia off limits, the Issaq might have encountered resistance from other northern populations—Dir clans and Darod subclans—had they decided to seek independence for themselves. The Issaq needed a polity that could provide a plausible foundation for a pluralist state. Expressing self-determination in a postcolonial setting made the participation of other groups possible. Although the Darod have so far maintained a rather defiant posture, the state's postcolonial pluralism was effectively illustrated by the election of President Rayale, a Dir, in 2002.

Patterns

By and large, the groups discussed in this section face greater potential returns to separatism because of their claim to postcolonial statehood by virtue of separate colonization. They demand their own juridical sovereignty. Unless the exclusionary politics of the main state are too severe to make compliance possible, as was the case between Eritrea and Ethiopia, this demand is usually part of a broader strategy for autonomy and the acquisition of local sovereign institutions, as illustrated by Somaliland's initial emphasis on federalism.

The claim to postcolonial statehood highlights the decolonization rather than secessionist nature of these self-determination movements and promotes greater conformity to international principles of recognition of new states. Thus, organizing rebellions along the lines of previous colonial boundaries maximizes the chances of recognition under the international sovereignty regime. The greater odds of recognition raise the relative returns of separatism over national integration.

The postcolonial claim also facilitates the domestic mobilization of diverse groups and interests because the juridical state is neutral. All subregional elites within the new territory will be able to make a claim to legal command in their region. Hence, the apparent paradox that, in a continent plagued by ethnic divisions, self-determination insurgencies are usually multiethnic and based on colonially defined territories. The neutrality of the postcolony contrasts with the frequently exclusive nature of the state to which these regions first belong. By making state-derived domination harder for local elites, exclusionary states lower the relative returns of compliance over separatism. In this respect, religious or dynastic control of the state makes a difference because of its monopolistic qualities.[101]

Sovereignty Variations

The Ethiopian Exception

As the previous section hinted, studying secessionism in Africa is unavoidably biased by Ethiopia's deviance from the continental norm. Ethiopia is by far the African country with the greatest propensity for separatism. Afar, Eritreans, Ogadenis, Oromos, and Tigrai have all at rather numerous times fought to break free from Ethiopia. Ironically, Ethiopia is also the only African country that successfully resisted colonization in the late nineteenth century. Emperor

Menelik II's troops crushed the Italians at the battle of Adowa in 1896, preserving Ethiopia's independence while the rest of the continent was being partitioned by Europe. The battle also allowed him to consolidate the allegiance of several previously wavering vassals, strengthening his state in the process.[102]

Paradoxically, Ethiopia's separatist deviance might have something to do with its successful resistance to colonization. It is the only contemporary African state not to be postcolonial. The first to recognize Ethiopia's "unqualified independence" were actually the Italians in 1896.[103] This was an act of *ex post* recognition of a victorious, empirical state by a European power, rather than the *ex ante* constitution of a juridical state. Ethiopia had not only beaten Italy in war, but had existed as Abyssinia for several centuries. Being endogenous rather than granted by the international system, its sovereignty was produced and remained largely "owned" by the Amharic and, to a lesser extent, Tigrinya core of the Abyssinian state until the 1990s.[104] Its origins might reduce the availability of Ethiopian sovereignty for domestic distribution. The exclusionary character of the Ethiopian state, compounded by the kingdom's religious foundations, made it more difficult than elsewhere in Africa for peripheral elites to credibly partake in sovereignty and derive local authority from it.

Moreover, Ethiopia's own imperialism, largely concealed by its public role in the vanguard of Pan-Africanism, resulted in many of its secessionist challenges. After defeating the Italians, Menelik II waged a quasi-colonial expansion of his own, consolidating or grabbing control over areas not previously under his control. He acquired from the French some of their Somali possessions around today's Djibouti, and from the British, the part of Somaliland that is today's Ogaden region. He waged military campaigns against populations in the south and more than doubled the size of his empire. In Thomas Pakenham's words, "it was imperial expansion and *Realpolitik*, African-style, and it brought greater rewards than any European war in Africa."[105]

Imperial expansion may have brought Menelik II great rewards, but it also brought his successors grave problems. For Ethiopia proved too weak over time to successfully integrate these regions and resist their aspirations for independence. As the rest of Africa decolonized, many of the recently acquired Ethiopian subjects began to feel the same urge for freedom, particularly those of regions like Ogaden, which shared very little history and culture with the core Ethiopian state. Their alienation was compounded by the monopolistic nature of the Ethiopian state whose administration was centralized. Amharic was imposed across the country as the language of the state, and Amhara formed the bulk of the bureaucracy and government. Even provincial governors tended to be Amhara.[106]

The fall of the Mengistu regime in 1991, at the hands of the Ethiopian Peoples' Revolutionary Democratic Front (EPRDF), led to a significant evolution in the nature of Ethiopia, as Amharic rule was replaced by a multiethnic coalition under Tigrinya (Tigre) leadership. The Tigre People's Liberation Front (TPLF), which had been fighting the Ethiopian government since 1975, was at the core of the EPRDF. The Tigre differ from other Ethiopian minorities by their historical role as the junior imperial partner to the Amhara. Some emperors, like Yohannes IV in the 1880s, had been Tigre. For the Tigre and the TPLF, ending Amharic dominance of the state was therefore more important than challenging Ethiopia per se.[107]

Upon seizing power, the TPLF genuinely tried to reform the state to accommodate minorities. It revoked the Amharization policies of its predecessors and embarked on a highly unusual experiment in ethnic federalism, granting minorities local autonomy.[108] The TPLF at first enjoyed the collaboration of most other minorities. Insurgencies abated. The 1995 federal constitution marked the high point of the new accommodationist outlook. It recognized minority rights and created ethnically defined federated regions for the Afar, Amhara, Oromo, Somali, and Tigre. The new Ethiopian state distributed its exclusionary sovereignty to peripheral groups and their elites as titular groups were given "proprietary rights" over their territory in each region.[109] Moreover, "nations, nationalities, and peoples" received the constitutional right to secede.

In practice, however, the new system showed its limitations. First, while minorities were formally given a large degree of autonomy, the government established proregime official organizations deemed to represent them, de facto limiting the rewards of the system to a coterie of collaborators. Second, the secession option was accompanied by so many constitutional hurdles that it remained largely theoretical.[110] Given these limitations, it was not surprising that Ogadenis and Oromos returned to armed insurgency after 1996.

Merged into Ethiopia at a late date through colonial bargaining, the Ogadenis have consistently resisted their integration. They share very little in common with the rest of Ethiopia.[111] They are Somali and most of their clans straddle the border with Somalia. On both parts of this border, irredentist Somali nationalism has been alive since the 1950s, when the Ethiopian government began its effective occupation of the region.[112] The Western Somali Liberation Front was formed in 1960 to promote the reattachment of Ogaden to Somalia. Armed resistance escalated in the 1970s under the Ogaden National Liberation Front (ONLF). In 1977, an invasion by Somali government forces was repelled.

Under the 1995 constitution, Ogaden became the Somali Regional State. This arrangement at first improved relations with Addis Ababa. The ONLF won the first regional elections and took control of the local administration. Yet, an attempt by the ONLF to push its luck and organize a referendum on self-determination soured relations with Addis Ababa and led to the imprisonment and exile of many of its leaders.[113] The government replaced the ONLF with the more subservient Ethiopian Somali Democratic League (ESDL), which took over local administration. Defectors from the ONLF later joined the ESDL to form the Somali People's Democratic Party (SPDP) and went on to win the 2000 and 2004 local elections.[114] The rest of the ONLF returned to guerrilla tactics, demanding an independent "Ogadenia," control of the Somali region within Ethiopia, and eventual merger with Somalia if it reunifies.[115]

The Oromos of southern Ethiopia were conquered by Menelik II after his defeat of the Italians. They are now Ethiopia's largest group, with some 32 percent of the population. Their relatively central geographical situation (compared to Eritrea and Ogaden) and their own lack of homogeneity have made separatism a more ambiguous goal for this group.[116] Nevertheless, Addis Ababa's policy of Amharization contributed to the formation of the Oromo Liberation Front (OLF) in 1973 to "lead the national liberation struggle of the Oromo people against the Abyssinian colonial rule."[117] Since 1976, the OLF has waged a low-intensity secessionist insurgency with apparently limited popular backing.[118]

As in Ogaden, the TPLF takeover of 1991 brought about a lull in the Oromo conflict. Instruction and administration in the Oromo language were again authorized, and Oromia was granted status as an autonomous region. Yet, here too, actual improvements in the Oromos' political lot soon proved limited. According to Alemseged Abbay, it has been "almost exclusively the co-opted and/or invented leaders who have access to political resources, not only in Oromia but at the federal level as well."[119] Violent secessionist activity resumed after 1996, although it still appears to gather minimal popular support. Ed Keller notes that "many Oromos are torn between wanting to exercise their right to self-determination and separating Oromia from the Ethiopian state, or sticking with it, but demanding their equal-citizenship rights."[120]

Time Variations in the Supply of Sovereignty

There are rare times when the possibility of gaining sovereignty for nonpreviously recognized entities seems greater than usual. In other words, while the supply of sovereignty is generally fixed, it goes through historical moments of greater liberalism when possibilities for recognition appear to increase. Ceteris paribus, peripheral groups are likely to try to benefit from these normative changes and seek secession rather than collaboration with the state.

These variations in the supply of sovereignty may be region-specific or worldwide. For Africa, the first such moment took place at independence, when the principle of postcolonial self-determination was not yet fully established or tested. For many regional elites, seeking independence on their own rather than partaking in existing states still appeared like a credible option in the first half of the 1960s. The second, more universal moment happened in the early 1990s, in the wake of the end of the Cold War, the breakdown of the Soviet Union, and the collapse of Yugoslavia, which saw the recognition of Slovenia and Croatia as new separatist states in 1991. Several regional African elites interpreted these events as the signal of a normative shift in the international sovereignty regime and adjusted their strategies accordingly, giving greater weight than before to separatist options. This was a short-lived moment, however, and the Balkans remained exceptions rather than precedents. Most African regional elites adjusted their strategies and the brief separatist surge abated. Figures 6.1 and 6.2 illustrate the two secessionist moments in Africa, respectively, for the whole continent and excluding Ethiopia. From 1971 to 1989, Ethiopia and Sudan account for all of Africa's separatist conflicts. Setting them aside, the figures clearly depict a bimodal distribution with bumps in the 1960s and in the 1990s, which broadly correspond to the two inflections in the international sovereignty regime.

In addition to Southern Sudan, which has already been discussed, the main separatist insurgencies of the 1960s took place in the Katanga and Kasai provinces of Congo, and in Nigeria's Biafra. To understand the Congolese cases, the very uncertain future of Congo as a nation-state in 1960 must be borne in mind. Ambiguous Western attitudes toward the Congolese government, army mutinies, and the stalemate opposing Prime Minister Patrice Lumumba and President Joseph Kasavubu buttressed Moise Tshombé's declaration of independence of Katanga. Tshombé bet on the possibility that the Congolese state might not survive and foresaw a better future in regional rather than in national politics. The assassination of Lumumba in 1961 altered the fate of the secession, as the West no longer objected to the government in Kinshasa. The UN intervention and the lack of foreign recognition of the breakaway state affirmed the principle of territorial integrity of Africa's post-colonies and doomed the Katanga experiment. It is not surprising then that

Figure 6.1   Time Trends in African Separatism

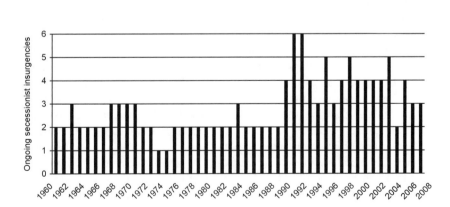

Source: Adjusted PRIO (2002, 2007) data.

Figure 6.2   Time Trends in African Separatism, Without Ethiopia

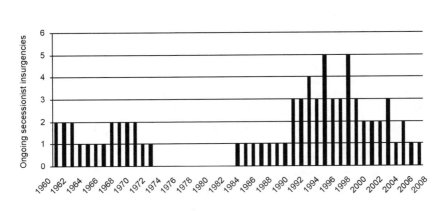

Source: Adjusted PRIO (2002, 2007) data.

Tshombé later became prime minister of Congo, having adjusted his strategy of access to power as a function of the locus of sovereignty.[121]

Kasai followed suit. After the massacre of Luba civilians by government troops in 1960, Albert Kalonji proclaimed the "Great Mining State of South Kasai" in 1961, and organized for autonomous rule. Kalonji, a Luba, was one of Lumumba's main rivals in the Mouvement National Congolais (Congolese National Movement, MNC) and was embittered by his failure to secure an influential position in the national government. He derived popular support from the fear of many Luba that the government would gain control of Kasai's diamond mines. More than Tshombé, Kalonji was a political opportunist who, in the words of Georges Nzongola-Ntalaja, "saw in the chaotic environment of the period the opportunity to realize his dream of becoming supreme leader somewhere," and had himself proclaimed king by local traditional rulers.[122] The autonomous state functioned until September 1962. As with Katanga, no country recognized the sovereignty of South Kasai, and Kalonji eventually turned his attentions to the national political stage, becoming agriculture minister in the 1964 Tshombé government.

There were some other, less salient, instances of separatist activism around the time of independence. In 1958, Tuareg notables from Mali and Niger wrote a letter to French president Charles de Gaulle calling for the creation of an independent Saharan state.[123] Once they realized this would not happen, in 1961, the Tuareg of Mali launched a rebellion, which was eventually repressed in 1964.[124] In Barotseland, Litunga Lewanika pushed for separate independence in 1961, before the amalgamation with Zambia.[125] In Uganda, the Buganda kingdom was also separatist in the early 1960s and the Rwenzururu kingdom was quite successful at establishing its own government

and administration away from Kampala's reach.[126] Through the 1960s, it collected local taxes, ran schools, raised an army, and developed a bureaucracy.
This experiment partly seems to find its origins in the refusal of the government
to give them their own district and the exclusion of the Bakonjo of Rwenzururu
from administrative positions and educational opportunities in the Toro district
to which they formally belonged. According to Nelson Kasfir, Rwenzururu's
new king, Isaiah Mukirane, "may have been ready to go it alone on the theory
that the rewards flowing from separate district status were apt to be multiplied
by United Nations membership with the possibilities of foreign aid."[127] Back in
Congo, there were also unsuccessful plots for the secession of Kivu and the creation of a Mongo state in the Equateur Province.[128]

In all these instances, perceived weaknesses in state sovereignty triggered
local strategies of power by regional elites, which were aborted when the respective sovereignty statuses of central and provincial authorities were clari-
fied. The then Western-dominated UN system conditioned these local dynamics with its capacity to grant sovereign status to territorial entities. Particularly,
the extent to which the UN eventually came out in favor of Congolese territorial integrity in the Katanga conflict sent a signal to all Africans and reduced
the appeal of separatist strategies. Still, Biafra fought a war of secession
against the Nigerian federal government as late as the period 1967–1970. Yet,
for the Igbo leaders of the secession, this was a second-best option. Their first
choice had been to take over power in Nigeria as a whole. It is only after the
Igbo officers' coup of January 1966 had been reverted by the countercoup of
northerner General Yakubu Gowon in July—followed by numerous massacres
of Igbos throughout the north—that the military governor of the Eastern region, Lieutenant-Colonel Emeka Ojukwu, proclaimed its independence as the
Republic of Biafra. By then, the possibility of Igbo elites taking over state
power or being plausible agents of Nigerian sovereignty in their region had all
but evaporated, and Nigeria had de facto become an exclusionary system to
them. After the war, the efforts of Nigerian elites to reintegrate the Igbos and
the multiplication of states in the Nigerian federation largely undid this exclusionary bias.

The period from the end of the Biafra secession to 1990 was characterized
by the virtual absence of separatism in Africa, with Sudan and Ethiopia the
lone exceptions. African regional elites could no longer entertain hopes for
more favorable rules of self-determination than elsewhere, and the benefits of
the sovereignty regime became more entrenched. In 1990, however, the end of
the Cold War, the partition of the Soviet Union, the ideological push by the
West for the spread of electoral democracy, and the new focus by donors on
nongovernmental organizations combined to affect, and in many cases undermine, the existing international legitimacy of African states. The perception of
changing international norms regarding territorial integrity, partly fed by the
recognition of Slovenia and Croatia in 1991, led to a renewal of autonomy-

seeking activities by regional political leaders around the world, Africa included. To some extent, the secession of Eritrea in 1991 and its recognition in 1993 greatly contributed to the impression of a relaxation of norms of sovereignty. The secession of Somaliland, which occurred in 1991 after Somalia had all but collapsed as a functional state (not unlike Yugoslavia), provides an illustration of the ensuing contagion. Senegal's Casamance conflict, although it had begun in 1982, took on renewed military vigor in 1990. In Mali and Niger, the Tuareg insurgencies reemerged in the early 1990s. Cameroonian Anglophone agitation also heightened at the time, simultaneously with its democracy movement, as did Barotseland's self-determination discourse, with the Litunga taking a trip to England to demand the restoration of the Barotseland Agreement.

There were also numerous other less salient autonomist initiatives across the continent in the 1990s. In Ghana, Uganda, and South Africa, there was a reaffirmation of subnational precolonial political systems (the Ashanti, Buganda, and Zulu kingdoms), which appeared for a while to undermine the postcolonial order.[129] But it is once again in Congo that politicians proved the readiest to embrace these new opportunities. After Etienne Tshisekedi of Kasai, a long-time Mobutu opponent, was appointed prime minister in 1992, amid chaos in Kinshasa, in replacement of Nguza Karl I Bond, a Lunda from Katanga, anti-Kasaian violence unfolded in Katanga (then named Shaba). Nguza stated that his province did not recognize the authority of the new prime minister, and the province's governor, Gabriel Kyungu Wa Kumwanza, recommended that people from Kasai living in Shaba be expelled. Refugees were gathered in concentration camps for repatriation to Kasai. Nguza vowed that there would be no national reconciliation under the auspices of the current government and refused to rule out the possibility of a secession, saying that the course of events depended upon how far the ongoing Sovereign National Conference, which had appointed Tshisekedi, pushed the people of Katanga. In the following months, this competition among national political elites via regional ethnic polarization took on an increasingly separatist content. Governor Kyungu decreed that all military officers of Luba origin had to leave Shaba and called for permanent and strict control of people's movements between Shaba and the two Kasai provinces. In addition, he stressed that the top jobs in companies based in the region, including the copper mining company, Gécamines, should be handed over to locals. Finally, in December 1993, Kyungu proclaimed his province's autonomy and announced the imposition of taxes at the borders. A few days later, Nguza's party, the Union des Fédéralistes et Républicains Indépendants (Union of Independent Federalists and Republicans, UFERI), stated its unconditional support for the autonomy of Katanga. These local leaders still recognized the constraints of the international sovereignty of Congo, however, and kept alive their options as national politicians by systematically referring to autonomy rather than independence.

Kasai Oriental followed Katanga in its drive for autonomy, although its main politician, Etienne Tshisekedi, never played the regional separatist card but maintained his aspirations for the prime ministership and presidency of the country. Kasai Oriental's autonomy from 1993 to 1996 reflected the actions of local Luba elites, mainly from the Catholic Church and the state diamond-mining company, the Compagnie Minière de Bakwanga (Bakwanga Mining Company, MIBA), who erected their own institutions in the wake of the apparent collapse of the central state. The role of the Shaban ethnic cleansing of 1992–1994 was important in getting Kasai started on its own drive for autonomy. With the influx of highly skilled Luba refugees, including engineers from the Katanga copper mines, Mbuji-Mayi began to boom and MIBA's operations were reinforced. Autonomous Kasai enjoyed relative prosperity, at least by the standards of the rest of Congo, and developed its own university and a Conference for the Economic Development of Eastern Kasai (CODEKO), which took over regional development planning. By refusing to recognize new banknotes introduced by the Kinshasa regime, Kasai also essentially adopted its own currency and exchange rate and altogether avoided inflation while the rest of the country experienced annual price rises above 8,000 percent.[130]

These episodes of provincial near self-determination illustrate the extent to which secessionist decisions are predicated upon the strategies of elites, which are conditioned by the international status of the state and the availability of legal command. In part because of the changing international climate, the post-1991 period saw tremendous political disruption in the national government of Congo. Kinshasa was all but paralyzed and opportunities for partaking in the state at the center abated together with perceptions of Western support for Congo. Although not quite as far-reaching as in the 1960s, this variation in the perceived sovereignty of Congo and in its domestic returns partly underwrote the autonomist strategies of Congolese regional elites.

These experiments in autonomy came to an end with the rise of Laurent-Désiré Kabila's Alliance des Forces Démocratiques pour la Libération du Congo and the Rwandan invasion of 1996. Preoccupied with a regime that supported its Hutu-based opposition, the Kigali government embarked on a military campaign that took it all the way to Kinshasa for Mobutu's overthrow. In doing so, it restored an internationally recognizable authority in Kinshasa and ironically (given its own border-crossing origins) provided a new boost to Congo's fledgling sovereignty. By supporting Kabila as representative of Congo's sovereignty, the international community contributed to putting an end to local movements of self-determination. Local politicians rejoined the fold of national politics (especially in Kabila's native Katanga) and local experiences in state substitution folded in the face of renewed state authority and command.

Table 6.1 illustrates Africa's see-saw pattern between national allegiance and separatism as a function of the strength and perceived benefits of sovereignty in comparison to the rest of the world. Because Ethiopia is an outlier

Table 6.1 Proportion of Country-Years with Secessions, Africa and the Rest of the World

	Africa (*n*)	Others (*n*)	Probability (%)
With Ethiopia			
1960s	0.08 (315)	0.07 (960)	88
1970s and 1980s	0.05 (878)	0.10 (2,263)	0
1990s	0.09 (477)	0.12 (1,361)	24
2000–2006	0.07 (336)	0.09 (973)	49
Without Ethiopia			
1960s	0.05 (305)	0.07 (960)	48
1970s and 1980s	0.01 (858)	0.10 (2,263)	0
1990s	0.07 (467)	0.12 (1,361)	4
2000–2006	0.03 (329)	0.09 (973)	3

Source: PRIO (2002, 2007). Somaliland and Sudan's SPLM are coded as territorial insurgencies (in contrast to their coding in PRIO 2007); some other PRIO entries are omitted for specific years either because they were territorial but not separatist insurgencies or because the group's agenda deviated from separatism.

Note: "Probability" refers to the probability that the difference between the two means is due to chance. It is based on two-sample two-tailed *t* tests with equal or unequal variances. When a probability is less than 10 percent, the difference is considered statistically significant; (*n*) is the number of observations (country-years) in each sample.

when it comes to both juridical sovereignty and secessions, the table compares Africa to the rest of the world with and without Ethiopia. In both cases, there is no statistically significant difference in the propensity for separatism in the 1960s. Thus, before the establishment of the juridical sovereignty regime, African regional elites demonstrate a similar willingness to resort to secession as regional elites elsewhere. The picture changes dramatically in the following two decades, when Africa, including Ethiopia, experiences about half the rate of secessions as elsewhere in the world, and one-tenth of it when Ethiopia is excluded. This is worth restating. From 1970 to 1989, the incidence of secessions in postcolonial Africa is only 10 percent of that in the rest of the world. While the incidence of separatism rises across the world, it falls precipitously in Africa. This pattern supports the claim that the benefits of partaking in the juridical sovereignty regime reduced the incentives of African regional elites to pursue separatist strategies of power, in contrast to most other regions of the world. Following the end of the Cold War, the data converge again. With Ethiopia included, there no longer is a significant difference between Africa and the rest of the world after 1990. Both regions experience a separatist surge in the early 1990s, which fades away as norms of state stability and territorial integrity are broadly restored. However, excluding Ethiopia, Africa's separatist surge remains significantly short of what it is elsewhere, and its secessionist deficit persists. Moreover, after the 1990s, there is again a sharp drop in African separatism, while the post-1990s decline is less pronounced in other regions. These trends suggest that the appeal of sovereignty in Africa continues to stifle separatism there compared to the rest of the world. By the end of 2001, the events of 9/11 in the United States finish the decade of deflated sovereignty and bring back, with a vengeance, an emphasis on "nation-building," which largely translates into support for state stability and territorial integrity. Because Africa has many weak states and is perceived more than other regions as a potential breeding ground for anti-Western nonstate actors, it has possibly seen a greater relative restoration of its sovereign structure than elsewhere.

Patterns

Two patterns that emerge from the cases in this chapter allow us to refine and deepen the theoretical argument. The first one deals with the importance of the "plural softness" of the African state derived from its juridical and exogenous sovereignty. The second reveals the extent to which acquiescence with the state is a variable that depends on the relative returns of legal command compared to other opportunities for advancement.

Chapter 2 mentioned Benyamin Neuberger's argument about the "plural softness" of the African state, its unwillingness or incapacity to fully enforce itself upon its minorities.[131] African states do not commonly have titular groups. Although the elites of some specific groups do at times appropriate the state, the latter is not defined in ethnic terms and other groups have equal grounds to claim sovereign power, especially at the local level. Tools of legal command are broadly available across minorities and equally unassailable by all groups as exogenous to all of them.

To a large extent, this plural softness derives from the exogenous and juridical nature of the African postcolonial state. By locating the ultimate source of state power outside the state and its populations, juridical sovereignty maximizes both opportunities for legal sovereign domination and the distribution of these opportunities across communities and their elites within countries. It "de-ethnicizes" the sources of power and promotes the universality of its rewards. The examples from Chapter 5 illustrated the resulting compliance. The regional elites of Cameroon, Congo, Nigeria, and Zambia surrendered claims of self-determination in part because they were able to make credible local claims of access to legal command.

The cases of Ethiopia, Sudan, and Somalia, however, suggest that ownership of the state by a specific group negates this plural quality. It reduces the odds of partaking in sovereign power for other minorities, making the distribution of sovereign command less universal, and increasing the relative returns of exit for these minorities. Ownership of the state can derive from specific historical conditions, as in the case of Ethiopia, which differs from the continental norm and more closely approximates empirical statehood. It can also result from the adoption of exclusionary ideologies by ruling elites, as in

Sudan. The impossibility of black Christian southerners to be the agents of a state intent on being Arab and Islamic partly accounted for their separatism. Linguistic discrimination, as existed in Oromia and Anglophone Cameroon, is another variant of this exclusion and reveals *a contrario* the importance of colonial languages in the feasibility of sovereign legal command. Like the juridical state, colonial language is exogenous and universal.

The cases in this chapter have shown that deviations from the African norm of plural softness are associated with separatist challenges. Although separatism appears to indicate a breakdown of the state, it also reflects genuine attempts at state formation and resistance to them. Whereas the pluralism of the juridical state allows it to reproduce as a weak exogenous state, the politics of the few African exclusionary states are thus more akin to the violent dynamics generally associated with state formation.[132]

The second pattern highlights the extent to which sovereignty-induced acquiescence to the state in Africa is a variable rather than a constant. The dominant role of sovereignty in accounting for state reproduction does not imply that there are not circumstances where alternative resources or alternative sources of command can lead to nonsovereign initiatives. The financing role of diaspora, for example, was an important facilitator of nonsovereign politics for Eritreans and Somalilanders, as it allowed their elites to function without access to the resources of legal command. Direct access to oil played a similar role in the Niger Delta. Likewise, the time variations in the supply and benefits of sovereignty discussed in this chapter point to the fact that legal command does not always trump other sources of authority. While this chapter focused on how the occasional deflation of international sovereignty undermined legal command and altered the calculus of compliance of regional elites, there are also occasions where legal command is steady but faces competition from other sources of authority. These might include religion, cultural traditions, or guns. The challenge to the state brought about by the autonomous Bungu dia Kongo sect in Congo provides an example of religion-derived authority. Tradition-derived authority no doubt contributed to the defiance of Rwenzururu and Buganda in Uganda in the 1960s. More recently, the "taxation" of people by the rebel forces of Laurent Nkunda in eastern Congo relied on their control of the means of violence rather than on any legal claim.[133] Generally, these alternative sources of command do not match the potential returns of sovereignty. Yet, understanding these variations in the origins of resources and command allow us to better explain variations in compliance with the state.

Notes

1. Boone, *Political Topographies,* 20.
2. Bayart, *The State in Africa,* 134–138.

3. Some of the material here was previously published as Englebert, "Compliance and Defiance."

4. Charpy, *Historical Testimony on Casamance*; Beck, "Sovereignty in Africa."

5. See Beck, "Sovereignty in Africa"; Diouf, *Sénégal*; Foucher, "Les 'évolués'"; Gasser, "'Manger ou s'en aller'"; Marut, "Le Problème."

6. Sidy Badji died in 2003 and Diamacoune in 2007. Following their deaths, the MFDC remained divided and some smaller factions continued to engage in local skirmishes and violent crime.

7. MFDC, "Plate-Forme Revendicative."

8. Because of its physical proximity to Gambia, the "Northern Front" was able to accept an arrangement in 1991 that did not involve the delegation of sovereign authority but allowed for nonsovereign economic opportunities.

9. Foucher, "Senegal: The Resilient Weakness," 184.

10. Boone, *Political Topographies*, 101; see also Pélissier, *Les paysans du Sénégal*; Darbon, *L'administration*.

11. Interview with Landing Badji, Casamançais lawyer, Dakar, July 2002.

12. Boone, *Political Topographies*, 117.

13. Foucher, "Les 'évolués.'"

14. I owe all MFDC biographical information to the knowledge and generosity of Vincent Foucher.

15. Foucher, "Senegal: The Resilient Weakness," 174–175.

16. Gasser, "'Manger ou s'en aller'"; Humphreys and Mohamed, "Senegal and Mali."

17. Foucher, "Les 'évolués,'" 308.

18. Humphreys and Mohamed, "Senegal and Mali."

19. Foucher, "Pas d'alternance"; Foucher, "Senegal: The Resilient Weakness," 182.

20. Bourgeot, "Révoltes et rébellions."

21. Ibid., 94.

22. Humphreys and Mohamed, "Senegal and Mali," 274. Given their privileged status, it is not surprising that the chiefs remained on the side of the state throughout the conflict.

23. Ibid., 274.

24. Iyad Ag Ghali, quoted by Imperato, *Historical Dictionary of Mali*, xlv.

25. *Africa Contemporary Record*, Vol. 23 (New York: Holmes and Meier, 1998), B84.

26. Lode, "Civil Society Takes Responsibility."

27. *Africa Contemporary Record*, Vol. 25 (New York: Holmes and Meier, 2001), B103.

28. Quoted in Humphreys and Mohamed, "Senegal and Mali," 41; see also Norris, "Mali-Niger: Fragile Stability."

29. "Pacte National conclu entre le gouvernement de la République du Mali et les mouvements et fronts unifiés de l'Azawad consacrant le statut particulier du nord du Mali," obtained from www.kidal.com/docs.

30. Seely, "A Political Analysis."

31. Ibid., 500.

32. Drisdelle, *Mali*, 29.

33. *Africa Research Bulletin*, May 2006, 43(5):16656–16657.

34. Ibrahim, "The Weakness of 'Strong States,'" 64.

35. *Africa Contemporary Record*, Vol. 23 (New York: Holmes and Meier, 1998), B107; Vol. 25 (New York: Holmes and Meier, 2001), B138.

36. Bourgeot, "Révoltes et rébellions," 13.

37. Salifou, *La question,* 109–110.

38. Bourgeot, "Révoltes et rébellions," 14.

39. Document reproduced in Decoudras and Abba, *La rébellion,* 31–42.

40. "Accord de paix entre le Gouvernement de la République du Niger et la Co-ordination de la Résistance Armée (CRA)," Ouagadougou, 9 October 1994.

41. Regis Guyotat, "Niger: La paix des dunes." *Le Monde,* 7 December 1996.

42. *Africa Contemporary Record,* Vol. 27 (New York: Holmes and Meier, 2003), B163.

43. Sikainga, "Sudan: The Authoritarian State,"191.

44. On this period, see Pakenham, *The Scramble for Africa,* chapter 13.

45. Prunier and Gisselquist, "The Sudan," 109–112.

46. Young, *The Politics of Cultural Pluralism,* 492.

47. Ibid., 496.

48. Johnson, *The Root Causes,* 35.

49. Ibid., 39–40.

50. Kok, "Adding Fuel to the Conflict," 107–108. See also Alier, *Too Many Agreements Dishonoured;* and Badal, "Oil and Regional Sentiment."

51. For more on the southern regional governments, see Johnson, *The Root Causes,* 42–43, 51–54.

52. Garang, *The Call for Democracy,* 253.

53. Deng, "Self-Determination and National Identity," 267.

54. The preference of both Western donors and Arab countries for a united Sudan further constrained the SPLA's agenda.

55. The Koka Dam Declaration, 24 March 1986 (a proposed program for national action) in Garang, *The Call for Democracy,* 142–143.

56. Mampilly also notes that "despite the elaborate structure of the [SPLM's] legislative system," it became clear in his fieldwork that "these were little more than paper institutions." In contrast, he observes that the presence of NGOs in the region is "overwhelming." Mampilly, "Stationary Bandits,"129–130.

57. Crossley, "Why Not to State-Build," 137.

58. Ibid., 148.

59. *Africa Research Bulletin (Political, Social and Cultural Series),* January 2005, 42(1):16056.

60. This reasoning assumes, however, that the government will indeed hold the referendum in 2011, which is far from certain. The fact that the international community sponsored the agreement illustrates how sovereignty is not in more limited supply in Africa than elsewhere.

61. Bayart, *The State in Africa,* 134.

62. See Buchheit, *Secession;* Coppieters and Sakwa, *Contextualizing Secession;* and Crawford, "State Practice and International Law."

63. UN, "Declaration"; OAU, "The Organization"; OAU, "Border Disputes."

64. Jackson, *Quasi-States,* 76, 77, 151.

65. Deng, "Beyond Cultural Domination."

66. Gasser, "'Manger ou s'en aller.'"

67. Gérard-Libois, *La sécession katangaise;* Lemarchand, "The Limits of Self-Determination."

68. Gorenburg, "Nationalism for the Masses."

69. Hale, "The Parade of Sovereignties," 49.

70. As noted by Young, "Comparative Claims," 219.

71. Ibid., 212–213.

72. Ibid., 215.

73. Pateman, *Eritrea*, 5; Pool, "The Eritrean People's Liberation Front," 21. Despite their similar ethnonyms, the Tigrinya (Tigre) and Tigrai are two distinct ethnic groups.

74. Pateman, *Eritrea*, 9.

75. Iyob, *The Eritrean Struggle*, 1, 41, 106.

76. Ibid., 57.

77. Ibid.

78. Ibid., 100–101.

79. Ibid., 122.

80. Quoted in ibid., 127 and 139.

81. Pool, "The Eritrean People's Liberation Front," 21.

82. Quoted in Clapham, "Ethiopia," 33. See also Adam, "Formation and Recognition," 30.

83. Adam, "Formation and Recognition," 24.

84. ICG, "Somaliland," 5.

85. Adam, "Formation and Recognition," 25.

86. Ibid., 29.

87. Lewis, *A Modern History,* 221–222.

88. Reno, "Somalia," 164.

89. Shinn, "Somaliland," 1; Adam, "Formation and Recognition," 29.

90. Bryden, "State-Within-a-Failed-State," 167.

91. Anonymous, "Government Recognition in Somalia," 262.

92. Quoted by ibid., 263.

93. In 1998, some Harti leaders of eastern Somaliland had declared the Puntland Autonomous Republic of Somalia. The Harti are a subgroup of the Darod clan that reaches from the tip of the horn to parts of the south (Barre was Darod). The subset of Harti that predominate in Puntland are the Majerteen. Inside Somaliland, the Harti clans are the Warsangeli and the Dulbahante who live in the regions of Sanaag and Sool, which are claimed by Puntland and where support for independence was least. See Mukhtar, *Historical Dictionary of Somalia.*

94. Mukhtar, *Historical Dictionary of Somalia,* 71.

95. ICG, "Somaliland," 6.

96. Clarke and Gosende, "Somalia"; Adam, "Formation and Recognition," 28.

97. Reno, "Somalia," 161–164.

98. Ibid., 170.

99. Anonymous, "Government Recognition in Somalia," 256.

100. Lewis, *A Modern History*, 266.

101. Christopher Clapham writes: "Like Sudan, too, Ethiopia was a state whose 'ownership' by a particular segment of the population, in this case the Orthodox Christian and the Amharic-speaking peoples especially of the central province of Shoa, was always liable to prompt resistance from other peoples" (Clapham, "Introduction," 3).

102. See Pakenham, *The Scramble for Africa,* 470–486.

103. Ibid., 486.

104. Clapham, "Ethiopia."

105. Pakenham, *The Scramble for Africa,* 486.

106. Abbay, "Diversity and State-Building," 598.

107. Young, "The Tigray People's Liberation Front," 38.

108. Clapham, "Ethiopia," 24.

109. Ibid., 29.

110. See Abbay, "Diversity and State-Building," 608.

111. Clapham, "Ethiopia," 23.
112. Keller, "Making and Remaking," 97.
113. Hagmann, "Beyond Clannishness and Colonialism," 514–515.
114. Ibid., 515.
115. Ibid., 525.
116. See Smith, "The Challenges of National Unity."
117. From www.oromoliberationfront.org/OLFMission.htm.
118. Abbay, "Diversity and State-Building," 604.
119. Ibid., 605.
120. Keller, "Making and Remaking," 119.
121. For more details on the Katanga secession, see Gérard-Libois, *Le sécession katangaise*; Young, "Comparative Claims"; Struelens, *The United Nations*; O'Brien, *To Katanga and Back*.
122. Nzongola-Ntalaja, *The Congo,* 103.
123. Humphreys and Mohamed, "Senegal and Mali," 37 (manuscript). This observation was not included in the published version of their chapter.
124. Bourgeot, "Révoltes et rébellions," 11–13.
125. Caplan, "Barotseland."
126. Kasfir, "Cultural Sub-Nationalism in Uganda."
127. Ibid., 101.
128. Young, *The Politics of Cultural Pluralism*, 158 and 248.
129. See Englebert, "Back to the Future?"
130. *The Economist,* "Zaire: A Provincial Gem," 27 April 1996; French, "A Neglected Region."
131. Neuberger, "Irredentism and Politics," 105.
132. Cohen, Brown, and Organski, "The Paradoxical Nature of State-Making."
133. See Polgreen, "Congo's Riches."

Part 3
Sorrow

The sovereign reproduction of Africa's weak states comes at a price. For sure, continued international recognition allows for the maintenance of structures of authority among the continent's weakest states, which provide elements of stability and predictability in people's lives. Yet, the arbitrariness of legal command and its propensity for underwriting strategies of domination shed a depressing glow on the meager benefits of state resilience. In this part, I address two dimensions of Africa's sovereign sorrow. In Chapter 7, I show that the critical role of citizenship in supporting individual claims of access to legal command promotes the development of a particularly nefarious brand of nationalism. Rather than being the expression of bonds of communal solidarity and togetherness, this nationalism is solitary and polarizing. As state retrenchment and political liberalization have increased the scarcity of legal command, extreme variations of this nationalism have developed in several countries under the guise of autochthony discourses, with the purpose of excluding entire communities from citizenship and its benefits.

In Chapter 8, I turn to the effects of the sovereignty regime on the continent's prospects for better governance, democratization, and development. I argue that the command bias of state institutions limits the reach of democratic reforms. I show that the lack of a credible exit option reduces incentives to good governance by effectively shielding government institutions from societal sanction and institutional competition. Africans are cheated of a tool of accountability. Finally, I contend that legal command fosters predation as a mode of economic (non)production. People extract from each other via the state with little corresponding productive activity. The pervasiveness of predatory relations reduces the capacity of state institutions to organize collective action and promotes social and economic atomization. While the subsequent widespread adoption of private solutions to public problems allows for individual survival and bears witness to the creativity and resilience of Africans, they foster inequality without significantly mitigating poverty.

7

The Politics of
Unity and Estrangement

*"Devant la Nation et le Peuple congolais seul détenteur de la souveraineté,
Moi, SASSOU-NGUESSO Denis, Président de la République, je jure
solennellement. . . ."*[1]

"Tous Congolais à part entière et donc tous apparentés."[2]

"Who is Ivorian, and who is not?"[3]

Students of African politics share a common puzzlement at the suc-
cess that African countries have demonstrated at developing national identities
in contrast to their failure at constructing actually functioning states. Sam
Nolutshungu, writing on Chad, mentions the "powerful attachment within
African societies to the idea of the nation-state."[4] Richard Joseph notes that "the
more illusory the idea of the nation, the more firmly it is proclaimed" in Africa.
Invoking Nigeria, he questions "the tenacity of the nation-state ideal despite the
profound failure to realize it."[5] Focusing on the DRC, Herbert Weiss and
Tatiana Carayannis observe a strengthening of "the identification of the Congolese with the Congolese nation over the last forty years . . . despite predatory
leaders, years of war and political fragmentation, devastating poverty, ethnic
and linguistic diversity, and the virtual collapse of state services."[6] And Crawford Young singles out the "remarkable contemporary paradox" of the "persistence of an affective attachment to a territorial nationality" in Africa, "even
when the state institutions are derelict."[7] In his eloquent words, the "naturalization of nationhood despite the historical artificiality and illegitimacy of the territorial partition of Africa . . . flies in the face of the debilitated condition of a
number of states."[8]

The facts of the matter are unambiguous. In ten democratic African countries surveyed by the Afrobarometer in the late 1990s and early 2000s, 94 percent of respondents professed strong national identities. The region with the
next highest score is Latin America with 91 percent, while all other regions are

in the low to mid-80s.[9] Nationalism is also vibrant among less democratic African countries. Despite their deep societal cleavages, 72 percent of the citizens of Sudan, 88 percent of those of the DRC, 95 percent of Sierra Leoneans, and 97 percent of Ugandans affirm that national unity is more important than group interests.[10] These trends are largely reproduced elsewhere across the continent.[11]

While the paradoxical spread of nationalism in Africa is often perceived as one of the few notable achievements of African leaders, a closer look at some of its dimensions reveals a propensity for alienation that certainly rivals its unifying qualities. This propensity, I argue, partly derives from the centrality of legal command in African politics. First of all, nationalists live a lie in Africa possibly more than anywhere else. African elites relentlessly engineer nationalist sentiments to downplay the exogenous origins of their state, conceal the private nature of state theft, and remove exit from the politically thinkable. As such they sacralize colonial structures whose intrinsic absolutism and arbitrariness make for poor conduits for individual emancipation. Second, nationalism also derives from individual expressions of national identity produced as evidence of citizenship, the main rationing criterion for access to legal command. This is not a liberating affirmation of the self as member of a cultural community. Rather, it is solitary nationalism, the proclamation of an identity as evidence of individual admissibility to a state-centered system of survival based on command, predation, and parasitism. Finally, African nationalist and patriotic discourses frequently promote polarization and exclusion among people and communities and occasionally underwrite agendas of intranational political violence.

For sure, political excess in the name of nationalism is as universal as nationalism itself. Yet, I show in this chapter that nationalist alienation relates in Africa to the sovereign structuration of social life. Legal command, I argue, contributes to the rise of a form of nationalism that disenfranchises people and separates communities more than it unites them. Of course, there are other sources of the national identities of Africans and other more positive manifestations of nationalism across the continent. In keeping with this book's argument, however, I focus here on the extent to which sovereignty produces identity in Africa, and on the manner in which it does so, which is largely inimical to Africans themselves.

Diversionary Nationalism

My first argument is rather simple. To a large extent, nationalist sentiments are stirred by African elites to make juridical states appear natural, hide the private nature of state theft, reduce the realm of the politically thinkable, and divert the blame for development failure onto others, particularly the West. African elites promote nationalism in part to imprint the state's external sovereignty into the hearts and minds of their citizens. The constant reaffirmation of the inevitability of state authority that nationalism promotes keeps many Africans captive of their state and relegates alternative modes of political actions—such as exit—to the realm of the unthinkable. Such nationalism from above engineers the fiction that sovereignty is popular, that it emanates from the people, whereas in reality it transcends them.

The excerpt of Denis Sassou-Nguesso's presidential oath at the beginning of this chapter provides a fitting illustration to start my argument. Of relevance is the claim that there are such things as a "Congolese nation and people" and that they possess sovereignty. Of course, the imputation of sovereignty to the nation in official proclamations or in countries' constitutions is not uncommon across the world, but its fictional quality is particularly salient here in view of the exogenous nature of African sovereignty. It is inaccurate that the Congolese people possess sovereignty. Congolese sovereignty belongs to the state, to which it was granted by outside recognition, on the grounds of past colonial existence. It is embodied in the agents of the state, starting with the president. The people of Congo—whether or not they form a Congolese people or nation—have no control of, or power over, their country's sovereignty. It is not theirs to give or take, although many of them use it in their social relations.

Yet, Sassou's words illustrate the relentless extent to which African elites manufacture nationalism and its intimate relationship to sovereignty. The promotion and production of nationalist sentiment by African elites is nothing new. In the 1950s already, James Coleman had identified the role of Westernized elites in the rise of African nationalism: "the drive behind African nationalism . . . is the movement of racially-conscious modernists seeking to create new political and cultural nationalities out of the heterogeneous peoples living within the artificial boundaries imposed by the European master."[12] Coleman also stressed the allegiance of these new elites to the colony as the relevant political arena, which correlates with the sovereign realm of today's nationalism. These modern elites used nationalism both against white rule and, at home, "against the dead hand of tradition."[13] Nationalism thus served a similar purpose then as sovereignty does now—to shield outsiders away and exert hegemony at home. It promoted domestic hegemony by "legitimat[ing] state power and those that exercised it."[14] Nationalism gave meaning to the struggle of modern elites beyond the mere acquisition of power. By presenting the postcolony as a nation or nation-in-making, these elites differentiated themselves from the colonials, while maintaining the latter's realm against the claims to rule of so-called traditional leaders. Thus, from the beginning, African nationalism and the postcolony were undissociable.

Nationalism from above in the late colonial and early postcolonial periods had ideological dimensions associated with racial equality, freedom, emancipation, and modernization. In contrast, the goals of contemporary elite-driven

African nationalism are more uniquely focused on the legitimation of the holders of sovereign power. As Crawford Young once pointedly remarked, Africa's dominant class is "the principal advocate and main beneficiary of the idea of nationalism, as it has been appropriated as state ideology."[15]

The first diversionary benefit of nationalism from above is to make the sovereign state appear natural or organic, as when Sassou claims that the Congolese nation is the possessor of Congolese sovereignty. By fabricating nationalism and equating it with the sovereign state, African state elites produce domestic respect for the institutions of the state, which they inhabit. As such, nationalism supports the domestic value of international state recognition in terms of domination and predation. Thus, African governments are often heard brandishing the twin ingredients of nation and sovereignty as rationales for their exactions and shields of their impunity. While jailed by the Cameroonian government in 1990 for having published an editorial critical of President Paul Biya, Célestin Monga was invited by the US ambassador, Frances Cook, to a conference in Washington, DC. Monga recalls the Cameroonian government's reaction that this invitation was a "gross provocation against the Cameroonian people . . . interference in domestic affairs . . . [and] disrespect for Cameroonian sovereignty [which is] recognized by the Organization of African Unity."[16] Of course, the Cameroonian government was not particularly entitled to speak in the name of the Cameroonian people at a time when it was coming under increased popular pressure for democratization, a pressure that Monga came in part to represent. However, when equating the Cameroonian people with Cameroon's sovereignty, which it rightly highlighted as deriving from outside recognition, the government was able to recapture a claim to popular representation, since there was no doubt as to the government's embodiment of sovereignty. And although sovereignty does not emanate from the people, the equation was nevertheless correct to the extent that the Cameroonian people emanate at least in part from Cameroon's sovereignty.

The second diversionary benefit of the nationalist discourse for elites is that it hides the private nature of their sovereign theft, as they commit it in the people's name (whether the people are fooled is another matter, but from my experience in the DRC, some of the people appear to be fooled at least some of the time). The following example from Chad illustrates the incantatory use of the nation to cover sovereign theft and displace popular anger toward the developed world. The government of Chad reneged in January 2006 on a previous agreement with the World Bank to allocate a certain amount of its oil profits to fight long-term poverty. The government did so simply by passing a law that abolished the "future generation fund," which had kept 10 percent of its oil revenue for antipoverty interventions. In doing so, it took money away from poverty reduction programs—which could conceivably have benefited Chad's poor population—and allocated it to the purchase of weaponry in order to defend itself against insurgencies, the benefits of which, for the majority of Chadians, are not straightforward. Yet, this is how Chad's finance minister characterized the World Bank's ensuing decision to freeze another oil-derived account it held in escrow for Chad at Citibank of London: "It is unacceptable that *a nation* should have its access blocked to revenues generated by the sale of its own resources. Chad's government . . . will take appropriate action to recover the legitimate rights of *the Chadian people*."[17] Chad's president subsequently denounced the bank's move as an attack on Chad's sovereignty.[18]

What is interesting for our purpose in this episode is the minister's mention of nation and people. He blamed the World Bank for blocking the nation's access to oil revenues, but it is debatable whether the Chadian nation ever had such access. The government presents its policies of control of the resources from oil as one of national control. It claims that it is the rights of the Chadian people that have been violated. References to the nation give a layer of legitimacy to sovereign prevarication. They pitch the World Bank, representing the rich developed world, against the Chadian people, represented by its government. Thereby, national invocation dilutes the exploitation by the Chadian government of its people's resources and rephrases it as domination by the World Bank against the Chadian people and government united. Meanwhile, the use by the government of some US$2 billion of oil revenue between 2003 and 2007 remains broadly undocumented and likely financed purchases of weaponry.[19] Nationalism is used here as an ideological smokescreen, the probable victims of which are Chad's poor.

In the same vein, elite nationalist discourse is also helpful as an ideological justification for all the state agencies put in place to extract resources. A frequent belief, supported by the colonial experience and reinforced by African authorities, is that foreign companies are stealing the resources of Africa. This is a rather pervasive sentiment in the DRC, for example, where most people I have interviewed over several years imputed the country's poverty to unfair contracts ("*contrats léonins*") of mineral exploitation with the West. Thus, the need for national control over natural resources and for resisting international exploitation justifies regulatory overload and government arbitrariness. These in turn compound the existing international exploitation with domestic exploitation. In the end, in addition to the compliance generated by the near-universality of sovereign command, societal agreement to sovereign statehood is produced by the nationalist discourse, which keeps together what predation takes apart. In this respect, the irony of African nationalism is that it sets the stage and provides the mechanism for the private dismemberment of African states' assets.

A third and related benefit of nationalism for African elites is that it focuses attention on other countries, generally the West, for the failings of African governments. The above example of Chad illustrated this dimension. In the DRC, nationalist feelings make it more palatable for people to be victims of theft by

Congolese authority than by Rwandan ones. Beyond Rwanda, many Congolese seem convinced that their misfortunes are imposed from abroad, in a conspiracy to stifle their country. Shocked that the many Congolese deaths of the 1998–2003 war triggered little international outrage, and puzzled that the United States helped Kuwait against Iraq but not Congo against Rwanda and Uganda, the Congolese suspected the West of silently backing the invaders. The subsequent anti-US sentiments are loaded with nationalist fervor, for the United States is believed to hold back the rise of a strong Congo. Mobutu was himself quite effective at mobilizing such sentiment for his own benefit. In fact, the Zaire-anization of foreigners' assets in 1974, a clear example of theft through the state if there ever was one, found its official justification in the alleged foreign exploitation of Congo. In Mobutu's own words,

> Zaire is the country which, up till now, has been the most heavily exploited in the world. . . . That is why, given the constitutional oath to guarantee the total independence of the Republic of Zaire, which I swore before you in this room, I announce to you the great decisions I have taken to put an end to exploitation. That is why farms, ranches, plantations, concessions, commerce, and real estate agencies will be turned over to sons of the country.[20]

The irony is that, by embracing the postcolonial state, anti-Western nationalism ends up embracing a Western concept, Western forms and ideas. The affirmation of African national sovereignty is but a reaffirmation of structures derived from colonialism. And despite frequent African beliefs to the contrary, postcolonial nationalism probably conforms to Western desires to see the former colonies endure. A Belgian colonial official summarized all the essential themes of African nationalism at a speech before the Katanga provincial assembly in 1958: "It is beyond doubt that the only formula which, now and for many years to come, will fit this country is the unitary one. We created Congo and we have every reason to be proud of it. We have endowed it with strongly centralized institutions, in conformity with the genius of our race, and which should necessarily engender, over time, a concept of nation and the birth of nationalism among populations which used to live in ignorance of each other."[21]

Finally, elite-engineered nationalism contributes to excluding secessionism and other forms of political exit from the realm of the politically thinkable or practically plausible. As a southern opposition journalist once told me in Brazzaville, "secession is not in people's mind. People do not think about it."[22] Such ideological production of compliance is not necessary if everyone is clearly aware of the available benefits of sovereignty. But not everyone is and these benefits cannot be shared equally. Hence, nationalism raises the threshold for separatist action, particularly for those at the receiving end of sovereign relations of domination and exploitation. Francis Nyamnjoh, writing about Cameroon, puts it best: "The effect of this policy is to blind Cameroonians to the fact of the system as their real problem, and to diffuse all momentum and potential unity on the basis of common interests and aspirations . . . the whole business of national unity and national integration is a smoke-screen perpetuated with the hidden aim of thwarting all attempts at meaningful change."[23]

Solitary Nationalism

African nationalism is not only engineered from above; it is also produced at the grassroots of society, in everyday interactions. Because partaking in the bounties of legal command is conditioned upon citizenship, affirmation of national identity becomes a tool of access to the state. Africans proclaim their belonging in the nation to legitimate their demands upon sovereign institutions. Nationalism results from this voicing of one's qualifications for access to the benefits of sovereignty and to the community defined by the sovereign realm.

The centrality of legal command in many people's eking out a living is at the core of the production of this form of nationalism. Because the supply of legal command is limited and monopolized by the state, access to it is conditioned by citizenship, that is, by one's status as belonging in the postcolonial nation. Proclamation of one's postcolonial identity becomes evidentiary of one's qualification for access to legal command and enjoyment of its benefits. Sovereignty engenders national identity, as the aggregation of the multitude of claims to legal command, made any given day across Africa, results in a broad-based discourse in which belonging to the nation figures prominently. The existence of the nation derives from the very fervor of the sentiments expressed in defense of one's rights to sovereign participation.

There is thus necessity to national identity. People embrace the postcolonial signifier in order not to be left out. Their claim to belong is formative of identity. Africans may have other compelling identities, including ethnicity, but the only identity that gives them access to command and command-derived opportunities is the national one. People become Burkinabè, Central African, Chadian, Congolese, Kenyan as they seek to be associated with access to the state.

The intimate bond between sovereignty and nation was well illustrated by the delegates to Benin's Sovereign National Conference in 1990. Recall from Chapter 4 that one of the conference's main achievements—however ambiguous it turned out to be—was to claim sovereignty away from the government, to imbue itself with the power to make new rules. The moment the delegates voted this power to themselves was a defining one, and they were well aware of its historical significance. As Eboussi Boulaga recalls, they were legitimately "swept with enthusiasm."[24] The manner in which they expressed their emotions, however, was more telling of sovereignty's grip on them than of their control over it. They stood up and sang the national anthem. They were sovereign. They were in charge of tools of legal command. They were Beninese.

No cynical ploy is implied in this argument, no ruthless instrumentalization of nationality by Africans as a conscious stratagem for public employment or access to the tools of domination. Rather, this dimension of African nationalism corresponds to a fetishization of sovereignty, a structuration of social relations through the sovereign realm. It develops as a by-product of necessity and of the overwhelming role of the state in people's lives. There are few opportunities outside the state. To claim part ownership of it, one must also claim membership in it. It is then the defining nature of sovereignty in African social relations that induces the development of postcolonial identity through the spreading of a discourse of belonging.

Lest this argument appear too utilitarian, postcolonial national identity is also meaningful, for, by linking individuals to the sovereign realm, it links them to each other, however unequal and polarized the terms of this connection might be. There is meaning to being, say, Congolese; it is the way to belong to the postcolony, which defines and structures social, economic, and political relations. National identity is how one absorbs the sovereign structuration of life in postcolonial Africa. One claims the right to participate in society, to function and survive in it, and one finds meaning in the surrounding arbitrariness, by being a citizen, a national. The necessity to function in societies whose containers are authoritatively defined from above leads therefore to the indigenization of the colonial state. To belong in Congo demands one be Congolese.[25]

As useful and meaningful as it might be, this form of nationalism also contains elements of individual alienation. The state exists by juridical fiat and legally forms the nation. National identity then spreads through individual affirmations of belonging. People claim that they are, say, Senegalese rather than (or together with being) Wolof, because the state and the law are Senegalese. They become Senegalese. Yet, defined by the law, national identity never fully emancipates from its colonial origins. The Senegalese proclaim their identity as Senegalese, but the Senegalization of their living space was a colonial act, which endures through the legal structuring of social relations. Of course, despite the original sin of their conception, it is not written in stone that postcolonial states cannot become instruments of emancipation. Yet, the nationalist embrace of the state by Africans for the sake of individual survival falls short of collective ownership and remains unlikely to infuse it with liberating impulses.

In addition, because this type of nationalism arises from competitive contact with others from the same country, it is solitary and mutually alienating, rather than the expression of bonds of community. Competition, rather than solidarity, defines the common grounds of identity. Lacking this component of natural solidarity of the national community, which usually characterizes the nationalist ideology,[26] solitary nationalism is not particularly conducive to nation-building. Individuals and groups compete in voicing their attachment to the nation but hardly come together as a people. From this perspective, claims of successful nation-building in Africa's postcolonies may be somewhat illusory, conflating it as they might with national identity and nationalism.

Understanding solitary nationalism might help us solve two paradoxes. The first one is the occasional tendency for the populations of failed states to display vibrant nationalism. Why would people profess attachment to such derelict structures? When African states function along conventional neopatrimonial lines, the informal redistribution of financial resources is the key ingredient in the reproduction of regimes. Informal financial transfers necessitate the identification and reward of potential supporters and opponents, but the system's very informality does not put a large premium on the national identity of these actors. The national question goes broadly unaddressed, while issues of ethnic identity, upon which claims for redistribution might be made, are more salient. As the state becomes bankrupt, however, financial flows dry up and rulers are left with command alone to distribute, which people can then use to extract their own resources from each other. But command is legal, and thus formal. Access to it is conditioned by legally established entitlement via national identity. Thus, as the state fails and the relative importance of command rises, so do the material returns to national identity and the necessity to voice one's membership in the nation.

The second paradox that solitary nationalism might shed light on is the allegiance to the state of groups who are victims of its policies. In a world where the supply of sovereignty is fixed, groups that are discriminated against need to make a loud claim as to their rightful membership in the nation in order to abate discrimination or secure access. Their only escape from persecution is to be more royalist than the king. The nationalist outlook of Congo's RCD rebels comes as less of a surprise now. Their goal was partly to secure the citizenship status of Rwandophone populations in the Kivus. In order to do so, they needed to gain access to the tools of sovereign command. It made sense, therefore, for their leadership to adopt a nationalist tone, even though their history within Congo was one of repeated exclusion. A similar logic applies to the FN rebels of Côte d'Ivoire, whose insurgency followed the development of a citizenship policy that largely excluded northerners from meaningful access to the state. Celebrating national holidays and maintaining national institutions, their goal was to redefine the conditions of eligibility for national identity in a manner that would no longer exclude them. They claimed their attachment to the country in order to reclaim a participatory right in it.

Exclusionary Nationalism

In recent years, the increased premium of citizenship brought about by diverse but simultaneous trends has compounded the divisiveness of solitary nationalism and promoted the rise, in some countries, of a more extreme politics of nationalist exclusion. The salience of citizenship has risen largely in parallel with political liberalization and the spread of elections across the continent. To some extent, citizenship has taken on greater political substance as the right to vote has become less choiceless.[27] Additionally, some authoritarian rulers have found that raising citizenship questions about their opponents or segments of their populations allowed them to push back democratization efforts.[28] Alassane Ouattara in Côte d'Ivoire and Kenneth Kaunda in Zambia were both subjected to this exclusionary treatment.

But citizenship has also become more important in the wake of the fiscal crisis of the neopatrimonial state, as discussed in the previous section: as financial resources have dried up, legal command has become relatively more important in political and survival strategies. The fact that legal command endures in periods of fiscal crisis does not mean, however, that there is enough of it to go around for all. Particularly in times of significant scarcity, the appropriation power of legal command can be bitterly fought over, as it allows those who have it to seize the assets of those who do not. In such circumstances, rulers find great political benefits in selectively allocating this tool of legal command to their supporters and denying it to others. One way to do this has been to challenge the citizenship of certain groups. In countries like Côte d'Ivoire and the DRC, such challenges have been couched in a new type of nationalist discourse that singles out certain communities as more authentically national than others. Because the fixed supply of sovereignty and the lack of significant non-state-controlled economic activities deprives the excluded of alternatives, victims of this exclusionary nationalism have typically responded by fighting for their reinsertion in the nation. In doing so, they too have produced a nationalist discourse and proclaimed their attachment to the state. The paradoxical result of these dynamics has been for increased societal cleavages to parallel the maintenance of very weak states and the rise of intense nationalist discourse among their populations.

In Nigeria, which is one of Africa's rare federal countries, similar challenges to the citizenship of some communities have tended to occur at a more decentralized level and to trigger more decentralized responses. Because many of the benefits of legal command are allocated at the level of the states of the federation and of the local government authorities, that is where exclusionary policies of indigeneity have developed. Some state authorities have proclaimed some communities to be nonindigenous to their state and therefore ineligible for access to the local benefits of citizenship. People who belong to these communities have had to relocate to states where they are deemed autochthonous or have supported demands by their elites for obtaining their own state or LGA. In either case, exclusion and divisiveness again take place while the state as a whole is reproduced (and multiplied) by both dominant and dominated.

The appeal of strategies of sovereign appropriation in times of increased political competition or fiscal distress correlates thus with new restrictive interpretations of citizenship. Autochthony discourses invent or stress ethnic or territorial foundations to citizenship in order to preclude access to legal command by some individuals in at least some parts of the country. They reduce local competition for positions of legal command and for access to resources managed at least in part by legal process—such as land. The fluidity of population movements in many parts of Africa, the ambiguity of colonial boundaries, and the even greater ambiguities of many people's ethnic affiliations have offered ample fodder for those who wish to exclude others from access to the state and its authority.

Policies of autochthony are based on an exclusionary conception of national identity. They exclude while glorifying national unity.[29] Both their proponents and their victims end up contributing to the spread of nationalism and to the apparent paradox of African postcolonial unity. Their proponents couch their policies in a discourse of authenticity that frequently emulates notions of ancestral *terroir* more familiar to other latitudes. The victims fight back by loudly reaffirming their right to belong in the nation. Although divisiveness or conflict ensues, the idea of the nation ends up reinforced, as do professions of attachment to it.

Policies derived from autochthony have wreaked havoc in Côte d'Ivoire and Nigeria since the early 1990s, but can also be found in other countries.[30] In Côte d'Ivoire, for example, the question of who is a national and who is a foreigner has become paramount since the mid-1990s and has found expression in a new type of nationalist mobilization based on the territorially and "traditionally" defined concept of *Ivoirité* (Ivorianness). In Nigeria, indigeneity to specific states has become the litmus test of effective citizenship.

Ivoirité

Richard Banégas has called the Ivorian civil war (2002–2007) a "war of rival patriotisms," fought over the question of "Who is Ivorian, and who is not? . . . Who is included in the nation?" It is a conflict "about the rights . . . that are conferred by possession of a national identity document."[31] To be sure, Côte d'Ivoire's nationality law is rather liberal by African standards, providing citizenship for those born in the country or those born of Ivorian parents. Foreigners residing in the country before independence can also become citizens, and there are numerous opportunities for naturalization for those who came later. Unlike some other countries, which confer their citizenship based on membership in ethnic groups deemed autochthonous, no reference is made to ethnicity in the Ivorian law, which does not explicitly state how one is to establish that one's parents were Ivorian. This inclusiveness turned out not to be a problem for much of the presidency of Félix Houphouët-Boigny (1960–1993). Although Houphouët was a Baoulé, a subset of the Akan ethnolinguistic grouping, and his regime was anchored around core Akan interests, all Ivorians were treated more or less equally in terms of citizenship, and nationality rules were applied liberally and inclusively to accommodate the large number of West African migrants who provided the engine of the Ivorian economy. During that time, residency certificates were easy to obtain for foreigners and gave them rights of access to land and most other benefits of citizenship, including voting (which was hardly a meaningful benefit under Houphouët's one-party personal rule). The system seemed so liberal at the time that many foreigners who married Ivorians or became otherwise eligible for citizenship did not bother to obtain certificates of nationality.

Things changed in the early 1990s, following the introduction of multi-party electoral politics. Northerners began to organize as a separate voting block—the Grand Nord—seeking greater political participation under the leadership of Allassane Ouattara and his Rassemblement des Républicains.[32] When Ouattara declared his intention to run in the 1995 presidential election, Henry Konan-Bédié (Houphouët's successor as president and himself a Baoulé) sought ways to exclude him and his supporters.[33] Certificates of nationality became a crucial tool in this politics of exclusion, since they allowed the holder the right to vote. As a result, the application of the law became increasingly arbitrary, with more and more people being denied certificates of nationality on account of their alleged foreign status.

At first, however, the attempt by the north to compete for control of the state and challenge the political hegemony of the southern Akans was met with legal manipulations aimed mostly at their candidate. A 1994 reform of the electoral code, which required the president to be born in Côte d'Ivoire of parents both born in Côte d'Ivoire, was targeted at Ouattara, whose mother had been born in what is now Burkina Faso.[34] Thus, Ouattara was prevented from standing as a candidate on the ground of insufficient nationality, despite having previously served as the country's prime minister. But it did not take long for his electoral exclusion to transform into a broader movement of redefinition of citizenship and exclusionary nationalism toward northerners and associated populations of migrant descent. Around 1996, Bédié launched the idea of *Ivoirité*, a discourse about the purity of national identity, which revoked the liberal and inclusive approach to Ivorian citizenship that had prevailed since the 1960s. *Ivoirité,* which was deemed to be acquired from being "born of Ivorian parents themselves belonging to one of the autochthonous ethnic groups" of Côte d'Ivoire, squarely put the country among those raising ethnic identity at the core of national identity.[35] Although it did not define specific groups as more Ivorian than others, it stressed the concept of "ancestral village," which undermined the citizenship claims of migrant populations and those of ancestry outside the contemporary Ivorian borders. In Ruth Marshall-Fratani's judicious words, local autochthony became the "grounds for national belonging."[36] Richard Banégas and Bruno Losch have gone so far as to say that *Ivoirité* effectively created an Akan ethnonational foundation to the Ivorian idea.[37] And Francis Akindes notes that the state engineered the "retribalisation" of Ivorian society.[38]

Although not a formal change in the law, *Ivoirité* soon became central to government discourse and affected administrative practices. Village chiefs were particularly empowered as they became the assessors of one's local ancestry. When a new Land Law in 1998 explicitly limited land ownership to citizens, the non-"autochthonous" in the south became all the more vulnerable, and many saw their land confiscated and redistributed by local customary and state authorities.

The exclusionary nationalist discourse of *Ivoirité* served as a restricting mechanism of the right to participate in legal command. It developed at a time when the formal conditions for access to command were liberalized by electoral politics and proceeded to undo this liberalization.[39] Moreover, as Akindes notes, it also coincided with a reduction in the resources available to the state for redistribution.[40] Instead of financial resources, it gave supporters of the regime the legal authority to chase others from their land, or exclude them from civil service and other sinecures reserved to citizens. The large number of expropriations of northerners from land in the south on account of their contested citizenship testifies to the legal use of national identity for the acquisition of income-generating assets.

Bédié was overthrown in a military coup in 1999, following a mutiny largely engineered by northern and other non-Akan officers and petty officers.[41] Brigadier-General Robert Gueï, a former chief of staff of the armed forces recently demoted by Bédié, emerged as the new leader and denounced *Ivoirité*. As a member of the Yakouba, a relatively marginalized ethnic group from the western part of the country, he had little interest or affinity for this ideology. After the coup, Ouattara returned from exile, as did Laurent Gbagbo, the leader of the main southern non-Akan opposition party, the Front Populaire Ivoirien. Yet, developing a taste for the presidency, Gueï revised the constitution in 2000 to stipulate that "The President . . . must never have used another nationality," an attempt again at the legal exclusion of Ouattara who had once served on the staff of international organizations with a diplomatic passport from Burkina.

With Bédié in exile in France and Ouattara unable to compete, many voters decided to boycott the October 2000 elections, which became a race between Gueï and Gbagbo. To the surprise of the former, Gbagbo won. A Bété from the southwest of the country and rival to the Baoulé, Gbagbo embraced the concept of *Ivoirité*, which was flexible enough to serve the interests of his supporters, who could claim ancestral autochthony in their region and benefit from discrimination against migrants.

Gbagbo took *Ivoirité* much further than his predecessor. In 2002, he set up the Office National de l'Identification, a government agency in charge of identifying citizens along new rules. Eligibility for a national identity card now required the production of a "statement of origin" from a committee of one's village. This requirement implied that people without a village of origin (such as urban dwellers and those of foreign descent) were not Ivorian. In addition, as with the 1998 Land Law, the village-of-origin requirement gave great power to the "local notables and village chiefs who sat on these committees" and who promoted a certain idea of ethnic purity.[42] The new law allowed them to refuse recognition *as a local*, and thus as Ivorian, to certain individuals. This increased the vulnerability of people belonging to ethnic minorities, who may not have had representatives in positions of customary authority in their village. These people found it more difficult to obtain certificates of origin, especially where local competition for land and public employment was fierce. The recognition of one's national identity and of citizenship rights along the criterion of village of origin resulted, as Banégas points out, in a "nativist concept of citizenry, founded on roots in a micro-territory"[43] It glorified the idea of the Ivorian nation, while crystallizing, dividing, and eventually undermining its component entities.

The adoption and implementation of the national identification program led to the rebellion of the excluded, as northern petty officers and former student activists launched an insurgency in October 2002, which ushered in a war and the partition of the country. The rebel movement, eventually known as Forces Nouvelles, initially called itself the Patriotic Movement of Côte d'Ivoire as it attempted to wrestle national identity back from the southerners. Discriminated against, rejected, and terrorized by Côte d'Ivoire, the northerners fought for their reinclusion in the nation. They too were patriotic, for they wanted to remain Ivorian. They were soldiers, students, politicians, with few material options outside the sovereign realm. They needed citizenship to share ownership of Côte d'Ivoire. Thus, Côte d'Ivoire per se was never at stake. The Ivorian conflict was a war of national unity. The rebels demanded the abandonment of the national identification program, a facilitation of naturalization for longstanding immigrants, and the repeal of the 1998 Land Law. In the towns they captured in rapid succession in the last months of 2002, they destroyed national identity records.[44]

The different peace agreements between the FN and the Gbagbo government, beginning with the Linas-Marcoussis Accord of 2003 and ending with that of Ouagadougou of March 2007, illustrate the rebels' overarching goal of maintaining the plural softness of the state in order for their community to reclaim membership in the nation and retain access to partial and local ownership of the state and of state-defined opportunities and resources.[45] In addition to integrating the rebel forces into the national army and creating governments of national unity with rebel participation (including, eventually, the prime ministership for Guillaume Soro in 2007), the agreements revisit the conditions for eligibility to nationality and the acceptable evidence for establishing one's status. Moving away from the restrictive requirements of *Ivoirité*, the agreements explicitly reiterate the provisions of Côte d'Ivoire's original nationality laws and suspend the *Ivoirité*-based operations of identification. Citizenship is granted to people born of one or two Ivorian parents (or born on Ivorian soil of unknown parents). How these in turn became Ivorians is not revisited. For those without a birth certificate or otherwise unable to prove the conditions of their birth, the agreements set up *audiences foraines*, local court sessions where people can obtain judgments (from magistrates, and not from customary authorities), which are legally equivalent to original birth certificates. In order to be eligible for these judgments, individuals born in Côte d'Ivoire merely need to go to their village or place of birth, as opposed to their village of "ancestral origin," and produce two older adult witnesses.[46]

The rebels' demands rely on, and reproduce, the domestic currency of Côte d'Ivoire's sovereignty. Judges, who say the law, are to impart people with their citizenship. This contrasts with the earlier efforts of southerners to use ancestry or tradition as tools to impart citizenship. The FN demands the restoration of the plural softness of the state. At the time of writing, it remains to be seen whether the northerners will be successful at their reintegration efforts. Many doubt that Gbagbo will faithfully carry on with a process whose outcome, by recognizing the citizenship of many northerners, might create conditions inimical to his reelection. Yet, if the *audiences foraines* turn out to be successful, northerners will have regained membership in the nation. At any rate, the nation will have endured throughout the conflict and its resolution, with nationalism the dominant discourse on both sides of the conflict.

Indigeneity in Nigeria

In Nigeria, the politics of exclusionary nationalism unfold mostly at the level of the states of the federation, where sovereignty and oil revenues are most often accessed for local elites. Within many states, there are ethnically defined rules for access to positions of legal command. The "original" residents of a state, as determined by the ethnic affiliation of their parents or grandparents, receive preference in state-sponsored allocations, appointments, and employment. There are no official lists of what groups constitute indigenous ethnicities. Instead, LGAs have a large degree of discretion in handing out "certificates of indigeneity," which are necessary for public employment, access to higher education, and eligibility for different forms of state financial assistance. Frequently, LGAs rely on the assessment of local traditional authorities in certifying people's indigeneity.[47]

Indigeneity allows some groups to establish local domination over others. It also magnifies the powers of those in positions of legal command. As Human Rights Watch writes, "local officials' power to grant or deny indigenous status to their residents . . . gives them a *de facto* veto power over any individual's attempt at attaining federal government employment" and, one could add, education and other benefits.[48] Thus, indigeneity maximizes the declaratory authority of the sovereign power holder. It increases the potential for domination of the state and its agents.

Indigeneity seems to have derived in part from the idea of parity to federal office, known in Nigeria as the principle of "federal character." Because the constitution mandates the president to appoint an equitable number of officials from the different states of the federation, the issue arose of whether, say, a Hausa residing in Lagos could be appointed and imputed to Lagos's tally.[49] In order to avoid such a situation, the notion of there being indigenous peoples to specific states gained currency and was eventually extended to state positions.[50] As a result, only people who descend from ethnic groups deemed indigenous to a certain state are allowed to seek public employment in that state or to represent that state in federal employment or contracts. Given widespread in-country migration, this has created numerous problems. It is a particularly troubling issue when new states are created, which happens by excision from existing ones. The rump state then tends to chase away civil servants who had heretofore been indigenous and now find themselves strangers at home.

While providing opportunities for some groups and individuals, indigeneity imposes an indigenous-versus-outsider logic onto social and political relations within some states, giving more legitimacy to some groups' claims for access than to others. The principle serves in part to limit access to sovereignty and its resources, as a large number of Nigerians, despite being obviously Nigerian, fail to establish the local foundations of their national identity and find themselves deprived of access to federal positions or to the local appendages of the state. In addition to its polarizing effects and the vulnerability it creates for people in the excluded group, this system also has quasi-exponential features since it produces new minorities each time a state is created. In order to escape its nonindigenous status, which shields it from state benefits, the minority then must make its own claim to statehood, embracing and reproducing the idea of Nigeria while fighting against local marginalization. Nigeria not only goes on but actually multiplies (metastasizes?), while more Nigerians become disenfranchised and antagonized. Federalism and state multiplication in Nigeria embody the creation of disunity in the replication of unity.

Indigeneity also favors the descrambling of ethnicity, that is, its geographical redistribution in more homogeneous groups. It increases localized homogeneity, as people denied local indigeneity in their state of residence tend to migrate toward states where they might be considered indigenous by descent (although this is not an option available to all). Where once an individual's ethnicity might have been diluted in a sea of heterogeneity, there are now more territorialized group identities. The sovereign reproduction of the Nigerian nation parallels its increased internal differentiation.

The End of Plural Softness?

Exclusionary nationalism challenges the plural softness of the postcolonial African state, as autochthony represents a monopolization of the state by some groups. By denying the claims of some communities for equal access to the postcolony, it prevents their members from making a plausible claim to legal command.

To some extent, autochthony corresponds to the historical trajectories of nation-states elsewhere in the world. As Akindes notes about Côte d'Ivoire, it is a "version of modern nationalism," which seeks to exclude others in terms of some criterion of racial purity.[51] Thus the recent trend toward exclusionary nationalism in several African countries might well mark an evolution of the postcolonial state away from its inclusive softness and toward ownership by certain subgroups. For as violent and repulsive as policies of autochthony can be, they might also, in this perspective, signal the formation of more effective states imbued with greater social ownership. After all, the birth of successful states is never pretty.

Yet, the fixed nature of African sovereignty largely prevents exclusionary nationalism from acquiring any politically productive quality. By depriving the excluded of any opportunity to design their own alternative political arrangement, it forces them to fight back for the maintenance of the plural soft state and for their reintegration into it. What the FN rebels of Côte d'Ivoire have done, like the RCD in Congo, is to fight for the continued universalism of legal command. Similarly, those excluded by indigeneity in Nigeria have responded to their exclusion by demanding more states, that is more units of legal command to compensate for their loss. In neither case have the excluded groups fought the state that excludes them and offered a new political vision for their members.

This situation is characterized by contradiction. The sovereign structure of political and economic life in countries plagued by scarcity promotes policies of exclusion as rationing mechanisms of access to legal command. Yet, this very same sovereignty regime prevents the victims of these policies from responding to their exclusion in any manner that might question their belonging to the state. The only plausible option is to fight back for the maintenance of the plural soft state and reinsertion in it, as Côte d'Ivoire and the DRC illustrate. The result is to push weak states into complete failure. But, at the same time as it engineers their demise, sovereignty guarantees that these states endure through failure, since the very object of their conflict is belonging to the state. Expectations about what peace and state reconstruction can bring about in these countries should be understood with this contradiction in mind. Excluded groups wish for a return to the pluralist state, and for their own recovery of the tools of command. They wish for a renewed universality of mutual exploitation and domination through the state. It might be unreasonable to expect too much from such states in terms of long-term development and human emancipation.

All three forms of nationalism—diversionary, solitary, and exclusionary—relate to sovereignty. The main implication of the argument is that sovereignty produces identity in Africa, yet it does so in a manner that tends to be unemancipatory and divisive. To some extent, sovereignty-derived nationalism lacks a nation. It is individual and solitary. It promotes a communal idea for the self that is wielded largely against the other. In this respect, African nationalism differs from European nationalism, which was, at least in the nineteenth century, reformist of undemocratic political structures. African nationalism, in contrast, is conservative of existing colonial structures.

This is not to say that there are not other forms of nationalist sentiment in Africa that might offer more constructive bonds of solidarity and meaning. For instance, people in weak or failed states may derive a certain degree of comfort from nationalism, which may be the political expression of a preference by citizens for established, if dysfunctional, state institutions over unpredictable reconfigurations of power and economic life. When people have little left of material value, when much has been taken from them and hardly anything given, when they are poor, when they have been hurt, injured, and exploited, nationalism may also bring them some sense of belonging to a continuous whole that predates and will survive them, of being part of a meaningful human society, something larger than themselves. As such, nationalist sentiment may be similar to religious sentiment.[52] Nationalism also probably offers some comfort by painting the state as better than it appears, that is, by offering the fiction that some successful structure, fallen upon hard times, underlies current failed states. Far from contradicting their misery, the nationalist discourse may help Africans in weak states conceal from themselves that their own state may lie at the roots of their dispossessions.

It is also quite possible that people derive a sense of national belonging from their shared history, including that of colonial and postcolonial misery. Crawford Young mentions the "shared experience [of] common colonial subjugation within a given territorial container" as a source of African nationalism.[53] He stresses that "particularized forms of oppression gave rise to distinctive narratives of suffering" as "the ramifying web of regulation and extraction followed the territorial contours."[54] Writing about former Soviet populations, Dmitry Gorenburg notes in turn that the "strength of an individual's cultural identity is mediated by state institutions," which "can play a key role in determining the depth of the sense of common identity."[55] The institutions he refers to—schools, museums, state universities, and national-language periodicals—are also those that have shaped postcolonial identity in Africa. In his milestone treatment of the origins of nationalism, Benedict Anderson had also noticed that the rise of national sentiment in Latin America was structured around administrative structures, which brought together local bureaucrats in distinct careers from those born in Spain.[56] Similar patterns of "banal nationalism" may be relevant to Africa as people from distinct regions and cultural backgrounds come in contact with each other through administrative structures as they seek birth certificates, judgments, and other officially stamped documents.[57]

Finally, there is also the distinct possibility that people are lying, or at least "falsifying their preferences," which makes some sense if they wish to stay out of trouble in potentially polarized multiethnic environments.[58] Citing Václav Havel, Nyamnjoh suggests that Cameroonians might well only pretend to be attached to their state and not necessarily believe in its "mystifications," but "they must behave as though they did, or they must at least tolerate them in silence, or get along well with those who work with them. For this reason, however, they must *live within a lie*. They need not accept the lie. It is enough for them to have accepted their life with it and in it. For by this very fact individuals confirm the system, fulfill the system, make the system, *are* the system."[59] These words echo Achille Mbembe's notion of conviviality, his observation that dominated Africans share in the "phantasm of power" of their elites and fully participate in the postcolonial system, even if it is with an element of duplicity or "simulacrum."[60] In this case, observed African nationalism may not be real but may reflect a shared pragmatic interest among elites and masses in complying with state institutions.

All these theories have great explanatory merit. There are clearly other sources to African nationalism than legal command and there are clearly other effects of African nationalism than individual alienation and group divisiveness. For many Africans at many points in time, bonds of national identity provide meaning and utility. Yet, the pervasiveness of legal command in Africa also promotes the spread of a brand of national identity and nationalist sentiment that is not emancipatory but contributes to a regime of sorrow.

Notes

1. These are the first few words of the presidential oath of Republic of Congo president Denis Sassou-Nguesso, 2002. It translates broadly as, "Before the Congolese Nation and People sole possessor of sovereignty, I, Denis Sassou-Nguesso, President of the Republic, solemnly swear that. . . ."

2. Baloji, "Tout Ceci." Translation: "All fully Congolese and therefore all related."

3. Banégas, "Côte d'Ivoire," 536.

4. Quoted by Joseph, "Nation-State Trajectories,"15.

5. Ibid.

6. Weiss and Carayannis, "The Enduring Idea of the Congo," 135.

7. Young, "Nation, Ethnicity, and Citizenship," 241.

8. Ibid., 244.

9. From Afrobarometer, Eurobarometer, World Values Survey (1990–1997) for Asia and Latin America.

10. Larémont, *Borders, Nationalism.* Simple average of subnational samples. Afrobarometer data for Uganda.

11. For more detailed evidence on the case of the DRC, see Englebert, "Why Congo Persists."

12. Coleman, "Nationalism in Tropical Africa," 419. See also Davidson, *The Black Man's Burden,* particularly chapter 4.

13. Young, "Evolving Modes of Consciousness," 66.

14. Ibid., 69.

15. Ibid., 71.

16. Monga, *Un Bantou à Washington*, 46 (translation mine).

17. Quoted in BBC News, "World Bank" (emphasis mine).

18. On the dynamics of the Chad–World Bank oil relationship, see also Soares de Oliveira, *Oil and Politics,* 278–286.

19. See Dougueli, "Pétrole."

20. Quoted by Young and Turner, *The Rise and Decline*, 326.

21. Gérard-Libois, *La sécession katangaise,* 25 (translation mine).

22. Anonymous interview, Brazzaville, July 2001.

23. Nyamnjoh, "Cameroon: A Country United," 106 and 110.

24. Quoted by Buijtenhuijs, *La conférence nationale*, 61.

25. One might add that, not only does national identity qualify for membership in the state and the community it physically defines, but it also conditions participation in humanity on a world-scale. Without national identity, without a country, one is not a member of the world community either. National identity thus also offers Africans a measure of equality with people elsewhere, which might well partly compensate for the inequalities that more often characterize their relations to the rest of the world.

26. Young, "Nation, Ethnicity, and Citizenship."

27. Ibid., 255.

28. Bayart, Geschiere, and Nyamnjoh, "Autochthonie, Démocracies, et Citoyenneté."

29. The unifying properties of exclusion are nothing new. See Marx, "Race-Making and the Nation-State."

30. Other cases include the DRC, where the nationality status of the Rwando-phones has been cyclically challenged since the early 1960s. I discussed the case of eastern DRC in Chapter 5 and do not return to it here. For an interesting argument on the multiple levels at which autochthony surfaces over time in Congo, see Jackson, "Sons of Which Soil?" Autochthony has also gained salience in Cameroon, where it supports threats to the land rights of Bamiléké in Yaoundé (see Socpa, "Bailleurs Autochthones").

31. Banégas, "Côte d'Ivoire," 536.

32. Akindes, "The Roots," 18.

33. Boone, "Africa's New Territorial Politics," 75.

34. Ironically, the south of Burkina Faso was part of Côte d'Ivoire between 1933 and 1947, when the colony of Upper Volta was divided and parceled out to three of its neighbors.

35. Document published by a pro-Bédié think tank, quoted by Marshall-Fratani, "The War," 23.

36. Marshall-Fratani, "The War," 23.

37. Banégas and Losch, "Côte d'Ivoire."

38. Akindes, "Côte d'Ivoire: Socio-Political Crises," 11.

39. Bayart, Geschiere, and Nyamnjoh, "Autochthonie, Démocracies, et Citoyenneté."

40. Akindes, "The Roots," 20.

41. There were other sources of discontent underlying the soldiers' mutiny that led to the coup, including a general repression of the opposition, increased criminality, and discontent over pay and conditions in the military.

42. Banégas, "Côte d'Ivoire," 540.

43. Ibid., 541 and 543.

44. Marshall-Fratani, "The War," 26.

45. The implementation of these accords has been partial at best. My analysis focuses on the rebels' demands rather than on what they were able to achieve in practice.

46. For details, see the site of the United Nations Mission in Côte d'Ivoire, www.onuci.org/audienceforaine.htm.

47. For an excellent overview and analysis of the problem of indigeneity in Nigeria, see Human Rights Watch, "'They Do Not Own This Place.'" My own analysis owes much to the insights and clarifications generously provided to me by Chris Albin-Lakey, Darren Kew, and Rotimi Suberu, who are not, however, in any way responsible for what I actually wrote.

48. Human Rights Watch, "'They Do Not Own This Place,'" 19.

49. Text of the constitution (1999), Chapter II, art. 14(3) (as per ICG, "Nigeria's Faltering Federal Experiment," 11): "The composition of the government of the federation or any of its agencies and the conduct of its affairs shall be carried out in such a manner as to reflect the federal character of Nigeria and the *need to promote national unity, and also to command national loyalty* [emphasis mine], thereby ensuring that there shall be no predominance of persons from a few States or from a few ethnic or other sectional groups in the Government or any of its agencies." Furthermore, "the President shall appoint at least one Minister from each State, who shall be an indigene of such State" (section 147).

50. The system also derives from the multiplication of federated states. As minorities in larger states seek their own statehood, they promote the concept of indigeneity to avoid losing control of these new states to larger ethnic groups who may also have residents there. Thus, the concept is often couched in a discourse of minority rights and affirmative action, which hides its discriminatory nature.

51. Akindes, "The Roots," 26.

52. Benedict Anderson has suggested that they are of the same nature, although his discussion of the rise of nationalism in Europe sees it more as a substitute in a time when the universality of religious claims was declining. See his *Imagined Communities,* particularly 12–19.

53. Young, "Nationalism and Ethnicity," 7.

54. Young, "Nation, Ethnicity, and Citizenship," 247.

55. Gorenburg, "Not With One Voice."

56. Anderson, *Imagined Communities,* 53–56.

57. Billig, *Banal Nationalism.*

58. For a theoretical treatment of the logic of this behavior as applied to other questions than nationalism, see Kuran, *Private Truths, Public Lies.*

59. Nyamnjoh, "Cameroon: A Country United," 107.

60. Mbembe, *On the Postcolony,* 128.

8

Sovereignty's Shackles

The widespread distribution of internationally acquired sovereign legal command and its convertibility into a private resource promote the reproduction of the African state. Immune to the erosion of state capacity, legal command endures and, with it, the state itself, however weak. While the survival of Africa's states is in many ways a remarkable achievement, the nature of their sovereign reproduction is not without harmful consequences to the continent's political economy. For one, the exogeneity and absolutism of Africa's sovereign institutions foster relations of domination, which weaken the substance and limit the scope of democratic experiments. Second, the instrumentalization of sovereignty by people in positions of state authority undermines the quality of governance, while the unconditional recognition of African states reduces the domestic accountability of public institutions by preventing credible sanction and the effectiveness of aid conditionality. Finally, the propensity for legal command to underwrite strategies of domination and extraction induces predatory economic relations, which contribute to the continent's poverty and inequality.

Legal Command and Democracy

There is no doubt that, on average, African countries are more democratic now than they were before 1990. Looking, as a convenient shortcut, at their political rights as coded by Freedom House, Figure 8.1 indicates that the continent improved (on Freedom House's inverted scale) from a mean score of 5.8 in 1972 (the first year for which data are available) to 4.4 in 2008.[1] From being, on average, "not free" in the 1970s, Africans are now "partly free." A large element in this evolution has been the generalization of multiparty competitive elections across the continent. Some scholars have seen significant achievement in this

Figure 8.1   Political Rights

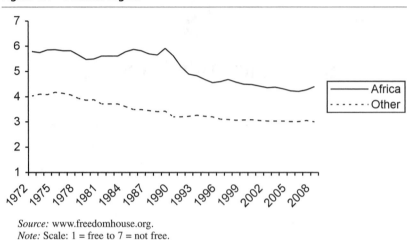

Source: www.freedomhouse.org.
Note: Scale: 1 = free to 7 = not free.

trend. Staffan Lindbergh, for example, has argued that the repetition of elections across Africa since 1990 has spread democratic ideas and led to greater civil liberties.[2] Daniel Posner and Daniel Young have also shown that African rulers faced with constitutional limits to their time in power increasingly resort to legal and norm-based transitions. Even when they refuse to let go of power, they do so by following rule-based procedural paths that contrast with the arbitrary ways of the past.[3]

As positive as this evolution has been, one cannot help but also notice the limits of Africa's democratic progress. First of all, as Figure 8.1 makes clear, the average level of democracy in Africa was still worse in 2007 than it was for the rest of the world in 1972, in the middle of the Cold War, and before the first stirrings of what Samuel Huntington has characterized as the "third wave" of worldwide democratization.[4] Second, the score of 4.4 that Africa had reached by 2008 was still above the middle point in the range of possible values. In other words, despite all its progress, Africa still is on the nondemocratic side of political regimes. Third, Africa's democratic transition already appears to be a thing of the past. As the graph suggests, there was a rapid improvement in democracy in the first half of the 1990s, but it has since largely stalled. While the continent's average score dropped by 1.3 points between 1989 and 1995, its decline over the following thirteen years was less than 0.2 points with no visible improvement since 2001. Many African countries now mix the trappings of democracy with authoritarian or neopatrimonial practices, a trend scholars have identified as "partial reform" or regime hybridity.[5] The stalling of Africa's democratization illustrates the resilience of its regimes, their capacity to adapt to new environments and survive, somewhat changed, but essentially similar to what they were in terms of generation, control, and distribution of power. Fourth and finally, the improvement in the continent's average score owes a lot to a relatively small list of eleven countries that have shown rapid democratization or steady democratic performance. Several of these countries—Benin, Botswana, Cape Verde, Lesotho, and São Tomé—have small populations, which further limits the reach of democracy for African individuals. In comparison, fourteen authoritarian African regimes never even embarked upon any attempt at democratization, eight experienced an authoritarian reversal after a few promising years, and another fourteen perfectly represent the concept of partial reform, having experienced some improvement, such as allowing opposition parties and some freedoms of the press, but remaining no more than "partly free." The most recent trend, with botched or stolen elections since 2007 in Kenya, Nigeria, and Zimbabwe (all large states) and military coups in Guinea and Mauritania in 2008, suggests that the number of authoritarian reversals might still increase and the number of Africans living in democracies decrease.

It also bears highlighting that Africa's transition to electoral systems has not generally produced a corresponding transition among ruling elites. Among African countries holding elections, the rate of incumbent success remained an astonishing 86 percent as of 2005.[6] While there is nothing undemocratic per se about an incumbent being reelected, this level of success suggests a particularly significant progovernment bias in elections. Such a rate of reelection also begs the question of how African governments can expect to be returned to office when they typically fail to provide their populations much in terms of development or other public goods. The lack of electoral sanction to bad governance in Africa is indeed rather puzzling and might illustrate Africans' lack of substantive expectations from their government. Moreover, Africans might have more limited real choice than many others when selecting their governments, for there is a lack of ideological differentiation among political parties.[7] The main characteristic differentiating opposition movements from governments is usually the former's claim of being more democratic. Yet, not a few opponents have developed authoritarian tendencies after being elected to office. Côte d'Ivoire's Laurent Gbagbo, Zambia's Frederick Chiluba, and Kenya's Mwai Kibaki come to mind. Thus, rather than challenging dysfunctional and authoritarian states, some opponents have adopted the qualities of the states they initially opposed.

The difficulties of African democracy have many sources. One of them, I argue, is the pervasiveness of legal command. The reliance of many people, in and out of government, on the declaratory, regulatory, and appropriative powers of legal command to eke out a living or move ahead biases state institutions and the practice of politics toward domination and absolutism, and away from responsiveness and accountability. However beneficial the holding of elections may be, and however improved certain civil liberties across the continent, the institutions and agents of the state are predisposed by legal command toward undemocratic behavior.

The absolutism of African sovereign power derives from its acquisition by international legal fiat, which tends to shield its excesses from social sanction and remove its practices from the realm of accountable behavior. By and large, the exogeneity of African statehood renders African citizens voiceless and promotes the disconnection of authority from the public. Holders of legal command operate with some impunity, where public office is often equated with license to abuse and exploit. Manifestations of the private exchange of sovereignty are not typically censured or prosecuted. Public office is expected to be arbitrary, dominant, and irresponsive. As Mahaman Tidjani Alou notes, the law in Africa is terrifying.[8]

To some extent, the tools of sovereign rule allow the authoritarian leaders of weak states to retain the residual capacity to stifle substantive change. Incompetent as they might be in matters of service provision, the dictators of places like Cameroon, Chad, or Zimbabwe steal elections and actively repress opponents through the law. More important, however, the absolutist nature of legal command undermines the democratic potential of public office at any level of government. Thus, while some democratic improvements, such as holding elections or liberalizing the media, are possible, democratization only goes so far and eventually hits the wall of the undemocratic nature of African sovereignty. For the same reason, democrats who win office through elections see their reformist impulses curtailed by the irresponsiveness of the tool they inherit.

There is little doubt that the African colonial experience set the tone for the absolutist and dominating nature of the postcolony. As Crawford Young has noted, "In the [African] colonial polity no real *état de droit* existed to restrain its domination of subject society."[9] This makes African law genetically on the side of domination: "The historical logic which led to the appearance of constitutionalism in Europe is a logic of resistance by civil society, the dominated vis-à-vis the dominators. The constitution serves to limit the power of the state. . . . In Africa it served to guarantee the authority of the state and the uncontrollable and uncontrolled exercise of power by the occupants of the state apparatus."[10] As Young puts it, the colonial state "lives, absorbed into the structures of the independent polity," which has retained its "operational code."[11] Achille Mbembe has made a similar argument. He highlights the "arbitrariness and intrinsic unconditionality that may be said to have been the distinctive feature of colonial sovereignty" and suggests its postcolonial continuity: "Postcolonial state forms have inherited this unconditionality and the regime of impunity that was its corollary."[12] This continuity, I argue, is based on international sovereignty, which, in its postcolonial African incarnation, is but an extension of colonial sovereignty. While one often stresses the boundary rigidity of the African postcolonial state, the rigidity of its power foundations is no less significant. Postcolonial sovereignty not only maintains the territory of the colonial state, but also its absolutism.

The lack of sustained popular demand for democracy on the continent might not therefore come as a surprise, but instead reflect a realistic absence of faith in its eventual success. Of course, Africans share universal desires for freedom, representation, and government accountability. Yet, they might not expect these conditions to obtain on their continent. They might perceive that political life is constrained by other factors that prevent sustainable full-fledged democracy. Opinion surveys by Afrobarometer capture this erosion of democratic preferences. On average, among twelve relatively democratic countries, support for democracy eroded from 69 percent of respondents in 2000 to 61 percent in 2005. Ten out of the twelve countries saw declines in support, including as much as 16 percent in Botswana and Nigeria, 19 percent in Uganda, and 46 percent in Tanzania. Similarly, satisfaction with democracy fell from an average of 58 percent around 2000 to 45 percent around 2005.[13]

Legal Command and Governance

Judging Africa's progress on governance quality rather than political rights paints an even bleaker picture. Democratic or not, most African governments have remained mired in patterns of bad governance, unable or unwilling to reduce corruption, promote the rule of law, and develop effective bureaucratic capacity. Given the decade or more of governance focus by aid donors and by African governments themselves, this trend illustrates the remarkable resilience of unaccountable public practices and of the instrumentalization of public office. Table 8.1, based on World Bank data, captures this dimension of Africa's political inertia, and the equilibrium nature of bad governance that characterizes its weak states.

Table 8.1   Governance in Africa, 1996–2007: Same or Worse

	1996	2007	Paired t-Test	One-Tail Probability
Voice and accountability	–0.60	–0.56	–0.58	0.28
Political stability	–0.54	–0.52	–0.12	0.45
Government effectiveness	–0.66	–0.78	1.54	0.07[a]
Regulatory quality	–0.61	–0.75	1.33	0.10[a]
Rule of law	–0.68	–0.75	0.93	0.18
Control of corruption	–0.59	–0.63	0.46	0.32

Sources: World Bank, *Africa Development Indicators 2007;* Kaufmann, Kraay, and Mastruzzi "Governance Matters."

Note: There are forty-eight observations. These indicators are distributed with a mean of 0 for the whole world and range from –2.5 to 2.5. Missing data for 1996 were replaced with 1998 observations; missing data for 2007 with 2006 observations.

a. Indicates a means difference significant at the 10 percent level in one tail.

The table shows that no improvement in governance quality has taken place between 1996 and 2007 on average for all forty-eight countries of sub-Saharan Africa for any of the indicators. The continent remains below the world's mean performance on all these dimensions of governance. Moreover, there has actually been a statistically significant decline in the average continent's performance on two of these indicators: government effectiveness and regulatory quality. These are the indicators that relate more closely to the daily administration of the country, to bare-bone state capacity. For sure, if we look at country-by-country performances, there have been some improvements. But these have not been dramatic. Governance in Africa tends to improve or worsen within a relatively small band of values that remains at the low end of the worldwide range. The extent to which discourses of good governance dominate the agendas of donors cannot be overstated, however. Thus, the degree to which Africa's weak states resist, ignore, or are incapable of adjusting to these demands is quite remarkable.

As with democracy, there are many reasons for Africa's crisis of governance. One of them, I argue, is the pervasiveness of legal command. The continent's resistance to stimuli for governance improvements is linked to the very resilience of the state itself, which derives from the centrality of legal command in social relations. Aid conditionality attempts to create policy incentives through fiscal means: misbehaving governments find themselves deprived of the tools of neopatrimonial redistribution. The better-behaving ones receive aid but agree to restrain themselves in their use of it. While empty or emptier coffers have indeed prevented African rulers from using fiscal resources with the same degree of freedom as before, they have not triggered any significant change in governance quality because they have not prevented these rulers from maintaining their control of sovereign command and of its distribution. The recipients of command have, in turn, continued to be able to use it to extract resources from others, compensating for dried-up fiscal flows. And there are very many such recipients at many levels of society. Ironically, for all the talk about the extent to which policy conditionality violates the sovereignty of African states, the one thing it has left untouched is actually their sovereignty.

The rise in the relative returns of legal command as a function of aid conditionality might help us understand why some dimensions of governance, such as administrative effectiveness and regulatory quality, have actually worsened. As donor pressure increases, the fiscal resources necessary for neopatrimonial redistribution dry up. As they do, the relative importance of command rises among strategies of survival and advancement. Regulation, for example, is a prime manifestation of legal command. Given the extractive nature of regulatory command, the quality of the regulatory environment declines as donor pressure for governance rises. In this case, sovereignty has not only undermined but actually reversed the path of reform.

Not only does the availability of sovereign command shield African governments from donor pressure to reform, but it also reduces domestic incentives for change. Domestically, the main consequence of the continued ability of African states to widely distribute the benefits of command lies in the fact that beneficiaries have no incentive to demand better governance. Universal command impedes the rise of significant groups of discontented citizens and elites for which improved governance would be a salvation. There certainly are plenty of discontented citizens and elites, but many victims of the state and its incompetence find that they are still locally better off from riding on the state's coattail than from challenging it. Their participation deprives them of the option of challenging the state. They decline to exit, whether physically or by rising as an independent force opposite the state. Universal command limits the size and strength of potential constituencies for change. It impedes the reformist potential of civil society.

This is not to say that there are not Africans who are genuinely dedicated to bringing about more accountability in government performance and more democracy. They certainly exist, and they tend to work at great risk to themselves and their family. What it does indicate, however, is that they are likely to be weak and to face difficulties in finding followers and in generating bona fide social movements, for the command-derived resilience of the state translates into a tendency for social and political inertia, which tends to abort or prevent the full-fledged development of initiatives for change.

The effective lack—however self-imposed—of an exit option in African politics has far-reaching consequences. In discussing them it might be worthwhile to take a few steps back and revisit the work of Albert Hirschman on "exit, voice, and loyalty." Hirschman argues that, at least in market situations, people (customers) can react to organizational decline (as manifested, for example, by declining product quality) by shopping elsewhere. Their exit from transaction triggers a "managerial reaction function," which is likely to lead to organizational recovery.[14] The alternative method for promoting organizational recovery is the use of voice—"any attempt at all to change, rather than to escape from, an objectionable state of affairs, whether through individual or collective petition"—which is more frequent in politics.[15] Although Hirschman derives ingenious insights from comparing the uses of exit and voice and the dynamics of their interaction, the distinction between them is somewhat overstated for our purpose. Both imply a measure of differentiation of citizens from the state apparatus, which is hampered in Africa by the pervasiveness of sovereign command in social relations. From our perspective, disengagement and voice both effectively represent exit patterns from the reach of, and the structuration of social life by, the state. This may seem too much of an amalgamation and one may argue that Africans frequently voice their displeasure at the poverty of governance, whether through elections, street demonstrations and protest, or even rebellions. While such a claim is not inaccurate, these instances of voice tend to be more frequently over issues of control of or succession within the system rather than challenges to the system itself. The more radical use of voice challenging the system and demanding an overhaul of existing structures is considerably rarer. It is the scarcity of this voice-as-challenge that I equate with the scarcity of exit in Africa.

The general prevention of exit confers an organization with certain monopoly advantages, particularly the enjoyment of the possibility of slack. The monopolist, Hirschman writes, has a "proneness to inefficiency, decay, and flabbiness," which derives from the lack of alternatives available to customers or citizens.[16] Sovereignty and the universality of legal command constitute a near-monopoly of forms of social, economic, and political exchange in Africa. The subsequent lack of exit, manifested through the sovereign stifling of constituencies for change, shields African rulers from any substantial pressure for a "reaction function" of their own, no matter the pressures of foreign aid.

Poor governance, weak state capacity, and institutional inertia can be partly construed as effects of the sovereign fetishization of social relations. As long as African governments remain imbued with the sovereign monopoly and the capacity to share it across their societies, they also remain largely shielded from sustained and broad-based domestic pressure for accountability. For sure, depriving them of the material resources of aid or threatening them with such deprivation (assuming the threat is credible) is likely to represent a significant nuisance and may well occasionally lead to improved performance. But, it leads to no sustained aggregate gain, for fiscal pressure will be offset by the continued availability, for personal use and for distribution, of the command resources of sovereignty.

These monopoly effects are further compounded by the contrast between fixed sovereignty and notions of accountability in many parts of the continent. Exit used to be an important tool of political accountability and self-preservation in precolonial Africa. Through it, Jeffrey Herbst writes, "it was possible for whole communities to escape permanently from their rulers."[17] Tim Kelsall notes that, in precolonial Africa, "production, persons and identities were mobile, with accountability being secured through the threat of flight."[18] There may not have been direct accountability, as characterized by the politics of voice that defines Western-style democracies, but the prevailing regimes of "Big Men" were kept on their toes by the possibility of exit of their subjects. This threat promoted better governance, expressed in terms of protection and provision of basic needs.[19] The first Banyamulenge, for example, probably settled in South Kivu as part of lineage exit and moved around the region as a mode of exit from abusive chiefs. The fixity of current African sovereignty precludes such creative exit.

The lack of accountability of African governments is an essential element in the poverty of their governance. The relationship between accountability and institutional quality is well established.[20] In his classical study of Italian governance, Robert Putnam has shown that government responsiveness to citizens correlated with performance.[21] By preventing the rise of effective domestic accountability, the African sovereignty regime is broadly inimical to good governance and development.

Not only is institutional accountability hampered by sovereignty in the short run, but the sovereign monopoly also stifles opportunities for institutional evolution over time. Around the world and throughout history, political institutions develop largely as a function of elites contracting with social forces to adjust to changing material conditions. Institutions are dynamic.[22] Some specific institutional form might rise with some enabling conditions and subsequently be supplanted by alternative arrangements when these conditions change. In Chapter 3, I briefly mentioned Hendrik Spruyt's work on this process as it unfolded in Western Europe.[23] Spruyt sees the late eleventh century as a time of growing economic production, long-distance trade, and rising towns. He notes that the increased importance of towns changed the balance of political order and led to several possible institutional outcomes, one of which was the territorial state.

France's Capetian dynasty (987–1328) is a prime example of the rise of the centralized territorial state. It came about, according to Spruyt, as the result of an alliance between the towns and the king, against the feudal lords. The towns wished to see their franchise recognized and protected against the overlapping loyalties of feudalism. The king offered such recognition and protection in exchange for an acceptable tax levied on the towns. For the king this was an opportunity to impose the principle of "territorial exclusivity" against rival lords.[24] The resulting features of the state were sovereign authority, territorial demarcation, royal justice, and a codified body of law, as opposed to the personal ties of feudalism and the universal claims of empire.

The sovereign state was only one among several possible institutional configurations at the time, as different material conditions prevailed across the region. In Germany, the emperor was domestically weak, busy as he was claiming universal holy power over Italy. Hence, the lords were unchecked. The cities could not find advantage in allying with a weak emperor. Instead, they went ahead and coalesced among themselves, which was made possible because they all produced similar types of bulk goods with little mutual competition. The Hanseatic League was a business association of towns, but it developed statelike institutions such as a parliament, representation abroad, legal texts, and so on. It acted like a nonterritorial confederation.[25]

We know the end of the story. The sovereign state won and became the dominant mode of political organization in Western Europe because of its superior features of internal hierarchy and territorial demarcation. Internal hierarchy led to standardization and certainty and helped prevent free-riding, increasing the credibility of the state's commitments toward other units. Territorial jurisdiction made it clear where state hierarchy applied and reduced opportunities for defections. Finally, other "units" followed suit, exiting the system they were in and mimicking statehood.

In Spruyt's theory, as new material forces unfold, they promote the reconfiguration of social alliances, which in turn lead to new institutional forms. An initial "shift in material power" contributes to defining "new rules of authority."[26] It might be unreasonable to expect the continuation of such dynamics in the contemporary world, given the domination and rigidity of the now universal territorial state. Nevertheless, the relative effectiveness of the sovereign state in different regions, and the different material conditions prevailing in them, might conceivably promote institutional adjustments of the territorial state, if left unimpeded. In Belgium, for example, the economic rise of Flanders in the second half of the twentieth century, and its ability to rely on new technologies and European economic integration for its own development, presided over a progressive dissolution of the state. Belgium might still exist (at the time of writing) as a recognized unit in a world of sovereign territorial states, but its functions have been largely delegated up and down, to the European and the local levels, in response to material changes between Belgium's regions and across Europe. Belgium has evolved.

One does not tend to see similar institutional evolutions in contemporary Africa, although the territorial state has not demonstrated any particular comparative advantage in bringing about development and successful social alliances in the continent.[27] Whatever historical alliance between modern elites and other segments of society may have prevailed in the sovereign state at the time of independence (for example, between Houphouët-Boigny as the "king" and cocoa planters in Côte d'Ivoire), it has not usually brought about sustained development.[28] Lacking the anticipated superior characteristics of their genus, African states are kept alive mostly by the effects of sovereign recognition. While this survival is often painted as a lone achievement in African political development, Spruyt's theoretical framework hints at the costs involved in the rigidity of African sovereignty. In short, sovereignty prevents institutional innovation and institutional responses to decay; it reduces the institutional elasticity of the state. By substituting an international arrangement for a set of domestic alliances, it removes the state from the realm of the institutionally negotiable. By promoting universal domestic acceptance through the distribution of legal command across society, it reduces incentives for social contracting among subnational elites. We may not be dealing here with the towns of the late European Middle Ages, but the same logic applies. Customary authorities, for example, faced with distracted and incompetent states, do not have any incentive to league together and solve their own problem. On the contrary, their frequent partaking in the sovereign bounty gives them the opposite incentives. They are more likely to compete with their peers for access to legal command than form alliances to reform the state. The same logic applies to other potential institutional competitors to the contemporary state, be they rebel groups or civil society organizations. By and large, the failure of institutional evolution in Africa is a failure of social contracting.

Practically, sovereign rigidity translates into a lack of institutional competition, which serves the interests of incumbent elites. The resilience of the African state is thus also that of established patterns of domination. One is not surprised, therefore, to see African ruling elites continually reasserting—and demanding allegiance of others to—the territorial integrity, sovereignty, and unity of the state. The very preamble of the Ouagadougou Accord of 2007 between the Ivorian government and the FN, for example, begins by setting the stage for the maintenance of a political environment from which institutional innovation and competition are banned. As is customary of most similar documents in Africa, the participants to the accord "reiterate" their "attachment to the respect of the sovereignty, independence, territorial integrity of and unity of Côte d'Ivoire."[29] This may read to some like some benign ritual incantation. But it is also the reinforcement of an institutional context at a time when complete state failure might conceivably have ushered in new institutional arrangements and progress. From a Spruytian point of view, the reiteration of the sovereignty of Côte d'Ivoire is stifling of institutional adjustment.[30] Although the Ivorian state has been unable to represent an institutional solution to the social upheavals engendered by Côte d'Ivoire's unresolved economic contradictions, its evolution is legally ruled out *ex ante*. The resulting treaty merely focuses on redefining the conditions of access to the state of different groups. It misses an opportunity for these social forces to come together and renegotiate the substance of their political union. It precludes social contracting.

The institutional protectionism of African sovereignty is also local. The national submission of regional elites reinforces their local domination via the conferring of local monopolies of sovereign authority, which stifle local institutional competition. The example of Zambia's Barotse Royal Establishment was particularly illustrative of this effect. Empowered with legal command in its region, the BRE maintained the dependence of local Lozi on its authority for their access to land, the adjudication of labor and family disputes, solutions to problems of sorcery, and even their access to state and international resources. Particularly, the power of giving land to people was a crucial element of the BRE's capacity to maintain its local hegemony. In my interviews in the region in 2003, I came across considerable frustration from the few local business people about their difficulties in operating independently of the BRE. Multiplied many times across the territories of African states, legal command effectively guarantees that there is no escape from domination in Africa.

Legal Command and the Economy

Although African poverty and inequality have many other sources, they partly result from Africa's sovereignty regime. The main effect of legal command on the economy lies in its inducement of predatory relations. Offices of declaratory power, of regulation and control, and of state appropriation offer their occupants the tools and authority to extract resources from others. Intermediaries participate in this predation by making it more bearable for its victims. As a result, mutual predation has become a significant element of the mode of production of some African societies.[31] Yet, predation does not actually produce anything. Legal command extracts what can hardly be termed a surplus from many Africans without any compensating productive activity. It defines an economic system in which the capacity of one to eat—in the sense of Bayart's politics of the belly—takes place at the expense of the other. Crawford Young termed the "hollowing out" of the state at the hands of its predatory agents a "self-cannibalization" of society.[32] The African state is maintained, but African societies and their potential for development are torn apart in the process.

Spreading beyond the confines of state power, predatory legal command is destructive of the social and economic fabrics of the societies that it plagues. The prevalence of "coop" as a survival strategy in the DRC illustrates this contagion. Coop—characterized by informal bargaining, trickery, negotiation, and imaginative new solutions to survive by "striking deals"—is occasionally and accurately analyzed as evidence of the resourcefulness of the Congolese in the failed state environment. Yet, as Theodore Trefon notes, it also involves a great deal of amorality, as the sentiment develops that "socially unacceptable [behaviors] such as fraud, violence or corruption are necessary to meet vital needs."[33] While people survive day to day by resorting to coop, "society becomes its own prey."[34] In Nigeria too, predatory social and economic relations contribute to a web of corruption from which it is hard to escape.[35] Daniel Smith notes that the frustration that results from this type of lifestyle might well be partly responsible for the country's prevailing violence. He details the "419" industry, frequently manifested in rich countries through e-mails promising some percentage of fraudulently acquired state funds. This practice is so widespread in Nigeria that it has become a verb, as in "I got 419'd." People rent houses they do not own, sell goods they do not have, promise services they do not deliver or finish. Capitalizing on distrust as a mode of economic activity is inherently limited, however. While there is money to be made from chaos, its generalization is inimical to productive activities, which require some stable property rights, a willingness of state agents to enforce contracts, and a minimum level of social capital. The predatory nature of economic and political relations, structured by legal command, prevents the spread of social trust and sabotages possibly one of the most fundamental sources of long-run growth.[36]

The debilitating environment of legal command also promotes state incompetence. As bureaucratic agents focus on extraction, and as people expect this much from them, state capacity erodes. A human rights activist in Lubumbashi told me in 2002 of the decay of the two large local parastatals, the mining company Gécamines and the Société Nationale des Chemins de Fer Congolais, the national railroad company. Workers were going unpaid, he noted, for no other reason than managers were stealing their salaries. It was understood that they would do this and thus they faced no sanction from above (or from below). On the contrary, they were probably expected to return a percentage of their loot to those who had appointed them to such profitable positions. Actual management could not be expected from them in these circumstances.[37] Similarly, few Congolese expect traffic-control police—so-called *roulages*—to actually control traffic. In Kinshasa, most people perceive traffic enforcement as little more than a racket. When the Kinshasa police received some motorbikes from the European Union in 2007, blogger Cédric Kalonji reported that they quickly became popular among *roulages* as they allowed for hot pursuit of those who refused to be pulled aside for the ritual of extraction. The motorbikes' multiplier effect on the revenues from legal command resulted in higher-ranking officers charging traffic officers for their use. A gift from donors meant to promote state capacity increased instead the extractive potential of a position of state authority.[38]

The incapacity of state institutions not only deprives Africans of public services and public goods; it also increases the costs that they encounter while trying to transact among themselves. In discussing the supply of food to Kinshasa, Eric Tollens notes that networks of food provision "do not benefit from any support from public authorities. The latter constitute on the contrary one of the principal obstacles to the free circulation and commercialization of goods, through the imposition of artificial prices, the levies of miscellaneous taxes and the intensive use of miscellaneous other means of more coercive extortion." He then goes on to note how the "voracity" of public authorities has generated the rise of many "ghost markets" in Kinshasa, that is, minuscule temporary markets out of someone's car trunk, in someone's compound, or under the cover of night, which appear when someone has goods to sell and disappear as soon as public authorities show up.[39] Again, such practices may illustrate the remarkable resourcefulness of Africans before the state, but they are no way to build an economy.

Of course, state officers are paid very little and practice their deviant trade of necessity. That they would pay themselves from their position of authority is the very foundation of the regime of legal command. It is thus the expectation of all that they will abuse their office. My point here is to highlight how the assignment of such income prebends *necessarily* undermines the performance of bureaucratic, control, or regulatory functions of the state. The problem is not one of corrupt individuals who can be righted by incantations for good governance, better training, or threats of punishment. What is corrupt is the very purpose of the institution, the very nature of the state-society relations it underwrites. Legal command is corruption. It is theft. And it is the state.[40]

Predation and weak state capacity are significant contributors to African poverty. To reiterate, African poverty has many more sources than legal command, including commodity dependence, climatic obstacles, the trade policies of developed countries, colonization, economic extraversion, poor infrastructure, low agricultural productivity partly related to a lack of irrigation and unpredictable rain patterns, counterproductive aid policies, and more. My focus on the causal link between sovereignty and poverty is not meant to deny or minimize the role of other factors. It is meant to point out, however, that sovereignty is one of these factors, which might be insufficiently appreciated by students of African underdevelopment.

Sovereignty is often perceived as a good thing for Africa and Africans, one of the few things they can rely on to protect themselves from unequal worldwide economic conditions. This might well sometimes be true. Yet, this chapter and much of the rest of this book have articulated how the domestic currency of international sovereignty in Africa—its conversion into legal command—reduces the quality of public governance and promotes predatory political, social, and economic relations that induce poverty over and above whatever other obstacles Africans may already be confronted with. Legal command reduces the accountability of public institutions by depriving Africans of credible exit mechanisms. Unaccountable institutions are in turn less responsive to demands for development and poverty alleviation. Even if they wished to provide public goods—such as growth—legal command's predatory nature also reduces the very capacity of state institutions to do so. Furthermore, it promotes unproductive extraction and mutual exploitation as a dominant economic system. It is through these mechanisms that sovereignty induces poverty in Africa.

Occasional rumors of economic takeoff on the continent may seem to belie my assessment or make it seem particularly pessimistic. The World Bank, for example, published a report in 2008 that vaunted renewed economic growth across the region and imputed it, in part, to better governance. According to the bank, continentwide economic growth averaged 5.4 percent in 2005 and 2006, and "many African economies appear to have turned the corner and moved to a path of faster and steadier economic growth."[41] The bank acknowledged that these positive results were largely affected by surging oil and other mineral commodity prices, but insisted that policies and governance had improved, noting particularly "more assaults on corruption."[42]

A closer look at the World Bank's own data makes it hard to share its enthusiasm, however. First of all, as discussed with respect to Table 8.1, there is no evidence of any improvement in governance across the continent, including corruption. Second, setting aside the growth rates of oil producers like Equatorial Guinea (30.8% annual growth from 1996 to 2005), of countries receiving massive oil-related investments like São Tomé and Príncipe (7.1% over the same period), and of postconflict aid-saturated countries such as Mozambique (8.3%), Rwanda (7.6%), and Sierra Leone (5.2%), the average economic performance of the continent barely exceeds its rate of population growth. The World Bank itself acknowledges that growth rates need to average 7 percent to sustain poverty reductions. Third, claimed achievements in poverty reduction are little more than the reversal of previous further deteriorations and are based on flimsy evidence. According to the bank, the number of Africans living in poverty has fallen from 47 percent in 1990 to 41 percent in 2004.[43] Although there seems to be a reduction in poverty rates from the 1990s to the 2000s, this trend seems to involve no more than sixteen countries. Averaging the nine observations for which the bank actually provides data in the appendix for the period 2000–2005 yields an unweighted mean rate of 49 percent of people below the poverty line.[44] Moreover, many countries have data available for the 1990s, then no longer. But the capacity to collect data usually correlates with the quality of other policies. The absence of data is therefore more likely to suggest decline than improvements. Finally, the poverty improvements suggested by the bank come in the wake of a rapid worsening of poverty in Africa in the previous decades. Between 1981 and 2001, the share of Africans living on less than $1 a day rose from 41.6 to 46.4 percent.[45] Thus, if the World Bank's latest figures are correct, they would merely indicate a return to the poverty rates of 1980.

By and large, recent African economic growth is a matter of oil and other minerals and is driven by Chinese demands and strategic developments in other parts of the world. The usual opacity of the public finances of oil producers does not augur well for this surplus to be reinvested productively. There may be some significant improvements in economic policies among Africa's smallest states, whose aid dependence is greatest. But the majority of Africans, who live in large states, remain mired in poverty. In general, not only is African governance not showing significant signs of improvement, but some analysts of the continent suggest instead that many African states increasingly act like criminal institutions, particularly the fast-growing oil producers of the Gulf of Guinea.[46]

Hopefully, the World Bank is right and I am wrong. However, it is not the first time that the World Bank or some other donor institution has suggested that Africa had turned the corner of development. Moreover, the gaps in the data are so large as to make it unreliable to infer any trend. The fact is that, despite its recent performance, Africa remains by far the poorest region of the world, with still about four out of ten individuals living in poverty despite fifty years of development efforts, per capita income lower than thirty years ago, and many Africans worse off than they were at the time of independence.[47] Only a handful of countries are likely to meet even half of the eight Millennium Development Goals laid down by the UN to reduce poverty by 2015.[48]

My argument is that Africa remains trapped in a crisis of bad governance, which derives in large part from the incentives associated with the sovereign regime. Without improved governance, the continent is unlikely to develop sustainably, and its population is unlikely to escape poverty in significant numbers. Perfect institutions might not be necessary for development, but the credible commitment of authorities is.[49] Policy reforms in Africa lack credibility because Africans know that their elites can continue to derive power and resources from legal command, however fiscally constrained they may be by donors.

In addition to their effects on poverty, predation and weak state capacity are also significant contributors to African inequality. While many African economies have failed to register significant per capita growth since the 1960s, they have, however, become increasingly unequal in the manner in which they distribute income (and probably also assets). The average Gini coefficient (a measure of income inequality that can range from 0 [most equal] to 100 [most unequal]) for sub-Saharan Africa as a whole averages about 49.[50] Not only is this increase in inequality a negative trend per se, but it is also discordant with Africa's general poverty. Usually, inequality rises with development and industrialization and tends to peak for countries at middle levels of income, while low-income countries, like those of Africa, and rich countries typically display lower Gini coefficients. As Table 8.2 makes clear, this trend is empirically verified for most regions of the world. Latin American countries, for example, which are typically middle-income countries and are notorious for their widespread economic inequality related in part to patterns of land ownership, average 52 on the Gini index. The rich countries of Europe and North America, in contrast, have Gini scores around 32. Thus, Africa displays a much more substantial degree of economic inequality than would be warranted by its overall poverty and failure to industrialize. Its Gini average is very close to that of Latin America, which is already an outlier among middle-income countries.[51]

Again, it is not my purpose to impute all African inequality upon sovereignty. Yet, sovereignty does contribute to increased inequality in several ways. First, the very extractive nature of legal command and its association with positions of state authority render its exercise automatically productive of inequality. Access to command is widespread throughout society, but it is nevertheless scarce. It remains the privilege of political elites, state employees,

Table 8.2 Income Inequality in Africa and the Rest of the World

Region	Gini Coefficient	Per Capita Income (US$)
Asia	38.0	6,535
Europe and North America	32.4	27,080
Latin America and Caribbean	52.2	5,073
Middle East and North Africa	37.7	9,944
Sub-Saharan Africa	49.2	1,473

Sources: http://hdrstats.undp.org/indicators/147.html; http://imf.org/external/pubs/ft/weo/2008/02/weodata/index.aspx; van de Walle, "The Institutional Origins."

Note: Gini coefficients calculated over the 1990–2007 period. Per capita GDP in nominal 2007 dollars. The countries in the regional samples occasionally differ from one variable to the other.

and those who manage to otherwise associate with the state. Because command allows for resource extraction, political inequality produces economic inequality. Those associated with power have a formidable capacity for resource appropriation. At the bottom of the state hierarchy, this may not translate into much inequality, as command may merely be a tool of survival. But, among national and regional elites, the degree of economic differentiation from the rest of society is large indeed. In the DRC, for example, amid the collapse of public infrastructure and the visible indigence of many citizens, the wealth of the political class appears unfathomable. Across Africa's weak states, as regional elites exchange their compliance with the state for the tools of local sovereign domination, they in turn multiply the production of domestic inequality. The very resilience of the weak state is thus an inequality-inducing process. This observation echoes Richard Sklar's claim that African social classes form around relations of power rather than of production.[52]

There is also a less obvious path by which sovereignty promotes inequality. When the state fails to provide some public good like security, energy, infrastructure, or communications, those who can afford to will find alternative sources of provision. In the case of security, for example, private companies may remedy police deficiencies (which may sometimes involve the private contracting of police or military personnel). Achille Mbembe has called "private indirect government" the practice whereby "functions supposed to be public, and obligations that flow from sovereignty, are increasingly performed by private operators for private ends."[53] A similar individual logic prevails for energy, infrastructure, and communications. The World Bank notes that, in a sample of six African countries, electrical outages occurred ninety-one days out of the year. In a comparative sample of fifty other developing countries, outages occurred twenty-nine days out of the year.[54] The frequent power interruptions almost throughout Africa have made individual gasoline-powered electricity generators ubiquitous—48 percent of African firms maintain their own generation equipment, as opposed to 32 percent elsewhere in the developing world.[55] In Monrovia, which was still without public electricity in 2008, Abdoulaye Dukule reports that "'big shots' maintain two to three generators—one at their home, another at their 'second home' and a third at the 'other home.'"[56] And, according to a South African electricity regulator quoted by the *New York Times*, "I've been on the 20th floor of an apartment building in Luanda, and there would be generators on all the verandas, with the racket, the fumes. . . . And the lift isn't working, because the main power supply is off."[57]

Similarly, bad roads go unrepaired for long periods of time. Herbst has shown that there is little difference between road networks in Africa at the time of independence and forty years later.[58] And many roads exist only on maps. Even in relatively small Congo-Brazzaville, one has to fly almost everywhere outside Brazzaville. Those who cannot afford to fly will spend days or weeks traveling short distances and will risk their belongings and sometimes their lives at many roadblocks manned by troops, militias, or mere bandits. For shorter trips, local and foreign elites—including UN and development NGO personnel—use four-wheel drives to negotiate the potholes. There is no other short-term alternative. The use of air transport reduces the need for the elites to have the roads fixed. The generalization of all-terrain vehicles has the same effect, with the additional negative impact of further deteriorating the roads.

The immense popularity of cell phones in Africa follows a similar logic, although it is somewhat more democratic. In many African countries, it has become very difficult to obtain a landline connection. Existing ones are poorly maintained and few governments are still investing in expanding infrastructure. Because cellular phones require very little infrastructure, many cell phone companies have become very active on the continent. They sell telephones and air time, which people can purchase in small increments. Their relatively cheap price has allowed many individuals who would never have been able to get a landline to have access to a phone. As a result, the number of phones per 1,000 workers in Africa has jumped from twenty-one in the 1990s to ninety in the 2000s.[59] This has had beneficial effects. In Niger, Jenny Aker has found that the use of cell phones among grain traders was associated with a decrease in price variations around the country and a small but significant decrease in the average price of grain.[60]

Setting aside the possible exception of the benefits of cellular phones, the attempts of the better-offs to cope with shortcomings of the state by designing private solutions to government failure generally produce additional inequalities. Stressing another insight from the work of Albert Hirschman, the effective exit of these wealthy individuals from the collective realm reduces the incentives for the system to adjust and improve. Those left behind end up worse off. From this perspective, even the relatively democratic spread of cellular telephony in Africa is likely to worsen the communication lot of the 90 percent of citizens who do not have access to these phones and are now less likely than before to see landlines extended to their region or village. Returning to energy, while many rich Nigerians generate their own electricity, only nineteen of seventy-nine power plants worked in the country as of July 2007. According to the Nigerian Council for Renewable Energy, quoted in the *New York Times*, "daily electricity output has plunged 60 percent from its peak, and blackouts cost the economy $1 billion a year."[61]

In conclusion, multiple facets of the African sovereignty regime coalesce to keep African countries underdeveloped. Unaccountable governance, ensconced in patterns of legal command, appears immune to reform and sheltered from institutional competition. Mutual predation pervades economic activity, producing poverty and inequality. In the streets of N'djamena and Abidjan, the hills of Kivu, the creeks of the Niger Delta, the plains of the Zambezi, the woods of Casamance, and many other places across the continent, life can be short, nasty, and brutish. Yet, it is not, as Hobbes would have it, for lack of a Leviathan. In Africa, sorrow comes at the hands of the state.

Notes

1. The Freedom House index ranges from 7 (not free at all) to 1 (completely free).
2. Lindbergh, *Democracy and Elections.*
3. Posner and Young, "The Institutionalization of Political Power."
4. Huntington, *The Third Wave.*
5. On "partial reform," an expression initially coined with respect to economic reforms, see van de Walle, *African Economies*; Lewis, "Governance and Political Space." On electoral autocracies, see Joseph, "Africa: States in Crisis." On hybrid regimes, see Diamond, "Thinking About Hybrid Regimes"; and Villalón and Von-Doepp, *The Fate,* 6. See also Joseph, "Africa, 1990–1997"; Mwandakire, "Crisis Management"; and Young, "The Third Wave."
6. Posner and Young, "The Institutionalization of Political Power."
7. Yet, the lack of substantive policy choices for governments constrained by donor agendas might partly account for the absence of ideological differentiations among parties. See Mwandakire, "Crisis Management."
8. Tidjani Alou, "Corruption in the Legal System," 157. See also Vansina, "Mwasi's Trials."
9. Young, *The African Colonial State,* 30.
10. Ibid., 285.
11. Ibid., 2.
12. Mbembe, *On the Postcolony*, 26.
13. Bratton and Cho, "Where Is Africa Going," 17 and 19.
14. Hirschman, *Exit, Voice, and Loyalty,* 23.
15. Ibid., 30.
16. Ibid., 57.
17. Herbst, *States and Power in Africa*, 228.
18. Kelsall, "History, Identity, and Collective Action," 54.
19. Kelsall's own theory, linking the de-agrarianization of African economies to the breakdown of identifiable communities that could have provided the continued foundation for exit-based accountable governance, is particularly insightful.
20. See van de Walle, *Overcoming Stagnation.*
21. Putnam, *Making Democracy Work.*
22. See North, *Institutions, Institutional Change.*
23. Spruyt, *The Sovereign State.*
24. Ibid., 77.
25. Another arrangement mentioned by Spruyt was the city-state of Northern Italy.
26. Spruyt, *The Sovereign State,* 67.
27. For a related claim, focused instead on large territorial states, see Herbst, *States and Power in Africa.*
28. The notable exception is Botswana, where the Tswana cattle-raising class has done very well out of the territorial state. See Samatar, "Botswana."
29. République de Côte d'Ivoire, "Dialogue Direct: Accord Politique de Ouagadougou," March 2007, 2, Mimeo.

30. Note that, in underwriting the sovereign system, Western countries deny Africans the benefits of institutional competition from which they themselves greatly benefited. Ironically, this denial takes place in a context that seems to extend to Africans the qualities and benefits of Western states.

31. For another discussion of Africa's "economy of predation," see Mbembe, *On the Postcolony*, 46.

32. Young, "Reflections on State Decline," quoted in Lemarchand, "The Democratic Republic of Congo," 37.

33. Trefon, "The Political Economy," 487.

34. Bilakila, "La 'coop' a Kinshasa," 45.

35. Smith, *A Culture of Corruption.*

36. While I have doubts on the validity of much of the "social capital" or "social trust" literature, there is great intuitive appeal to the notion that bonds of trust facilitate investment and capital accumulation. Their relative absence in Africa correlates with the continent's deficit of investment (see van de Walle, "Economic Reform," 34–35), and with the preference of political elites for capital flight and luxury consumption over accumulation (see Soares de Oliveira, *Oil and Politics*, 140–146).

37. Anonymous interview, Lubumbashi, April 2002.

38. Cédric Kalonji. "Motos pour les policiers de la route, bon moyen pour maximiser les recettes." Congoblog, 19 November 2007. http://cedric.uing.net/1802/page_d_accueil.html?b_st=0&b_d=&b_cd=20090309&b_m=&b_u=&b_pi=0&b_k=0&b_s=roulage&b_o=DESC.

39. Tollens, "Sécurité alimentaire a Kinshasa," 67.

40. The structuring of state-society relations by sovereign theft is the general rule, but it is not without exceptions. There are people of integrity who resist this system all over Africa.

41. World Bank, *Africa Development Indicators 2007*, 1.

42. Ibid.

43. Ibid., 8.

44. Ibid., 48.

45. UNDP, *Human Development Report*, 34.

46. On the criminalization of African states, see Hibou, "The Social Capital." On the particular case of criminal African petro-states like Angola, Chad, or Equatorial Guinea, see Soares de Oliveira, *Oil and Politics.*

47. Leonard and Straus, *Africa's Stalled Development*; Lancaster, "Development in Africa," 222.

48. "A Glimmer of Light at Last?" *The Economist*, 22 June 2006.

49. See the recent comparison of institutions and development in Nigeria and Indonesia by Lewis, *Growing Apart.* Lewis shows that Indonesia was able to take off economically with less than ideal institutions, but with sufficient governance credibility to induce a market response.

50. Van de Walle, "The Institutional Origins."

51. Nicolas van de Walle ("The Institutional Origins") has called attention to the unusually high levels of income inequality in Africa and has also offered explanations for it that relate to politics more than to economics.

52. Sklar, "The Nature of Class Domination." For a more detailed discussion of the inequality-producing nature of the African state, see Bayart, *The State in Africa.*

53. Mbembe, *On the Postcolony*, 80.

54. World Bank, *Africa Development Indicators 2007*, 6.

55. Ibid.

56. Dukule, "Life in Monrovia."

57. Wines, "Toiling in the Dark."
58. Herbst, *States and Power in Africa.*
59. World Bank, *Africa Development Indicators 2007,* 6.
60. Aker, "Does Digital Divide or Provide?"
61. Wines, "Toiling in the Dark."

Part 4
Conclusion

In Chapter 9, I conclude with some possibly far-fetched policy impli-cations of my argument. The irony of all Western approaches to African underdevelopment is that, no matter how conditional or selective they might be regarding policies and government behavior, they never challenge the very existence and sovereignty of African states (although Jeffrey Herbst offers a major exception to this in his *States and Power in Africa*). While this restraint is often perceived as a form of respect for Africans, I argue that the maintenance and reinforcement of the sovereign state system by donors not only facilitates the continuation of sovereign predation, but also represents a form of Western validation of African politics essentially based upon the colonial blueprint. To use a lapidary shortcut, the protection of African sovereignty is an extension of colonialism. Consistent with this understanding, I offer a menu of policy recommendations—addressed to some hypothetical international community presumably interested in African development—which starts with withdrawing the postcolonial recognition of African states before moving to more realistic suggestions, all of which are based on the idea of altering the behavioral incentives of African elites away from sovereign inertia and toward improved governance, while recognizing their self-interests and the potential costs and benefits of their actions.

9

Rational Policy Fantasies

Despite their crisis, African states are stable, prodded by the inter-national recognition of their sovereignty. They not only endure, but often represent optimal short-term outcomes for individual strategies of survival. Attempts by outsiders at promoting change in Africa typically have not accounted for the equilibrium qualities of the African sovereign regime. Donor responses to weak state performance have included calls for better governance based on conditionality (the exchange of aid for a promise of better behavior) or selectivity (the awarding of aid to better-behaving countries); promotion of greater state capacity through training, technology, or material incentives; and sheer reconstruction of collapsed states by outsiders. Yet, none of these approaches accounts for the role of sovereignty in these countries' predicament. They tinker with elements of the state's public manifestation, but take the state itself for granted. But if state reproduction occurs in a way that undermines the emancipation of Africans, what is the redeeming value of state stability? Does it contribute anything that trumps African development and democracy? Given the centrality of the domestic uses of sovereignty in the reproduction of Africa's failed states, it is hard to sidestep the conclusion that they should no longer benefit from the automatic recognition of the rest of the world.

Questioning states can be heretic. Not only African elites, but scholars, international organizations, and even humanitarian groups tend to be favorably disposed toward existing states. Paul Collier in *The Bottom Billion*, for example, complains that poor landlocked African countries should probably not have been permitted to become independent, yet "the deed is done, and we have to live with the consequences."[1] Why this should be the case is unclear, however. In contrast this conclusion tries to rationally follow the book's argument to its logical implications and policy recommendations. Of necessity, these revolve around deflating state sovereignty in Africa. In a world of sovereign territorial states, such recommendations might sound like fantasies. Yet, as unrealistic as they might be, there must be some merit in fostering a discussion of these options, in bringing them into the realm of the thinkable. Jeffrey Herbst has already blazed this trail.[2] Some of his prescriptions have greatly inspired mine.

In general, the logic of my recommendations relies on incentives. Rather than assuming altruism or benevolence, they highlight the circumstances under which it would be rational for African elites to pursue policies that maximize public welfare rather than predation. Reliance on incentives is not new and lies in fact at the heart of both conditionality and selectivity. The US Millennium Challenge Account, for example, provides monetary incentives to the governments of developing countries to compete with each other on matters of governance. Yet, conditionality is easily bypassed and incentives like those of the Millennium Challenge Account tend to apply only to those states that already are the best performing. More important, depriving a government of fiscal resources does not deprive it of the domestic tools of sovereignty, which it can distribute as a resource. In keeping with the logic of the book's argument, modifications in the practices and norms of recognition might have the most powerful effects on the rulers' and reformers' incentives. Some form of institutional resuscitation can be achieved in Africa if political elites are given incentives to pursue their own interests in a manner that also benefits institutional development and the welfare of the greatest number. These incentives are more likely to be effective if the "international community" relaxes its guarantee of the existence of currently weak and failed states.[3] In other words, Africans must be empowered with some form of exit option in order to constrain the individual maximization exercise of their elites. The development of the capacity of African states may therefore be linked to a renunciation of their sanctity.

I do not discuss the pros and cons of current aid policies toward Africa's weak states at any significant length, except for occasional passing references. There have been several excellent recent books on this topic.[4] The focus here is instead on the argument that, if state sovereignty is a cause of Africa's predicament, then it must be altered. I present three versions of it, from most to least radical.

The End of Western Validation

There is an overwhelming bias in the practice of international relations in favor of sovereign states, irrespective of the negative nature of their sovereignty or of all other doctrinal claims in favor of state responsibility or the human rights of citizens. For international actors, the sovereign, by default, is always endowed with some presumption of popular domestic legitimacy, even in the absence of any evidence. For example, the UN Panel of Experts on the

Illegal Exploitation of Natural Resources and Other Forms of Wealth of the Democratic Republic of Congo stated in its October 2002 report that a "step towards halting the [illegal] exploitation of natural resources" in the DRC would be to "ensure that central government control is reinstated."[5] This statement came in the wake of pages of evidence related to the abuses and exploitation of government officials and rebels alike. How reinstating the state would reduce rather than magnify their exploitative behavior was not demonstrated, nor did it make intuitive sense, apart from its convenience to donors. In addition, it has not proven empirically valid since the relative restoration of centralized state authority in the DRC in 2003. Similarly, the typical recommendations of reports by the International Crisis Group stress resumption of state authority and strengthening of its institutions. The Kimberley Process, to stem the flow of "blood diamonds" in Africa, demands producing states to issue certificates of origin, as if they were less likely than rebels to organize violence in the areas they control. Somehow, a diamond produced in Katanga, under control of government forces, is more legitimate than a diamond produced in Kivu under rebel control. But what made the Congolese government—then nothing more than successful rebels—more legitimate than rebels, apart from recognition?

Sovereignty, however, constrains the realm of the thinkable in domestic and international relations of power. Michel Oksenberg, looking at the introduction of the concept of sovereignty by Western powers in East Asia, has aptly shown that it "tilts" us "toward some solutions over others." In the case of China, sovereignty "affected the way in which the rulers . . . approach[ed] their policies toward Taiwan, Tibet, and Hong-Kong."[6] In the early 1800s, the Qing emperor ruled over the area through a model of cultural superiority, Oksenberg argues, with ill-defined boundaries and rituals of obedience from lesser peripheral lords. Peripheral populations were not literally forced to choose between being Chinese or something else. Ambiguity in formal status allowed for the coexistence of several forms of authority. Sovereignty put an end to this because of its territorially exclusive nature, and its monopolistic impulse.

In Africa, too, our recognition of the sovereignty of states limits what policies are possible. And because African sovereignty is acquired from past colonial existence, one can argue that, almost fifty years after most independences, colonialism still defines the realm of the possible and, more stunningly even, the foundations of political authority in Africa. Colonially derived institutions, however reviled, remain imbued with the seal of sovereign sacredness. The maintenance of the recognition of their state status in international relations is paramount to the hegemonic strategies of African rulers, and of their potential challengers. African rulers are adept at wielding the presumption of representation that comes from sovereign recognition. When criticized by the international NGO Global Witness for its opaque management of oil revenues,

Congo's president Denis Sassou-Nguesso declared, "What is the legitimacy of Global Witness? In whose name does this NGO speak? As for us, we speak in the name of the Congolese people."[7]

My first policy fantasy, then, is to wipe away this sovereign bias with a blanket removal of the recognition of Africa's postcolonial states. Considering them to be the contemporary manifestation of colonialism, one could simply refuse to recognize them. This is not to imply that one could not trade with their producers, arrange air links with them, or develop other forms of economic interactions, but there would be no diplomatic recognition. Other countries would not recognize their governments, their sovereignty, their membership in the international system of states. For anyone who cares about the emancipation of Africans from the remaining shackles of colonialism, this policy would spell freedom at last. The Berlin Conference would be undone; the business of decolonization finished once and for all. While African rulers would certainly attack such a policy as a disregard for their people's sovereignty, it is really only their own prerogatives as sovereign rulers that would be affected.

Thus, the United States, for example, could adopt a new doctrine, according to which it does not recognize African states. If many other non-African countries followed suit, it would effectively undermine, and possibly altogether erase, the supply of sovereignty to African states, thereby fundamentally altering the power and self-interest calculations of African elites. If sovereignty no longer were exogenously available to those occupying positions of state authority, it would deprive them of the tools of legal command. Without it, these elites might find greater incentives to establish social contracts with citizens in order to obtain domestic legitimacy and endogenous foundations to their right to rule and make rules. It might be rational for them to offer services, provide welfare, and otherwise behave with accountability in exchange for the recognition of their authority, in a domestic bargain that has historically been absent from postcolonial Africa. In other words, the withdrawal of international recognition might force African state authorities to seek domestic recognition.

Somaliland provides an example of what dynamics could unfold. Unrecognized by the rest of the world, it has developed better governance than the majority of African countries, despite being ensconced in a neighborhood rather inimical to quality government. Some have even argued that it would be a mistake to recognize Somaliland, for it would undermine existing incentives for good governance.[8] The logical extension of this argument, however, is that recognition should be withdrawn from other states if it will not be extended to Somaliland. What accounts for Somaliland's success in state-building? Political and business leaders located in the part of the country that was a former British colony effectively seceded from Somalia after it collapsed in 1991. After demobilizing and reinserting their combatants on their own, they developed public structures of basic stability and order, enabling the resumption of commercial activities. They also organized a constitutional succession and several credible local and national elections.[9] Remaining diplomatically unrecognized, the state has bargained with powerful local interests such as businessmen and clan elders. William Reno explains that, relying on businesses for revenue, authorities "are forced to take into account business interests in promoting economically efficient policies and in limiting commercial risk within Somaliland. Thus unlike southern political actors, Somaliland's authorities have an immediate interest in imposing uniform order and controlling coercion."[10] While Somaliland displays capacity, its authorities lack effective command—the reverse image of the rest of Africa. Its president needs permission from local clan leaders to travel through their region, unable as he is to impose his state on them without international sovereignty. In the struggle between loci of power that characterizes the process of state formation, the president is forced, without sovereignty, to seek *domestic* legitimacy.

Particularly interesting is the fact that the political and clan leaders of Somaliland decided that their region provided a better container for their ambitions than Somalia as a whole. With Somalia in chaos, they chose the level of political action that maximized their chances of success. This level was both regional—because of language and clan affinities—and postcolonial—because Somaliland's previous existence as a state offered an institutional skeleton to flesh out. In the absence of international recognition, African elites will be free to choose the arena in which to operate.

Somaliland demonstrates that it is possible to function without juridical sovereignty. It does not have any ambassador with any other country, but it hosts an Ethiopian trade office and has a Somaliland Liaison Office in Ethiopia, where Somaliland passports are recognized for official business. The Ethiopian Commercial Bank and the Central Bank of Somaliland have an agreement that facilitates transactions with the rest of the world, and Ethiopian Airlines flies to Hargeysa. There is also a Somaliland Liaison Office in South Africa. Senegal hosted the Somaliland president on a visit to Dakar in 2003, and Djibouti has signed agreements with his government.[11]

Outside of Africa, Taiwan offers maybe the best example of successful nonsovereign political and economic development. After being recognized since 1949 as the legitimate government of China, Taiwan lost its sovereignty in the 1970s. It first lost its seat at the UN in 1971. In the ensuing years, it was kicked out of other international organizations. In 1979, the United States switched its own diplomatic recognition from Taipei to Beijing, and in 1980, Taiwan was ousted from the World Bank and the IMF.[12] If such a derecognition happened to an African country, one would expect claims of injustice. Yet, after losing its sovereignty to the People's Republic of China, Taiwan not only endured as an effective state, but it liberalized its economy and thoroughly democratized. In fact, Taiwan went from a score of 6 on Freedom House's political rights variable in 1972 to 1 in 2005. Over the same period, its economy grew by close to 10 percent per annum.

Robert Madsen argues that their loss of recognition led the Taiwanese authorities to "implement policies that broadened the state's base of support among its citizenry."[13] After progressively allowing for a measure of economic liberalization, the Kuomintang government legalized opposition groups, abolished martial law, organized elections, and even issued an apology to the Taiwanese people for past misrule. In contrast, when the Kuomintang was still under the protection of the United States during the Cold War—a situation similar to the current shielding of African sovereignty—its rule was "founded on brute force" with a suspended constitution and no elections.[14] The Kuomintang was essentially using its international recognition to exert unaccountable authority at home. "Extrapolating from Taiwan's experience," Madsen writes, "it is clear that a state can do many things to mitigate the negative effects of losing formal legal sovereignty. By enacting sound domestic policies a government can develop a popular legitimacy that is largely independent of its stature among other countries."[15]

This is not to imply that losing recognition was not deeply problematic for Taiwanese authorities. Yet, they were able to maintain or build alternative paths of connection with other governments and international markets, which illustrates the possibilities for nonsovereign states to function in this world. The Taiwanese government constructed an "informal diplomatic structure . . . [with] new diplomatic mechanisms . . . unofficial embassies . . . [a] wide variety of semiofficial and private institutions . . . [acting] as agents of [the] Nationalist State . . . trade or cultural centers . . . China Airlines . . . [and an] American Institute in Taiwan to manage most aspects of US-[Taiwan] intercourse."[16] It also set up a China External Trade Development Council and maintained an active private diplomacy, illustrated for example by the 1995 visit of President Lee Teng-Hui to the United States.

The experience of Taiwan suggests two important patterns. First, when a state is derecognized internationally, the returns to its government of good domestic governance increase dramatically. For sure, other courses of action are possible, including increased domestic repression, from which no further international isolation can be feared. Yet, ceteris paribus, rulers face fewer incentives to provide effective governance from being recognized than from not. Second, and related, withdrawing recognition does not necessarily imply the disappearance of the state or its lack of international agency. In fact, domestically as well as internationally, derecognition leads to institutional innovation.

Deprived of sovereignty, some African states might succeed in engineering a similar transformation, and some might not. Some states might find themselves incapable of striking such a bargain, whether because of their advanced degree of decrepitude or because of their lack of credibility as agents of collective action within their societies. Some other groups might challenge them and rise as more successful providers of governance. These challengers may find it optimal to operate within existing states, find utility in merging states with neighboring reformers, or prefer to work at the subnational level. Logically, without recognition, if political entrepreneurs must rely on domestic legitimacy, we can expect them to focus their actions at the level of aggregation that maximizes governance quality and, therefore, to contribute to the creation of more empirical states in Africa. We should thus expect considerable but not systematic territorial reconfiguration from a blanket derecognition. Some elites might find that the institutions inherited from the postcolony facilitate their effectiveness and might thus try to negotiate a new social compact within the existing nation-state framework. Others might find the cultural homogeneity of subregions to provide more fertile ground. Because of their connections to sovereignty, national identities could very well dissolve and would not prevent such reconfigurations. Exit would once again become available and loyalty would have to be earned.

This is the best-case scenario. But derecognition could also unleash significant violence. In fact, the loss of sovereignty would raise the relative returns of controlling lootable natural resources and encourage some local political entrepreneurs to turn into violent warlords. Conflict may ensue with the authorities of the rump state. While this cannot be ruled out and presents a considerable potential liability to derecognition, one must bear two important arguments in mind when assessing this danger. First, the risk of nonsovereign violence must be weighed against the prevalence of political violence in the current sovereign system. Recall from Chapter 2 that thirty-two out of Africa's forty-eight states have witnessed at least one violent conflict since the 1960s and many of them more than one. The sovereignty of the DRC, for example, did not prevent its collapse into warlord-controlled zones of mineral exploitation. Yet, political violence in Africa has not typically been productive, if one may use that word, because of the continued appeal of the state's sovereign shell. Several authors have argued, however, that long-term state formation cannot take place without a certain amount of warfare and political violence.[17] Jeremy Weinstein, for example, has shown that effective national leadership tends to emerge in situations where well-organized insurgencies claim victory in wars whose outcome is not negotiated by outsiders.[18] Recent claims by the "Young Patriots" militia of southern Côte d'Ivoire that what the country needs is a "good civil war" echo this idea.[19] It is far from my intention to condone or encourage any type of violence. From a long-term state-formation point of view, however, the risks of political violence must be weighed against the potential of such violence to result in the formation of stable and developmental political systems. Conceivably, this potential is greater in a derecognized Africa than in a sovereign one.

Second, one can also justifiably question the premise that uncontrolled violence would follow derecognition. There might be pockets of violence, but one should also expect pockets of safety as some communities and their leaders organize collective action and provide public order. Some regions have already experienced potential alternative authorities to the state, which could exercise significant authority in a postrecognition environment. Somaliland, of course, comes to mind. So do the Kasai provinces of the DRC, which were largely autonomous in the latter years of the Mobutu regime under leadership from Catholic religious authorities.[20] Similarly, the Rwenzururu Kingdom of Uganda demonstrated in the 1960s its capacity for unrecognized self-rule. It should also be borne in mind that Africa was not an ocean of indiscriminate violence *before* the recognition of contemporary states, which originated with colonization. While there were large zones of statelessness, conflict, and enslavement, there were also some well-developed polities. Even the writings of Henry Morton Stanley testify to this. Stanley was swept off his feet by the extent of institutional capacity, social peace, and agricultural production he encountered in the Buganda Kingdom in the 1870s, to the point that he believed they only needed Christianity to complete their civilization. And, going as far back as the thirteenth century, the Charter of Kurukan-Fuga of the Mandingue Empire established political institutions, checks and balances, and a broad set of human rights.[21] Why would Africans be less capable of organizing public life today than then?

Another obvious criticism of the derecognition idea is that, to be effective, it must be followed by many states, including the most influential ones. To undo sovereignty, derecognition must be collective. African states, derecognized by the United States, would be unlikely to turn into Taiwans if their sovereignty were still recognized by Russia or China. The fact that respect for sovereignty is the main diplomatic pillar of China's massive return to Africa in the twenty-first century augurs ill for the possibility of collective action on this question.[22] Clearly, it would take an unusual diplomatic effort to yield derecognition. Non-African countries would have to perceive it as overwhelmingly in their interest to undertake such a collective step. It is unlikely to take place. On the other hand, the colonization of Africa also represented a massive diplomatic undertaking and, a mere ten years before the scramble of the 1880s, also looked rather unlikely to take place.

Let a Thousand Nations Bloom?
Liberalizing the Supply of Sovereignty

An alternative to the previous fantasy, which involved stifling the supply of sovereignty to African states, might be to liberalize its supply after first rationing it. One could start with a policy of derecognition and complement it with an offer of recognition to those public authorities that demonstrate benevolent rule. The logic would be the same as selective aid, which allocates funds

to countries with the best governance. But since sovereignty has a more enduring utility to rulers than money, the crucial mechanism would be selective
recognition. There would be no illusion as to the altruistic nature of rulers.
Recognition would be granted with the understanding that it represents a significant tool of domestic power, which is what would make it desirable for
African elites. Yet, these elites would be constrained in their domestic use of
sovereignty by the requirement for good governance. Because sovereignty
would be granted *ex post* to authorities that have already demonstrated their
willingness and capacity to serve their populations, it would endorse effective
states rather than create fictitious ones. Thus, by altering the criteria for recognition of states from postcolonial sovereignty to effective institution-building,
Western governments could foster the rise of indigenous forms of accountability. If a state's recognition were a function of the quality of its performance,
rather than of its previous existence as a colony, the pursuit of effective institutions would be compatible with individual and communal quests for resources. I borrow this idea from Jeffrey Herbst's concept of "decertification"
of states and recognition of breakaway units if they provide greater political
order than existing ones.[23]

This approach would be more likely to promote state-building than chaos
and would thereby avoid some of the uncertainties of complete derecognition.
By conditioning recognition upon good governance and making the maximization of elite self-interest compatible with public welfare, it would reduce
the returns to violence, as well as the rents associated with legal command
(and increase the relative returns of private paths of accumulation). Theoreti-
cally, elites would choose the level of political action that maximizes the development of state capacity to the extent that this level would also maximize
their chances of obtaining sovereignty. Although they can be expected to continue to seek the appropriation of the rents from state control for their own private advantage, they would now do so in a context that would neutralize the
benefits of sovereignty associated with weak statehood and make such pursuits compatible with public welfare. As with complete derecognition, this
context could be subnational, promote the adoption of a new developmental
social contract at the national level, or even encourage regional integration.

There is no a priori in this fantasy as to what or who should be recognized.
Although recognition is an outsider's act, it would be reactive to African initiatives. Under the incentive of recognition, African political entrepreneurs
might redefine more functional political units for themselves and their con-
stituents. They would choose the mode and level of governance that maximizes the chance of policy success and development, if these are the conditions for recognition. In some cases, new states would arise as local leaders
find that they provide them with better terrain for collective action. In other
cases, this new set of incentives would encourage new nationwide social contracts. At any rate, the potential for violence would be limited by the linking

of recognition to good governance, which implies human security at the very least. This approach would bypass criticisms of partition in Africa along the lines of "any new states would be just as arbitrary as what exists now," since whatever new state were to emerge would be an endogenous African creation. One often hears arguments that no new partitioning of Africa could be inherently better than what we have now. Every region has its own heterogeneity and would simply multiply existing predicaments. It should be clear, however, that the argument here does not advocate any ethnic-based or other preestablished pattern of state reconfiguration. Similarly, any outside redrawing of African boundaries would be foolish at best and, more likely, neocolonial. My argument instead is to offer recognition to effective units of governance, whatever geographical or ethnic form they take. If the Ashanti find it more convenient to organize within an Ashanti polity, they will be successful at providing security and services in this context and deserve recognition (provided the security, services, and legal rights are recognized to all residents, not just Ashanti). If, on the contrary, collective action appears easier to organize at the level of Ghana, Ghana could be recognized as an effective state. If, finally, Ghanaian authorities were to be more successful in organizing collectively with Burkina Faso or part thereof, the resulting union would be recognized. The point is that recognition is not based on any principle regarding the nature of the polity, but on its effectiveness as an agent of human protection. The problem with the postcolonial versus ethnic self-determination debate is that it focuses on identity rather than effectiveness. It asks "Is there a more legitimate level of recognition in principle?" while the right question is "Are there some effective units of governance that warrant recognition?"

The argument is thus not about promoting partition but about allowing it. If people have a right to leave and start their own government with a realistic chance of eventual recognition, existing governments might be more responsive to their needs. If they are not, then some or all of their citizens may organize along alternative lines that facilitate accountable collective action. The point is not to force African states to split, but to offer this option by making recognition conditional on effective institutional capacity. It may well be that current states would provide the best setting for this to happen; or they could merge; or they could split. It matters little in the end whether Africans would avail themselves of such options if they were given them. But making territorial partition politically feasible by altering the norms of recognition would at least modify the parameters of African elites' political calculus. Improved governance can be expected because of its requirement for recognition and because it would foster rulers' domestic legitimacy before recognition.

Note that there is nothing particularly radical about this fantasy. In fact, it applies principles of empirical sovereignty to Africa that have long prevailed in international society. Before decolonization, states were typically recognized only after they had established their domestic existence. The Montevideo Convention of 1933 on the rights and duties of states stipulates the conditions for statehood as including a territory, a stable population, effective government, and the capacity to enter into relations with other states. These conditions were abandoned with UN Resolution 1514 in 1960, which stipulated that lack of preparedness for independence could not be used as a reason for delaying it. Faced with lingering neocolonial threats, there were good reasons for such protection of new states at the time. But the liabilities of the system have now more than offset its benefits, and it is time to undo this provision. African rulers are unlikely to promote the transformation of their states into effective states unless they have to.

Recent examples of conditional recognition based on specific government behavior could be used as precedents. In 1991, faced with the Yugoslav situation, the European Union endorsed specific "Guidelines on the Recognition of the New States in Eastern Europe and the Soviet Union." Among these guidelines were the conditions that the new states "have constituted themselves on a democratic basis, have accepted the appropriate international obligations and have committed themselves in good faith to a peaceful process and to negotiations."[24] Moreover, the new states were explicitly required to offer "guarantees for the rights of ethnic and national groups and minorities." Similarly, when the Soviet Union broke down, the United States recognized Moldova, Turkmenistan, Azerbaijan, Tajikistan, Georgia, and Uzbekistan but withheld full diplomatic relations until "we are satisfied that they have made commitments to responsible security policies and democratic principles."[25] Why would African governments not be held responsible for such basic commitments?

There is a double hypocrisy to the prevailing system of international recognition. On the one hand, existing African states get a free pass, receiving recognition without meeting conventional or normative prerequisites for statehood. On the other hand, however, their constituent parts are subject to a more stringent application of the rules of self-determination and territorial integrity than elsewhere—although the rules themselves are the same. The principle of territorial integrity demands that there be no change in boundaries of existing states. This does not prevent, however, the recognition of constitutive units of existing states, on the grounds that they are part and parcel of these states. Such recognition is only possible, however, if the existing state itself agrees to its own dissolution, as happened with the Soviet Union in 1991. In the case of Yugoslavia, there was partly an agreement by the remainder of the Federal Republic to let go of some of its units (beginning with Slovenia and Croatia), and there was a judgment by the European Union that the country had dissolved, which allowed it to pretend that there were no secessionist republics per se but just successor states. At any rate, the recognition of countries such as the Baltic states in the former Soviet Union or Serbia in the former Yugoslavia was based in part on the fact that they had been seen as partial repositories of the sovereignty of their container state beforehand. In other words, they embodied part of it. This argument relied on the fact that they had been recognized as independent states in an earlier period: the Baltic states in the 1920s; Montenegro and Serbia as early as the Berlin Congress of 1878. Other republics, like Kazakhstan, Kyrgyzstan, Tajikistan, and Turkmenistan, were administrative creations of the Soviet Union but had been formally granted sovereignty in the Soviet constitution. The root of hypocrisy, however, lies in the fact that—with the exception of Ethiopia—the sovereignty of existing precolonial African political systems was never recognized by Western powers (even though Europeans signed treaties with most of them). Simply put, Africa was not part of the international system of states before its forceful integration into it. Thus, many African subnational systems have no legal ground on which to stand nowadays in terms of self-determination. As a result, even when their state collapses or dissolves, they cannot claim successor status.

Although the legal principles of recognition of states are universal, their application is biased against Africans—and more generally against post-colonies everywhere—who are denied certain rights based on Europe's unwillingness to recognize some of their systems as states in the nineteenth century. This is, of course, both an insult and an injury to Africans. It is an extension of colonialism, a denial of Africa's history. There may be very little that is emancipatory nowadays about precolonial political entities in Africa, but their institutional evolution could have taken a different path had it not been stifled by the sovereignty of the postcolonial states. At any rate, Africans are left in the current system with no recognizable institutional foundation to fall back on apart from the postcolonial state. Adopting a policy of recognition based on effective and benevolent governance would go a long way toward undoing this injustice.

If we were to adopt this approach, most existing African states might be derecognized. Botswana, Mauritius, and South Africa would endure, as might a few others that have invested more in their populations than their average counterpart. The likes of Chad, the Central African Republic, the DRC, Nigeria, Somalia, or Sudan would see their sovereignty revoked at once. In contrast, Somaliland would be recognized, having established a track record since the early 1990s of good governance and democratization, against overwhelming odds. Somaliland's "credible presidential elections" of 2003 stand indeed in sharp contrast with the deeply flawed elections in Kenya, Nigeria, and Zimbabwe in 2007 and 2008 where ruling elites were able to ignore international outcry as they shoved their sovereign powers down the throats of their opponents.[26] While the government of Kenya managed to undermine meaningful choice in constitution-making in 2005, the Somaliland constitution was approved by 97.9 percent of participants in a 2001 referendum, who represented 66 percent of the country's adult population. After President Mohamed Egal died in May 2002, "within hours the vice president, Dahir Rayale Kahin, was sworn in by Parliament as Egal's successor, in accordance with Article 86 of the new constitution."[27] In Togo, when Gnassingbé Eyadéma died in 2005, a coterie of senior officers took it upon themselves to immediately violate the constitution, which provided for temporary succession by the head of parliament, and appointed instead Eyadéma's son. Again, general outcry did not prevent the latter from consolidating his rule. In the 2003 elections, Kahin won by a mere eighty votes. Somaliland is not only democratic, it is also relatively well run. Its government successfully implemented a disarmament, demobilization, and reinsertion program for veterans of the civil war in the 1990s without any significant foreign assistance. Eighty percent of its minimal US$25 million annual budget goes to providing for security, which has helped provide one of Africa's safest environments, in sheer contrast to neighboring Somalia.

There remain, however, some substantial potential drawbacks with this policy. First, in contrast to the previous one, recognition based on effective governance maintains Western validation to African governance. It favors the continued extraversion of African politics, although it does not require it. Second, like the previous argument, it suffers from the implausibility of coordination among outsiders. Derecognition and selective rerecognition might have only limited effects on African rulers if their states continue to receive unconditional recognition from, say, China and Russia. This is a problem beyond the reach of my argument and it should not per se undermine consideration of its logical merits. Third, I assume that Western governments and other outsiders with the power to recognize favor development and good governance in Africa. But, just as African rulers cannot be assumed to care about the development of their countries, so too might outsiders benefit from failure in Africa. From this point of view, dysfunctional but stable states might trigger discursive lamentations from donors but not truly motivate them to provoke substantive changes. If that is the case, then there would be a larger struggle to be waged in rich countries by groups and segments of society interested in African development to affect the policies of their governments.

The last three potential problems are more immediately related to the internal logic of the argument. The first deals with the danger that selective recognition of political entities might lead to a chain reaction of separatism across Africa. Could successful recognition of a breakaway republic promote additional splinters? Could a thousand tiny nations establish effective local governance and make demands for sovereignty? The fact is that if they do provide effective governance to their citizens and thus prove viable, there may not be any problem with such an outcome. People concerned with the breakup of African states often warn against the Balkanization of the continent. But, truth be told, Africa was never unified, and its political units before colonization were typically much smaller and numerous than afterward.[28] Thus such a fragmentation pattern might be neither historically new nor necessarily negative. Moreover, such an outcome would be rather unlikely beyond some level of reconfiguration because of the high costs of organizing a new polity for elites, not least the uncertainty with respect to the dynamics unleashed by such realignments.

Second, this system might suffer from its intrinsic instability. If nothing else, postcolonial recognition has the merit of stability. States are recognized once and for all, and there is little they can do to change that, apart from endorsing their own dissolution. With selective recognition, there would first be a period of nonrecognition, which would last different lengths for different polities, leading to some being recognized while their neighbors are not. In addition, what if a new state gets recognized on account of its good governance only to turn predatory later? Would one derecognize it again and send all ambassadors packing? The practice of selective recognition in other regions seems to deal only with the initial recognition. This could be short-sightedness or derive from the hope that state benevolence is path dependent. At any rate, the interstate system needs a modicum of stability, which this model could not quite accommodate in this version.

Finally, what if some autochthony-crazed group adopted an autonomist agenda after derecognition of its state? Say it engaged in ethnic cleansing, kicking people out, organizing pogroms in order to create a homogeneous region based on a son-of-the-soil ideology, and claiming natural resource ownership. Years of violence would ensue and, clearly, this group would not be recognized as legitimately sovereign. What if, however, some ten years later, having established a homogeneous and internally legitimate polity, they run a successful state with good governance? Should they be recognized? Doing so would be endorsing the violent origins of their development. It would send the signal to every group that it is worth engaging in violence if it might produce the conditions for admission to sovereignty. This is clearly a problem. One could possibly conceive of rules of recognition that would take account of such original sin of violence, but there might be complex issues of regime succession that could wreak havoc on such logic. What if the government in power ten years down the road is composed of former opposition politicians who originally stood against the violence but now benefit from its long-term effects? I do not have a clear answer to this conundrum. But there is a matter of fairness to be considered, however repulsive political violence is. If we were to reject the recognition of effective states that were born of internal violence, we should agree that the United States or France should also no longer be recognized. When countries recognize the United States nowadays, they do not typically hold against it the decimation of the native populations during the colonial and postcolonial settlement of the country. Neither is France's diplomatic status hampered by the excesses of the French revolution. While, in the short run, violence and good governance are antithetical, it is nevertheless a fact that many developmentally successful and democratic states were born of political violence (as were dysfunctional postcolonial ones). Short of providing incentives for rulers to avoid violence, such as individual prosecution by

some international court, it might be unrealistic to expect political development to become a systematically nonviolent affair.

The Twilight Zone:
Institutional Competition and Empirical Statehood

If the first two fantasies were to prove too unrealistic, a milder option might
consist of maintaining the sovereignty of postcolonial African states while
granting groups or regions the power to develop their own institutions in order
to administer their own affairs in more or less complete autonomy from the political center. Existing states would continue to be recognized, but their sovereignty would be hollowed out, diluting its effects by providing alternate forms
of recognition to nonstate actors and thus giving them quasi-sovereign benefits. This dual system might foster institutional competition for the state and
deflate the returns to sovereignty for state elites. If offered some measure of
international recognition, some form of associate status by the UN in exchange
for providing public goods in their region, local elites might trade off their current sovereign benefits for this new status, provided it gives them effective
power. The goal would be to sever them from their need of the state by giving
them competing sources of recognition and authority. As for state elites, they
would no longer enjoy the monopoly rents of the pure sovereignty regime and
would be forced to compete with these institutions, which might result in improved governance. Such alternative recognition could take place in favor of
local state structures—provinces, districts, and so on—or nonstate ones, like
NGOs, chieftaincies, or even rebel organizations.

In the early 1990s, Western donors began working increasingly with
NGOs in Africa, bypassing states as a result of a liberal economic agenda and
triggering some institutional evolution in the process. The number of NGOs
exploded and they started representing alternative career paths to offices of the
state. Many of these NGOs were little more than individual instrumentalization strategies and provided little or no public goods, but the fabric of civil society might nevertheless have been thickened and strengthened from the exercise, with some groups eventually rising as providers of public services and
benefiting from the recognition of this new legal status. In fact, it was very
much its international recognition as a legitimate form of organization that
gave the NGO its domestic significance at the time. Recognition of NGOs as
bona fide forms of social organizations by donors opened up an avenue for
collective action outside the state. Not much came out of this in terms of challenge to state authority, in part because donors and Africans alike continued to
conceive of NGOs as subsidiary institutions to the state and residual providers
of services and because the wave of state failures that hit the continent at
around the same time diverted donors' focus toward state reconstruction rather

than state evasion.[29] Yet, the institutional response from Africans to the signaling by donors that nonstate organizations would be considered appropriate counterparts is what matters here. It suggests that a similar normative shift, offering a degree of diplomatic recognition to subnational entities, might trigger a supply response that would enrich Africa's institutional landscape and hold the state more accountable.

For such a shift to take place, however, it might be essential that these nonstate actors be provided with some equivalent power to sovereignty and not merely that created in domestic law. Many states were able to tame NGOs in the 1990s because they retained legal command over them. From this perspective, a suggestion such as Paul Collier's "independent service authorities," which would offer an "alternative system for spending public money" in failed states, is probably insufficient although it is on the right track.[30] Collier uses the example of Chad's Collège de Contrôle et de Surveillance des Ressources Pétrolières, which was established to wrestle control of oil resources away from the state, as an example. However, Chad's Collège illustrates the necessity of providing these alternative actors with some equivalent resource to state sovereignty for them to be really "independent." Indeed, the Collège was so effective at managing oil resources that its functions were eventually largely scrapped by the government. If these nonstate actors can be given a source of institutional authority outside the state—through some equivalent of international recognition—then they might be able to resist legal command, having similar powers of their own.

There are in fact numerous precedents for quasi-sovereign status to substate entities in the practice of international relations. Andorra, Hong Kong, Northern Ireland, or the Palestinian Authority are some instances of groups granted elements of sovereignty short of full recognition as states, which has allowed them to resist the hegemonic ambitions of the states that legally control them. They all exercise some dimension of executive authority over specific populations also formally covered by the sovereignty of a recognized state. What these require is a renunciation of the dichotomous nature of sovereignty—you have it or you don't—and an acceptance that it can be sliced. Lee Seymour has shown that the international system is already evolving toward such a fluid understanding of sovereignty. Looking at the outcome of self-determination conflicts, he points to the increasing instances of "governance arrangements that deviate from a sovereign ideal, including conditional independence, *de facto* states, occupied territories, neotrusteeships, and arrangements for autonomy and minority rights."[31] Such sovereign heterogeneity could be extended to African nonstate and subnational actors without having to wait for conflict and its outcome.

In its attempt to convince the world of its right to exert sovereignty over Taiwan, the government of the People's Republic of China coined the concept of "one nation, two systems," whereby Taiwan would be given autonomy and maintain substantial elements of its capitalist system in exchange for accepting the sovereign power of Beijing. Although the idea failed to gain sufficient diplomatic leverage at the time, it is worth exploring as relevant to the contemporary conundrum of Africa's weak states. It was later put into practice with Hong Kong, which maintained its own government and a measure of autonomy while being reattached to China after 1997. Hong Kong's autonomous status was not merely granted by Beijing but resulted from an agreement with the UK. Thus, its domestic status derived from outside recognition. One could similarly conceive of African governments being offered continued recognition in exchange for accepting partial recognition of some of their subnational components: one nation, many systems. These entities might then be allowed to develop their own fiscal powers, enter into trade or other international instruments with third countries, and otherwise develop features of statehood.[32] Since such partial recognition would be conditioned upon good governance, the average degree of empirical statehood of these states should rise. Returning to the example of Taiwan after its derecognition by the West might be helpful to illustrate possibilities of partial recognition of entities that are not fully sovereign. After severing diplomatic relations with Taiwan, the United States passed the Taiwan Relations Act in April 1979, which provided, among other things, for the continued supply of weapons to the island. Taiwan also maintained ambassadorial "privileges and immunities" for its "unofficial" representatives in Washington, DC.[33]

This policy prescription is equivalent to a forced decentralization of the state. But, as with the recognition of NGOs, it does not simply ask African states to decentralize from within, which can lead merely to a multiplication of their sovereign authority at the local level and of opportunities for sovereign predation and domination (witness Nigeria's federalism).[34] What this policy calls for, instead, is for outsiders such as Western governments and international organizations to recognize effective and accountable decentralized governance units and use their leverage to force governments to accept the separate status and authority of these entities. The underlying premise is that local institutions might be better suited at providing accountable governance than absolutist postcolonial states. Nadia Horning, for example, has shown that local communities have better natural resource management capacities than the state in Madagascar.[35] And James Wunsch has argued that local institutions are superior because they benefit from "fairly similar socio-economic status [in regions where] shared values and social equality may work to reduce organization costs . . . while face-to-face relationships and social pressure work to reduce or control 'free-riding' and 'individualistic suborning' of rule sets."[36] At any rate, such regional quasi recognitions, involving simultaneous decentralization and a reform of the sovereignty regime, might dilute some of the benefits of the central state and raise the returns of organizing regional collective action for local elites.

Although such an approach would fail to undermine the sovereignty regime that sustains Africa's weak states, it would also avoid the systemic instability that the first two fantasies were likely to trigger. As a result, it might be more palatable to many and, as such, more feasible. Like the second fantasy, however, it maintains outside validation—the granting of sovereignty—as its main building block. Thus it puts emphasis on the extraversion of political action in Africa as well as on its internal logic. From this respect, it might fall short of the disalienating power of the first fantasy. Another possible weakness of "one nation, many systems" is that it might face considerable reluctance from state authorities. Governments forced by donors to concede such reforms at a time of great weakness might later repress these initiatives when the opportunity arises. Enforcing the recognition of subnational entities might therefore involve a degree of peacekeeping-like military involvement that makes the policy less attractive.

Conclusion

There are other ways to deflate the domestic benefits of sovereignty for African elites. The US government's Millennium Challenge Account, created in 2000, follows the same incentive logic without directly confronting the supply of sovereignty. Instead it makes aid grants available to those governments that demonstrate better-than-average governance, thereby raising the returns to good governance and constraining the exercise of sovereign power. This might still prove an effective tool for development, although its implementation is restricted by virtue of its own selectivity.

For the most failed of states, the idea of "neotrusteeships" also has the merit of undermining the sovereign authority of rulers, transferring it to some multilateral body until the local government demonstrates its readiness to use it for the greater welfare.[37] Under this system, failed states would be placed under prolonged international administration with phased-in transfer of authority to locals over decades. This effectively constitutes benevolent recolonization. It appears to consider that Africans themselves are currently incapable of self-rule, while this book has suggested that their agency is structurally constrained. These constraints would not be alleviated by neotrusteeships, which would also require unrealistic levels of donor financial commitments.

As an alternative to reducing the benefits from sovereignty, one might also try to raise opportunities for material advancement outside the state. The lack of significant private economic opportunities in Africa is partly responsible for the unusual returns of legal command. Policies that promote the rise of a middle class independent from the state would tweak material incentives away from the sovereign realm.[38] Deborah Brautigam has shown, for example, that private Chinese foreign direct investments were much more likely to result in collaborative efforts with African capital in Mauritius, which had an enabling policy environment, than in Nigeria.[39] The question remains, however, of what can trigger the initial impetus in policy reform. If anything, the net effect of Chinese penetration in Africa may be more inimical than favorable to private interests. Most of China's loans and investments in Africa since 2000 have been either directly to state authorities (as in the case of Angola, where the Chinese government guaranteed its loan to the government with oil futures) or in projects that sustain state-dominated industries (as with infrastructure for mineral exploitation in the DRC).[40]

Finally, there are also numerous small-scale and private initiatives that can accomplish much in the lives of many people and should not be discounted. For example, the Program of African Studies at Northwestern University launched the "Consortium for Development Partnerships" in 2005 with African institutional counterparts, which promotes collaborative institution-building and develops capacity irrespective of the failings of the state. Similarly, the Afrobarometer center at Michigan State University systematically collaborates with African polling institutes in running its surveys, training numerous African pollsters in the process and contributing to the creation of a skilled class of nonstate actors with tools relevant to democratization.

While these initiatives are significant, the emphasis of this book has been on the overarching and overwhelming structural constraints imposed by sovereignty on the lives of Africans. Its policy prescriptions have retained this broad perspective. Despite its good intentions, granting sovereignty to Africa's postcolonies has been poisonous to Africans. Possibly one of the greatest challenges for those interested in African development will be to separate the notion of sovereignty from that of welfare and distance themselves from the fallacy that African postcolonial sovereignty is a net asset to Africans. Africans can reasonably expect better lives from a reform of the current sovereignty regime. They and the people in richer countries who care about African development should be encouraged to let go of their compliance with this regime.

Notes

1. Collier, *The Bottom Billion*, 107.
2. Herbst, "Responding to State Failure."
3. The questions of the existence, homogeneity, and benevolence of the international community are another matter altogether, which I do not get into here. While I will occasionally highlight the problems that arise from divergent interests among donors, I typically assume here the existence of an outside agent with the capacity and desire to promote African economic development and good governance, and which sees it to be in its interest.
4. Easterly, *The White Man's Burden*; van de Walle, *Overcoming Stagnation*; and Collier, *The Bottom Billion*.
5. UN, "Report of the Panel," 28.

6. Oksenberg, "The Issue of Sovereignty," 84 and 87.

7. Soudan, "Denis Sassou Nguesso," 73 (translation mine).

8. See Bryden, "State-Within-a-Failed-State."

9. Menkhaus, *Somalia*, 17 and 22.

10. Reno, "Somalia: State Failure," 170.

11. Bryden, "State-Within-a-Failed-State," 173–174.

12. Madsen, "The Struggle for Sovereignty."

13. Ibid., 170.

14. Ibid., 149.

15. Ibid., 180.

16. Ibid., 175–176.

17. Tilly, "War Making and State Making"; Cohen, Brown, and Organski, "The Paradoxical Nature"; Herbst, *States and Power in Africa.*

18. Weinstein, "Autonomous Recovery."

19. As reported to the author in January 2006 by a US diplomat recently returned from a mission to Abidjan.

20. See Chapter 6.

21. OECD, *The Charter of Kurukan-Fuga.*

22. See Taylor, *China's New Role.*

23. For more details on this and other original policy suggestions from Herbst, see *States and Power in Africa.*

24. Quoted by Rich, "Recognition of States," 6.

25. Quoted by ibid., 9.

26. Bryden, "State-Within-a-Failed-State," 169.

27. Ibid., 172.

28. Also see Herbst, *States and Power in Africa.*

29. See Englebert and Tull, "Post-Conflict Reconstruction," 114.

30. Collier, *The Bottom Billion*, 118–119.

31. Seymour, "Conflict Management and Hierarchy," 2.

32. In Belgium, Flanders and Wallonia enjoy such partial sovereignty, including their own representation abroad in the matters for which they have constitutional competence.

33. Madsen, "The Struggle for Sovereignty," 162 and 165.

34. See also Gina Lambright, "Silence from Below," 324; she finds that decentralization does not further democracy in Africa.

35. Horning, "Madagascar's Biodiversity Conservation Challenge."

36. Wunsch, "Refounding the African State," 494.

37. For a discussion of this concept, as well as the germane ideas of "shared sovereignty" and "protectorates," see Krasner, "Sharing Sovereignty"; Ellis, "How to Rebuild Africa"; and Fearon and Laitin, "Neotrusteeship."

38. For a discussion of how aid could at least not undermine Africa's middle class, see Birdsall, "Do No Harm."

39. Brautigam, "Close Encounters."

40. See Taylor, *China's New Role.*

Acronyms

AAC	All Anglophone Conference
ACB	Association of Cameroonians for Biya
AFDL	Alliance of Democratic Forces for the Liberation of Congo-Zaire
ANR	National Intelligence Agency (Congo)
AU	African Union
BBC	British Broadcasting Corporation
BCA	Barotse Cultural Association
BLA	The Barotseland Agreement
BPF	Barotse Patriotic Front
BRE	Barotse Royal Establishment
CNS	National Sovereign Conference
CODEKO	Conference for the Economic Development of Eastern Kasai
CONAKAT	Confederation of Tribal Associations of Katanga
CPA	Comprehensive Peace Agreement
CST	Superior Council of the Transition (Chad)
DIRMOB	Direction for Resource Mobilization
DRC	Democratic Republic of Congo
ELF	Eritrean Liberation Front
EPLF	Eritrean People's Liberation Front
EPRDF	Ethiopian Peoples' Revolutionary Democratic Front
ESDL	Ethiopian Somali Democratic League
EU	European Union
FN	New Forces
FROLINAT	National Front for the Liberation of Chad
GDP	gross domestic product
ICG	International Crisis Group
IFC	International Finance Corporation

IYC	Ijaw Youth Council
LGA	local government authority (Nigeria)
MAR	Minorities at Risk
MASSOB	Movement for the Actualization of the Sovereign State of Biafra
MEND	Movement for the Emancipation of the Niger Delta
MFDC	Movement of Democratic Forces of Casamance
MIBA	Bakwanga Mining Company
MMD	Movement for Multiparty Democracy
MNC	Congolese National Movement
NDPVF	Niger Delta People's Volunteer Force
NGO	nongovernmental organization
NRA/M	National Resistance Army/Movement
OAU	Organization of African Unity
OCC	Congolese Office of Control
OFIDA	Office des Douanes et Accises (Customs Office)
OLF	Oromo Liberation Front
ONLF	Ogaden National Liberation Front
PRESBY	President Biya's Youth
PRIO	Peace Research Institute of Oslo
RCD	Congolese Rally for Democracy
RDPC	Democratic Rally of the Cameroonian People
RPF	Rwandan Patriotic Front
SCNC	Southern Cameroons National Council
SCYL	Southern Cameroons Youth League
SDF	Social Democratic Front
SNM	Somali National Movement
SOMIGL	Great Lakes Mining Society
SPDP	Somali People's Democratic Party
SPLA	Sudan People's Liberation Army
SPLM	Sudan People's Liberation Movement
SWELA	The South West Elites' Association
SYL	Somali Youth League
TGE	Transitional Government of Ethiopia
TPD	All for Peace and Development
TPLF	Tigre People's Liberation Front
UFERI	Union of Independent Federalists and Republicans
UK	United Kingdom
UN	United Nations
YOSUPO	Youth for the Support of Those in Power

Bibliography

Abbay, Alemseged. "Diversity and State-Building in Ethiopia." *African Affairs*, 2004, 103(413):593–614.

Adam, Hussein M. "Formation and Recognition of New States: Somaliland in Contrast to Eritrea." *Review of African Political Economy*, 1994, 59:21–38.

Addison, Tony, ed. *From Conflict to Recovery in Africa*. Oxford: Oxford University Press, 2003.

African Studies Review, "Special Issue: Autochthony and the Crisis of Citizenship," September 2006, 49(2).

Afrobarometer. "Citizens and the State in Africa, New Results from Afrobarometer Round 3. A Compendium of Public Opinion Findings from 18 Countries, 2005–2006." Cape Town: Afrobarometer, 2006.

Airault, Pascal. "Où va l'argent du cacao?" *Jeune Afrique*, 2365, 7 May 2006, 32–33.

———. "La Vie au Nord: Mode d'Emploi." *Jeune Afrique*, 2383, 3–9 September 2006, 38–40.

Aker, Jenny. "Does Digital Divide or Provide? The Impact of Cell Phones on Grain Markets in Niger." Paper presented at the Working Group on African Political Economy, Stanford, CA, December 2007.

Akindes, Francis. "Côte d'Ivoire: Socio-political Crises, 'Ivoirité' and the Course of History." *African Sociological Review*, 2003, 7(2):11–28.

———. "The Roots of the Military-Political Crises in Côte d'Ivoire." Research Report No. 128. Uppsala: Nordiska Afrikainstitutet, 2004.

Akinyele, R. T. "Ethnic Militancy and National Stability in Nigeria: A Case Study of the Oodua People's Congress." *African Affairs*, 2001, 100(401):633–634.

Alapiki, Henry E. "State Creation in Nigeria: Failed Approaches to National Integration and Local Autonomy." *African Studies Review*, 2005, 48(3):49–65.

Alier, Abel. *Too Many Agreements Dishonoured*. Exeter: Ithaca Press, 1990.

Amuri, Sid, and Alain Gourdon. "Etude diagnostic des organisations et des procédures de la filière café-cacao de Côte d'Ivoire." Rapport réalisé pour le compte du gouvernement de Côte d'Ivoire sur financement de l'Union Européenne, n.d.

Anderson, Benedict. *Imagined Communities: Reflections on the Origins and Spread of Nationalism*. New York: Verso, 1991.

Anonymous, "Government Recognition in Somalia and Regional Political Stability in the Horn of Africa." *Journal of Modern African Studies*, 2002, 40(2):247–272.

Arifari, Nassirou Bako. "'We Don't Eat the Papers': Corruption in Transport, Customs and the Civil Forces." In Giorgio Blundo and Jean-Pierre Olivier de Sardan, eds., *Everyday Corruption and the State: Citizens and Public Officials in Africa*, 69–109.

Austin, John. *The Province of Jurisprudence Determined and the Uses of the Study of Jurisprudence.* New York: Noonday, 1954.

Autesserre, Séverine. "Local Violence, National Peace? Postwar 'Settlement' in the Eastern D. R. Congo (2003–2006)." *African Studies Review*, 2006, 49(3):1–29.

Ayodele, Thomson, Franklin Cudjoe, Temba Nolutshungu, and Charles Sunwabe. "African Perspectives on Aid: Foreign Assistance Will Not Pull Africa out of Poverty." Cato Institute Economic Development Bulletin No. 2, 14 September 2005.

Ayres, R. William, and Stephen M. Saideman. "Is Separatism as Contagious as the Common Cold or as Cancer? Testing the International and Domestic Determinants of Secessionism." *Nationalism and Ethnic Politics*, 2000, 6(3):92–114.

Azarya, Victor, and Naomi Chazan. "Disengagement from the State in Africa: Reflections on the Experience of Ghana and Guinea." *Comparative Studies in Society and History*, 1987, 29:106–131.

Badal, Raphael K. "Oil and Regional Sentiment in the South." In M. A. Al-Rahim, R. Badal, A. Hardallo, and P. Woodward, eds., *Sudan Since Independence: Studies of the Political Development Since 1956.* London: Gower, 1986.

Baker, Bruce. *Escape from the State: Political Disengagement and Its Consequences.* Oxford: James Currey, 2000.

Baloji. "Tout ceci ne vous rendra pas le Congo." *Hotel Impala,* musical recording. EMI France, 2007.

Banégas, Richard. "Côte d'Ivoire: Patriotism, Ethnonationalism and Other African Modes of Self-Writing." *African Affairs*, 2006, 105(421):535–552.

Banégas, Richard, and Bruno Losch. "La Côte d'Ivoire au bord de l'implosion." *Politique Africaine*, 2002, 87:139–161.

Barotse National Conference. "Resolutions of the Barotse National Conference Held at Lealui." 3–4 November 1995.

Barotseland Agreement 1964: Background Documents. Lusaka: Mulungushi International Conference Center, December 1992.

Bartkus, Viva Ona. *The Dynamic of Secession.* Cambridge: Cambridge University Press, 1999.

Bassett, Thomas J. "Dangerous Pursuits: Hunter Associations (Donzo Ton) and National Politics in Côte d'Ivoire." *Africa*, 2003, 73(1):1–30.

Bayart, Jean-François. "Africa in the World: A History of Extraversion." *African Affairs*, 2000, 99(395):217–267.

———. *L'Etat au Cameroun.* Paris: Presses de la Fondation Nationale de Sciences Politiques, 1985.

———. *The State in Africa: The Politics of the Belly.* New York: Longman, 1993.

Bayart, Jean-François, Stephen Ellis, and Béatrice Hibou. *The Criminalization of the State in Africa.* Oxford: James Currey, 1999.

Bayart, Jean-François, Peter Geschiere, and Francis Nyamnjoh. "Autochthonie, Démocraties et Citoyenneté en Afrique." *Critique Internationale*, 2001, 10:177–194.

BBC News. "World Bank Shuts Chad Oil Account." 13 January 2006, news.bbc.co.uk/ go/pr/fr//2/hi/business/4608900.stm.

———. "Yes, It's Good to Be King." 14 October 2005, news.bbc.co.uk/1/hi/world/ africa/4294208.stm.

Beck, Linda J. "Sovereignty in Africa: From Colonial Inheritance to Ethnic Entitlement? The Case of the Casamance Secessionist Movement." Paper presented at the American Political Science Association Annual Meeting, Atlanta, GA, 2–5 September 1999.

BERCI. "Le rapport préliminaire de l'enquête SUNY." Kinshasa: BERCI, 2003.

Bierschenk, Thomas, and Jean-Pierre Olivier de Sardan. "Local Powers and a Distant State in Rural Central African Republic." *Journal of Modern African Studies*, 1997, 35(3):441–468.

Biersteker, Thomas J., and Cynthia Weber. "The Social Construction of State Sovereignty." In Thomas J. Biersteker and Cynthia Weber, eds., *State Sovereignty as Social Construct*. Cambridge, MA: Cambridge University Press, 1996, 1–21.

———, eds. *State Sovereignty as Social Construct*. Cambridge, MA: Cambridge University Press, 1996.

Bilakila, Anastase Nzeza. "La 'coop' a Kinshasa: Survie et Marchandage." In Theodore Trefon, ed., *Ordre et désodre à Kinshasa. Réponses populaires à la faillite de l'Etat*. Paris: L'Harmattan, 2004, 33–46.

Billig, Michael. *Banal Nationalism*. London: Sage, 1995.

Birdsall, Nancy. "Do No Harm: Aid, Weak Institutions and the Missing Middle in Africa." Washington, DC: Center for Global Development Working Paper 113, 2007.

Blundo, Giorgio. "La corruption comme mode de gouvernance locale: Trois décennies de décentralisation au Sénégal." *Afrique Contemporaine*, July–September 2001, 199:115–127.

———. "Négocier l'Etat au quotidien: agents d'affaire, courtiers et rabbateurs dans les interstices de l'administration sénégalaise." *Autrepart*, 2001, 20:75–90.

Blundo, Giorgio, and Jean-Pierre Olivier de Sardan, eds. *Everyday Corruption and the State: Citizens and Public Officials in Africa*. London: Zed Books, 2006.

Boli, John. "Sovereignty from a World Polity Perspective." In Stephen D. Krasner, ed., *Problematic Sovereignty: Contested Rules and Political Possibilities*. New York: Columbia University Press, 2001, 53–82.

Bookman, Milica Z. *The Economics of Secession*. New York: St. Martin's Press, 1992.

Boone, Catherine. "Africa's New Territorial Politics: Regionalism and the Open Economy in Côte d'Ivoire." *African Studies Review*, 2007, 50(1):59–81.

———. "Open-Economy State Building: Neoliberalism and National Integration in Africa." Paper presented at Pomona College, Claremont, CA, 4 March 2004.

———. *Political Topographies of the African State: Territorial Authority and Institutional Choice*. Cambridge: Cambridge University Press, 2003.

Bourgeot, André. "Révoltes et rébellions en pays touareg." *Afrique Contemporaine*, 1994, 170:3–19.

Branch, Adam, and Zachariah Mampilly. "Winning the War but Losing the Peace? The Dilemma of SPLM/A Civil Administration and the Tasks Ahead." *Journal of Modern African Studies*, 2005, 43:1–20.

Bratton, Michael. "Beyond the State: Civil Society and Associational Life in Africa." *World Politics*, 1989, 41(3):407–430.

———. "Peasant-State Relations in Postcolonial Africa: Patterns of Engagement and Disengagement." In Joel Migdal, Atul Kholi, and Vivienne Shue, eds., *State Power and Social Forces: Domination and Transformation in the Third World*. Cambridge: Cambridge University Press, 1994, 231–254.

Bratton, Michael, and Wonbin Cho. "Where Is Africa Going: Views from Below. A Compendium of Trends in Public Opinion in 12 African Countries, 1999–2006." Afrobarometer Working Paper No. 60, May 2006.

Bratton, Michael, and Nicolas van de Walle. *Democratic Experiments in Africa: Regime Transitions in Comparative Perspective*. Cambridge: Cambridge University Press, 1997.

Brautigam, Deborah. "Chinese Business and African Development: 'Flying Geese' or 'Hidden Dragons'?" In Daniel Large, J. Christopher Alden, and Ricardo Soares de Oliveira, eds., *China Returns to Africa: A Rising Power and a Continent Embrace*. New York: Columbia University Press, 2008, 51–68.

———. "Close Encounters: Chinese Business Networks as Industrial Catalysts in Sub-Saharan Africa." *African Affairs*, 2003, 102:447–467.

———. "Substituting for the State: Institutions and Industrial Development in Eastern Nigeria." *World Development*, 1997, 25(7):1063–1080.

Bryden, Matt. "State-Within-a-Failed-State: Somaliland and the Challenge of International Recognition." In Paul Kingston and Ian Spears, eds., *States Within States: Incipient Political Entities in the Post–Cold War Era*. New York: Palgrave Macmillan, 2004, 167–192.

Buchheit, Lee C. *Secession: The Legitimacy of Self-Determination*. New Haven: Yale University Press, 1978.

Buijtenhuijs, Robert. *La conférence nationale souveraine du Tchad: Un essai d'histoire immédiate*. Paris: Khartala, 1993.

Caplan, Gerald L. "Barotseland: The Secessionist Challenge to Zambia." *Journal of Modern African Studies*, 1968, 6(3):343–360.

———. *The Elites of Barotseland: A Political History of Zambia's Western Province*. Berkeley: University of California Press, 1970.

Chabal, Patrick, and Jean-Pascal Daloz. *Africa Works: Disorder as Political Instrument*. Bloomington: Indiana University Press, 1999.

Charpy, Jacques. *Historical Testimony on Casamance*. Dakar: Republic of Senegal, Ministry of Communication, 1994.

Christopher, A. "Laurent Gbagbo: Je n'ai pas lutté pour la démocratie pour supprimer les contre-pouvoirs." 2006, www.cotedivoireisback.com.

Clapham, Christopher. *Africa and the International System: The Politics of State Survival*. Cambridge: Cambridge University Press, 1996.

———. "The Challenge to the State in a Globalized World." *Development and Change*, November 2002, 33(5):775–795.

———. "Degrees of Statehood." *Review of International Studies*, 1998, 24(2):143–157.

———. "Ethiopia." In Christopher Clapham, Jeffrey Herbst, and Greg Mills, eds., *Big African States*. Johannesburg: Wits University Press, 2006, 17–38.

———. "Introduction: Analysing African Insurgencies." In Christopher Clapham, ed., *African Guerrillas*. Oxford: James Currey, 1998, 1–18.

Clark, John. "Explaining Ugandan Intervention in Congo: Evidence and Interpretations." *Journal of Modern African Studies,* 2001, 39:261–287.

Clarke, Walter S., and Robert Gosende. "Somalia: Can a Collapsed State Reconstitute Itself?" In Robert Rotberg, ed., *State Failure and State Weakness in a Time of Terror*. Cambridge, MA: World Peace Foundation, 2003, 129–158.

Cohen, Youssef, Brian Brown, and A. F. K. Organski. "The Paradoxical Nature of State-Making: The Violent Creation of Order." *American Political Science Review*, 1981, 75:901–910.

Coleman, James. "Nationalism in Tropical Africa." *American Political Science Review*, 1954, 48(2):404–426.

Collier, Paul. *The Bottom Billion: Why the Poorest Countries Are Failing and What Can Be Done About It*. Oxford: Oxford University Press, 2007.

Collier, Paul, and Anke Hoeffler. "Greed and Grievance in Civil Wars." *Oxford Economic Papers*, 2004, 56(4):563–595.

————. "The Political Economy of Secession." In H. Hannum and E. F. Babbitt, eds., *Negotiating Self-Determination*. Lanham, MD: Lexington Books, 2006, 37–59.

Comaroff, Jean, and John Comaroff, eds. *Law and Disorder in the Postcolony*. Chicago: University of Chicago Press, 2006.

Connor, Walter. "The Politics of Ethno-Nationalism." *Journal of International Affairs*, 1973–1974, 27–28(1):1–21.

Cooper, Frederick. *Africa Since 1940: The Past of the Present*. Cambridge: Cambridge University Press, 2002.

Coppieters, Bruno, and Richard Sakwa, eds. *Contextualizing Secession: Normative Studies in Comparative Perspective*. Oxford: Oxford University Press, 2003.

Crawford, James. "State Practice and International Law in Relation to Unilateral Secession." 19 February 1997, http://canada.justice.gc.ca/en/news/nr/1997/factum/craw_pt4.html.

Crossley, Ken. "Why Not to State-Build New Sudan." In Paul Kingston and Ian Spears, eds., *States Within States: Incipient Political Entities in the Post–Cold War Era*. New York: Palgrave Macmillan, 2004, 135–151.

Cummins, Chip. "Exxon Oil-Fund Model Unravels in Chad." *Wall Street Journal*, 28 February 2006, A4.

Darbon, Dominique. *L'administration et le paysan en Casamance: Essai d'anthropologie administrative*. Paris: Pédone, 1988.

Davidson, Basil. *The Black Man's Burden: Africa and the Curse of the Nation-State*. New York: Random House, 1992.

Decoudras, Pierre-Marie, and Souleymane Abba. *La rébellion touarègue au Niger: Actes des négociations avec le gouvernement*. Bordeaux, France: Centre d'Etudes d'Afrique Noire, Travaux et Documents No. 45–46, 1995.

De Herdt, Tom, and Stefaan Maryssse. *L'économie informelle au Zaire: (Sur)vie et pauvreté dans la période de transition*. Brussels: Institut African-CEDAF, 1996.

Deng, Francis M. "Beyond Cultural Domination: Institutionalizing Equity in the African State." In Mark R. Beissinger and Crawford Young, eds., *Beyond State Crisis? Postcolonial Africa and Post-Soviet Eurasia in Comparative Perspective*. Washington, DC: Woodrow Wilson Center Press, 2002, 359–384.

————. "Self-Determination and National Identity Crisis: The Case of Sudan." In Wolfgang Danspeckgruber, ed., *The Self-Determination of Peoples: Community, Nation, and State in an Interdependent World*. Boulder: Lynne Rienner, 2002, 253–286.

Diamond, Larry. "Thinking About Hybrid Regimes." *Journal of Democracy*, 2002, 13(2):21–35.

Diouf, Makhtar. *Sénégal, Les Ethnies et La Nation*. Dakar: Les Nouvelles Editions Africaines du Sénégal, 1988.

Dougueli, Georges. "Pétrole: Ou va l'argent du brut?" *Jeune Afrique*, 16 December 2007, 2449:16–22.

Drisdelle, Rheal. *Mali: A Prospect for Peace?* Oxford: Oxfam Publication, 1997.

Dugard, John. "A Legal Basis for Secession: Relevant Principles and Rules." In Julie Dahlitz, ed., *Secession and International Law: Conflict Avoidance—Regional Appraisals*. The Hague: Asser Press, 2003, 89–96.

Dukule, Abdoulaye. "Life in Monrovia." *The Perspective,* 26 November 2001, www.theperspective.org/lifeinmonrovia.html.

Easterly, William. *The White Man's Burden: Why the West's Efforts to Aid the Rest Have Done So Much Ill and So Little Good*. New York: Penguin, 2006.

Eboussi-Boulaga, Fabien. *Les conférences nationales en Afrique noire: Une affaire à suivre*. Paris: Karthala, 1993.

EIU (Economist Intelligence Unit). *Country Report: Côte D'Ivoire,* December 2003.

———. *Country Report: Cameroon,* February 2005.

Ellis, Stephen. "How to Rebuild Africa." *Foreign Affairs*, 2005, 84(5):135–148.

Emerson, Rupert. "The Problem of Identity, Selfhood, and Image in the New Nations: The Situation in Africa." *Comparative Politics*, 1969, 1(3):297–312.

Englebert, Pierre. "Back to the Future? Resurgent Indigenous Structures and the Reconfiguration of Power in Africa." In Olufemi Vaughan, ed., *Indigenous Political Structures and Governance in Africa*. Ibadan, Nigeria: Sefer Books, 2003, 26–59.

———. "Born-Again Buganda or the Limits of Traditional Resurgence in Africa." *Journal of Modern African Studies*, 2002, 40(3):1–24.

———. "Cameroon: Background to a Crisis." *CSIS Africa Notes,* No. 130. Washington, DC: Center for Strategic and International Studies, 1991.

———. "Compliance and Defiance to National Integration in Barotseland and Casamance." *Afrika Spectrum,* 2005, 39(1):29–59.

———. "Patterns and Theories of Traditional Resurgence in Africa." *Mondes en Développement*, 2002, 30(118):51–64.

———. *State Legitimacy and Development in Africa*. Boulder: Lynne Rienner, 2000.

———. "Why Congo Persists: Sovereignty, Globalization and the Violent Reproduction of a Weak State." In V. Fitzgerald et al., eds., *Globalization, Self-Determination and Violent Conflict*. New York: Palgrave, 2006, 119–146.

Englebert, Pierre, and Katharine Boyle. "The Primacy of Politics in Separatist Dynamics." *African Prospective*, 2008, 2:31–63.

Englebert, Pierre, and Denis Tull. "Post-Conflict Reconstruction in Africa: Flawed Ideas About Failed States." *International Security,* 2008, 32(4):106–139.

Eyoh, Dickson. "Conflicting Narratives of Anglophone Protest and the Politics of Identity in Cameroon." *Journal of Contemporary African Studies*, 1998, 16(2):249–276.

Fearon, James, and David Laitin. "Ethnicity, Insurgency, and Civil War." *American Political Science Review*, 2003, 97(1):75–90.

———. "Neotrusteeship and the Problem of Weak States." *International Security*, 2004, 28(4):5–43.

———. "Weak States, Rough Terrain, and Large-Scale Ethnic Violence." Paper presented at the annual meeting of the American Political Science Association, Atlanta, GA, September 1999.

Forrest, Joshua B. "State Inversion and Nonstate Politics." In Leonardo Villalon and Philip A. Huxtable, eds., *The African State at a Critical Juncture: Between Disintegration and Reconfiguration*. Boulder: Lynne Rienner, 1998, 45–56.

———. *Subnationalism in Africa: Ethnicity, Alliances, and Politics*. Boulder: Lynne Rienner, 2003.

Foucher, Vincent. "Les 'évolués,' la migration, l'école: Pour une nouvelle interprétation de la naissance du nationalisme casamançais." In Momar Coumba Diop, ed., *Le Sénégal contemporain*. Paris: Karthala, 2002, 375–424.

———. "Pas d'alternance pour la Casamance." *Politique Africaine*, October 2003, 91:101–119.

———. "Senegal: The Resilient Weakness of Casamancais Separatists." In Morten Boas and Kevin Dunn, eds., *African Guerillas: Raging Against the Machine*. Boulder: Lynne Rienner, 2007, 171–197.

French, Howard. "A Neglected Region Loosens Ties to Zaire." *New York Times*, 18 September 1996, A1, A4.

Frynas, Jedrzej George. "Corporate and State Responses to Anti-Oil Protests in the Niger Delta." *African Affairs*, 2001, 100(398):27–54.

Frynas, Jedrzej George, and Manuel Paulo. "A New Scramble for African Oil? Historical, Political, and Business Perspectives." *African Affairs*, 2007, 106(423):229–251.

GANVE (Groupe d'Actions Non-Violentes Evangéliques). "La participation nationale pour une paix sociale durable en République Démocratique du Congo." Lubumbashi: Société Civile du Katanga (published by GANVE with Bureau de la Société Civile and Développement et Paix), 2001.

Garang, John. *The Call for Democracy in Sudan*. New York: Kegan Paul International, 1992.

Gasser, Geneviève. "'Manger ou s'en aller': Que veulent les opposants armés casamançais?" In Momar Coumba Diop, ed., *Le Sénégal contemporain*. Paris: Karthala, 2002, 459–498.

Gérard-Libois, J. *La sécession katangaise*. Brussels: CRISP, 1963.

Gleditsch, Nils P., Peter Wallensteen, Mikael Eriksson, Margareta Sollenberg, and Håvard Strand. "Armed Conflict 1946–2001: A New Dataset." *Journal of Peace Research*, 2002, 39(5):615–637.

Global Witness. *Digging in Corruption: Fraud, Abuse and Exploitation in Katanga's Copper and Cobalt Mines*. Washington, DC: Global Witness Publishing, 2006.

Gorenburg, Dmitry. "Not With One Voice: An Explanation of Intragroup Variation in Nationalist Sentiment." *World Politics*, 2000, 53(1):115–142.

———. "Nationalism for the Masses: Popular Support for Nationalism in Russia's Ethnic Republics." *Europe-Asia Studies*, 2001, 53(1):73–104.

Gurr, Ted R. *Minorities at Risk: A Global View of Ethnopolitical Conflicts*. Washington, DC: United States Institute of Peace, 1993.

Hagmann, Tobias. "Beyond Clannishness and Colonialism: Understanding Political Disorder in Ethiopia's Somali Region, 1991–2004." *Journal of Modern African Studies,* 2005, 43(4):509–536.

Hale, Henry. "The Parade of Sovereignties: Testing Theories of Secession in the Soviet Setting." *British Journal of Political Science*, 2000, 30(1):31–56.

Hall, Richard. *Zambia*. New York: Praeger, 1975.

Harbeson, John W., Donald Rothchild, and Naomi Chazan. *Civil Society in Africa*. Boulder: Lynne Rienner, 1994.

Harnischfeger, Johannes. "The Bakassi Boys: Fighting Crime in Nigeria." *Journal of Modern African Studies*, 2003, 41(1):23–49.

Hechter, Michael. "The Dynamics of Secession." *Acta Sociologica*, 1992, 35(4): 267–283.

Heilbrunn, John R. "Social Origins of National Conferences in Benin and Togo." *Journal of Modern African Studies*, June 1993, 31(2):277–299.

Herbst, Jeffrey. "The Creation and Maintenance of National Boundaries in Africa." *International Organization*, Fall 1989, 43(4):673–692.

———. "Let Them Fail: State Failure in Theory and Practice." In Robert Rotberg, ed., *When States Fail: Causes and Consequences*. Princeton, NJ: Princeton University Press, 2004, 302–312.

———. "Responding to State Failure in Africa." *International Security*, 1996/1997, 21(3):120–144.

———. *States and Power in Africa: Comparative Lessons in Authority and Control*. Princeton, NJ: Princeton University Press, 2000.

Herbst, Jeffrey, and Gregg Mills. "Africa's Big Dysfunctional States: An Introductory Overview." In Christopher Clapham, Jeffrey Herbst, and Greg Mills, eds., *Big African States*. Johannesburg: Wits University Press, 2006, 1–15.

Hibou, Béatrice. "The Social Capital of the State as an Agent of Deception or the Ruses of Economic Intelligence." In Jean-François Bayart, Stephen Ellis, and Béatrice Hibou, eds., *The Criminalization of the African State*. Oxford: James Currey, 1999, 69–113.

Hirschman, Albert O. *Exit, Voice, and Loyalty: Responses to Decline in Firms, Organizations, and States*. Cambridge, MA: Harvard University Press, 1970.

Holsti, Kalevi J. *The State, War, and the State of War*. New York: Cambridge University Press, 1996.

Horning, Nadia R. "Madagascar's Biodiversity Conservation Challenge: From Local-to National-Level Dynamics." *Environmental Sciences*, 2008, 5(2):109–128.

Horowitz, Donald L. "The Cracked Foundations of the Right to Secede." *Journal of Democracy*, 2003, 14(2):5–17.

———. *Ethnic Groups in Conflict*. Berkeley: University of California Press, 1987.

———. "Patterns of Ethnic Separatism." *Comparative Studies in Society and History*, 1981, 23(2):165–195.

Hoyos, Carola. "Shipping Replaces Diamonds in Liberia War Chest." *Financial Times*, 24 October 2001, 16.

Human Rights Watch. "'They Do Not Own This Place': Government Discrimination Against 'Non-Indigenes' in Nigeria." April 2006, 18(3).

Humphreys, Macartan, and Habaye Ag Mohamed. "Senegal and Mali." Manuscript, 2002.

———. "Senegal and Mali." In Paul Collier and Nicholas Sambanis, eds., *Understanding Civil War: Evidence and Analysis (Volume 1: Africa)*. Washington, DC: World Bank, 2005, 247–302.

Huntington, Samuel. *The Third Wave: Democratization in the Late Twentieth Century*. Norman: University of Oklahoma Press, 1993.

Hyden, Goran. "Problems and Prospects of State Coherence." In Donald Rothchild and Victor Olorunsola, eds., *State Versus Ethnic Claims: African Policy Dilemmas*. Boulder: Westview, 1983, 67–84.

Ibrahim, Jibrin. "The Weakness of 'Strong States': The Case of the Niger Republic." In Adebayo Olukoshi and Liisa Laakso, eds., *Challenges to the Nation-State in Africa*. Uppsala: Nordiska, 1996, 50–73.

ICG (International Crisis Group). "Congo's Elections: Making or Breaking the Peace." Washington, DC: ICG Africa Report No. 108, 2006.

———. "Congo's Transition Is Failing: Crisis in the Kivus." Washington, DC: ICG Africa Report No. 91, 2005.

———. "Fuelling the Niger Delta Crisis." Washington, DC: ICG Africa Report No. 118, 2006.

———. "Nigeria's Faltering Federal Experiment." Washington, DC: ICG Africa Report No. 119, 2006.

———. "Somaliland: Time for African Union Leadership." Washington, DC: ICG Africa Report No. 110, 2006.

———. "The Swamps of Insurgency: Nigeria's Delta Unrest." Washington, DC: ICG Africa Report No. 115, 2006.

———. "Tchad: Vers le Retour de la Guerre?" Washington, DC: ICG Africa Report No. 111, 2006.

Ikelegbe, Augustine. "The Perverse Manifestation of Civil Society: Evidence from Nigeria." *Journal of Modern African Studies*, 2001, 39(1):1–24.

Imperato, Pascal J. *Historical Dictionary of Mali*. Lanham, MD: Scarecrow Press, 2008.

Innocenti, Nicol Degli. "Diluted Deal on Conflict Diamonds Agreed." *Financial Times*, 31 October 2003, 2.

Iyob, Ruth. *The Eritrean Struggle for Independence: Domination, Resistance, Nationalism, 1941–1993*. Cambridge: Cambridge University Press, 1995.

Jackson, Robert H. *Quasi-States: Sovereignty, International Relations and the Third World*. Cambridge: Cambridge University Press, 1990.

Jackson, Robert H., and Carl G. Rosberg. "Personal Rule: Theory and Practice in Africa." *Comparative Politics*, 1984, 16(4):421–442.

———. "Why Africa's Weak States Persist: The Empirical and the Juridical in Statehood." *World Politics*, 1982:1–24.

Jackson, Stephen. "'Our Riches Are Being Looted!' War Economies and Rumour in the Kivus, D. R. Congo." *Politique Africaine*, 2001, 84:117–136.

———. "Sons of Which Soil? The Language and Politics of Autochthony in Eastern D. R. Congo." *African Studies Review*, 49(2):100–109.

Johnson, Douglas. *The Root Causes of Sudan's Civil Wars*. Bloomington: Indiana University Press, 2003.

———. "The Sudan People's Liberation Army and the Problem of Factionalism." In Christopher Clapham, ed., *African Guerillas*. Bloomington: Indiana University Press, 1988, 53–72.

Joseph, Richard. "Africa, 1990–1997: From Abertura to Closure." *Journal of Democracy*, 1998, 9(2):3–17.

———. "Africa: States in Crisis." *Journal of Democracy*, 2003, 14(3):159–170.

———. *Democracy and Prebendal Politics in Nigeria*. Cambridge: Cambridge University Press, 1987.

———. "Nation-State Trajectories in Africa." *Georgetown Journal of International Affairs*, 2003, 4(2):13–20.

Jourdan, Luca. "New Forms of Political Order in North Kivu: The Case of Governor Eugène Serufuli." Paper presented at the conference "Beside the State: New Forms of Political Power in Post-1990s Africa," Milan (Italy), December 2005.

Junger, Sebastian. "Blood Oil." *Vanity Fair*, February 2007.

"Kaiama Declaration by Ijaw Youths of the Niger Delta Being a Communiqué Issued at the End of the All Ijaw Conference Which Was Held in the Town of Kaiama This 11th Day of December 1998," http://ijawcenter.com/kaiama_declaration.html.

Kasfir, Nelson. "Cultural Sub-Nationalism in Uganda." In Victor Olorunsola, ed., *The Politics of Cultural Sub-Nationalism in Africa*. Garden City, NY: Anchor Books, 1972, 51–148.

Kaufmann, Daniel, Aart Kraay, and Massimo Mastruzzi. 2008. "Governance Matters VI: Governance Indicators for 1996–2007." Washington, DC: World Bank Policy Research.

Keller, Edmond. "Making and Remaking State and Nation in Ethiopia." In Ricardo Larémont, ed., *Borders, Nationalism, and the African States*. Boulder: Lynne Rienner, 2005, 87–134.

Kelsall, Tim. "History, Identity and Collective Action: Difficulties of Accountability." In Ulf Engel and Gorm Rye Olsen, eds., *The African Exception*. London: Ashgate, 2005, 53–69.

Kennes, Eric. "The Mining Sector in Congo: The Victim or the Orphan of Globalization?" In Stefaan Marysse and Philip Reyntjens, eds., *The Political Economy of the Great Lakes Region in Africa: The Pitfalls of Enforced Democracy and Globalization*. Houndmills, UK: Palgrave Macmillan, 2005.

Kingston, Paul. "States-Within-States: Historical and Theoretical Perspectives." In Paul Kingston and Ian Spears, eds., *States Within States: Incipient Political Entities in the Post–Cold War Era*. New York: Palgrave Macmillan, 2004, 1–13.

Kingston, Paul, and Ian Spears, eds. *States Within States: Incipient Political Entities in the Post–Cold War Era*. New York: Palgrave Macmillan, 2004.

Knight, Cassie. *Brazzaville Charms: Magic and Rebellion in the Republic of Congo*. London: Frances Lincoln, 2007.

Kok, Peter Nyot. "Adding Fuel to the Conflict: Oil, War and Peace in the Sudan." In Martin Doornbos, Lionel Cliffe, Abdel Ghaffar M. Ahmed, and John Markakis, eds., *Beyond Conflict in the Horn: The Prospects for Peace, Recovery and Development in Ethiopia, Somalia, Eritrea and Sudan*. Trenton, NJ: Red Sea Press, 1992, 104–112.

Konings, Piet. "Anglophone University Students and Anglophone Nationalist Struggles in Cameroon." 2003. http://asc.leidenuniv.nl/pdf/conference24042003-konings.pdf.

Konings, Piet, and Francis Nyamnjoh. "The Anglophone Problem in Cameroon." *Journal of Modern African Studies*, 1997, 35(2):207–229.

———. *Negotiating an Anglophone Identity: A Study of the Politics of Recognition and Representation in Cameroon*. Leiden: Brill, 2003.

Krasner, Stephen. *Sovereignty: Organized Hypocrisy*. Princeton, NJ: Princeton University Press, 1999.

———. "Sharing Sovereignty: New Institutions for Collapsed and Failing States." *International Security*, 2004, 29(2):85–120.

Kraxberger, Brennan. "The Geography of Regime Survival: Abacha's Nigeria." *African Affairs*, 2004, 103(412):413–430.

Kuran, Timur. *Private Truths, Public Lies: The Social Consequences of Preference Falsification*. Cambridge, MA: Harvard University Press, 1995.

Laakso, Liisa, and Adebayo Olukoshi. "The Crisis of the Post-Colonial Nation-State Project in Africa." In Adebayo Olukoshi and Liisa Laakso, eds., *Challenges to the Nation-State in Africa*. Uppsala, Sweden: Nordiska Afrikainstitute, 1996, 7–39.

Laitin, David. "Secessionist Rebellion in the Former Soviet Union." *Comparative Political Studies*, 2001, 34(8):839–861.

Lambright, Gina. "Silence from Below? Central-Local Relations and Institutional Performance in Africa." Manuscript, 2008.

Lancaster, Carol. "Development in Africa: The Good, the Bad, the Ugly." *Current History*, 2005, 104(682):222–227.

Lapidus, Gail W. "Contested Sovereignty: The Tragedy of Chechnya." *International Security*, 1998, 23(1):5–49.

Larémont, Ricardo, ed. *Borders, Nationalism, and the African State*. Boulder: Lynne Rienner, 2005.

Le Billon, Philippe. "Angola's Political Economy of War: The Role of Oil and Diamonds, 1975–2000." *African Affairs*, 2001, 100(398):55–80.

Lemarchand, René. "The Democratic Republic of Congo: From Failure to Potential Reconstruction." In Robert Rotberg, ed., *State Failure and State Weakness in a Time of Terror*. Cambridge, MA: World Peace Foundation, 2003, 29–70.

———. "The Limits of Self-Determination: The Case of the Katanga Secession." *American Political Science Review*, 1962, 56(2):404–416.

Leonard, David K., and Scott Straus. *Africa's Stalled Development: International Causes and Cures*. Boulder: Lynne Rienner, 2003.

Le Vine, Victor. *The Cameroons from Mandate to Independence*. Berkeley: University of California Press, 1964.

———. *The Cameroon Federal Republic*. Ithaca, NY: Cornell University Press, 1971.

Lewis, I. M. *A Modern History of the Somali*. Oxford: James Currey, 2002.

Lewis, Peter. "Governance and Political Space in Africa's Poor Democracies." Paper prepared for the conference "Governance and Insecurity in West Africa," Northwestern University, 13–15 November 2003.

———. *Growing Apart: Oil, Politics, and Economic Change in Indonesia and Nigeria*. Ann Arbor: University of Michigan Press, 2007.

Lindbergh, Staffan. *Democracy and Elections in Africa*. Baltimore, MD: Johns Hopkins University Press, 2006.

Lode, Karl. "Civil Society Takes Responsibility: Popular Involvement in the Peace Process in Mali." 1997, www.prio.no/page/Publication_details/Staff_alpha_ALL/9429/38063.html.

Lund, Christian. "Bawku Is Still Volatile: Ethno-Political Conflict and State Recognition in North Ghana." *Journal of Modern African Studies*, 2003, 41(4):587–610.

———. "Precarious Democratization and Local Dynamics in Niger: Micro Politics in Zinder." *Development and Change*, 2001, 32(5):845–869.

———. "Twilight Institutions: Public Authority and Local Politics in Africa." *Development and Change*, 2006, 37(4):685–705.

Madsen, Robert. "The Struggle for Sovereignty Between China and Taiwan." In Stephen D. Krasner, ed., *Problematic Sovereignty: Contested Rules and Political Possibilities*. New York: Columbia University Press, 2001:141–193.

Malkki, Liisa. *Purity and Exile: Violence, Memory, and National Cosmology Among Hutu Refugees in Tanzania*. Chicago: University of Chicago Press, 1995.

Mamdani, Mahmood. *Citizens and Subjects: Contemporary Africa and the Legacy of Late Colonialism*. Princeton, NJ: Princeton University Press, 1996.

———. *When Victims Become Killers: Colonialism, Nativism and the Genocide in Rwanda*. Princeton, NJ: Princeton University Press, 2002.

Mampilly, Zachariah. "Stationary Bandits: Understanding Rebel Governance." Ph.D. dissertation, Department of Political Science, University of California, Los Angeles, 2007.

Mararo, Stanislas Bucyalimwe. "L'administration AFDL/RCD au Kivu (novembre 1996–mars 2003): Stratégie et bilan." In Stefaan Marysse, ed., *L'Afrique des grands Lacs: Annuaire 2002–2003*. Paris: L'Harmattan, 2003, 171–205.

———. "La guerre des chiffres: Une constante dans la politique au Nord Kivu." In Stefaan Marysse, ed., *L'Afrique des Grands Lacs: Annuaire 1999–2000*. Paris: L'Harmattan, 2003, 225–262.

Marshall-Fratani, Ruth. "The War of 'Who Is Who': Autochthony, Nationalism, and Citizenship in the Ivorian Crisis." *African Studies Review*, 2006, 49(2):9–43.

Marut, Jean-Claude. "Le Problème casamançais est-il soluble dans l'Etat-nation?" In Momar Coumba Diop, ed., *Le Sénégal contemporain*. Paris: Karthala, 2002:425–458.

Marx, Anthony. "Race-Making and the Nation-State." *World Politics*, 1996, 48(2):180–208.

Mbalanda, Daddy. "La gestion des rumeurs à l'Office Congolais de Contrôle." Thesis presented to the Faculté des Communications Sociales des Facultés Catholiques de Kinshasa, 2005.

Mbembe, Achille. *On the Postcolony*. Berkeley: University of California Press, 2000.

Mbembe, Achille, and Janet Roitman. "Figures of the Subject in Times of Crisis." *Public Culture*, 1995, 7:323–352.

Médard, Jean-François. "The Underdeveloped State in Africa: Political Clientelism or Neo-Patrimonialism?" In Christopher Clapham, ed., *Private Patronage and*

Public Power: Political Clientelism and the Modern State. London: Pinter, 1982:162–189.

Menkhaus, Ken. *Somalia: State Collapse and the Threat of Terrorism.* Adelphi Paper No. 364. Oxford: Oxford University Press, 2004.

MFDC (Mouvement des Forces Démocratiques de Casamance). "Plate-Forme Revendicative." Congrès de Banjul (21–25 June 1999). www.ifrance.com/Casamance/casamance%20Kunda.htm.

Migdal, Joel. *The State in Society.* Cambridge: Cambridge University Press, 2001.

Minorities at Risk. "The Lozi." www.cidcm.umd.edu/inscr/mar.

Monga, Célestin. *Anthropology of Anger:Civil Society and Democracy in Africa.* Boulder: Lynne Rienner, 1996.

———. *Un Bantou à Washington.* Paris: Presses Universitaires de France, 2007.

Moore, Sally F. "Post-Socialist Micro-Politics: Kilimanjaro, 1993." *Africa,* 1996, 66(4):587–606.

Mukhtar, Mohamed Haji. *Historical Dictionary of Somalia.* Lanham, MD: Scarecrow Press, 2003.

Murphy, Alexander B. "The Sovereign State System as Political-Territorial Ideal: Historical and Contemporary Considerations." In Thomas J. Biersteker and Cynthia Weber, eds., *State Sovereignty as Social Construct.* Cambridge: Cambridge University Press, 1996, 81–120.

Mwandakire, Thandika. "Crisis Management and the Making of 'Choiceless Democracies.'" In Richard Joseph, ed., *State, Conflict and Democracy in Africa.* Boulder: Lynne Rienner, 1999, 119–136.

Neuberger, Benyamin. "Irredentism and Politics in Africa." In Naomi Chazan, ed., *Irredentism and International Politics.* Boulder: Lynne Rienner, 1991, 97–110.

Nolutshungu, Sam C. *Limits of Anarchy: Intervention and State Formation in Chad.* Charlottesville and London: University Press of Virginia, 1996.

Norris, Carolyn. "Mali-Niger: Fragile Stability." UNHCR Center for Documentation and Research, Writenet no. 14/2000, 2001, www.unhcr.org/publ/RSDCOI/3bc5aaa66.pdf.

North, Douglas. *Institutions, Institutional Change and Economic Performance.* New York: Cambridge University Press, 1990.

Nugent, Paul. *Africa Since Independence.* New York: Palgrave, 2004.

Nyamnjoh, Francis B. "Cameroon: A Country United by Ethnic Ambition and Difference." *African Affairs,* 1999, 98(390):101–118.

Nyamnjoh, Francis B., and Michael Rowlands. "Elite Associations and the Politics of Belonging in Cameroon." *Africa,* 1998, 68(3):327–328.

Nzongola-Ntalaja, Georges. *The Congo from Leopold to Kabila: A People's History.* London: Zed Books, 2002.

Nzouankeu, Jacques Mariel. "The Role of the National Conference in the Transition to Democracy in Africa: The Cases of Benin and Mali." *Issue: A Journal of Opinion,* 1993, 21(1/2):45.

OAU (Organization of African Unity). "Border Disputes Among African States." AHG/Resolution 16(I). First Ordinary Session of the Assembly of Heads of State and Government Held in Cairo, UAR, 17–21 July 1964, www.africa-union.org/Official_documents/Treaties_Conventions_Protocols.

———. "The Organization of African Unity (OAU) Charter." Addis Ababa, 1963, www.africa-union.org/Official_documents/Treaties_Conventions_Protocols/OAU_Charter_1963.pdf.

Obi, Cyril I. "Global, State and Local Intersections: Power, Authority and Conflict in the Niger Delta Oil Communities." In Thomas M. Callaghy, Ronald Kassimir, and

Robert Latham, eds., *Intervention and Transnationalism in Africa: Global-Local Networks of Power.* Cambridge: Cambridge University Press, 2001:173–193.

O'Brien, Conor Cruise. *To Katanga and Back: A UN Case History.* New York: Grosset & Dunlap, 1966.

OECD (Organization of Economic Cooperation and Development). *The Charter of Kurukan-Fuga.* www.oecd.org/dataoecd/56/56/38874847.pdf.

Office of the Ngambela. "Resolutions of the People of Barotseland from the Special Meeting Held at Lealu." 3–4 November 1995.

Oksenberg, Michel. "The Issue of Sovereignty in the Asian Historical Context." In Stephen D. Krasner, ed., *Problematic Sovereignty: Contested Rules and Political Possibilities.* New York: Columbia University Press, 2001, 83–104.

Olson, James S. *The Peoples of Africa: An Ethnohistorical Dictionary.* Westport, CT: Greenwood Press, 1996.

Pabanel, Jean-Pierre. "La question de la nationalité au Kivu." *Politique Africaine,* 1991, 41:36.

Paden, John. "Unity with Diversity: Toward Democratic Federalism." In Robert Rotberg, ed., *Crafting the New Nigeria: Confronting the Challenges.* Boulder: Lynne Rienner, 2004, 17–38.

Pakenham, Thomas. *The Scramble for Africa: White Man's Conquest of the Dark Continent from 1876–1912.* New York: Random House, 1991.

Pateman, Roy. *Eritrea: Even the Stones Are Burning.* Lawrenceville, NJ: Red Sea Press, 1998.

Pegg, Scott. "What They Really Want: Survey Evidence from the Niger Delta on Self Determination, Resource Control and Conflict." Paper presented to the 47th annual meeting of the African Studies Association, New Orleans, November 2004.

Pélissier, Paul. *Les paysans du Sénégal: Les civilisations agraires du Cayor à la Casamance.* Saint-Yrieix: Imprimerie Fabrègue, 1966.

Pitch, Anthony. *Inside Zambia—and Out.* Cape Town: Howard Tummins, 1967.

Pole Institute. "Rules for Sale: Formal and Informal Cross-Border Trade in Eastern DRC." Goma: Pole Institute, 2007.

Polgreen, Lydia. "Congo's Riches, Plundered by Renegade Troops." *New York Times,* 16 November 2008, 1, 20–21.

Pool, David. "The Eritrean People's Liberation Front." In Christopher Clapham, ed., *African Guerillas.* Oxford: James Currey, 1998, 19–35.

Posner, Daniel. *Institutions and Ethnic Politics in Africa.* Cambridge: Cambridge University Press, 2005.

Posner, Daniel, and Daniel Young. "The Institutionalization of Political Power in Africa." *Journal of Democracy,* 2007, 18(3):126–140.

Pratten, David, and Charles Gore. "The Politics of Plunder: The Rhetorics of Order and Disorder in Southern Nigeria." *African Affairs,* 2003, 102:211–240.

Prunier, Gérard, and Rachel Gisselquist. "The Sudan: A Successfully Failed State." In Robert Rotberg, ed., *State Failure and State Weakness in a Time of Terror.* Cambridge, MA: World Peace Foundation, 2003, 101–127.

Putnam, Robert. *Making Democracy Work: Civic Traditions in Modern Italy.* Princeton, NJ: Princeton University Press, 1992.

Reintjens, Filip, and Stefaan Marysse. "Conflits aux Kivus: Antécédants et Enjeux." Antwerp, December 1996.

Reno, William. "The Changing Nature of Warfare and the Absence of State-Building in West Africa." In Diane E. Davis and Anthony W. Pereira, eds., *Irregular Armed Forces and Their Role in Politics and State Formation.* Cambridge: Cambridge University Press, 2003, 322–345.

―――. "How Sovereignty Matters: International Markets and the Political Economy of Local Politics in Weak States." In Thomas Callaghy, Ronald Kassimir, and Robert Latham, eds., *Intervention and Transnationalism in Africa: Global-Local Networks of Power*. Cambridge: Cambridge University Press, 2001:197–215.

―――. "Shadow States and the Political Economy of Civil Wars." In Mats Berdal and David M. Malone, eds., *Greed and Grievance: Economic Agendas in Civil Wars*. Boulder: Lynne Rienner, 2000, 43–68.

―――. "Somalia: State Failure and Self-Determination in the Shadow of the Global Economy." In Valpy Fitzgerald, Frances Stewart, and Rajesh Venugopal, eds., *Globalization, Violent Conflict and Self-Determination*. Houndmills, Basingstoke, UK: Palgrave Macmillan, 2006:147–178.

―――. *Warlord Politics in African States*. Boulder: Lynne Rienner, 1999.

Rich, Roland. "Recognition of States: The Collapse of Yugoslavia and the Soviet Union." *European Journal of International Law*, 1993, 4(1):36–65.

Roitman, Janet. *Fiscal Disobedience: An Anthropology of Economic Regulation in Central Africa*. Princeton, NJ: Princeton University Press, 2005.

Ross, Michael. "What Do We Know About Natural Resources and Civil War?" UCLA Department of Political Science, 2005.

Rotberg, Robert I. "Failed States, Collapsed States, Weak States: Causes and Indicators." In Robert I. Rotberg, ed. *State Failure and State Weakness in a Time of Terror*. Cambridge, MA: World Peace Foundation, 2003, 1–27.

―――. "What Future for Barotseland." *Africa Report,* 1963, 8(7):21–23.

―――, ed. *When States Fail: Causes and Consequences*. Princeton, NJ: Princeton University Press, 2004.

Salifou, André. *La question touarègue au Niger*. Paris: Karthala, 1993.

Samatar, Abdi. "Botswana: Comprehending the Exceptional State." In Abdi Ismail Samatar and Ahmed I. Samatar, eds., *The African State: Reconsiderations*. Portsmouth, NH: Heinemann, 2002:17–51.

Sambanis, Nicholas. "Partition as a Solution to Ethnic War: An Empirical Critique of the Theoretical Literature." *World Politics*, 2000, 52(4):437–483.

Sandbrook, Richard. "Patrons, Clients and Factions: New Dimensions of Conflict Analysis in Africa." *Canadian Journal of Political Science*, March 1972, 5(1):104–119.

Schatzberg, Michael. *The Dialectics of Oppression in Zaire*. Madison: Wisconsin University Press, 1989.

―――. *Political Legitimacy in Middle Africa: Father, Family, Food*. Bloomington: Indiana University Press, 2001.

Seay, Laura. "Authority at 'Twilight': Civil Society, Social Services, and the State in the Eastern Democratic Republic of Congo." Ph.D. dissertation, University of Texas at Austin, Department of Government, forthcoming.

Seely, Jennifer. "A Political Analysis of Decentralization: Coopting the Tuareg Threat in Mali." *Journal of Modern African Studies*, 2001, 39(3):499–524.

Seymour, Lee. "Conflict Management and Hierarchy: Unbundling Authority in Secessionist Conflicts." Paper presented at the African Studies Association Annual Meeting, Chicago, November 2008.

―――. "The Surprising Success of 'Separatist' Groups: The Empirical and Juridical in Self-Determination." Paper presented at the International Studies Association Annual Convention, San Diego, March 2006.

Shinn, David. "Somaliland: The Little Country That Could." *CSIS Africa Notes,* No. 9. Washington, DC: Center for Strategic and International Studies, 2002.

Sikainga, Ahmad. "Sudan: The Authoritarian State." In Abdi Ismail Samatar and Ahmed I. Samatar, eds., *The African State: Reconsiderations*. Portsmouth, NH: Heinemann, 2002, 191–216.

Sklar, Richard L. "African Polities: The Next Generation." In Richard Joseph, ed., *State, Conflict, and Democracy in Africa*. Boulder: Lynne Rienner, 1999:165–178.

———. "The Nature of Class Domination in Africa," *Journal of Modern African Studies*, 1979, 17(4):531–551.

———. *Nigerian Political Parties: Power in an Emerging African Nation*. Princeton, NJ: Princeton University Press, 1963.

———. "Unity or Regionalism: The Nationalities Question." In Robert Rotberg, ed., *Crafting the New Nigeria: Confronting the Challenges*. Boulder: Lynne Rienner, 2004, 39–60.

Smith, Daniel J. *A Culture of Corruption: Everyday Deception and Popular Discontent in Nigeria*. Princeton, NJ: Princeton University Press, 2007.

Smith, Lahra. "The Challenges of National Unity and Self-Determination Rights: The Case of the Oromo of Ethiopia." Paper prepared for presentation at the Annual Meetings of the African Studies Association, Chicago, November 2008.

Soares de Oliveira, Ricardo. *Oil and Politics in the Gulf of Guinea*. New York: Columbia University Press, 2007.

Socpa, Antoine. "Bailleurs Autochthones et Locataires Allogènes: Enjeu Foncier et Participation Politique au Cameroun." *African Studies Review*, 2006, 49(2):45–67.

Soudan, François. "Denis Sassou Nguesso: L'Afrique, le Congo et lui." *Jeune Afrique*, 19–25 February 2006, 2354.

———. "Pourquoi les Africains ne votent plus." *Jeune Afrique*, 29 July 2007, 2429:72–78.

Spruyt, Hendrik. *The Sovereign State and Its Competitors*. Princeton, NJ: Princeton University Press, 1994.

Struelens, Michel. *The United Nations in the Congo, or O.N.U.C., and International Politics*. Brussels: Max Arnold, 1976.

Suberu, Rotimi T. "Democratizing Nigeria's Federal Experiment." In Robert Rotberg, ed., *Crafting the New Nigeria: Confronting the Challenges*. Boulder: Lynne Rienner, 2004, 61–84.

Taylor, Ian. *China's New Role in Africa*. Boulder: Lynne Rienner, 2009.

Tegera, Aloys. "Nord-Kivu: Une rébellion dans une rébellion?" *Regards Croisés*, 2003.

Tidjani Alou, Mahaman. "Corruption in the Legal System." In Giorgio Blundo and Jean-Pierre Olivier de Sardan, eds., *Everyday Corruption and the State: Citizens and Public Officials in Africa*. London: Zed Books, 2006, 137–177.

Tilly, Charles. *Coercion, Capital and European States: A.D. 990–1992*. Malden, MA: Blackwell, 1990.

———. "War Making and State Making as Organized Crime." In Peter Evans, Dietrich Rueschemeyer, and Theda Skocpol, eds., *Bringing the State Back In*. Cambridge: Cambridge University Press, 1985, 169–191.

Tollens, Eric. "Sécurité alimentaire à Kinshasa: Un face-à-face quotidien avec l'adversité." In Theodore Trefon, ed., *Ordre et désodre à Kinshasa. Réponses populaires à la faillite de l'Etat*. Paris: L'Harmattan, 2004, 61–79.

Tostensen, Arne, Inge Tvedten, and Mariken Vaa, eds. *Associational Life in African Cities: Popular Responses to the Urban Crisis*. Stockholm: Elanders Gotab, 2001.

Trefon, Theodore. *Parcours administratifs dans un Etat en faillite: Récits de Lubumbashi (RDC)*. Paris and Brussels: L'Harmattan/Cahiers Africains, 2007.

————. "The Political Economy of Sacrifice: Kinois and the State." *Review of African Political Economy*, 2002, 29(93/94):481–498.

Treisman, Daniel. "Russia's 'Ethnic Revival': The Separatist Activism of Regional Leaders in a Postcommunist Order." *World Politics,* 1997, 49(2):212–249.

Tull, Denis. "The Dynamics of Transnational Violence in the Great Lakes Region: State Collapse and Social Crisis in Kivu (Democratic Republic of Congo)." 2001. Mimeo.

————. "The Limits to State Substitution: Constraints of Collective Action in North Kivu (DR Congo)." Paper presented at the Eighteenth International Biennial Conference of the African Studies Association in Germany (VAD), Hamburg, May 2002.

————. *The Reconfiguration of Political Order in Postcolonial Africa: A Case Study from North Kivu (DR Congo)*. Hamburg: African Studies Center, 2004.

Tull, Denis, and Andreas Mehler. "The Hidden Costs of Power-Sharing: Reproducing Insurgent Violence in Africa." *African Affairs*, 2005, 104(416):375–398.

UN (United Nations). "Declaration on the Granting of Independence to Colonial Countries and Peoples." *General Assembly Resolution 1514* (XV). 14 December 1960, www.gibnet.com/texts/un1514.htm.

UNDP (United Nations Development Programme). *Human Development Report 2005*. New York: UNDP, 2005.

UN IRIN News Report, 19 April 2005.

UN Security Council. "Report of the Panel of Experts on the Illegal Exploitation of Natural Resources and Other Forms of Wealth of the Democratic Republic of the Congo." 2001 (S/2001/357).

Van de Walle, Nicolas. *African Economies and the Politics of Permanent Crisis, 1979–1999*. Cambridge: Cambridge University Press, 2001.

————. "Economic Reform: Patterns and Constraints." In E. Gyimah Boadi, ed., *Democratic Reform in Africa: The Quality of Progress*. Boulder: Lynne Rienner, 2004, 29–64.

————. "The Institutional Origins of Inequality in Sub-Saharan Africa." *The Annual Review of Political Science,* forthcoming.

————. "Neopatrimonialism and Democracy in Africa, with an Illustration from Cameroon." In Jennifer Widner, ed., *Economic Change and Political Liberalization in Sub-Saharan Africa*. Baltimore: Johns Hopkins University Press, 1994, 129–157.

————. *Overcoming Stagnation in Aid-Dependent Countries*. Washington, DC: Center for Global Development, 2005.

————. "Presidentialism and Clientelism in Africa's Emerging Party Systems." *Journal of Modern African Studies,* 2003, 41(2):297–321.

Van Rouveroy van Nieuwaal, E. A. B. "Chieftaincy in Africa: Three Facets of a Hybrid Role." In E. A. B. van Rouveroy van Nieuwaal and R. van Dijk, eds., *African Chieftaincy in a New Socio-Political Landscape*. Hamburg: LIT Verlag, 1999:21–48.

Vansina, Jan. "Mwasi's Trials." *Daedalus*, 1982, 111(2):49–70.

Verschave, François-Xavier. *La Françafrique*. Paris: Stock, 1998.

Villalón, Leonardo, and Peter VonDoepp. *The Fate of Africa's Democratic Experiments: Elites and Institutions*. Bloomington: Indiana University Press, 2005.

Vines, Alex. "Vessel Operations Under 'Flags of Convenience' and National Security Implications." Hearing Before the House Armed Services Committee, 13 June 2002, http://armedservices.house.gov/openingstatements and pressreleases/107th congress.

Vlassenroet, Koen. "Citizenship, Identity Formation & Conflict in South Kivu: The Case of the Banyamulenge." *Review of African Political Economy*, 2002, 29(93/94):499–516.

Wallis, William. "Africa's Conflict Diamonds: Is the UN-Backed Certification Scheme Failing to Bring Transparency to the Trade?" *Financial Times*, 29 October 2003, 13.

Weinstein, Jeremy. "Autonomous Recovery and International Intervention in Comparative Perspective." Washington, DC: Center for Global Development, Working Paper No. 57, April 2005.

———. *Inside Rebellion: The Politics of Insurgent Violence*. Cambridge: Cambridge University Press, 2007.

Weiss, Herbert F., and Tatiana Carayannis. "The Enduring Idea of the Congo." In Ricardo Larémont, ed., *Borders, Nationalism, and the African State*. Boulder: Lynne Rienner, 2005, 135–177.

Willame, Jean-Claude. *Banyarwanda et Banyamulenge: Violences ethniques et gestion de l'identitaire au Kivu*. Paris: L'Harmattan, 1997.

Wines, Michael. "Toiling in the Dark: Africa's Power Crisis." *New York Times*, 29 July 2007.

———. "We Welcome You to Lush Zimbabwe! Your Wallet, Please!" *New York Times*, 18 November 2003, A13.

World Bank. *Africa Development Indicators 2007*. Washington, DC: World Bank, 2008.

———. *African Development Indicators Online*. Washington, DC: World Bank, 2008.

———. *World Development Indicators Online*. Washington, DC: World Bank, 2008.

Wunsch, James. "Refounding the African State and Local Self-Governance: The Neglected Foundation." *Journal of Modern African Studies*, 2000, 38(3):487–509.

Yashar, Deborah. *Contesting Citizenship in Latin America*. Cambridge: Cambridge University Press, 2005.

Young, Crawford. *The African Colonial State in Comparative Perspective*. New Haven, CT: Yale University Press, 1995.

———. "Comparative Claims to Political Sovereignty: Biafra, Katanga, Eritrea." In Donald Rothchild and Victor Olorunsola, eds., *State Versus Ethnic Claims: African Policy Dilemmas*. Boulder: Westview, 1983, 199–232.

———. "The End of the Post-Colonial State in Africa? Reflections on Changing African Political Dynamics." *African Affairs*, 2004, 103:23–49.

———. "Evolving Modes of Consciousness and Ideology: Nationalism and Ethnicity." In David E. Apter and Carl G. Rosberg, eds., *Political Development and the New Realism in Sub-Saharan Africa*. Charlottesville and London: University of Virginia Press, 1994, 61–86.

———. "Nationalism and Ethnicity in Africa." *Review of Asian and Pacific Studies*, 2002, 23:1–19.

———. "Nation, Ethnicity, and Citizenship: Dilemmas of Democracy and Civil Order in Africa." In Sara Dorman, Daniel Hammett, and Paul Nugent, eds., *Making Nations, Creating Strangers: States and Citizenship in Africa*. Leiden: Brill, 2007.

———. *The Politics of Cultural Pluralism*. Madison: University of Wisconsin Press, 1976.

———. "Reflections on State Decline and Societal Change in Zaire." Typescript. January 1997.

———. "The Third Wave of Democratization in Africa: Ambiguities and Contradictions." In Richard Joseph, ed., *State, Conflict, and Democracy in Africa*. Boulder: Lynne Rienner, 1999, 15–38.

Young, Crawford, and Thomas Turner. *The Rise and Decline of the Zairian State.* Madison: University of Wisconsin Press, 1985.

Young, John. "The Tigray People's Liberation Front." In Christopher Clapham, ed., *African Guerillas.* Oxford: James Currey, 1998, 36–52.

Zartman, I. William, ed., *Collapsed States: The Disintegration and Restoration of Legitimate Authority.* Boulder: Lynne Rienner, 1995.

Index

About the Book

Though the demise of one or another African state has been heralded for nearly five decades, the map of the continent remains virtually unchanged. By and large, these states have failed to protect and promote the interests of their citizens. And yet they endure.

Pierre Englebert asks why: Why do these oppressive and exploitative, yet otherwise ineffective, structures remain broadly unchallenged? Why do Africans themselves, who have received little in the way of security, welfare, or development, continue to embrace their states and display surprising levels of national attachment? He finds his answer in the benefits that sovereign weak states offer to Africa's regional and national elites—and to those who depend on them.

Englebert carefully articulates the manner in which international sovereignty is translated into domestic legal command—and the sorrow that ensues. He also offers some corrective "policy fantasies." Effectively combining theory, quantitative evidence, and detailed case studies, his book reveals a pattern of reproduction of a predatory, dysfunctional state in which human integrity is sacrificed to its territorial counterpart.

Pierre Englebert is professor of politics at Pomona College. His previous publications include *State Legitimacy and Development in Africa.*